Government Budgeting and Financial Management in Practice

Logics to Make Sense of Ambiguity

Government Budgeting and Financial Management in Practice

Logics to Make Sense of Ambiguity

Gerald J. Miller

CRC Press
Taylor & Francis Group
Boca Raton London New York

CRC Press is an imprint of the
Taylor & Francis Group, an **informa** business

CRC Press
Taylor & Francis Group
6000 Broken Sound Parkway NW, Suite 300
Boca Raton, FL 33487-2742

Printed in the United States of America on acid-free paper
Version Date: 20110818

International Standard Book Number: 978-1-57444-753-8 (Hardback)

Visit the Taylor & Francis Web site at
http://www.taylorandfrancis.com

and the CRC Press Web site at
http://www.crcpress.com

For Milan Nelson and Jack Rabin

Contents

Preface

When recently asked about government budgeting, finance, and financial management's[1] foundational idea, I described the many different fields of study and schools of thought that battle to dominate what's done in practice and research. This fact came to mind again when an accreditation committee asked for the set of core competencies we require students to demonstrate to pass the core course in the university's master's program. Again, the many fields–many schools of thought answer underlays the competencies, as it did in the effort to institute government finance office accreditation (Hildreth, 1998).

Answering the question of where the critical assumptions come from to drive government budgeting, finance, and financial management, the field is blessed with varied frames of reference or logics. There's also a political contest going on over the relationship between government and market. There's another one over how the U.S. federal, state, and local governments will finance their commitments to an aging population. Students, colleagues from a variety of academic areas, and I have fairly intense interest in the practice and study of government budgeting, finance, and financial management. These budgeting and finance battles resonate.

What fundamental ideas will dominate the way we do research and how we practice the craft? So far there are no clear winners; the field is multidisciplinary, not yet interdisciplinary.

The idea that a field of academic research could define government financial management as a profession may be naïve. However, there does seem to be some agreement between research and practice, agreement that forms the starting point of this book. Consider three ideas from the research side that help understand this field.

First, a substantial research tradition has followed Simon's (1947) start in administration behavior. Roughly and simplistically, Simon argued that people, having defined the situation in a certain way, readily choose the one best way in which to act. The problem lies in the definition of the situation, in a sense, a value premise. Therefore, if one can control the value premise—the definition of the situation—one can control the decision (March and Simon, 1958). Normative approaches espoused by practitioners make it clear that battling for the value premise is what they spend their time doing (Miller, Rabin, and Hildreth, 1987).

Second, traditional and not so traditional financial management research dwells less on technique than in direction, that is, the idea that much of what organization members know comes from stories and narratives, as in justifications for budgets; symbols, such as "the budget" as a single decision, one comprehensive document produced by a chief executive; contextual realities, as in debt management networks; metaphors, particularly "efficiency"; and language, especially that surrounding merit, need, and rights as the basis for allocation of scarce resources among competing uses. Much of this is conveyed through postevent construction of meaning (Miller, 1991).

Third, the glue that holds these concepts together, giving action to what goes on in financial management, is the idea of interpretation. By interpretation, I mean "the immediate apprehension ... of an objective event as expressing meaning" (Berger and Luckmann, 1966, p. 129). With interpretation, one acts in social structures in ways that modify, but eventually enable internalization, of the apprehensions. Internalization takes place in a social setting, one in which plausibility structures emerge for maintenance of what is internalized.

The practice side of public budgeting and financial management has a major impact on what researchers find important enough to spend time and money investigating. The third chapter of this book, and the conceptualization that underlies the entire book, develops the idea that practice is theory.

Good government, and the budget management that is a part of the good government reform movement, have come under fire from the political right and even neoliberals at all levels of government in the United States. The good government critics call government the problem, not the solution in society. They feel it necessary to bring to an end the era of big government and good government along with it. Yet, the political left also attacks good government, particularly when executive budgets scorn particularistic interests. The left, with ostensible opposition from the right, created direct spending entitlements, tax expenditures, and nonconventional spending through loans, loan guarantees, insurance, and other narrowly focused guarantees to solve problems ranging from disaster relief to corporate insolvencies.

Good government has never had the popular appeal public administration writers expected from public administration theorists. Academic theorists have called good government's orthodoxy a set of proverbs, politically credulous, blind to socioeconomic inequity, and committed to making the road to serfdom efficient. Good government advocates find it more and more difficult to explain their quest as commonsensical, and even less as idealistic.

So, what is good government, if a basis for government budgeting, finance, and financial management? The argument here places good government within an orthodox approach to public administration generally. Then, the argument places orthodox public financial management theory within its public finance complement in rational decision making. The question arises: Is orthodoxy in public financial management and public finance a set of absolutes that corresponds to realism in social theory?

Realism should contrast with constructivism. We can't construct a reality at odds with the way the world really works. Yet, within the social world, traditions, expectations, socialization, and even power help socially construct a reality that gets accepted and is for all intents and purposes the reality. Social constructions of reality can be as realistic and operate as rationally as any physical world phenomenon.

As a social construct, good government has both a humanistic and a political side. These more relaxed sides prevail among good government advocates; a prevailing theory of public financial management exists. The constructed element of good government—if good government is not an absolute or realistic theory of public financial management—rests on idealistic views of human nature (cooperation rather than conflict) and politics (conflicts among interest groups and between anti- and pro-activist government social movements that often lead to partisan mutual adjustment, but rarely to standoffs that close down legislative processes and even government operations).

Social constructs are flexible and useful. They are subject to changes of mind, of frames of reference. Social construction of reality rather than realism can depict abstract ideas about the context and application of the tools of public financial management. The argument in this book rests on the importance of social constructions in public financial management. Realism is more apparent than real, we claim.

The battle waged in financial management, and in organizations that have an important concern with financial matters, is one over the interpretation of complex events. Financial managers find themselves engaged in interpreting, and finally gaining the upper hand in determining critical assumptions. In financial management terms, consider an application in public budgeting (Schick, 1988, pp. 64–65). The process by which resource claimants and allocators meet brings together interpretations of fiscal problems and solutions in specific areas in which indirect communication of subject matter, participation, and appropriate models of discourse and choice are understood. Ultimately, the process influences and is modified by a value premise: efficiency, sometimes equity, and parsimony.

This book uses the question as the motivating force to understand critical assumptions of today's government budgeting, finance, and financial management: Where do they come from to drive financial management? The book takes developments in the field as sources for these assumptions: fiscal policy, conventional and nonconventional budgeting, citizen participation in decision making, direct democracy, debt management networks, and revenue decision making particular to tax incentives. Together or apart, developments in these areas should tell something about what leads to constructions of the government finance world. The critical assumptions guiding people working in the activities described in this book, we argue, differ often from the single rational system many prefer or take for granted.

Because this book emerges from work with so many colleagues, I (Jerry Miller), rather than we, want to recognize and thank my coauthors in this book first— Lyn Evers, Iryna Illiash, Jonathan B. Justice, Jaeduk Keum, and Donijo Robbins.

Awhile back, Bob Golembiewski immersed (baptized?) me in organization theory, behavior, and especially development, and that background underlies this book. So, the baptism took. The late Jack Rabin, always enamored with the latest gadget but doubtful about the latest finance fad, introduced me to government budgeting, finance, and financial management in the MPA program and with the Public Budgeting Laboratory. His work on small-group decision making—he came out of Bob Golembiewski's shop, too—had a profound effect on my way of looking at the subjects in this book. I miss him and his singular ability to put me on the defensive to justify anything I took for granted. I hope those justifications show through here. Finally, I recognize my friend and frequent coauthor, Bart Hildreth, for all he's done to bring new ideas to the field and to increase its research quality. This book was done in the same spirit as Bart's efforts.

Endnotes

1. To make all easier to read, we will use *government budgeting, public budgeting, public finance, finance, financial management, public financial management, government financial management,* and various other usages representing the people doing these tasks, interchangeably in the book.

References

Berger, Peter L., and Thomas Luckmann. (1966). *The Social Construction of Reality: A Treatise in the Sociology of Knowledge.* New York: Doubleday.

Hildreth, W. Bartley. (1998). Should there be an accreditation program for finance and budget offices? *Public Budgeting & Finance* 18(2):18–27.

March, James G., and Herbert A. Simon. (1958). *Organizations.* New York: Wiley.

Miller, Gerald J. (1991). *Government Financial Management Theory.* New York: Dekker.

Miller, Gerald J., Jack Rabin, and W. Bartley Hildreth. (1987). Strategy, values, and productivity. *Public Productivity Review* 11:81–96.

Schick, Allen. (1988). An inquiry into the possibility of a budgetary theory. In *New Directions in Budget Theory,* ed. Irene Rubin, 59–69. Albany: State University of New York Press.

Simon, Herbert A. (1947). *Administrative Behavior.* New York: Free Press.

Contributors

Lyn Evers
Piscataway, New Jersey

Iryna Illiash
School of Public Affairs and
    Administration
Rutgers University
Newark, New Jersey

Jonathan B. Justice
School of Public Policy and
    Administration
University of Delaware
Newark, Delaware

Jaeduk Keum
Department of Public Administration
College of Public Affairs and
    Economics
University of Seoul
Seoul, South Korea

Gerald J. Miller
School of Public Affairs
Arizona State University
Phoenix, Arizona

Donijo Robbins
School of Public, Nonprofit, and
    Health Administration
Grand Valley State University
Grand Rapids, Michigan

Chapter 1

Socially Constructed Decisions about Public Money

Is the government financial manager's work what government budgeting, finance, and financial management[1] are about? We argue here that it is—that practice is theory.

Practice in all fields follows logics that are based on some set of expectations about ends and means, preferences and consequences, roles and behavior. Practitioners may derive the logics from technology, what financial engineers or even accountants do. They may come from theory and research: good government reformers, supply-side and Keynesian economics, fiscal policy analyses, and tax system designs.

More important, the logics driving decisions made by practitioners could be the critical assumptions and foundational ideas in the study of government budgeting, finance, and financial management. Distilled, the logics, assumptions, and ideas become theory suitable for verification and validation in research.

Financial managers act much as all other managers. They try to reduce ambiguity that comes with disagreement over the ends their decisions serve. Managers also calculate and minimize the uncertain consequences of the choices they make. They act by "aligning" the demands of critical outside interests or contingencies with the capabilities and interests of those inside the organization.

Financial managers, as do all managers, hope to achieve the same ultimate goal, and to "the extent that any truly overall objective might be identified [across organizations], that objective is probably organization survival" (Caplan, 1966, p. 418).

Another important goal is the development and maintenance of the legitimacy of their role in decision making.

However, financial managers' handling of ambiguity has strategic importance, if not always centrality, to organizations. While the ultimate goal in almost all government agencies is not a financial one, still, goal achievement requires financial resources. The centrality of resource acquisition and allocation makes the financial manager a critical, even pivotal, actor in organization life.

The strategic importance of government budgeting, finance, and financial management is permanent, diminishing only when there are no scarcity among resources and no perceived uncertainty about their availability. The greater the impression of unpredictability, however, the greater the likelihood of unforeseen dependencies, and the more importance given the finance function in managing them.

Financial Management as Socially Negotiated Process

Given the looming importance of finance in public organizations, knowing the "meaning" of procedures and the position financial managers take in the processes, an observer should be able to predict the future of organizations in government. Such is not the case, for the same reasons that an observer cannot predict the course of events in private organizations. The unpredictability in both sectors derives from administrative reality that is contextual, negotiated, and socially constructed (Astley, 1985). Financial management, no more or no less than any other management process, is not an ordered process deduced from some normative first principle, but a negotiated reality, constructed by the people involved.

Consider the budget process in a government. Jan Foley Orosz (2001) tells the story of a chargeback system used in the state of Ohio. Programs like Wildlife and Watercraft, which received dedicated funds, were charged the cost of central services, covering everything from invoices processed to staff position descriptions written. The chargeback system freed up general fund money to finance the governor's initiatives. A victory for technical rationality and the application of sound accounting principles, the chargeback system became symbol and narrative of a governor redirecting funds that the people had voted to a particular use. "In the socially constructed world of agency management, 'chargeback' took on a life of its own" (Foley-Orosz, 2001, p. 127). Certainly, the Wildlife and Watercraft people and the governor's budget office staff had socially constructed worlds that made sense of what they did. The trouble was they produced competing realities.

In all, the budget is a formidable tool when the views of all the participants can balance. What a budget will be is a matter in which all have a say by the information they provide or not, the arguments they offer or not, and the decisions they make or choose not to make. The budget's formulation is usually structured to be highly systematic. Ideas must survive an exacting process of scrutiny before they become budget items. In all, new budgets emerge as products of a socially negotiated consensus (Astley, 1985, p. 499).

We can view all of government budgeting, finance, and financial management in the same way. That is, there is no objective truth, in the sense truth has in physics or biology, on which to base management. There is only socially constructed truth formed through intense political struggle. These socially constructed models of financial management, it follows, are unique to their institutional and cultural contexts. They emerge from the interplay of individuals there. They tell us about the specific ways in which organizations use financial management technologies to make decisions with financial management specialists in the lead or in tow.

The Study of Government Budgeting, Finance, and Financial Management

The main purpose of this book is to explore a new avenue down which we might push financial management thinking. The new road centers on ambiguity as a motivator for accepting the existence of multiple rationalities, all of which people in organizations socially construct.

Ambiguity and social construction question the assumption about organization consensus held by more orthodox stories of the way the world of government budgeting, finance, and financial management works. Consensus becomes an object of research—when and why, so and not—rather than the assumption. Rational action becomes a focus of investigation, where research has led to the argument that managers or anyone else may never know what was intended until they act. Looking back, one can force order on the thought process—rationalize acts and decisions—but foresight may be a scarcer resource.

Therefore, helping or making people act more rationally is an ideology, often subjugating people, through a social process, to an abstract instrument, concept, or value that they would not hold if free. Making people act more rationally is an absolutist view of social phenomena. Many in financial management contest the existence of absolutes.

An alternative way of thinking about management, organization, people, and financial management is to view reality and its absolutes—the ideology existing in an organization—as whatever those in the organization build from their relationships. Organizing choices range from the authoritarian hierarchy to the loosely coupled system. The courses of action members of an organization choose can as often come from the ideas members project onto their world as from the realistic limits—brute facts—they face in trying to succeed in a common endeavor. Both projection and recognition of realistic limits exist under conditions that range from ambiguity to uncertainty to certainty.

The lesson? Research questions in government budgeting, finance, and financial management ask what happens in ambiguous circumstances, especially as the phenomena expected to help structure thought and action move toward randomness. Ambiguity is often the result of disagreement about goals. Studying life under these conditions tends to introduce, rather than ignore, preferences or values in public financial management theory and practice.

Ambiguity leads to an alternative way of thinking about financial management. In this way, anyone can describe public financial decision making without the premise of conscious, foresightful, intended action. Facing ambiguous preferences, goals, and ends conditions, anyone can argue that there is no verifiable "best interest" of an individual or collection of individuals. Rather, a decision made by an individual, in ordinary circumstances, is relatively random and unpredictable. What gives an otherwise random, unpredictable decision any meaning is either post hoc rationalization or the preemption of an individual's premises through organizational superiors' definitions of problems and situations (Simon, 1947).

Ambiguity Theory

This alternative to a rational or consensus model springs from two very different fields. The first, ambiguity theory, centers on the disconnectedness of ends and means and assumes inherent ambiguity in the effort to make any choice. March and Olsen (1976) explain:

> Intention does not control behavior precisely. Participation is not a stable consequence of properties of the choice situation or individual preferences. Outcomes are not a direct consequence of process. Environmental response is not always attributable to organizational action. Belief is not always a result of experience. (p. 21)

In a situation involving unknown or contradictory goals and technologies, as well as one in which individuals may differ in their levels of participation over time, according to March and Olsen, choice comes with difficulty because the actors seldom realize their preferences until they have made choices. Or, as Weick would put it (1980, p. 19), "How can I know what I think until I see what I say?"

Social Construction Theory

A second source for this alternative comes from a field of thought that emphasizes the relativity of meaning, a field that focuses on the social construction of reality (Berger and Luckmann, 1966; Goffman, 1961, 1974). This field argues that every organization, being in essence a social assemblage somewhere between evanescence and permanence, embodies a set of shared views of the world that give meaning to what organization members do. These views, or "interpretations of reality," build and gain legitimacy through the individuals' interaction with each other. Moreover, the existence of interpretations belies the notion that there exists an objective reality shared by all organizations.

The alternative idea we argue in this book holds that interpretation forces out ambiguity. That is, the greater the number of different, constructed realities, the greater the uncertainty that exists among and within organizations. For practical problems of management, the greater the uncertainty, the less likely management prescriptions—program budgeting, accrual accounting, or legislative postauditing—have any real applicability. Not agreeing about what a budget, accounting, or auditing system means or should do, financial managers employ procedures that are loosely coupled to any one view of reality (Weick, 1976).

As a result, the greater the compounding of differences among views in a group of individuals having some collective interest, such as an organization or a government, the greater the influence of randomness—in terms of events and specific people shaping meaning—and the larger the amount of interpretation needed by members to make sense and to act in a concerted way (Weick, 1979). Thus, it is in the interest of a financial manager to find a role that makes for gate keeping within this randomness. In one organization, for example, the finance officer may be an umpire among competing advocates, in another the guardian of the public purse which is under great pressure, and in still another, the prime institutional memory for past decisions made.

Moreover, the members of different organizations may develop different meanings for instruments of financial management, such as the budget. Among them we might find the budget is an analytical exercise, a pointless ritual, or the satisfaction of a mandate created somewhere else. In all cases, the set of roles and shared meanings are contextual, and therefore unique, belonging as they do to the particular actors who negotiated or constructed them there.

As a tool for research, the importance of the alternative way of looking at government budgeting, finance, and financial management lies in the perspective it provides on the ways we think. Emerging paradigms—ambiguity or social construction—could describe reality or predict behavior in ways that contrast with either orthodox or prevailing approaches.

All other views of finance decision making depend for their explanatory power on relatively large amounts of consensus about organization goals and technologies. Many research journals have published many articles that counted phenomena that exist or probably exist. Many, if not all, of the counts rest on a survey of opinion, a construction. Even more important, the questioner's construction probably differs from the respondent's in many, if not all, of the surveys. This consensus condition may not exist in many organizations, particularly public or governmental ones, and this alternative approach asks why and how. This alternative approach to research also seeks the fundamental, intersubjectively determined premises that make collective action possible.

A second difference among consensus-assumed and interpretive concepts exists in the assumption each holds about intention. The orthodox study of government budgeting and finance has followed a fairly simple route; public finance, political economy, and budget execution have held to the notion of rational actor.

Ideas based on Simon's notion of bounded rationality (1947), suggest the prevalence of uncertainty and the impossibility of an entirely rational actor. That is, individuals cannot know with certainty the consequences of given courses of action. Instead, courses of action are chosen when just enough information is available to predict consequences within reasonable tolerances. The rationality of management decision making is bounded by the costs and benefits of searches for satisfactory alternatives. Nevertheless, whether the rational effect of such decision making is more often than not produced, the intent purportedly exists.

"Making people rational" as a basis for management is, moreover, an ideology, others argue (Pfeffer, 1981). Some would say the ideology misuses the individual. The effect of intended rationality is to imply agreement among members of an organization about important ways of acting. Even if it is instrumentally important to gain agreement, assuming that action requires agreement tends to trivialize the basis for organized life—to connect too neatly the concept of organization with organized relationships among individuals, effectively subjugating an individual to an abstract concept (McSwain, 1987, p. 37). Organizations, it has been argued (White and McSwain, 1983; Weick, 1979) depend on the building blocks of relationships and the unconscious meanings and interpretations that develop out of them. Relationships may be managed in benign ways (Barnard, 1938, pp. 168–169) or in extremely harmful ones (Milgram, 1964). Not all facets of organized life mask the actual building blocks of organization; in fact, some, like "loosely coupled systems" (Weick, 1976), tend to encourage as well as sustain relationships.

Consider ideas that do not assume certainty. Assume instead a range of conditions from certainty to ambiguity. A researcher compares descriptions and explanations of actions that take place in all of these circumstances, especially as consensus moves toward randomness. Such may be valuable to know, and the investigation might be interesting and fruitful, especially as it influences human relationships in collective endeavors. Since ambiguity is often the result of disagreement about goals, studying life under these conditions is to introduce, rather than ignore, preferences or values in government budgeting, finance, and financial management.

Organization of the Book

The key ideas in this book are ambiguity and interpretations that move these unclear preferences, ends, and goals toward uncertainty and even consensus. The finance official is the critical interpreter, we argue. Implicit in the finance official's interpretation is a choice of logics. These logics come from technology, learned patterns of behavior, and even theory and research. The question we investigate in this book is what logic drives what interpretation when.

This book follows the alternative route of inquiry into government budgeting and finance discussed in this chapter. The genesis of this approach came in the

Carter-Reagan antigovernment era, when the basic premises of the Progressive Reform Era were first called into question by both Democrats and Republicans. We describe this history of financial reform to the present in Chapter 2.

The coalitions of interests, described in Chapter 2, are the primary influence on research that has gone on in government budgeting and finance, especially the topics chosen, the methods used, the explanations given, and the solutions found for problems. It is appropriate, then, that Chapter 2's history introduces the conceptual center of the book that leads to the third chapter's argument that practice is theory. Practitioners define what practice is. These are definitions or logics, economizing, responding, and democratizing. The logics serve as a conceptualization of government budgeting and finance. The interpretation argument practice is straightforward. Practice takes most, if not all, of its impetus and direction from the problems encountered in public organizations, and problem definitions depend on the lens through which finance officials see and the logics they apply.

The applications section of the book—all the chapters after our presentation of the practice is interpretation is theory argument—begins with a review of research on economizing. The review follows public finance research paths to determine what impacts fiscal policies can and do have.

The chapters on budgeting illustrate the responding or agency logic. The conventional budgeting chapter (5) deals with responsiveness to political masters. The nonconventional budget chapter (6) deals with cultural and value responsiveness.

The citizen participation and revenue regime change chapters (7 and 8) discuss two very different forms the democratization logic takes. The first form is an inclusive one, in which citizens are invited to take part in the traditional government budgeting and finance decision-making process. The second form, initiative and referendum or direct democracy efforts usually connected with tax limitations, is democratization's revolt form.

In the two other chapters, we expand the scope of the illustrations to show some combinations of logics and what they reveal. In the debt management networks chapter (9), we explain the logic of economizing interest costs in a debt sale. We contrast it with a responding logic found in the case study the chapter presents. The combination is definitely a hybrid, and we describe that hybrid as something very close to exploitation—debt network members take advantage of the opportunities each offers the others.

In the tax incentives for economic development chapter (10), we consider these incentives as an economizing measure and as a group of fiscal policies meant to respond to the needs of business firms a locality is trying to recruit. Indirectly, the incentives respond to citizens in need of jobs as well as political masters needing to show that they can do something about economic problems. We provide some data to show that economizing and responding may actually lead to business exploitation of intergovernmental competition. The winning government may actually be cursed with a business firm that leaders paid more than required to recruit or that will cost more than the benefits the locality will receive.

The alternative approach to research identified here forms the medium, by which we explain important facets of financial management. While we see this approach as following directly from events and problems in public organizations and from the ideological bent of many political actors in competition, we argue the alternative as but one of the ways to truth. We believe, like Golembiewski (1977, pp. 218–219), that in a field where sufficient agreement about a uniform perspective does not exist to focus research and practices, scientists must recognize the value of overlapping and competing metaphors. Competition takes account of diversity and builds on the creativity existing in initial stages of development of thought.

Endnotes

1. To make all easier to read, we will use all of these terms and other related ones interchangeably in this book.

References

Astley, W. Graham. (1985). Administrative science as socially constructed truth. *Administrative Science Quarterly* 30:497–513.

Barnard, Chester I. (1938). *The Functions of the Executive.* Cambridge, MA: Harvard University Press.

Berger, Peter L., and Thomas Luckmann. (1966). *The Social Construction of Reality: A Treatise in the Sociology of Knowledge.* New York: Doubleday.

Caplan, Edwin H. (1966). Behavioral assumptions of management accounting. *The Accounting Review* 61:496–509.

Goffman, Erving. (1961). *Asylums.* Garden City, NY: Doubleday.

Goffman, Erving. (1974). *Frame Analysis.* New York: Harper & Row.

Golembiewski, Robert T. (1977). *Public Administration as a Developing Discipline: Part 1: Perspectives on Past and Present.* New York: Dekker.

March, James G., and Johan P. Olsen. (1976). *Ambiguity and Choice in Organizations.* Bergen, Norway: Universitetsforlaget.

McSwain, Cynthia J. (1987). A structuralist perspective on organizational ethos. *Dialogue* 9(4):35–58.

Milgram, Stanley. (1964). *Obedience to Authority: An Experimental View.* New York: Harper & Row.

Orosz, Janet Foley. (2001). The truth is out there: Is postmodern budgeting the real deal? In *Evolving Theories of Public Budgeting*, ed. John Bartle, 125–156. New York: JAI.

Pfeffer, Jeffrey. (1981). *Power in Organizations.* Marshfield, MA: Pitman.

Simon, Herbert A. (1947). *Administrative Behavior.* New York: Free Press.

Weick, Karl. (1980). The management of eloquence. *Executive* 6:18–21.

Weick, Karl E. (1976). Educational organizations as loosely-coupled systems. *Administrative Science Quarterly* 21:1–19.

Weick, Karl E. (1979). Cognitive processes in organizations. In *Research in Organizational Behavior*, ed. B. M. Staw, 41–74. Vol. 1. Greenwich, CT: JAI Press.

White, Orion F., Jr., and Cynthia J. McSwain. (1983). Transformational theory and organizational analysis. In *Beyond Method: Strategies for Social Research*, ed. Gareth Morgan (pp. 292–305). Newbury Park, CA: Sage.

Chapter 2

History of Government Budgeting and Finance Reforms

Radically different imperatives have guided government budgeting and finance through modern history from the twentieth century on. The radical differences, and constant change toward each other, stand in stark contrast to the imperatives of nongovernmental, economic organizations.

Consider first market firms. Market-driven organizations unify tasks. To maximize value of the organization to the shareholder, managers must confront three issues: the investment decision (the allocation of capital to investment proposals whose benefits are to be realized in the future), the financing decision (determining capital structure), and the dividend decision (determining the amount of earnings paid to shareholders in cash) (Van Horne, 1986).

In contrast to maximizing value in market firms, ambiguity has characterized the environment, goals, and technologies of government financial management. The profession of those who manage the fiscal affairs of government involves both the spending and the husbanding of wealth. Episodically, widely different interests have tried to influence one or both of these halves. Ironically, the interests that coalesced have found common ground in forcing reform in government for often irreconcilable reasons.

The question "Why so?" is quite difficult to answer. For the public sector, knowing *how* disparate government finance activities such as budget, revenue, and debt management developed together is easier to understand than *why* the interests compromised to create the norms that came to exist. The question remains: Normatively, what propels government finance activities?

This chapter traces reform episodes. Reform episodes emerge as periods in which coalitions materialized to create an uncontested direction in which all financial activities might head. The first section of this chapter depicts the episodes in five stages, from the early Progressive movement to the beginning of a right turn in politics based on supply-side economics, that has an impact on government finance. The second part of the chapter distinguishes the episodes as three major stages, stages in which either efficiency, equity, or parsimony dominated. The last part of the chapter argues that the battles among reform coalition parties were bruising, profoundly affecting the practice of government finance, the formation of theories, and the conduct of research.

The significance of this chapter lies in the fact that unifying, normative concepts are hard to locate among the various government finance enterprises. The field has grown, but the ideas that form its imperative (do it this way!) come from different, sometimes even contradictory, points of view.

In treasury operations, for instance, contradictory values guide idle cash investment policy. Fiduciary values compel finance officers not to invest idle public funds for fear of risking their loss.[1] These values derive from the nature of speculative risk that has undergirded much private sector–public sector interaction over time (Myers, 1970; Nash, 1979; Dewey, 1930; Hammond, 1970; Bolles, 1869).

Other values advise the opposite. The time value of money concept,[2] along with the idea of opportunity costs, suggests that not investing idle funds is a method of losing the money's value.

Research in government budgeting and finance has proceeded and gained the respect it has by episodically rebalancing fundamental values revealed in unifying ideas. But why be concerned with ideas or values, rebalanced or not? Political leaders and government administrators, no less citizens, voice considerable concern about the work of government finance researchers and teachers; the lack of organizing concepts has provoked debate (Kioko et al., 2010; Rubin, 1988). The consequences of a lack of consensus, the debate suggests, are insufficient farsightedness when prescribing solutions as problems arise. The wages of disagreement could also lead to splintered and disjointed research efforts, slow comprehension of developing financial problems besetting government, insufficiently equipped students of programs that train for the public service, and the dissipation of effort in a long tradition of parity with the field of public administration in advancing inquiry.

The normative problem, this chapter argues, is not a problem so much as a political struggle. The field has bobbed, uncomfortably, among different normative and ideological coalitions.

Normative Development of Government Budgeting and Finance

We first review the history of the study of fiscal activities. We describe this as six basic stages of development thinking, from the early "reform government" movements to the current one sponsored by conservative economists.

The Efficient Citizenship Movement

The Progressive movement produced, through the National Municipal League and the New York Bureau of Municipal Research, the idea of a budget and a principle by which to unify all aspects of financial management. According to Waldo (1948, pp. 32–33):

> [Progressives] were sensitive to the appeals and promises of science, and put a simple trust in discovery of facts as the way of science and as a sufficient mode for solution of human problems.... They accepted—they urged—the new positive conception of government, and verged upon the idea of a planned and managed society.... [They] found in business organization and procedure an acceptable prototype for public business. They were ardent apostles of "the efficiency idea" ... [C]ivic awareness and militancy, efficiency, and "useful" education ... together form the core of the Efficient Citizenship movement.

Involved in this movement were three basic groups: positive government proponents, usually called progressives; governmental research bureau professionals or the analysts; and business interests to which openness provided a way to check large increases in tax bills. The movement[3] produced the principle that a well-informed citizenry, provided information through easily understood government budgeting and finance procedures—line-itemized budgets, competitively bid purchases, and audited financial statements—could check the moves of "detested politicians." Openness of government yielded a rudimentary medium through which action might follow. Efficiency stood as a "scientific" check on processes used in government, by providing a performance standard.

Openness became the great unifying principle that drew support and led to the coalition of interests supporting reform. The coalition members that produced the reforms implementing efficient citizenship had different goals; all of the goals were complementary only when the open government issue provided context. At other times, business favored restrained taxation. The researchers promoted the secular notion that "proper institutions and expert personnel" could create "good" government (Waldo, 1948, p. 23). The positive government proponents sought to use government authority to provide services needed as a result of the demand for more roads and schools.

Restrained taxation, responsible procedures, and government leadership in economic and social development were fundamental positions of members of the original coalition. The later developments integrating government budgeting and finance derive from rebalancing these three goals: parsimony, efficiency, and equity. Changes in the size of government could continually pull the coalition apart.

The upshot of the efficient government movement efforts to proceduralize government administration for accountability's sake led to the widespread institution of organizations for this purpose. The insistence on openness gave the institutionalizing movement momentum. The Budget and Accounting Act of 1921 became the major achievement. The act created a budget office and an auditing agency, both of which would open government to scrutiny through publication of a unified budget. Unification and openness put the spotlight on the executive; all could follow the decisions being made because they all took place in public view under the responsibility of a single official. Moreover, the implementation of these decisions could be checked by the other half of the act's purview: the expenditure audit.

The other members of the original coalition came off somewhat less well, even poorly. Researchers could look to the budget bureau and the accounting office as places where analysis might take hold. Greater faith in government decisions might come out of greater openness and might also lead to equity in vigorous government, a position of positive government proponents. Oddly enough, business interests, and parsimony, lost the biggest fight, that over the income tax when it was established just before the 1921 act, and their share of the outcomes of the efficient citizenship movement was earned from the movement's acceptance of business operations as the standard for appropriate and high-quality financial management.

The Positive Government Movement

If the muckrakers led the movement for the 1921 act, the positive government proponents could claim to lead the movement toward the New Deal. The economic debacle of the Great Depression prompted government action as a method of ameliorating its effects. The key word was *equity*, embellished with analysis.

In fact, the Brownlow Committee's major gripe about the ineffectiveness of the original Bureau of the Budget was its emphasis on preparing the budget rather than directing and controlling its execution (President's Committee on Administrative Management, 1937, pp. 15–24). In the Roosevelt sense of letting ideas grow even if in conflict with each other, the control had become secondary to finding solutions to pressing problems of economic growth and governance.

The report of the Brownlow Committee might be read as one faction of the positive government movement talking to another. The committee, by implication, saw the positive government movement splitting, and thereby diminishing, its effort. By devoting less attention to the ideal of comprehensive budget control and central direction, the movement had failed to capitalize on the returns of diversity. If the ideal—"the new positive conception of government [that] verged upon the idea of a planned and managed society" (Waldo, 1948, p. 32)—were to come true, a new orthodoxy must develop, especially one that integrated fiscal management under an executive with undivided powers, a clear chain of command, and sufficient planning, directing, and accountability mechanisms to bring these powers to effect. The upshot? Equity, to the positive government types, lay in a planned and managed society with a big, but disciplined government.

The Analytical Movement

Following on President Johnson's institution of the Planning, Programming, and Budgeting System (PPBS) in the federal government, financial systems became useful for analysis of any number of questions.

This movement was the later derivation of the efficiency emphasis in early Progressive literature, the idea that referred more generally to the movement that tried to apply rules of scientific inquiry to the solution of public problems through government.

Substantially, the PPBS reform changed the basic assumptions behind resource allocation—from equitable distribution to optimization. It also led to the analysis of programs, the establishment of goals, and the rational pursuit of goal and program achievement. Such an organization of inquiry was the basis of the idea in the first place: there is a principle by which all important aspects of management operate; discovery of that principle may come with disciplined inquiry.

Later embellishments of the original PPBS reform came with President Carter's sponsorship of U.S. Department of Housing and Urban Development's (HUD) Financial Management Capacity Sharing Program. Significant among the products of this program were analytical devices, especially the Financial Trend Monitoring System (Groves, Godsey, and Shulman, 1981), major initiatives in productivity measurement (Epstein, 1984), and a proposal for integrating fiscal systems (Grossman and Hayes, 1981).

Still more capacity building took place in President Nixon's first administration and continued into the Ford administration. The conservative, Republican presidents' effort to strengthen local government came through a three-pronged effort. The first prong involved revenue sharing with local and state governments. The greater capacity of the federal government to collect revenue would be matched with the greater (and often better, some said) local capability to deliver services and implement federal domestic policy. Local problems beset the country, and state and local governments were far closer and abler in solving them, the revenue sharing partisans argued.

The second prong of the effort developed through Nixon administration efforts to strengthen planning at the state and local government levels. The HUD programs that subsidized the regional, area, and city land use planning activities got new mandates to increase the management capacities of these units and the governments of which they were a part. In addition, a review and notification system for federal grants came into being to help coordinate local government planning and development efforts.

Third, the capacity building effort of the later Nixon years and the Ford years directed attention to intergovernmental management, and especially the relationship among policy management (leadership), resource management (organizational maintenance, adaptation and compliance with environmental constraints), and program management (productivity and responsiveness to client needs and policy guidance). The clearest statement of the nature of capacity building (Executive Summary, 1975) suggests that capacity building was an instrument of restraint. That is, building capacity and resources at levels of government other than the federal level would lead to federal spending and taxing restraint.

The implications of analyst dominance remain today, especially in assessing capacity building's features in common with privatization. The major plank in both President Carter's election platform and that of President Reagan was the need to put a stop to Washington administrative harmony with Congress. Capacity building, in other words, became a method of breaking up the positive government-bureau movement alliance that had made the efficient citizenship movement possible and which had produced the New Deal's infrastructure. In breaking apart analyst from progressive, the capacity building movement led unwittingly to privatization.

Supply-Side Economics

Supply-side economics gained favor in explaining the need for large tax cuts joined with genuine reform of the tax structure (Roberts, 1984) and almost single-handedly installed parsimony as the primary virtue in government finance. Tax cuts gained justification in the view of many that tax rates and revenue production have a curvilinear relationship—up to a point, both tax rates and revenue increase, after which rate increases lead to successively smaller total revenue increases.

Tax cuts, and even a flat rate for income taxes, would have an ameliorative effect on revenue because of two factors, supply-siders argue. First, tax rates would have a more neutral effect on economic production, leading to greater manufacturing and services output when profits were seen as a reward rather than a penalty. Second, lower taxes would stimulate economic production in its own right, as had been evident in earlier tax cuts in the Kennedy administration.

The timing of the increase in economic production and the by-product, greater government revenue, were never clear. The haziness became extremely consequential in marrying privatization to supply-side economics. The tax cuts in 1981, 1986, 2001, and 2003 produced large shortfalls in government revenue for the federal government without corresponding cuts in government expenditures. The deficit produced enormous pressure to cut spending further, to curtail debt increases, and to privatize still other government functions.

The Privatization Movement

The intellectual movement to reclaim private goods production from the government sector paralleled arguments for supply-side economic policies.[4] Although resting on a tradition in conservative political and economic thought (Schumpeter, 1942; Hayek, 1944; Buchanan and Tullock, 1962), privatization was popularized by E. S. Savas (1982). The revolt evident in privatization—government is "a horde of self-aggrandizing opportunists" (p. 1)—represents a return of business interests to paramount influence in the ruling coalition in government financial management.

Such influence finds its source in the tax revolts of the 1970s, but privatization also represents new thinking about the production of goods and services long dominated by positive government adherents. For instance, proposals have included rethinking toll goods: Could roads and bridges be financed as private property with use and pricing like any other consumer good? Could common pool resources, such as clean air, be regulated by allocating its pollution among competing abuses, through caps on the amount of pollutants, and allowing firms to trade any of the amount under the cap to other firms producing more than their capped amount (USEPA, 2010). Another proposal would give manufacturers the right to continue producing pollutants if they were willing to pay higher fees for the right (Hershey, 1989). Public goods come under special scrutiny, as managers explore ways to check expenditures by contracting out the production of such services as corrections.

Finally, federal government regulators, illustrated by the Securities and Exchange Commission and the Food and Drug Administration, have begun exploring the uses of fees to help the agencies become self-sustaining. Fees could be charged to the regulated industries in such a way that the industries' demand for permits of one sort or another could be matched with the "supply" of administrative and regulatory effort.

Moreover, the idea of a regulatory budget emerged (Crandall, 1978, pp. 93–94). The budget would reveal, limit, and allocate the cost of regulation. Like typical budget expenditures, the regulatory budget would include only the measurable costs incurred by firms in meeting regulatory requirements.

Cutback Management

The analysts' response to tax revolts, tax reform, and budget deficits was cutback management, the notion of managed reductions in force and program structure.[5] The hallmark of this line of thinking was the strength of hierarchy variable in determining orderly contraction of public organizations (Levine, 1980; Dunsire and Hood, 2010). Where hierarchy did not exist, it was argued, interest group resistance replaces orderliness, and interest groups adapt as they vie among themselves to preserve distributional patterns within policy areas they dominate (Rubin, 1985). Fiscal policy and government budgeting and finance problems created by recessions and other crises have added new insistence to cutback management and privatization (Miller and Svara, 2009).

Coalition Convergence and Divergence in Three Stages

The leaders of the successive movements who have swayed thinking in government budgeting and finance shared one important belief—that openness in government's financial dealings served their own interests, whether they were

parsimony. Those interests might be very different—pro-
̹ositive government, business interests low taxes, and research
̹sis (and muckrakers punishment for thieves). However, the coali-
̹ to pursue openness believed the basic currency of government bud-
gꜜ ̹g and finance to be procedures and routines that were able to be both
observed and evaluated.[6] Observable and able to be evaluated *for what* remained
to be seen.

Openness was the currency among the members of the reform coalition. It
united them all in opposition to what were referred to as political forces, widely
known as the political clubs that controlled local and often state government and
which were themselves controlled by a political boss.

Openness was also the plateau to reach before any of the reform coalition members could realize any of their beliefs. Positive government types had to have some
measure of fairness, and the data besides, to determine equity and to counter the
effects of discrimination and less than ideal levels of political participation. Only
openness could provide this measure and the necessary data. Analysts had to have
openness in order to determine efficiency. Business interests had to have openness
in order to pinpoint the threats to parsimony and the sources of inequity in their
taxes. (Muckrakers, finally, had to have openness, in order to root out thievery.)

Openness, itself, was not accountability. Openness was the necessary basis on
which to build accountable systems of work. Accountability was the belief, the
vision to be fulfilled, while openness was a way of employing technology and management to achieve the vision.

Systems of Accountability as Sources of Divergence

Reform coalition members held different beliefs, advocated different management
systems, and advanced the use of different technologies, all of which implied different systems of accountability. If we consider muckraking as essentially the primary
position of all members of the coalition, we are left with three major, sometimes
overlapping groups and systems of accountability: positive government types—
more government as service needs expanded; analytical and research types—efficient government first and foremost; and pro-business types—low taxes for greater
returns on investment in private enterprise. Consider Table 2.1 and its portrayal of
these systems.

Among the members of the group, differences existed over the accountability
premise. Positives and pro-business interests tended to see needs outside the organization as having primary control over what the organization did; they saw responsibility in equity. This responsiveness to clients or taxpayers tended to outweigh the
need for responsibility, especially that premised on efficiency calculations and held
by analyticals, and that premised on parsimony arguments and held by business
interests.

Table 2.1 Comparison of Accountability Systems Implied by Reform Coalition Members in Government Financial Management

	Group		
	Positives	*Analyticals*	*Pro-Business*
Accountability Premise	Equity	Efficiency	Parsimony
Technology	Marginality	Productivity	Monetized utility
Organization Theory	Negotiated	Hierarchical	Privatization
Belief System	Government as expanding sphere	Government as fixed sphere	Government as contracting sphere

Source: Adapted from Waldo, D., *The Administrative State: A Study of the Political Theory of American Public Administration*, The Ronald Press, New York, 1948; Schiesl, M. J., *The Politics of Efficiency: Municipal Administration and Reform in America, 1800–1920*, University of California Press, Berkeley, 1977.

Technologies differed as well. Positives tended to compare programs with other programs, defining the best programs as those whose rates of return at the margin outweighed others. Efficiency as technology demanded a calculation of material inputs and outputs with effort taken to ensure minimum loss in between. Typically, pro-business interests determined the worthiness of effort based on its perceived utility expressed in money terms and discounted for loss of value over time; the value of the preferred effort exceeded that of alternative ones.

Members of the coalition differed in their approach to the problems of management, in their organization theories. Positive government types wanted the goals and methods of organizations to be matters of cooperation reached through negotiation (Golembiewski, 1977). Analyticals, from the Brownlow Committee on, tended toward hierarchy (Gulick and Urwick, 1937). The pro-business interests favored private sector provision of most services that had before been produced by government (Wolf, 1988).

Finally, the belief system of the three elements of the reform coalition differed. Positive government types, by definition, believed in government as an expanding sphere of influence in direct proportion to the demand for public services. In contrast, pro-business interests lay in shrinking government's sphere for the sake of both increasing business opportunity and decreasing taxes. Analyticals, however, tended to waffle on the size of government issue, emphasizing the efficiency issue whatever the sphere of government.

The Long-Term, Lasting Effect of Divergences

The similarities and differences among the members of the earliest reform coalition have had a remarkably durable effect on thinking about government financial management. The three early versions of accountability—equity, efficiency, and parsimony—have competed as sources for technologies in present reforms, different points of view regarding the role government budgeting and finance should play in government organizations, cognitive styles to which financial managers lay claim, and the theories of government organization to which the field subscribes. A statement of government budgeting and finance theory, at any point, is an amalgam, or more accurately, a scorecard indicating which of the original sources of thought has greatest, current influence. Therefore, there has never been a stable belief structure—a consensus about the role of government finance in society or the role of government budgeting and finance in government—on which to base theory in the field of public financial management. Political coalitions evolve, and different beliefs have influence.

Consider three basic beliefs that still compete to dominate thinking in the field, as identified and contrasted in Table 2.2.

Table 2.2 Comparison of Theories Derived from Early Reform Efforts in Government Financial Management

	Theory		
	Cybernetics	*Pluralism*	*Public Choice*
Accountability Premise	Efficiency	Equity	Parsimony
Originating From	Analyticals	Positivists	Pro-business
Technology	Productivity	Marginality	Monetized utility
Organization Theory	Hierarchical	Negotiated	Privatization
Belief System	Government as fixed sphere	Government as expanding sphere	Government as contracting sphere
Culture	Hierarchical	Egalitarian	Individualistic

Source: Adapted from Waldo, D., *The Administrative State: A Study of the Political Theory of American Public Administration*, The Ronald Press, New York, 1948; Schiesl, M. J., *The Politics of Efficiency: Municipal Administration and Reform in America, 1800–1920*, University of California Press, Berkeley, 1977; Wildavsky, A., *Budgeting: A Comparative Theory of Budgetary Processes*, 2nd rev. ed., Transaction Books, Piscataway, NJ, 1986.

The first belief system is one derived from centralized planning and control. It is based in cybernetics and elaborated in accounting theory (Key, 1940; Simon, 1947; Beer, 1959; Smithies, 1955; Comptroller General of the United States, 1985).

The second approach and belief system, epitomized in budgeting theory, has a decidedly pluralistic, management orientation. This approach derives from an open-systems logic, and it achieves its highest elaboration in organization decision-making theory (Churchman, 1968; von Bertanffly, 1968; Johnson, Kast, and Rosenzweig, 1963; Lindblom, 1965; Cyert and March, 1963; Cohen, March, and Olsen, 1972).

The third approach, based in economics, influences thought as a normative device through public choice theories (Buchanan, 1987; Borcherding, 1977). Its influence extends to research methods, especially that in positive methodologies (Friedman, 1953) and to analytic technologies such as cost-benefit analysis (Kaldor, 1939; Hicks, 1940). The approaches compete; each, however, is strongest in different areas of analysis. Much of accounting and control theory has technical application, especially in the ability to characterize and classify data. Accounting theory vaguely implies a top-down management structure and even more vaguely a hierarchical culture and belief system based on maintaining distinctions (strata, castes) among groups.

Budgeting theory has a strong managerial flavor. It suggests a negotiation between bureaus and central guardian agencies—a sort of bottom-up flow of initiative and information subject to varying degrees of centralized discretion, control, or reconciliation. Budgeting theory implies but does not elaborate a technology based on marginal rates of substitution: each claimant's incremental demand is compared to each other claimant's demand rather than all past demands. It also implies an egalitarian belief system, as each source of initiative may be roughly, equally legitimate, even though distinctions—particularly those that limit political participation—still bar total equality. Economic analysis has very little to say about management but implies a quantification of productivity measures and their analysis. The major contribution made by this approach is the belief expressed by public choice theorists in a small or contracting sphere for government action. A pro-business culture would resemble that espoused by pro-market advocates: highly decentralized decision making that is individualistic rather than collectivist in its action.

A Continuing and Episodic Struggle

The three approaches continue today as diverging views. The struggle to dominate—to decide what government budgeting and finance will entail—is one that continues.

The struggle could be one for political dominance. Others who have given it some attention—in the budgeting literature (Schick, 1966; Hyde, 1978; Rubin,

1988) —view it in a different way. They suggest, instead, a gently unfolding succession of methods of analysis that build cumulatively. For instance, Schick's view is one of a control emphasis setting the stage for a management focus in budgeting, with the management focus requiring the data gathering that a control emphasis yielded. A planning gestalt succeeds control and management, adding a futuristic dimension to budgeting decision making, but not displacing the necessary tools of control and management. The "gently unfolding succession" idea may mask a truly titanic struggle, however, a struggle that befits an area of administration of such magnitude as financial management. Knowledge acquisition here has two competing explanations, and the subject deserves analysis.

As a method of depicting the way specific reforms gained support, consider the following model. Burchell and his colleagues (1980) and, in a more basic way, Thompson and Tuden (1959) represent different variations of consensus and disagreement as a matrix based on answers to two basic questions. First, do interests agree on what ends may be served by prevailing technologies? For example, can interests agree on what end openness would serve? Second, do interests agree on what means might be most suitable for achieving a given end? That is, do interests agree on what means might be most suitable to achieve equity, efficiency, and parsimony?

By answering each of the questions, we have the cells pictured in Table 2.3. The table may be interpreted, and illustrated with specific reforms, cell by cell. That is, cell 1 suggests agreement on means and ends. The case of complete agreement is best illustrated by interpreting the original coalition's action that created modern financial management. That is, agreement existed over means (openness in financial management) to achieve the given end (accountability).

Cell 2 portrays agreement on ends but disagreement over means. The most memorable illustration is the conflict that transpired in 1937 and 1938 between the President's Committee on Administrative Management and the Brookings Institution. Brookings (U.S. Senate Committee Investigating Executive Agencies, 1937) argued the validity of intensive analysis and classifications of activities into

Table 2.3 Preferences and Beliefs among Cybernetics, Pluralists, and Public Choice Interests

		Preferences about Ends	
		Agree	Disagree
Beliefs about Means	Agree	1	3
	Disagree	2	4

Source: Adapted from Burchell, S. et al., *Accounting, Organizations and Society*, 5: 14, 1980; Thompson, J. D., and A. Tuden, in *Comparative Studies in Administration*, ed. J. D. Thompson, P. B. Hammond, R. W. Hawkes, B. H. Junker, and A. Tuden, University of Pittsburgh Press, Pittsburgh, PA, 195–216, 1959.

major functions—reorganizing for reorganizing's sake. The President's Committee argued the value of solving the President's management problems, such as giving direction to budgeting through the transfer of the Bureau of the Budget to a newly created Executive Office of the President.

The same events have unfolded over the U.S. Bureau of Census model of municipal government (Fox, 1977; MacDonald, 1988). The bureau directors created functions that seemed common to city government activities. The functions became a means of reporting, in a comparable way, the data received from local governments. The end product, however, was a basis not only for classifying data but also for organizing departments and for developing early professions in local government.

The mirror image of cell 2 is that in cell 3, the agreement on means and disagreement on ends. Perhaps the best illustration of such is the use of PPBS in the Johnson administration (Rabin, 1975; Schick, 1973; Wildavsky, 1966; Novick, 1968). Understood to have worked well in the Defense Department as a method of maximizing choices over weapons systems (with operations research a long heralded success at the same thing), President Johnson decreed the spread to other agencies, with less spectacular results. Schick observed (1973, p. 416) that "analysis was to be a change agent; it would reorient budgeting by serving it." What PPBS may actually have been was a *means* (as opposed to end) of appearing frugal and centralizing decision making (Wildavsky, 1966, p. 306; Golembiewski, 1989).

In either case, the means—either deliberately or fortuitously—determined the end. Wildavsky (1966, p. 300) observed: "A (if not the) distinguishing characteristic of systems analysis is that the objectives are either not known or are subject to change." He quotes Hitch (1960, p. 19) to reinforce: "We may, of course, begin with tentative objectives, but we must expect to modify or replace them as we learn about the systems we are studying—and related systems."

Cell 4 represents an absence of consensus in either way, means or ends. It also represents a method of resolving disagreement. That is, cell 1 suggests the destination of thinking when disagreement over either ends or means exists. One expects to achieve consensus by working through disagreements whatever they may be. Cell 4 takes a different approach by suggesting the resolution of utter conflict (disagreement over both ends and means) through the redefinition or reinterpretation of the phenomenon entirely. In fact, cell 4 may be a destination of thinking itself. As agreement on either means or ends becomes remote in ambiguous situations, those parties who have a stake in the outcome may reinterpret the events and their context, often post hoc, in order to achieve agreement (Weick, 1979).

The Nature of Reform Episodes

This model, Table 2.3, also helps classify all reform episodes as a whole, or the idea of how knowledge is acquired. As pointed out earlier, Schick (1966) and others (Hyde, 1978; Lyden and Miller, 1978) have depicted these efforts as a "gently unfolding succession" of developments that build on the strengths of predecessor reforms. I have described them as titanic struggles that are more discontinuous than cumulative in their effects. There are still other views. What view has the greatest plausibility? What difference does it make?

Consider each cell in Table 2.3. Cell 1 reflects the no change position. This position is generally espoused by those who view the survival of a procedure or policy over a long period of reform as the survival of what was a stable state all along. Often, research has sought to interpret budgeting and tax reform legislation as failure-prone efforts to overhaul systems that require mere fine-tuning (Wildavsky, 1961; Wildavsky and Hammond, 1965). These research pieces have also related reforms to more general thinking in organization and accounting theory to show how different views of government budgeting and finance can easily coexist; control, management, and planning emphases in budgeting, for example, are not successors but complements. Each serves a different level of organization (Parsons, 1960; Thompson, 1967; Anthony, 1965).

Cell 2 in Table 2.3 portrays differences over means but agreement over ends. Cell 2 reflects a *linear* notion of reform. As events occur, particularly those unforeseen by the original reformers, the original reforms become "established types" and targets for new reformers who find it advantageous to attack the orthodox thinking and its unpopular results. In this instance, the struggle to dominate thought among finance professionals creates temporary solutions to a continuing problem—how to finance the aims of government adequately as well as guard the public treasury from plunder and abuse. Reforms to solve this tension gain support, are enacted, and then have foreseen and, more importantly, unforeseen consequences, this interpretation argues. Those unforeseen consequences show vulnerabilities, and they offer opportunities for opponents to attack. Early thinking about budgets, for example, suggested that line itemization might provide information for a public that had little idea for what and how its money was spent. Openness served the function of control. Yet, large itemized lists often toppled of their own weight; they actually provided more places to hide than less. In fact, the Hoover Commissions felt that less, rather than more, control was exerted through these types of budgets (Gross, 1969).

Cell 3 of Table 2.3 portrays the agreement on means but disagreement on ends. Such a situation—a set of means searching for an end—occurred in public financial management: in the PPBS and zero based budgeting (ZBB) episodes in budgeting and in the strategic planning movement in debt management. Particularly evident in PPBS, the means—greater use of analysis, particularly methods of operations research—gained credence from World War II on, leading to the development of a band of devoted disciples of analysis who found a succession of ends that the means could serve—bombing, strategic weapons, weapons costs analysis, and finally budgeting. ZBB, too, was a matter of taking an innovation from one context (Texas Instruments) and applying it in another (Georgia state government and then the U.S. government), in the former to force attention on innovation and in the latter to show frugality (Pyhrr, 1977). In the strategic planning movement, much store has been placed by early recognition of ends that the various tools of treasury or cash management—various put and call option variations—might be employed to optimize (Miller, 1991, pp. 152–160). In either case, the means are glorified, the ends found incidental: almost any will do.

This view of reforms suggests what popular historians (Schlesinger, 1986) call the cycles of history. That is, issues change and opportunities appear on which one or another set of interest groups finds it easiest to capitalize. Groups such as professions have vested interests, not so much in what to gain, but in where to apply the technologies that have been developed and fine-tuned. Dominance moves from one interest to another and back again. Therefore, cell 3 resembles a nonlinear view of reform or change in public financial management. Circumstances change and opportunities develop in which a group finds it advantageous to assert mastery over events (Kaufman, 1956, fn. 11; Ferguson and Rogers, 1986).

Cell 4 takes a different tack entirely in suggesting that differences over both means and ends can exist. Most closely following the logic in Wildavsky's cultural theory (1986), this position holds that preferences emanate from culture, as do appropriate means "to get people what they want" (p. 5). Cultures differ, and it follows that preferences and means to attain them differ as well.

Wildavsky sees variations among cultures in two ways. The groups with which people identify or to which they belong have more or less strong boundaries. These groups also have more or less emphatic prescriptions for members' actions. Thus differences over ends and means (cell 4) are defined by those involved as very basic, each preference "endogenous, formed through opposing and supporting institutions" (p. 5).

Ambiguity for finance officials is common in mixed cultures such as the United States. While some states, regions, and even institutions may suggest a single culture, few are, at least by the imprecise and deliberately abstracted categories Wildavsky uses.

The differences among the principal cells, cell 2/ends looking for means and cell 3/means looking for ends, suggest different theories of change and different political theories as well. Cell 2/looking for means suggests Kuhn's concept of change (1970): ideas (means) work until something better comes along. Cell 3/looking for an end resembles Kaufman's battles among forces underlying public administration doctrine (1956). Each interest, whether neutral competence, executive leadership, or representativeness, has control of the political universe in mind; the battle exists over how control will develop. Political theories change with the cells as well. In the cell 2/looking for means situation, a council of experts is called for (elite politics) in which falsification—as with scientific method—is the major determinant of appropriate means. In the case of cell 3/looking for ends, pluralist politics requires compromise in which a dominant set of groups achieves control.

The similarities between cells 2 and 3 are equally remarkable. In cell 2, events transpire that create anomalies that the working reform fails to comprehend, much less solve. In cell 3, events transpire that create dysfunction. In both, events beyond reforms' control have the crucial effect.

Second, both theories have interpretive features. That is, in both cells 2 and 3, ambiguity exists about what happened to cause the apparent need for reform and why. The resulting anomalies or dysfunctions lead to competition among explanations.

The implications for the plausibility of the gently unfolding succession could not be harsher. While Schick (1966) suggests that values smoothly and cumulatively evolve, such does not seem to be so, in either the logic of events surrounding financial systems reform or the evidence alone. Reform seldom represents a progressive accumulation of knowledge because it is so often prodded by anomalous events. At the very least, reform may come about because events create opportunities that vested interests exploit (cell 3). Reforms may also offer opportunities with which rationalization of the past or reinterpretation of the present changes the entire picture confronting all actors (cell 4). The entire frame of reference changes, in fact, so that no vested interest sees the world in the same way, no anomalous event can truly be said to be anomalous or not, and steady-state politics no longer exists. It is this last type of reform that leads to the plausibility of a titanic struggle.

This titanic struggle involves no less than the fight to change the entire premise by which individuals operate. This fight is over what Taylor (1961) calls "vindication" or "the standards and rules that make up a value system" (p. 129). The competition among value systems could not be keener, and the implications for what we know more profound. The logic of events allows the conceivability that professionals battle, instead of slowly and peacefully giving way to each other. Their norms are pitted against each other in a way that their entire reason for existence may be called into question. The threat to jobs, livelihoods, and even conceptions to self lurks. Events themselves suggest that change comes with conflict, and this view is not new. Morstein Marx (1957) portrays the battles that took place as far back as the Brownlow Committee in 1937, between the orthodox Brooking Institution crowd and the more insurgent New York City crowd from the Bureau of Municipal Research, as fierce. Kaufman (1956) has described many similar ideological battles in the second Hoover Commission. Evidence from Mosher (1984) comparing the development of the U.S. General Accounting Office (GAO) and the U.S. Office of Management and Budget (OMB) and from Walker (1986) on GAO leads one to believe that the successions of points of view, as OMB and GAO evolved, did not take place in a deferential way but in circumstances just short of force.

The logic of events and the events themselves support the idea of a titanic struggle for dominance of the premises behind government budgeting and finance and leads to analysis of current thinking in these terms. Who rules?

The Right Turn in Politics and Related Developments

The period from California's Proposition 13 in 1978 through Colorado's Taxpayer Bill of Rights in 1992 produced narratives about change in the practice and theory of subnational government budgeting and finance in the United States. President Reagan's idea that "government is not the solution to our problem; government is the problem" and President Clinton's "the era of big government is over" lead almost anyone to believe in the end of New Deal, Fair Deal, New Frontier, and Great Society eras that held a "good government is good" view—especially of fiscal management: "as the work and accomplishments of public agencies came to be regarded as benefits, the task of budgeting was redefined as the effective marshalling of fiscal and organizational resources for the attainment of benefits" (Schick, 1966, p. 249). Hacker and Pierson (2007, 2010) argue that the 1990 Bush tax increase,[7] over a promise not to create new taxes or raise rates among existing taxes, was the watershed event that changed the stories told to pursue fiscal policy, practice, and theory in the U.S. federal government.

The substance of change may be less important than its form. How, you ask, do narrative and storytelling encourage or discourage change? How do they fit within fiscal regime change?

The pivotal events led to a new social construction of taxing and spending. The watershed in politics, as Hacker and Pierson (2007) describe it, included the hegemony of a supply-side economics narrative, the rebellion of economic elites in the Republican Party, the rise of tax cut-driven think tanks, and the development of many more safe seats in Congress, reducing party competition in congressional districts.

The social construction followed the arguments used by supply-siders. That is, tax policies starve government of resources as entitlements drive public spending. Tax expenditures, policy designs enacted through "the deliberate manipulation of rhetoric and policy presentation" (Hacker and Pierson, 2007, p. 279), and relatively uncontrollable direct and nonconventional expenditures based on "rights," disaster, or "too big to fail" produce structural deficits.

Tax cuts and rights are both social constructions derived from basic but contested concepts, which we find in democracy, justice, and liberty. Or are they? Realism holds that there are "reasoned arguments concerning the great political issues [that] can persuade opponents" (Grafstein, 1988, p. 9). Realism also holds that there are concepts from which we all deduce constructions, such as the conceptual base and arguments for tax cuts or rights-based spending. Otherwise, "without shared political and social values, specific arguments about democracy, justice, or liberty are bound to end, at best, in a mutual shrugging of shoulders" (Grafstein, 1988, p. 9) or the use of power, as Foucault argues. What if realism is wrong, that there is no agreement about underlying but contested concepts? What if the world of tax cutters and the world of rights advocates are purely social constructions that share no basic worldview? How do government budgeting and finance questions get resolved? When deficits are not sustainable, what will happen? Who will bear the burden of making budgets sustainable or who will become the undeserving?

Since the antigovernment campaigns waged by Presidents Carter and Reagan, a premise has gained ascendance in which positive, activist government has become "part of the problem rather than the solution." The premise, along with the observation that the era of big (positive) government is over, has had substantial effects on government budgeting and finance, raising the importance of privatization, supply-side economics, cutback management, and public choice. As part of the movement to end positive government, direct democracy movements have spread. These movements include various forms of citizen participation in financial and policy affairs. The direct democracy movements also include drives to pass referenda questions controlling the size of government, the legislative procedures in dealing with financial matters, tax issues, and the allocation of cutbacks in budgets. The right turn in national politics has built momentum due to the post-1970s oil crisis that provoked economic insecurity, technological innovation and change, a reduction in manufacturing jobs and rise in service jobs, and the growth of nonunionized firms in the U.S. sunbelt. The right turn has included both antitax policies and market allocation of private, toll, and common pool goods once produced by government. The right turn led to top-down budgeting in various forms as well as proposals for more comprehensive budgeting that includes tax expenditures and other forms of nonconventional expenditure, as well as direct, conventional expenditure. The right turn has also led to market, instead of government, allocation of public goods. The issues faced in government budgeting and finance have mirrored the fundamental change in premises. To take only four issues, consider how premises have changed to force a new frame of reference in the following.

Direct Democracy, Citizen Participation, and Initiatives and Referenda

Direct democracy includes techniques used to have either a positive or a negative impact, both of which affected government budgeting and finance. On the positive side, citizen participation efforts began with President Lyndon B. Johnson's encouragement of "maximum feasible participation" in community development programs funded by the War on Poverty. From that point, dogged by controversy over who has the right to decide, citizen participation has grown as a worldwide movement influencing efforts, especially at the local government level in the United States (Participatory Budget Project, 2010).

On the negative side, a series of initiatives and referenda during the right turn imposed tax limits, budget limits, and fiscal policy decision-making limits on government leaders. Proposition 13 in California in 1978 is the best known of the tax limit referenda. That initiative provided that a property's assessed value was its value when acquired (through change in ownership or new construction), with assessments changing by no more than the smaller of 2% or the inflation rate.

Best known of the budget limit referenda was the 1992 Taxpayer Bill of Rights (TABOR) constitutional amendment in Colorado. TABOR restricted all tax increases by all governments and school districts to those approved by voters in an election. Revenue collected at existing rates beyond that attributable to increases in inflation and population had to be refunded unless voters approved spending instead. In a 2005 referendum, Colorado voters approved suspension of the 1992 TABOR until 2010 with a modified version in effect afterwards.

The far-reaching fiscal policy decision-making limits, pejoratively "ballot box budgeting," were voted in in several states. These measures required a legislative supermajority vote to increase taxes or change revenue system designs in any way that was not revenue neutral. Initiatives with successful referenda have directed spending to specific objects, creating a larger expenditure budget. Finally, voters have approved measures that require that any referendum-approved spending measure must have a dedicated revenue stream, and spending could not exceed the amount in the stream.

Top-Down Budgeting

Emerging in the privatization movement is a new coalition of neutral competents and fiscal conservatives. Neutral competents are intent on pursuing top-down budgeting, as Schick (1986) says, as a way of evening balance between the bottom-up, agency-dominated interest group liberalism of the recent past (Wildavsky, 1964) and the more ideological and insurgent politics of the right turn in the 1980s (Ferguson and Rogers, 1986). Fiscal conservatives have taken the mantle of executive leadership; their lock on the presidency has provided initiative in a battle over who will govern, a battle in which fiscal issues become major tests of will and offer chances for one side or the other to threaten stalemate and bring the government's fiscal machinery to a halt. In any case, executive branch budgeting no longer rests solely on base and fair share norms that underlay a bottom-up budget system of administrative agency, congressional appropriations subcommittee, and interest group alliances. Top-down budgeting places the president on continual collision courses with congressional leaders. Further efforts across English-speaking and Scandinavian worlds have led to "entrepreneurial budgeting." Trading control of the total revenue and expenditure in the budget, leaders have delegated the design, planning, and control of the details to neutral competents.

Market Allocation of Private Goods

The loss by the positive government proponents in the emerging conflict is the loss of faith in pluralism as a means of allocation as well as a means of formulating regulatory policy, and as a contributor to the redistribution. Privatization, to its adherents, is a means by which private interests served by government programs can become actual, private, individual rights that the market can allocate.

To illustrate (Linowes, 1988, pp. 248–249), a small farmer, through government programs, has received permission to use publicly provided and subsidized water for irrigation. The farmer cannot transfer or sell this permission even if it has higher value to a municipality nearby. Privatizing this permission by granting the farmer the right of transfer or sale would bring markets into the decision about the highest and best use of the water.

Market, Not Government, Allocation of Public Goods

Does government finance have a role in the emerging view of government budgeting and finance, or will the market allocate even public goods? What the new coalition of fiscal conservatives and neutral competents has provided is not only a more strident advocacy of business-like government finance administration, but the direct application of individualism as the assumed basis for decision making in allocating such collective goods as industrial and debt market regulation. For example, in matters involving the U.S. Office of Management and Budget, cost-benefit analysis has gained common use in guiding review of the quantity and type of regulatory rule making in agencies, to the point of creating a "regulatory budget" (Stockman, 1986, p. 103). The bias of cost-benefit analysis toward the individual (Meier, 1982) removes the public good aspect of regulatory rule making and, with privatization, reinterprets regulation as a private, market-allocated interest.

Hollow State

The net effect of privatization and market allocation of public goods is a "hollow state." At the very least, according to Milward and Provan (2000, p. 359), "the increasing use of third parties ... to deliver social services and generally act in the name of the state" left governments with more contract management responsibility and less direct service provision. And more, use of third parties hollowed out the state's function and threatened the state's legitimacy. Associated with contracting out the provision of services, the hollow state could also cover use and effect of tax expenditures, those reductions in tax levies used as an incentive given individual and organization taxpayers to encourage them to pursue particular policy goals.

The changed focus in emerging thinking has affected municipal debt markets as well. The competitive market has been used as a guide to state and local government capital investment and infrastructure improvement, through reliance on taxable debt instruments, as Congress has curtailed tax-exempt market uses by these governments for economic development purposes. Cash management, finally, has been pushed to join regulation and debt. Some have urged cash managers to define professional competence less in terms of fiduciary responsibility and more in terms of a business principle in which risk and return guide decisions (Miller, 1987).

The Retrograde Movement in Rights-Based Budgeting

Finally, as a countermovement of sorts, the courts have begun insisting that individuals have rights with fiscal mandates attached. These rights—often a matter of standards setting in prisons, mental hospitals, and schools—are deemed individual ones, and courts have taken the initiative in forcing through orders for the expenditure of the necessary funds to accommodate the rights (Harriman and Straussman, 1983).

The emerging conflict is one in which the courts enforce what has been called interest group liberalism (Linowes, 1988; Reich, 1964, 1965, 1966), while fiscal conservative forces push these private interests into the market through various privatization programs. The courts, nominally acting on the side of the unrepresented, stand in the way. Inexorably, fiscal policy and government budgeting and finance seem destined to enforce a move away from the provision of broadly defined classes of public goods and redistribution of income. Thinking has sided with, and now helps guide the implementation of, the premise that government is a part of the problem, not the solution.

The right turn has affected the Republican and the Democratic Party in the United States. It has prompted neoliberal hegemony in policy making and especially in government budgeting and finance. The upshot, Lindert (2004) finds, has been a broader-based, flatter-rate tax system in the United States (and other countries with highly developed economies). The tax system retains a progressive structure, and the spending that takes place redistributes across income classes. Nevertheless, income inequality has grown. Finally, nominal administrative and regulatory costs have dropped.

In a sweeping summary of developments across public and market sectors during the right turn, Davis (2009) describes them as the creation of an investor society in which maximizing the value of portfolios of each individual is the permanent goal. He says (p. 236) that individuals and their investments—houses and 401k retirement plans—along with their "friends, families and neighborhoods"—their social capital—are the equivalent of an investor who buys and sells securities for their economic and social portfolios. Truly, Davis says, government and all other institutions are managed by the market; that is, they are conditioned to respond to market incentives to maximize wealth. In the government budgeting and finance world, the metaphors signify a rejection of positive government as the reformers defined it and dominance of a pro-business, if not business-driven, government decision-making norm.

Summary

Different points of view exist at each point in the American federal, state, and local political-administrative system, and, unlike parliamentary government controlling a permanent bureaucracy, are not easily and comprehensively reconciled through elections and legislative votes of no confidence. The distribution of influence—or more likely the determination of ends and means linkages—is highly randomized. Problem solving is piecemeal as a result. On a problem-by-problem basis, the connection between how the problem is defined and what technologies, including organization and management knowledge, are used in solving it are highly contextual.

In the larger scheme of things, the problems and solutions are randomly connected with each other (Cohen and March, 1986). How do we make sense or gain meaning from a piecemeal fragmented system? We construct meaning, according to ambiguity theorists. After the fact, we rationalize information to make it meaningful. We interpret the situation beforehand in defining problems and in choosing solutions, but because of the fragmented nature of problem solving itself, we often make sense of it all after the fact in ways that provide continuity with the past and ignore the essentially random nature of the relationships.

The role of government budgeting and finance in ambiguous situations, then, is to interpret and act based on this interpretation. Government budgeting and finance is a repository of language, of processes in budgeting and revenue projection that reconcile, of networks that establish legitimacy, and of categorization devices. Language, reconciling devices, legitimacy granting structures, and means of classification are the tools of meaning construction. For government budgeting and finance theorists, the job is to conceive of ways it is used and to investigate the ways, their contexts, and their representation for the people they serve.

The emerging thinking represents the victory of parsimony over equity and efficiency. The three values have competed for control since government budgeting and finance became a topic of serious study. The victory is one of reconstructing meaning through the control of the premise guiding thought, as the "government is a part of the problem, not the solution" so vividly captures. The implication for theory building for once is *not* the capture of government budgeting and finance by economics and market devotees. It is the imperative to base government budgeting and finance theory on a foundation of meaning construction.

For the successors to the bureau movement analysts, the question of theory is largely left unanswered. During the Progressive Era, the analysts could cope using a theory that, at the time of the Brownlow Committee, was thought to be the leading thinking in the field of management. It was orthodoxy at its height, yet based on strict, deductive logic.

The successor, during a period of government growth, was incrementalism. Connected ineluctably to pluralist theories of politics, incrementalism served to counter the pretense of hierarchical power and executive leadership with an "invisible hand" of policy selection based on give-and-take among interests. Yet, incrementalism's resemblance to individualist theories of market behavior led to a counterrevolution in which the market forces themselves rebelled over, apparently, the cost of government growth based on pursuit of private gain by public interests.

At present, an alternative view has developed that challenges the orthodox and incrementalist approaches, in two different ways. First, ambiguity theory (Cohen, March, and Olsen, 1972) reflects the idea that neither planning/control theory nor pluralism provides a conceptual structure to qualify either alone as a full-fledged analytic approach with the three requisite parts: technique, management theory, and institutional value structure (Selznick, 1957; Parsons, 1960).

Second, social construction theorists (Berger and Luckmann, 1966) argue that developing an institutional-level approach is possible, even though it is no small task. The elaboration of an institutional level of analysis—the level of belief structure and values—on which to base a conceptual structure and from which we infer techniques in specific government finance systems comprises the task of the remainder of the book.

Endnotes

1. This imperative comes from the vault system (Advisory Commission on Intergovernmental Relations, 1961), which suggested that prudence in safekeeping public funds demands that money thus held might not circulate for fear that the bank holding the funds might fail.
2. The time value of money suggests that the value of a given sum is greatest at the present, and that foregoing its present use should be priced, as interest. Opportunity cost calculations are those in which one use of money is compared to another, and the difference between them is defined as a cost or the cost of an opportunity not chosen.
3. Supporting this political coalition argument, Adrian (1987) calls all of the groups, other than the progressives, "urban conservatives." Schiesl (1977) and Elkin (1987) take the more conventional, political science route to describing the composition of the coalition, placing forces on either the pro-machine side or in the antimachine block.
4. Private goods are defined in the context of market failure and nonappropriability, and the term *private goods* refers to those goods produced and sold by either government or private business or both. Since market failure comes about as a result of the inability of a provider of goods to receive all of the returns from the purchase of a service, "market success" is an instance of appropriability, or the ability to exclude nonbuyers of a good from its use and to prevent the concurrent use of a good by buyers and nonbuyers. What private goods are in practice and who should provide them is the subject of much speculation, of which Wolf (1988) is one of the best balanced analyses.
5. The large literature on cutback management has consumed thinking in public financial management for almost a decade. The apparent source of thinking on cutback management began with Simon (1962). For more of the bibliography on cutback management, see Levine (1980) and McCaffery (1981).
6. Later, these beliefs would be spelled out in implementation measures that developed into iron-clad principles, each viewed as good in and of itself. Herbert Simon called them proverbs (1947). Debt management norms are good examples of the trouble caused by conventional wisdom.
7. Omnibus Reconciliation Act, of which the Budget Enforcement Act was a part.

References

Adrian, Charles R. (1987). *A History of American City Government: The Emergence of the Metropolis, 1920–1945*. New York: Lanham.

Advisory Commission on Intergovernmental Relations. (1961). Investment of idle cash balances by state and local government. Washington, DC: U.S. Government Printing Office.

Anthony, Robert N. (1965). *Planning and Control Systems.* Cambridge, MA: Harvard University Press.

Beer, Stafford. (1959). *Cybernetics and Management.* New York: John Wiley & Sons.

Berger, Peter L., and Thomas Luckmann. (1966). *The Social Construction of Reality: A Treatise in the Sociology of Knowledge.* New York: Doubleday.

Bolles, Albert S. (1869). *The Financial History of the United States,* 3 vols. New York: D. Appleton & Company.

Borcherding, Thomas E., ed. (1977). *Budgets and Bureaucrats: The Sources of Government Growth.* Durham, NC: Duke University Press.

Buchanan, James M. (1987). *Public Finance in Democratic Process: Fiscal Institutions and Individual Choice.* Chapel Hill: University of North Carolina Press.

Buchanan, James M., and Gordon Tullock. (1962). *The Calculus of Consent: Logical Foundations of Constitutional Democracy.* Ann Arbor: University of Michigan Press.

Burchell, Stuart et al. (1980). The roles of accounting in organizations and society. *Accounting, Organizations and Society* 5:14.

Churchman, C. West. (1968). *The Systems Approach.* New York: Dell.

Cohen, Michael D., and James G. March. (1986). *Leadership and Ambiguity: The American College President.* 2nd ed. Cambridge, MA: Harvard Business School Press.

Cohen, Michael D., James G. March, and Johan P. Olsen. (1972). A garbage can model of organizational choice. *Administrative Science Quarterly* 17:1–25.

Comptroller General of the United States. (1985). *Managing the Cost of Government: Building an Effective Financial Management Structure.* Vol. 2, Conceptual framework (GAO/AFMC-85-35-A). Washington, DC: U.S. General Accounting Office.

Crandall, Robert W. (1978). Federal government initiatives to reduce the price level. In *Curing Chronic Inflation,* ed. Arthur M. Okun and George L. Perry, 165–204. Washington, DC: Brookings.

Cyert, Richard M., and James G. March. (1963). *A Behavioral Theory of the Firm.* Englewood Cliffs, NJ: Prentice-Hall.

Davis, Gerald F. (2009). *Managed by the Markets.* New York: Oxford University Press.

Dewey, Davis Rich. (1930). *The Financial History of the United States,* 12th ed. New York: Longmans, Green, & Co.

Dunsire, Andrew, and Christopher Hood. (2010). *Cutback Management in Public Bureaucracies.* Cambridge: Cambridge University Press.

Elkin, Stephen L. (1987). *City and Regime in the American Republic.* Chicago: University of Chicago Press.

Epstein, Paul. (1984). The value of measuring and improving performance. In *New Directions in Public Administration,* ed. Barry Bozeman and Jeffrey Straussman, 265–269. Monterey, CA: Brooks/Cole.

Executive summary (of Volume II of the Study Committee on Policy Management Assistance report, Strengthening public management in the intergovernmental system). (1975). *Public Administration Review,* special issue: 700–705.

Ferguson, Thomas, and Joel Rogers. (1986). *Right Turn.* New York: Hill & Wang.

Fox, Kenneth. (1977). *Better City Government: Innovation in American Urban Politics, 1850–1937.* Philadelphia: Temple University Press.

Friedman, Milton. (1953). The methodology of positive economics. In *Essays in Positive Economics,* ed. Milton Friedman, 3–43. Chicago: University of Chicago Press.

Golembiewski, Robert T. (1977). *Public Administration as a Developing Discipline: Part 1: Perspectives on Past and Present.* New York: Dekker.

Golembiewski, Robert T. (1989). *Men, Management, and Morality: Toward a New Organizational Ethic.* Transaction ed. Piscataway, NJ: Transaction Books.

Grafstein, Robert. (1988). A realist foundation for essentially contested political concepts. *Western Political Quarterly* 41(1):9–28.

Gross, Bertram M. (1969). The new systems budgeting. *Public Administration Review* 29:113–137.

Grossman, David A., and Frederick O'R. Hayes. (1981). Moving toward integrated fiscal management. *Public Budgeting and Finance* 1(2):41–46.

Groves, Sanford, Maureen Godsey, and Martha Shulman. (1981). Financial indicators. *Public Budgeting and Finance* 1(2):5–19.

Gulick, Luther, and L. Urwick. (1937). *Papers on the Science of Administration.* New York: Institute of Public Administration.

Hacker, Jacob S., and Paul Pierson. (2007). Tax politics and the struggle over activist government. In *The Transformation of American Politics*, ed. Paul Pierson and Teda Skocpol, 256–280. Princeton, NJ: Princeton University Press.

Hacker, Jacob S., and Paul Pierson. (2010). *Winner-Take-All Politics.* New York: Simon & Schuster.

Hammond, Bray. (1970). *Sovereignty and an Empty Purse: Banks and Politics in the Civil War.* Princeton, NJ: Princeton University Press.

Harriman, Linda, and Jeffrey D. Straussman. (1983). Do judges determine budget decisions? Federal court decisions in prison reform and state spending for corrections. *Public Administration Review* 43:343–351.

Hayek, Friedrich. (1944). *The Road to Serfdom.* Chicago: University of Chicago Press.

Hershey, Robert D., Jr. (1989). New market is seen for "pollution rights." *New York Times*, national edition, June 14, pp. 29, 32.

Hicks, John R. (1940). The valuation of the social income. *Economica*, May, pp. 105–124.

Hitch, Charles J. (1960). On the choice of objectives in systems studies. Santa Monica, CA: RAND Corporation. Quoted in Wildavsky, Aaron. (1966). The political economy of efficiency: Cost benefit analysis, systems analysis, and program budgeting. *Public Administration Review* 26:292–310.

Hyde, Albert C. (1978). A review of the theory of budget reform. In *Government Budgeting*, ed. Albert C. Hyde and Jay M. Shafritz, 71–77. Oak Park, IL: Moore Publishing Co.

Johnson, Richard A., Fremont E. Kast, and James E. Rosenzweig. (1963). *Organization and Management: A Systems and Contingency Approach.* New York: McGraw-Hill.

Kaldor, N. (1939). Welfare propositions of economists and interpersonal comparisons of utility. *Economic Journal*, 49(195):549–552.

Kaufman, Herbert. (1956). Emerging conflicts in the doctrines of public administration. *American Political Science Review* 50:1057–1073.

Key, V. O. (1940). The lack of a budgetary theory. *American Political Science Review* 34(6):1137–1144.

Kioko, Sharon, Justin Marlowe, David S. T. Matkin, Michael Moody, Daniel L. Smith, Zhirong J. Zhao. (2011). Why public financial management matters. *Journal of Public Administration Research and Theory* 21(1):i113–i124.

Kuhn, Thomas S. (1970). *The Structure of Scientific Revolutions.* 2nd ed. Chicago: University of Chicago Press.

Levine, Charles H. (1980). *Managing Fiscal Stress.* Chatham, NJ: Chatham House.

Lindblom, Charles E. (1965). *The Intelligence of Democracy.* New York: Free Press.

Lindert, Peter H. (2004). *Growing Public.* 2 vols. Cambridge: Cambridge University Press.

Linowes, David F. (1988). *Privatization: Toward More Effective Government.* Urbana: University of Illinois Press.

Lyden, Fremont J., and Ernest G. Miller. (1978). Introduction. In *Public Budgeting,* ed. Fremont J. Lyden and Ernest G. Miller. Chicago: Rand McNally.

MacDonald, T. J. (1988). A history of urban fiscal politics in America, 1830–1930: What was supposed to be versus what was and the difference it makes. *International Journal of Public Administration* 11:679–712.

McCaffery, Jerry. (1981). The impact of resource scarcity on urban public finance: A special issue. *Public Administration Review* 41:105–202.

Meier, Kenneth. (1982). Political economy and cost-benefit analysis: Problems of bias. In *Political Economy of Public Policy,* ed. Alan Stone and Edward J. Harpham, 143–162. Beverly Hills, CA: Sage Publications.

Miller, Gerald J. (1991). *Government Financial Management Theory.* New York: Dekker.

Miller, Gerald J., and James Svara. (2009). *Navigating the Fiscal Crisis: Tested Strategies for Local Leaders.* Phoenix, AZ: Alliance for Innovation and International City Management Association.

Miller, Girard. (1987). The investment of public funds: A research agenda. *Public Budgeting and Finance* 7:47–56.

Milward, H. Brinton, and Keither G. Provan. (2000). Governing the hollow state. *Journal of Public Administration Research and Theory* 10(2):359–380.

Morstein Marx, Fritz. (1957). *The Administrative State.* Chicago: University of Chicago Press.

Mosher, Frederick C. (1984). *A Tale of Two Agencies: A Comparative Analysis of the General Accounting Office and the Office of Management and Budget.* Baton Rouge: Louisiana State University Press.

Myers, Margaret G. (1970). *A Financial History of the United States.* New York: Columbia University Press.

Nash, Gary B. (1979). *The Urban Crucible: Social Change, Political Consciousness, and the Origins of the American Revolution.* Cambridge, MA: Harvard University Press.

Novick, David. (1968). The origin and history of program budgeting. *California Management Review* 11(1):7–12.

Parsons, Talcott. (1960). *Structure and Process in Modern Societies.* Glencoe, IL: The Free Press of Glencoe.

Participatory Budget Project. (2010). www.participatorybudgeting.org (accessed December 7, 2010).

President's Committee on Administrative Management. (1937). Report. Washington, DC: U.S. Government Printing Office.

Pyhrr, Peter A. (1977). The zero-base approach to government budgeting. *Public Administration Review* 37:1–8.

Rabin, Jack. (1975). State and local PPBS. In *Public Budgeting and Finance,* ed. Robert T. Golembiewski and Jack Rabin, 489–503. 2nd ed. Itasca, IL: F. E. Peacock Publishers.

Reich, Charles. (1964). The new property. *Yale Law Journal,* April, pp. 120–155.

Reich, Charles. (1965). Individual rights and social welfare: The emerging legal issues. *Yale Law Journal,* June, pp. 1–55.

Reich, Charles. (1966). The law of the planned society. *Yale Law Journal,* July, pp. 1255–1280.

Roberts, Paul Craig. (1984). *The Supply Side Revolution.* Cambridge, MA: Harvard University Press.

Rubin, Irene S. (1985). *Shrinking the Federal Government: The Effect of Cutbacks on Five Federal Agencies.* New York: Longman.

Rubin, Irene S. (1988). *New Directions in Budget Theory.* Albany: State University of New York Press.

Savas, E. S. (1982). *Privatizing the Public Sector: How to Shrink Government.* Chatham, NJ: Chatham House Publishers.

Schick, Allen. (1966). The road to PPB: The stages of budget reform. *Public Administration Review* 26:243–258.

Schick, Allen. (1973). A death in the bureaucracy: The demise of federal PPB. *Public Administration Review* 33:146–156.

Schick, Allen. (1986). Macrobudgetary adaptations to fiscal stress in industrialized democracies. *Public Administration Review* 46(2):124–134.

Schiesl, Martin J. (1977). *The Politics of Efficiency: Municipal Administration and Reform in America, 1800–1920.* Berkeley: University of California Press.

Schlesinger, Arthur. (1986). *The Cycles of History.* New York: Houghton Mifflin.

Schumpeter, Joseph A. (1942). *Capitalism, Socialism, and Democracy.* New York: Harper and Bros.

Selznick, Philip. (1957). *Leadership in Administration.* Evanston, IL: Row, Peterson.

Simon, Herbert A. (1947). *Administrative Behavior.* New York: Free Press.

Simon, Herbert A. (1962). The architecture of complexity. *Proceedings of the American Philosophical Society* 102(6):467–482.

Smithies, Arthur. (1955). *The Budgetary Process in the United States.* New York: Committee for Economic Development, McGraw-Hill Book Co.

Stockman, David A. (1986). *The Triumph of Politics: Why the Reagan Revolution Failed.* New York: Harper & Row.

Taylor, Paul W. (1961). *Normative Discourse.* Westport, CT: Greenwood Press.

Thompson, James D. (1967). *Organizations in Action.* New York: McGraw-Hill.

Thompson, James D., and Arthur Tuden. (1959). Strategies, structures, and processes of organizational decision. In *Comparative Studies in Administration*, ed. James D. Thompson, Peter B. Hammond, Robert W. Hawkes, Buford H. Junker, and Arthur Tuden, 195–216. Pittsburgh, PA: University of Pittsburgh Press.

USEPA (Environmental Protection Agency). (2010). Cap and trade. www.epa.gov/capandtrade (accessed December 7, 2010).

U.S. Senate Committee Investigating Executive Agencies, 75th Congress, 1st Session. (1937). Senate report 1275. Washington, DC.

Van Horne, James C. (1986). *Financial Management and Policy.* Englewood Cliffs, NJ: Prentice-Hall.

Von Bertalanffy, Ludwig. (1968). *General System Theory.* New York: George Braziller.

Waldo, Dwight. (1948). *The Administrative State: A Study of the Political Theory of American Public Administration.* New York: The Ronald Press.

Walker, Wallace Earl. (1986). *Changing Organizational Culture: Strategy, Structure, and Professionalism in the U.S. General Accounting Office.* Knoxville, TN: University of Tennessee Press.

Weick, Karl E. (1979). Cognitive processes in organizations. In *Research in Organizational Behavior*, ed. B. M. Staw, 41–74. Vol. 1. Greenwich, CT: JAI Press.

Wildavsky, Aaron. (1961). Political implications of budgetary reform. *Public Administration Review* 21:183–190.

Wildavsky, Aaron. (1964). *The Politics of the Budgetary Process.* Boston: Little Brown.

Wildavsky, Aaron. (1966). The political economy of efficiency: Cost-benefit analysis, systems analysis, and program budgeting. *Public Administration Review* 26:292–310.

Wildavsky, Aaron. (1986). *Budgeting: A Comparative Theory of Budgetary Processes*. 2nd rev. ed. Piscataway, NJ: Transaction Books.

Wildavsky, Aaron, and Arthur Hammond. (1965). Comprehensive versus incremental budgeting in the Department of Agriculture. *Administrative Science Quarterly* 10(3):321–346.

Wolf, Jr., Charles. (1988). *Markets or Governments: Choosing between Imperfect Alternatives*. Cambridge, MA: MIT Press.

Chapter 3

The Practice of Government Budgeting and Finance Is Interpretation[1]

Connections between ends and means in public policy making are made through analysis, bargaining, learning, or interpretation. Finance influences the way the connections are made because every policy depends on money. Money is scarce. Necessity forces the question: Is the activity worth the money? Need establishes finance as the ultimate contingency and leads policy makers to depend on finance officials for expertise and practical advice, leading finance officials to encourage analysis, bargaining, learning, or interpretation.

Finance officials use a lens for seeing the issues, one that's highly developed and tempered through time. A part of the lens comes from financial management norms. Norms direct the use of specialized knowledge that defines financial management. Another part, however, comes from the way finance officials define their job. This chapter explores the application of expertise, relying on finance officials to tell how they define and practice financial management, how they interpret ambiguous phenomena, and how they enact a world where their views of ends, means, and priorities dominate.

Practitioners Define Government Budgeting, Finance, and Financial Management

Two major authorities can help define financial management. One is composed of the texts provided for financial managers (Lehan, 1991). The other is the view financial managers take in focus groups and surveys (Miller and Evers, 2002; Alexander, 1999; Miller, 1998). From these sources, we find three definitions of financial management.

Economic Efficiency and Financial Control

An optimizing logic appears as received wisdom in the training materials finance officers use. Lehan (1991, p. 35) offers three major issues in which financial managers optimize: the availability of money, the cost of money, and the productivity of money. Availability may be defined as liquidity. Maintaining liquidity "focus[es] on a jurisdiction's credit repute, reserves, tax strategies, billing cycles, payment procedures, past-due receivables, and the investment of loan proceeds and cash balances. Liquidity is the *sine qua non* of finance management" (p. 35). Cost of money implies reduction of costs and may involve reducing interest costs on borrowed funds as well as reducing the cost of government work. Increasing the productivity of money may apply generally in raising "the net benefit earned by the allocation of funds to the various purposes of ... government" (p. 35).

The liquidity, cost, and investment goals often suggest behavior to maximize outcomes. These goals have strict efficiency tests, in other words. Efficiency can also carry a more relative test. Administrative efficiency traditionally hinges a given amount of performance to least cost or maximum performance to a given amount of resources (Thompson, 1967, p. 86).

In the relative sense, efficiency has become synonymous with a managerial emphasis rather than an economic one. As a way of defining the purpose of financial management, managerial ideas stress most heavily "the pursuit of maximum output with minimum inputs," a "faith in the tools and techniques of management science and an ability to use them to resolve problems," and faith in managers' skills and knowledge in acting as moral agents "to achieve the greatest good, not only for their organizations, but for society as a whole" (Edwards, 2001, p. 4).

The managerial position argues that a finance office is an institution with legitimacy to operate in the public sphere independently. The primary institutional value is neutral competence, a concept combining managerialism with economizing values and certainly with the willingness and ability to generate policy alternatives for debate.

In focus group discussions, CFOs agreed that they must act instrumentally, most of the time, to achieve consensus priorities (Miller and Evers, 2002). The rest of the time, finance officers must act as stewards or fiduciaries for the public. One

CFO said it best when he defined the purpose as "doing everything possible, with as little help from the taxpayer as necessary, to give citizens what they want." The CFO echoes a Latin proverb on choices and reality: no gain is so certain as that from the economical use of what you already have.

Loyalty and Responsiveness to the Elected Elite

Of the three purposes financial management could serve, the local government CFOs expressed the greatest amount of support for the loyalty purpose—that good finance officers should serve and support priorities.

The reason for this support is not hard to understand given these respondents. More than once, CFOs indicated that their job was to give advice, to produce options for elected officials—to "give them what they need to get what they want," one said. That person explained that a CFO cannot stand in the way of politicians bent on doing something; the best that can be done is to advise them on how to do it with the least financial damage. Ultimately, to have advice taken, to be viewed as a source of expertise and good judgment, the CFO must build confidence in this expertise among elected officials.

Supporting republican government follows a political logic. That logic hews closely to a modern-day ubiquitous budget strategy vividly described by Wildavsky (1964, pp. 74–84). Advocates everywhere try to build confidence among those examining their budget requests, he said. While it is a strategy related to the politics of budgeting, building confidence underscores the finance officer's role as an expert, conditioning political leaders to a reality that only the finance officer can divine. In building confidence, the normative basis moves beyond instrumentalism and neutral competence, the ordinary definition of expertise, to an interactive form of influence, with parts equally deferential, referential, and domineering.

Participation, Stewardship, and Direct Democracy

CFOs did not reject citizen participation as a way to promote greater democracy, the third purpose of financial management. After all, they subscribed to giving citizens what they want. Similar to and yet different than Alexander's (1999) respondents, these CFOs had significant doubts about some ways to bring it about. A later chapter here explores these doubts. CFOs defined successful participation far more broadly than the word *citizen* suggests: participation should involve the important stakeholders in the organization, whether the stakeholder is a taxpayer, an employee receiving a paycheck, the various parties in the debt market, or a vendor in the purchasing system. The CFOs also pointed out the necessary first step in participation—making financial information and processes clear and understandable to taxpayers, citizens, employees, elected officials, investors, and vendors.

In focus group discussions, however, CFOs argued that stakeholder participation often has roots in politics. They asked: Will demagogues take advantage of the tenuous control officials have over events to embarrass, or will political rivals take finance transactions out of context to defeat elected leaders? Not only are rivals a menace, but taxpayers and bond market professionals have leverage over important issues also, and the three groups are sometimes at odds with each other.

The CFOs also explained that budgeting frequently operates as a closed system, excluding many groups. Budgeters can intentionally bury decision making from outsiders to ensure a simpler affirmation of community goals and a more resolute effort to accomplish them. Only in the cases of referenda on bond, tax, and other fiscal policy issues, on the issue of tax increases, and the disclosure of budget and financial reports required by various legal and financial authorities did CFOs concede to broadening public knowledge, with some participation, to solve problems.

What texts argue and what managers report are dependent on context. The context may include dimensions related to instrumental ideas—maintaining liquidity, reducing costs, and increasing productivity—that dominate a finance officer's thinking, making efficiency an absolute or relative measure of good choices. As a primary advisor and executor, CFOs encounter an agency dimension when they consider acting for local leaders or important stakeholders, such as taxpayers, vendors, and investors. The finance official often stresses precedent, consistency, and predictability in the advice he or she gives, and other times associates experience with issues and problems. As a necessity of law and a sense of fair play, the dimensions at other times may relate to balancing a variety of interests, due process, creative participation, and equity for those without voice.

What Practitioners Ultimately Do

Is it fair to ask which definition of public financial management prevails? From what we understand, financial managers deal with decisions involving money, and through money they profoundly influence the work of government organizations. Analysis reveals that all CFOs do not see the world in the same way.

Differences exist among CFOs because they have differing amounts of discretion when compared across state and local governments. Some CFOs have very basic, core-level responsibilities running routine operations. Others have a more policy-oriented role and may have become high-level advisors to chief executives. Still others may be elected executives themselves, particularly city and state treasurers. These differences became apparent in the budgeting office research of Thurmaier and Willoughby (2001) and Rubin (1998), in which large differences in the structures and expectations of budgeting officials emerged. The differences are also apparent in cases and research on cash investment later in this chapter. Differences in place and time form a contingency theory of budgeting and, perhaps, financial management. Such differences may arise from legal structural sanction, political ideology, or the level of development of the profession locally, but the differences definitely exist.

Another strategic view argues that CFOs must capitalize legitimacy, functionalism, and independence. McCaffery and Jones (2001, pp. 62–65) argue that some budget officers and staff members are not useful enough and others are too useful. In not being useful enough, the budget office could exist as one part of an entire government regime dedicated to economizing. In such a situation, a budget office may not be useful in being just another voice for economy. In some circumstances, budget officers may not be believable enough, and in this way much less useful, in arguing impractical, inflexible managerial theories of organization or constitutional power in opposition to those who have managerial expertise at least equaling, if not surpassing, budget and finance officers—agency managers or outside consultants, all of whom have their own views of what will or will not work (p. 65). McCaffery and Jones spot instances where budget offices may be too useful, so good at what they do, that they tend "to get drawn into the role of general staff advisor, or even roles that would seem to be more political and belonging to … political staff," allowing fiscal values to be suppressed (2001, p. 65). The case in which a finance official could dominate revenue forecasting appears later in this chapter and illustrates the too useful view and a misuse of the efficiency definition of finance.

What is the inference of the not useful enough–too useful argument? Finance officials find ways to avoid being either useless or too useful to guard their legitimacy, functionalism, and independence.

Success lies in a sense of aptness. Financial managers can interpret the need to act appropriately as efficiency, agency, or stewardship imply. The interpretation emerges from the context in which issues have materialized. Contexts differ over time and reflect the financial manager's openness to politics and reference groups, as well as the risks associated with problems and solutions (Schneider and Ingram, 1997, pp. 36–38; Thompson, 1967, pp. 84–98).

Yet the basic motive behind structure and strategy remains: to preserve the institutional power of the finance office. The effort in building financial management theory bottoms on professionalization, institutionalization, and institutional survival premises, all of which are fundamental to understanding institutions universally (Scott, 2001; Merton, 1936, 1957; Selznick, 1957; Silverman, 1971; Zucker, 1991; Berger and Luckmann, 1966). How finance offices continue to be valuable—to avoid being useless or too useful—may seem to be irrelevant, since knowledgeable people can hardly conceive of a consequential government decision with no fiscal values at stake. If finance office influence is the issue, we can investigate whether influence serves efficiency, political masters (agency), or the public (participation, stewardship, and direct democracy).

Theories about Finance Officials' Work

To investigate the meaningful content of public financial management, we use decisions as a unit of analysis, assuming that decision making can encompass most of what financial managers do. The decision-making view has a long tradition. In general, decision making "is the core of administration, [all administration] being dependent on, interwoven with and existent for the making of decisions" (McCamy, 1947, p. 41; Simon, 1947). Considerable effort has led to orthodox, prevailing, and alternative explanations of decision processes and outcomes (Miller, 1991; Wildavsky, 1964; Jones, Sulkin, and Larsen, 2003; Kant, 1992; Smith, 1991; Schneider and Ingram, 1997; Martinez-Vazques, 2001; Miller, Hildreth, and Rabin, 2001; Forrester and Adams, 1997; Buchanan, 1977).

A theoretical view broad enough to build on existing theories must explore the connection between decisions and the social reality in which they take place. This approach involves interpretations. As Martin (2002, p. 261) points out, "Constructing a correct decision, a sound one, is always an interpretive project. Interpretation ... must range over a great number of dimensions ... and interpretive choices have to be made within each dimension." With the theoretical view taken in this chapter, we explore how financial managers make sense of reality in reaching decisions. We look at how managers recognize the possibility for making a decision, and the interpretive choices they make over numerous dimensions.

What Is an Interpretation?

A focus on interpretation comes from the body of research concerned with the construction of reality. That is, much of the world of financial managers exists because they want it to exist and because it customarily exists in the form in which they refer to it or grasp it. They—all financial managers in league with institutional leaders—could socially negotiate a change in many of the facts in their world if they wanted them changed. Consider, for example, deficits and taxes. Are unbalanced budgets a safe, risky, or foolhardy fiscal policy? Do tax increases dampen economic efficiency or encourage economic fairness?

Such a view comes from analytic philosophy. As Searle (1995, pp. 1–2) says: "There are portions of the real world, objective facts in the world, that are only facts by human agreement. In a sense there are things that exist only because we believe them to exist." Searle's examples are money, property, governments, and marriages. At first glance, these four concepts are very much objective in that they do exist for each of us. He explains that while all four "are 'objective' facts in the sense that they are not a matter of your or my preferences, evaluations, or moral attitudes," they could be changed by human action, specifically human action through institutions. Other media for exchange than money might be used if we prefer. Property is defined by constitutions as existing for private persons or not; if it does not exist for private use, it no longer exists as property. Governments exist by the social contracts that emerge among individuals, and when the contract is written, it may be written with the specific authority of the governed to change it or do away with it. Marriages exist in many different forms, based on many different attitudes, as a civil action, a religious action, a human growth action in procreating and developing families, or simply an agreement to cohabit. Any of these forms may be changed by human action. Searle calls the facts that exist by human agreement institutional facts.

He contrasts institutional facts with "brute facts." He illustrates brute facts as "Mount Everest has snow and ice near the summit" and "hydrogen atoms have one electron," both facts completely independent of human opinions.

Institutional facts contrast with brute facts "because they require human institutions for their existence." Searle recognizes that even brute facts depend upon human recognition and speech for part of their existence. Scientific research has to take place and the results reported, refereed, and accepted. A brute fact exists even though we may not know it fully or be able to say precisely what it is. He says, "Of course, in order to state a brute fact we require the institution of language, but the fact stated needs to be distinguished from the statement of it."

The more humans agree and the more institutional facts they accept, the more humans perceive the structure of opportunities and the consequences of their acts as reality. In areas where there seems to be full agreement among humans, we have "shared subjectivity" or a shared interpretation (Saaty, 1980, p. 15). Saaty argues (p. 15), "However we try to be objective in interpreting experience, our understanding is perceived and abstracted in a very subjective way.... Shared subjectivity in interpretation is actually what we mean by objectivity. Thus [the social constructions] we form are objective by our own definition because they relate to our collective experience." The world's finance officials know are constructed to benefit from their collective professional views, the opinions developed through social interaction in organizations, and the beneficial ideas they have accumulated through experience.

Golembiewski (1999, pp. 14–17) has straightforward arguments about interpretations and social constructions. He agrees with those theorists who "note that reality does not exist 'out there': it is enacted (or socially constructed) by each of us, and in some unspecified ways these individual enactments somehow come to constitute reality until they are somehow unenacted by enough of the appropriate people." He argues that, at least in some senses, social construction of reality applies since "much that constrains and motivates behavior exists by social consensus." He illustrates with Sherif's autokinetic experiment (Sherif, 1935) and recalls (p. 14):

> A point of light in a dark room seems to move; a consensus about distance moved often develops among groups observing that light; and that consensus persists when individuals are later brought back alone to observe the same light.

Although dramatic, the Sherif experiment is a narrow one, and Golembiewski points out that social construction of reality has "sharp limits." He notes (p. 14), "Enact as you will, stepping out of a seventh floor window is unlikely to have sanguine effects." He argues further that even when subject to human action, social constructions may be extremely hard to change. He uses slavery as the ultimate example of hardened social constructions.

Golembiewski identifies the root of socially constructed reality as power. He notes (p. 14) that "we are not ... equal when it comes to enacting some ... perhaps even the most important realities. Indeed, some power-wielders might be able to enact realities for many of us, most of the time."

His argument that power wielders enact reality has a potential significance for financial managers. Following an economic or managerial logic, financial managers' analyses and recommendations to leaders have certain legitimacy within the limits imposed by economic theory and the social consensus about that theory in the capitalist United States. Following a political logic, financial managers' actions to build confidence among their superiors may often serve to speak the truth that financial managers believe, or interpret as truth, to powerful leaders. Following a stewardship logic, finance officials guide the use resources held in common and balance the means-ends connections of disparate stakeholders—bond market professionals who want to maximize borrowings for a given cost, taxpayers who oppose new and increased taxes, customers and clients who want efficient and varied services.

Products and tools of finance—cash investments, information systems and revenue forecasts, as well as government budgets, debt structures, and revenue regime changes—are socially negotiated ones (Astley, 1985, p. 499). That is, there is no one best way, no objective truth on which to base management; there are very few brute facts.

This chapter argues that finance decision makers do much to create a reality for their organizations by strategically, symbolically, ritualistically, and rhetorically coping with the most critical problem facing them—resource constraints. Coping gives finance rights or legitimacy, the clout to be able to enforce the use of a special language and to force the justification of actions in unique ways. In that language, financial management becomes a general metaphor, one in which scarce means finance the highest and best ends chosen by the polity, through elected leaders who depend on reservoirs of expertise in bureaus, think tanks, consulting firms, and universities. Creating a reality in which resources are contingent and in which finance is the critical agency for commanding resources and wisely allocating them among uses, the financial manager provides many of the institutional facts in public organizations.

As for arguments that finance officials, or any other officials, are "rational actors," we have the counterargument by Olsen (2003, p. 2) that "theory may benefit from taking into account ... a great diversity in human motivation and modes of action. Actors are driven by habit, emotion, coercion, interpretation of internalized rules and principles, as well as calculated expected utility and incentive structures. Human character is variable and changeable, not universal and constant." The working hypothesis of many researchers, as with Olsen, may be characterized here as "finance officials interpret." The financial official's world is one in which he or she has customary ways of seeing objects, people, and their interaction. Customs and even norms come from interpretations that have a more vivid sense of fact as consensus grows among those people the finance official influences and is influenced by.

For more than a half century, theorists have argued that managers play a major role in interpreting critical contingencies, in giving meaning or sense to phenomena they find, and in interpreting the phenomena they find when problems, solutions, and people meet in random ways. We argue here that finance officials' interpretations act to assign phenomena in ways in which the phenomena can be acted on, especially in controlling the critical financial contingencies the government organization faces. Finance officials can interpret phenomena to require computation, learning, bargaining, or reinterpretation (see Table 2.3). What they choose depends on the amount of agreement about goals and about the technology most reasonably suited to achieve agreed upon goals (Miller, 1991, pp. 59–61; Burchell et al., 1980; Thompson and Tuden, 1959). By defining the phenomena in a particular way, the finance officials dictate a way to deal with them. A simple interpretive system appears in Figure 3.1.

The simple process outlined in Figure 3.1 attributes credibility and legitimacy to the financial manager. The ambiguous events that occur lead to a cycle of interpretation or making sense for the organization. Brute facts and institutional facts

---

Ambiguity—no clear ends, means, or ends-means connections—prevails with few constraints from a dominant power center.

↓

Interpretations make sense of ambiguity.

↓

The financial manager interprets ambiguity as the expert.

↓

Financial managers construct interpretations from what they know and sense through the filters their efficiency, agency, and stewardship logics provide.

↓

Interpretation pushes ambiguous phenomena into categories where they can be handled with computation, bargaining, or learning.

↓

Financial managers communicate their interpretations through arguments incorporating narratives, myths, symbols, and rituals.

↓

Financial managers enforce their interpretations through the work others expect them to do—making decisions about spending and its financing and, in those decisions, rationalizing interpretations.

Figure 3.1   A model of interpretation by financial managers.

help, but considerable ambiguity remains, enabling financial managers to interpret through the views of their networks. The networks include those others with whom the financial manager works closely, and the particular network chosen depends on the norm the financial manager senses as aptly fitting the ambiguous circumstances—economizing, building confidence among political leaders, or bringing the narrow or broad stakeholder public into the situation.

For example, liberty (or its synonym freedom) in economic affairs has resonance among finance officials. Liberty is a contested concept, however. One view holds that economic freedom is "a nonpolitical freedom ... at best ... guaranteed by government" (Grafstein, 1988, p. 21). A rival claim "argues that true economic freedom includes control over the range and structure of economic alternatives" (Grafstein, 1988, p. 21). In the contested concept of liberty, rivals argue the character of society. Is economic freedom a subspecies of political freedom or vice versa? In other words, shall activist, pro-positive governments manage the economy, or shall most, if not all, social relationships, including political ones, be managed by the market?

To prevent gridlock while the rivals contest the concept of liberty in economic affairs, finance officials must decide issues big and small every day. Our argument is that they interpret phenomena, not in activist government or managed by the market terms, but in terms of the logics that help them make sense of the world—optimizing, agency, and stewardship. By applying the appropriate logic, the finance official can reduce any problem to computation, bargaining, or learning.

In the sense that liberty is a contested concept in economic affairs, we can consider the problem of improving the U.S. federal tax system, improving to achieve what is at the heart of the rival claims over the meaning of freedom. Therefore, a finance official might use an optimizing logic, redefining the problem as to computation, promoting both a more efficient system and a more equitable one. Efficient and equitable tax system improvements have existed for centuries, and hot debate over different solutions takes place every day. Thus, the decision does not lack solutions. It lacks a definition of the problem, and optimizing efficiency and equity through computation is one approach that finance officials might use. Narratives tell how people stop working when they have earned just short of the amount that would increase their tax bill, and how some get tax breaks only because they have a good tax accountant or worse, contributed money to an influential legislator. Storytellers also invoke the myth that tax revenues collected will rise until at some rate they begin to fall; at some rates lower or higher than that pivot point, revenues collected are actually smaller. The symbol emerges as a flat tax, a tax system redesign solution that has a rate low enough to avoid penalizing work, high enough to provide the same revenue as the previous system, as well as a broad enough tax base to maintain horizontal equity. Ritual unfolds in which experts that have studied the tax system explain they have found the solution to a more efficient and fairer system: the flat tax. The experts report their findings to legislators, who then examine the flat tax and decide whether it is good for the country. The end result is finance officials' adoption of the flat tax.

The optimizing logic and computation decision-making strategy pushed the ambiguity and rivalry over economic freedom toward the determination of whether a flat-tax solution optimized efficiency and equity, increasing one without decreasing the other. If the computation showed that the solution optimized efficiency and equity under these conditions, finance officials would expect the solution to be acceptable. Acceptability or perhaps indifference might prompt a political bargain over economic stimulus spending during a recession, even though few would agree about the recession's causes, the problem the stimulus should target, and the optimal means for producing economic growth under these conditions. Finally, many more than not would accept learning through citizen participation in community development budgeting and planning, since rivals often dispute the goals of development, the present level of development of a community, the nature and severity of present development problems, and what projects to pursue for development. In the community development case, citizen participation—learning—works better than bargaining among political rivals, and much better than the computation that optimizes community wealth often with eminent domain proceedings.

The interpretations themselves depend on a variety of means through which the financial manager's frame of reference gives the interpretation intelligibility. The means include projecting precedent, experience, general public feeling, political history, community climate and culture, and simple, compelling arguments. The financial manager can project the logic of appropriateness rooted in popular, political, and professional norms, trial and error, precedent, custom, habit, and the meaning of experience (March, 1994); general feelings such as tax revolts (Lowery and Sigelman, 1981); fiscal individualism or fiscal socialism (Lexington: The Age of Fiscal Socialism, 2000); a dominating fiscal illusion (Downs, 1959–1960; Buchanan, 1977), or the premier conception of the community's social contract (Wildavsky, 2001); the particular point in the cycles of political history (Phillips, 1990); good policy arguments (Meyers, 1994, pp. 159–189); the extent of deference to expertise (Schneider and Ingram, 1997, pp. 158–159); and the sense of discretion one may have in order to make or oppose risky decisions (Miller, 1991, pp. 158–160; Thompson and Jones, 1986).

Interpretations, once chosen, evolve into narratives or texts, rituals evoking and manipulating symbols, and ultimately myths (Miller, 1991; Czarniawska and Gagliardi, 2003; Roe, 1994). The financial manager has substantial authority to enforce interpretations in the work related to taxing and spending, often in which financial managers rationalize interpretations or deftly handle punctuating events that alter stable interpretations. Both of these create new equilibria that give altered interpretations power in the future (Jones, Sulkin, and Larsen, 2003, pp. 151–169; Jordan, 2003, pp. 345–346, 358–360).

Studies

In the next sections, three studies describe the ways financial managers use the three definitions the chapter proposed initially. These three definitions reflect an efficiency logic, an agency logic in which finance officials give political leaders "what they need to get what they want," and a stewardship logic in which finance officials were "responsive to citizen demands" and anticipated citizen demands and acted in citizen interests to do all possible "with as little help from the taxpayer as necessary, to give citizens what they want."

In the first section, the cash investment study describes an activity's norms and limits as framed by finance officials in such a way that the appearance of taking risks is more dangerous than the risk itself. The information system study that follows demonstrates the symbolic and signaling uses to which finance officials put, much less the system's functional contributions to decisions. The third case on revenue forecasting demonstrates how problems connected with uncertain revenue streams and ambiguous economic and political phenomena allow, even force, finance officials to sequence decisions and, in so doing, socially construct reality.

Cash Investment

Research investigated cash management practices, particularly those involving investment. This work (Miller, 1991) investigated the acceptability of futures and options, early forms of derivatives, in cash investment practices of public managers. The findings revealed controversy over acceptance at two levels. At the ideological level, acceptance of financial innovations depends as much on the role and size of government in society as the inherent productivity potential of the techniques. A government that does little more than what is necessary may regard these innovations as irrelevant. A government that does everything may not need financial management, let alone financial innovations, since it faces no scarcity. In between, most financial managers find the language of risk and loss controlling their choices. At the instrumental level, in the public sector, risk is not opportunity that, when exploited, defines gain. Rather risk refers to the chance of mishap, the avoidance or prevention of which has a high priority. In fact, in public administration theory, risk may carry ethical connotations, one of the most traditional of which regards risk taking as a violation of a fiduciary relationship to the polity.

In the research financial officials were asked their ranking of the goals of cash investment and then their use of derivatives. In the rankings (Miller, 1991, p. 165), officials considered as most important the preservation of capital. In a significant sense, the first goal became the frame for all other goals and for all investments and investment risks. As Tversky and Kahneman (2000) suggest, most individuals, and in this case, public cash investment managers, are loss-averse. In an experiment with Ohio investment officers, McCue (2000) confirms these prospect theory predictions, as does Denison's survey (2002) and the comparative research by Mattson, Hackbart, and Ramsey (1990).

The Orange County, California, investment loss case proved to be a one-off case, but one widely discussed and supporting the risk aversion approach to cash management described here. Chapman (1996) describes the county's greater reliance on investment income in the early 1990s when compared to the other major county population centers. Contributing to the outcome was an apparent entrepreneurial strategy and willingness to take risks with investments (Chapman, 1996, pp. 26–30). The entrepreneurial strategy and heavy reliance on investment income led to multi-billion-dollar losses by the end of 1994, and the county filed for bankruptcy protection in the courts.

The lesson Chapman drew from the case taught that uncertainty increases when ambiguous cash investment goals get resolved to maximizing return. Reliance on self-interested private tresury advisors may not increase certainty.

The increasing uncertainty lesson yields another similar one about public entrepreneurship strategies. Chapman concludes:

> Entrepreneurship in the public sector is different from entrepreneurship in the private sector. Although neither can afford to fail, the public consequences can be very serious for the public entrepreneur. The public entrepreneur cannot be allowed to take chances that could lead to large failures. It may be that the public entrepreneur should be constrained from taking chances that could lead to any failures. Orange County missed this lesson. (p. 31)

The public consequences include stakeholder reaction and measures taken to overcome the failure. One measure being public humiliation, the Orange County case serves as a cautionary tale for entrepreneurial public treasurers.

Information Systems

The U.S. Office of Management and Budget (OMB) published, in October 1969, the set of guidelines called Circular A-95,[2] and research investigated their intent and practical use. These guidelines created, essentially, a process by which agencies at all levels of government were brought into the grant-in-aid review process, before the grant proposal was funded, through clearinghouses that distributed grant proposal information. This review consisted of examination and comment on the consistency of any proposed project with projects already in existence and those planned for the future. Moreover, Circular A-95 covered projects funded under nine federal cabinet departments and five independent agencies.

Later, in June 1970, OMB published another circular, A-98, which went beyond A-95. A-98 required federal agencies, for the first time, to inform both the grant applicant *and* the state and local agencies that originally reviewed the application of their decision on funding. Thus, Circulars A-95 and A-98 designed a complete grant information system. A-95, by the systematic review it prescribed, allowed agencies at lower levels of government to evaluate and coordinate requests for assistance on the basis of what had been done or was planned. A-98, as stated, went one step further and required that agencies be kept informed of the status of proposals they reviewed.

The A-95/A-98 grant information system, because of its circular flow of "messages," is an example of communications and control in government and may be understood best as a cybernetic model. The central purpose of the A-95/A-98 review and notification system was to coordinate policy making and the administration of domestic development programs[3] among agencies at all levels of government. The coordination concept was set forth by Congress and implemented by the Office of Management and Budget in the form of a *communications* system for grant applications to involve not only federal agencies, but also state and local agencies in the grant-in-aid decision-making cycle. The theme of intergovernmental grant coordination through a communications system may be traced from its legal background to its practical application in rules and regulations.

The A-95/A-98 system is similar to a cybernetic system, in that it can be studied not only as a flow of information on grants, but also as a self-regulatory device that keeps the plans and programs of governmental agencies coordinated (stable) by controlling grant applications so that the objectives of these plans and programs may best be fulfilled.

The evidence from research on the Project Notification and Review System (PNRS) highlighted its shortcomings. First, there existed inadequate area-wide plans to which to compare new projects, providing incentives to use randomly selected criteria for judging or not judging grant applications. Second, little staff commitment, in either interest or time–money–staff resources to devote to clearinghouse activity, may have led to a random selection of participants to enter or not enter the review process. Finally, federal grant sources lacked interest or were not forced by OMB to include clearinghouse comments in their decisions, providing another random process of solution-provider selection.

The research evidence relates to evidence compiled from other such studies of information use (Feldman and March, 1981, p. 174, fn. 1):

> (1) Much of the information that is gathered and communicated by individuals and organizations has little decision relevance. (2) Much of the information that is used to justify a decision is collected and interpreted after the decision has been made, or substantially made. (3) Much of the information gathered in response to requests for information is not considered in the making of decisions for which it was requested. (4) Regardless of the information available at the time a decision is first considered, more information is requested. (5) Complaints that an organization does not have enough information to make a decision occur while available information is ignored. (6) The relevance of the information provided in the decision-making process to the decision being made is less conspicuous than is the insistence on information.

The findings suggest that a decision outcome in the PNRS process did not necessarily relate to information gathered in that process. Why then were information, participants, and decision so disconnected? First, the clearinghouses had no direct incentive to curb or align information gathering in light of what was needed by decision makers. Clearinghouses were paid, often by decision makers themselves or the governments they head, to gather information, not to ensure its use. Moreover, the criticism of clearinghouses was likely to come from those who overestimated what they knew about events—were surprised by what they did not expect—and actually could have used more information. Less criticism came from those who underestimated what they knew and got more information than they could use.

Second, not knowing the exact shape community development should take, decision makers could not use information clearinghouse procedures provided to guide them to the best alternative. Economic change, for one thing, forced decision makers to contemplate new urban and rural development forms and goals, even as clearinghouses told them the best way to what were now relatively obsolete development forms and goals. Often the questions to ask, not the alternative answers, were needed.

Third, the information provided by participants in a clearinghouse process often had strategic importance for more than one participant in more than one way. Conflicts of interest were often apparent, as one community might compete with another, with each community's review of the other's projects jaundiced as a result. Strategic misrepresentation could be commonplace. Without trustworthiness, the information fell in value, and by virtue, all information became suspect.

Nevertheless, finally, the clearinghouse process had legitimacy, especially for its symbolic attention to the rational decision process, if not for PNRS's adherence to the rational decision process's substance. In government, legitimacy attached to decisions that were made in apparently rational ways, that is, made in accordance with long-standing norms about appropriate procedures (Olsen, 1970; March and Sevon, 1984; March and Weissinger-Baylon, 1986). Whether the clearinghouse procedure actually led to good or better decisions, or whether the procedures related to decision making at all, the clearinghouse process itself led participants to believe in the appropriateness of grant decisions and sometimes even the development plans and decisions related to them, and led to support for clearinghouses and their further development.

Analyzing the PNRS process, it resembled a garbage can in which various combinations of problems, solutions, participants, and choice opportunities attached to each other. The streams of each of the four elements were independent and exogenous to the system.

The garbage can choice process, according to Cohen, March, and Olsen (1972), results in an interpretive system. Since much of the problem solving in the PNRS may be random associations of problems and solutions, few conclusions may be made about the outcomes without elaborating some existing scheme of reference. Lacking definitive results, agencies such as the Advisory Commission on Intergovernmental Relations (ACIR) called for more federal funding (ACIR, 1977) and reported the general satisfaction government jurisdictions have with the system.

The important differences between a system that relies on cybernetics and much of the rest of the world that real people inhabit is the degree of ambiguity with which decision makers contend. Cybernetics requires the question to be known, the goal to be shared widely among organization members.

Seldom does this degree of certainty or agreement actually exist. More likely the case is a federalist system, where federal funding agencies may have far more concrete ideas about community development and where local governments are far more predatory in seeking these funds, than in a cybernetic system. Combining three different sets of participants in a choice structure in which funding solutions may have little relation to problems as they are comprehended by any or all of the participants prompts what we know as an organized anarchy.

Such a system relies on symbolic moves for creating progress. Creating a PNRS may have little direct, technological relevance to decision makers. Whatever technological relevance the process has lies in its random juxtaposition of problems, solutions, and participants. By random mating, some problems get solved, some solutions get used, and some participants feel they have actually created an outcome.

However, the PNRS has remarkable salience in legitimizing or even justifying decisions *after* they are made. In whatever way a decision was reached, a decision maker has incredible amounts of information on which to build a case for a decision already made.

In even going through the process, moreover, the decision makers achieve legitimacy for action. Following what is widely believed by voters to be a good decision-making process in which competing alternatives are weighed against each other in terms of contributing to a goal, the decision maker creates the potential for attachment and commitment by those who will carry out the decision as well as those who will live with the result.

Revenue Forecasting

Revenue forecasting in government is hardly ever the prerogative of only one group. Intergroup effort, in fact, describes what takes place when both legislative and executive bodies forecast (Kamlet, Mowery, and Su, 1987). Such effort is also required among different offices within the federal executive branch (Pierce, 1971), and at the local level, among the different activities within the finance department (Meltsner, 1971).

Common to all whose task is forecasting is uncertainty and ambiguity. Seldom is there a clear definition of economic base–tax base–revenue cause–effect relationships creating uncertainty. Less seldom is there agreement about what one wants to happen (beyond stable revenue) creating ambiguity. Thus forecasting is often a judgmental process, especially influenced by forecasters' social construction of reality. To understand the judgmental process, and thus revenue forecasting, requires insight into the elements that interact to construct cause-effect relationships and desired outcomes. The interaction among actors in forecasting, as in all other organizational and judgmental exercises, assumes that all want stability; all participants interact and confine behavior in ways to trade stable expectations about behavior.

Explaining reality construction solely as an economy of social interactions is incomplete. March and Olsen (1989, p. 62) suggest that the market centers on bias:

> Although there seems to be ample evidence that when performance fails to meet aspirations, institutions search for new solutions ..., changes often seem to be driven less by problems than by solutions.... When causality and technology are ambiguous, the motivation to have particular solutions adopted is likely to be as powerful as the motivation to have particular problems solved, and changes can be more easily induced by a focus on solutions than by a focus on problems. Solutions and opportunities stimulate awareness of previously unsalient or unnoticed problems or preferences.

All parties to making judgments have a solution in mind, we assume. Judgment in a collective choice situation depends on one party's convincing other parties that a preferred solution connects to the problem at hand. The argument about one's preferred solution may be easier to make when the party realizes the importance of sequential attention. Parties to the making of judgment have limited time and limited willingness to devote more than a fair share of that time to a given judgment call. Any party realizing the limited time problem can choose to focus attention, or not, on a given solution. One's ploy may well be to focus on the aspect of the problem that a given solution seems most capable of resolving. Or one's time may best be spent in defining a problem so that a favorite solution can solve it. In fact, Brunsson (1989) has argued that it is possible to sustain a coalition among members who have what appear to be strictly inconsistent objectives because of sequential attention.

The ploys can be illustrated with many state consensus forecasting units (Sun and Lynch, 2008), and especially the governor-house-senate consensus forecasting process in Florida (Klay and Vonasek, 2008). Better still, because of its documentation, the Troika portrays ploys vividly. The Troika was a 1960s' era federal executive branch forecasting group consisting of representatives of the U.S. Department of Treasury, the Council of Economic Advisors, and the Office of Management and Budget.

According to Pierce's research (1971), favorite solutions to budget and economic problems stand behind the Troika members' contributions and thus influence forecasts. Through the use of econometric models in policy analyses, members of the Troika ran any policy solution through the econometric model, varying the assumptions built into the model. Thus solutions, in the form of policies, often drove Troika forecasting. The members of the Troika also had their unique biases. According to Pierce (1971, p. 49), "Treasury technicians tend[ed] to place a higher priority on the goal of price level stability than on unemployment or growth," while the Council of Economic Advisors usually placed greater emphasis on full employment and economic expansion. The Office of Management and Budget was responsible to presidential norms: no budget action could lead to a depression or recession, at least not in an election year, and no forecast could create conditions for a self-fulfilling prophecy.

The procedure used by the Troika, according to observers (Kettl, 1986; Greider, 1987; Pierce, 1971) was sequential attention. First, Treasury forecast revenue. Then, OMB forecast expenditure. Finally, the Council forecast the economic outlook. By adroitly applying technology and expertise, Troika members could manage the assumptions and judgments that must be made to combine revenue and expenditure forecasts in some reasonable way and predict economic change.

The recognition of biases, and the understanding that differences may be useful, underscores much research in judgment making (Wright and Ayton, 1987). That is, differences create a healthy skepticism about others' views and assumptions, bringing them out in the open (Golembiewski and Miller, 1981). Research by Klay (1983, 1985) and Ascher (1978) suggests that airing such differences may reduce overreliance on outdated core assumptions, or "assumption drag," in forecasts, improving their accuracy. The structuring of forecasters to exploit their differences may not depend on simply adding more forecasters who distrust others' work. Subtly nudging forecasts in other ways may require more attention but may have substantially larger payoffs.

The sequential attention factor may have the most potential for improving or changing forecasting practice. Varying the sequence of attention may lead those who want to control attention to focus it on important matters. Such seemed to be the case in Crecine's study of local government budgeting (1969) and in Meltsner's study of local government revenue estimating and rate setting (1971).

A set of potential roles emerges from these models. Individuals assume and take responsibility for parts of an idealized process. A record keeper/data driver finds the average rate of change over previous years. Various other observers could determine why the average rate might be different in the future and offer another, higher rate of change with these potential events in mind. Another, more cautious officer could recommend that the two be averaged and rounded down.

Such may easily be the case in forecasting. One would assume that forecasts are computational exercises for the most part. If they are not completely computational, we would expect them to be a combination of interpretation and computation, using the full range of quantitative, qualitative, and sequencing methods.

If the latter is more reasonable as a surmise, interesting questions emerge. First, whose interpretations guide forecasts? In cases where there are different interpretations, how does a group of forecasters choose one or reconcile all of them? Second, is there an inherent bias in the forecasting process? Is such a bias toward high numbers, in someone's political interest, or toward low ones?

These research questions ask who rules assumptions and guides forecasting. Two competing explanations seem to draw agreement: sequence and institutional bias.

Sequence

The sequential attention partisans (Hammond, 1986; Plott, 1976) explain assumption rules in terms of structure. Sequential attention finds support in both agenda research on legislatures and hierarchy research in bureaucracies. First, agendas dictate what is considered first and so on through legislative work sessions. Plott (1976) models the agenda of a decision process and shows how the agenda may force decisions in certain ways. When, for example, three different preference orderings exist, each possible agenda yields a different outcome. Whoever controls the agenda controls the outcome.

Second, in more ambiguous circumstances where preferences are not known, agenda strategy can still have importance. March and Olsen (1976) argue the practical value in tactically loading agendas, for instance. Loading some agendas rather than others, such as university self-studies and budget deliberations, rather than investment committee meetings—takes high-pressure issues away from other agendas and permits work to get done. Moreover, they point out, loading meeting agendas at the front end with controversial items may work in favor of actually gaining acceptance (or encouraging ignorance) of other issues that are more serious and are placed in a less vulnerable position later in the agenda. Such front loading provides garbage cans in which all parties can put solutions, problems, and other such issues.

Compelling arguments have also been made by Padgett (1980) in bureaucracy studies. He shows that altering subordinates' attention rules—through variants of agendas such as structural stratagems—actually reduces the amount of close control and scrutiny required of the chief executive and, by sequencing attention, increases the amount of unclouded information the chief executive gets.

Institutional Bias

The second, role bias explanation (Wildavsky, 1964; Schick, 1988) holds that forecasting is inherently conservative, with all extreme positions moderated by the need for compromise. This view holds that institutions that have a stake in the outcome of a forecast must compel representatives to "vote" this bias in strategically important ways in interorganizational confrontations or cooperative ventures. Without staking out initial positions at the extreme, these institutions find that later decisions or compromises do not incorporate the institutions' points of view.

Research explored the sequencing vs. institutional bias alternatives in a Troika-like simulation (Miller, 1991, pp. 208–228). The research simulated the idealized roles and their preferences: average, higher, and lower rates of change.

The simulation assumed that there is no common set of preferences other than stable expectations or expected stability guiding forecasters. Rather, roles are played and the forecast depends on numbers actually generated through these roles.

Second, the simulation assumed three other matters. First, the forecast results from negotiation rather than computation. Second, the properties of a forecasting process include negotiation over the limits and middle ground. Third, this negotiation guides and dictates the outcome of that process.

We simulated three relationships among forecasters to eliminate either the sequencing or institutional bias explanation for the forecast. First, we would expect that whoever controls the agenda has a greater say in the outcome, corresponding to the sequential attention position.

Second, previous research focused on the neutrality of the agenda setter. If we assume that all parties consider one in their group as primarily neutral and that party's chairing the group as merely a way to open discussion on a neutral note, we could discard the idea of agenda setting. Instead, assuming the chair's forecasts rest on random values of a few variables, we could infer that a final forecast that neared the chair's forecast to a greater extent than the other parties' forecasts randomly influences the process. This point of view still supports sequential attention.

Pierce's third finding (1971) explains the effect of extreme positions and resembles the institutional bias position. The more extreme the initial position, the more likely the position will have some influence on the outcome.

Our research examined therefore the two competing positions in consensus revenue forecasting groups. The sequential attention factor represented the view that whoever controls the agenda controls the outcome. The institutional bias view supported the notion that representation of important biases contributed to extreme forecasts that were moderated, though not overcome, by group effort. The research suggested that sequential attention was the strongest and most defensible explanation of consensus revenue estimations. The chair in both conditions of the research design dominated the outcome. The relationship between the chair and bias seemed weak since the chair was as likely as not to have one of the extreme positions. Moreover, the chair, in providing the initial position, guided the outcome.

The research confirmed other studies to suggest that sequencing the attention of the forecasters might have a large impact on estimates. Work by Meltsner (1971), especially, argued this view. Meltsner's research on local government revenue systems, supports the idea that the structure for decision making applies to forecasting, and reveals the influence of sequencing work (separate sequences for large and small "other" revenue sources, and then property taxes) and a hierarchy of steps within these sequences.

Sequential attention explanations of behavior parallel agenda-setting functions in public administration and policy making. The literature following publication of work on organization anarchies and the garbage can model of decision making led by March and Olsen (1986) highlighted agenda setting and the impact it has on decision outcomes (Kingdon, 1984). The findings are straightforward: when ends are ambiguous and means uncertain, agendas resolve instability problems. Agendas resolve unstable preferences and estimates in revenue forecasting too. Forecasts have a large impact, and even sometimes drive other activities in budgeting and policy making. Ends or preferences about forecasts do exist and influence forecast negotiations, but agendas also influence revenue forecast negotiations.

Conclusion: Summarizing Practice as Interpretation

Financial issues loom large in policy deliberation. Leaders look to the institution-alized expertise of finance officials for help. Finance officials practice three fiscal values—efficiency, agency, and stewardship—to interpret ambiguous phenom-ena. These values represent interpretations of the ends, means, and their connec-tions that form policy goals and designs. The argument in this chapter claims that their institutional survival interests motivate finance officials to push or transform ambiguous events into categories in which there is some degree of agreement, whether about ends, means, or both. If the transformation succeeds in creating an objective view of both ends and means, finance officials may simply compute the answer to the problem. If less successful in gaining consensus, the result may call for bargaining or learning.

Three studies of fiscal policy ambiguity illustrated the interpretation phenom-enon in the chapter. Figure 3.2 provides a capsule version of the cases.

Ambiguity existed in the cash investment case because few could tell when public investment with derivatives became gambling rather than insurance. The study concluded that finance officials had gained consensus about ends and means. The end seemed to be take no risks and lose no taxpayer money through invest-ments. The means were investments that earned more than simply locking cash in a vault, but were nearly risk-free. The case leads to the conclusion that ambiguity about what investments to make for what reason got resolved with the take-no-risk approach. This strategy is usually based on stewardship and sometimes also respon-siveness to political masters' risk aversion. The relatively risk-free investments still permitted returns greater than no investment at all. The risk-free investment strat-egy allowed an optimizing or computational solution to a cash investment dilemma and illustrates the finance official's transformation of an ambiguity problem into a computational one through interpretation.

The information systems study described the intentional design of the A-95/A-98 Project Notification and Review System (PNRS) to resemble a cyber-netic one. Many entryways for information, clearinghouses, and communication channels for moving information about gave federal, state, and local officials access to land use plans, project grant applications, and development proposed project plans. Decision points permitted reviewers to provide feedback and to coordinate proposed efforts with past and future ones.

However, in use, the system resembled streams of problems, solutions, and deci-sion opportunities connected to each other in only random ways, a system known

Model Specification	Cash Investment Case	PNR System Case	Consensus Revenue Forecasting Case
Ambiguity	Insurance or speculation or guarding investment against loss	Who proposes and gets federal, state, or local financial support for what development project? How does the project fit with other organizations' land use plans and projects?	What revenue will the government collect in the future? How accurate, and thus how believable and useful, are the government's revenue estimators?
Interpretation	Preventing losses	At random, some grants (solutions) find problems to solve, some development problems find solutions, and some choice opportunities connect some problems to some solutions	Economic growth or slowdown with present fiscal policies, future fiscal policies, or the dynamics of fiscal policies that are likely to take place; the revenue the government is likely to be able to collect
Who interprets	Finance officials based on professional knowledge and fiduciary role	Government planners at all levels, real estate developers, federal grantors, state-local leaders with money from both, and other government leaders with projects to support	Revenue estimators in consensus forecasting units
How interpretation constructed	Professional norms; unwillingness to take risks	Random mating of problems, solutions, individuals, and choice opportunities	Sequence of decisions and agenda setting

Figure 3.2   Case study findings and interpretive model specifications.

Model Specification	Cash Investment Case	PNR System Case	Consensus Revenue Forecasting Case
How interpretation communicated	Narrative of gambling with the public's money	Narrative of progress along with the legitimacy and justification of decisions on plans and grant support for them	Narrative of estimate accuracy and the accepted scenario of economic and social change on which the estimate rests
How interpretation enforced	Investment policy	Grant support for development projects; consensus on long-term land use plans and projects necessary to implement them	Expenditure limits at the state-local level; size of the federal deficit and debt

Figure 3.2 (*Continued*)   Case study findings and interpretive model specifications.

as an organized anarchy. Ambiguity pervaded; no one could know whether all of the projects in the stream fit all the plans in the stream. Finance and other officials operating through information clearinghouses in the system worked in a choice structure in which connecting solutions was not the use PNRS found. Financial officials and others relied on the PNRS as a symbol of progress in communicating and cooperating, if not a system funneling information to decision makers who were negotiating grant-funded projects, and much less a system in which one agency's leaders got the sole power to decide the fate of a project and impose a view on a community.

Finance officials and others used the PNRS as a legitimizing or even justifying device after decisions were made. PNRS produced substantial information on which to build a case for a decision already made. Ambiguity about the appropriate ends and means could get rationalized after the fact, as if the decision made had been a computational and thereby rational one. Legitimacy increased with narratives about progress and orderly regional and community development, the myth of rationality as wisdom, and functionality symbolized by cybernetic, command and control systems.

In the revenue forecasting study, estimation appeared at first to be a computational problem. The study showed revenue estimation to have many features in common with political decision negotiation, but it is, in truth, another ambiguous decision situation. There is no agreement about whether the estimate should be optimistic or not, given the possibility that the estimate will influence a subsequent series of decisions and make the estimate a self-fulfilling prophecy. There is also uncertainty about the rate and direction of movement as well as interaction among a large number of dynamic socioeconomic factors.

Relying on models that can portray a part but not all of the socioeconomic complexity of society and the economy, estimators in consensus forecasting units will probably choose their favorite model. The simulation of revenue estimation reported in the study revealed how vulnerable the estimation process is to model competition and agenda setting in even consensus forecasting groups.

The findings from the simulation showed that ambiguity could give way to computation by way of sequencing the attention of estimators. The estimator who sets the sequence of choices—the chair and the agenda in the simulation—had the ability to determine which socioeconomic model estimates competed on a pairwise basis to guarantee a particular outcome. Ambiguity became computation through the finance official's sequential attention to problems and solutions.

Summarizing the institutional and interpretive meanings we find in the studies, the behavior of finance officials to transform ambiguous events to manageable ones was reasonable. To control critical contingencies, whether money or knowledge about how to get and use it, finance officials made shrewd suggestions or took sensible action. They promoted efficiency (revenue forecasting), conformed to the expectations of the public in stewarding resources (cash investment), and responded to leaders who needed to show how more information led to better decisions but also needed information to legitimize a bargained solution to a planning problem (information systems). Recognizing the variety of interpretations possible in ambiguous circumstances, finance officials were able to leverage their expertise and gain consensus, transforming the subjective into the objective. What finance officials practice is interpretation.

Endnotes

1. This chapter was adapted from Practice as interpretation in public financial management, by Gerald J. Miller, Jonathan B. Justice, and Iryna Illiash, in Aman Kahn and Bartley Hildreth, eds., *Financial Management in the Public Sector,* 89–114. Westport, CT: Praeger, 2004. Used with permission of ABC-CLIO, LLC.
2. The circular's full name was "Evaluation, Review, and Coordination of Federal Assistance Programs and Projects."
3. Programs included open-space land projects or planning and construction projects for hospitals, airports, libraries, water supply and distribution facilities, sewerage facilities and waste treatment works, highways, transportation facilities, law enforcement facilities, and water development and land conservation projects. Housing facilities were added in 1971.

References

Advisory Commission on Intergovernmental Relations (ACIR). (1977). *Improving Federal Grants Management: The Intergovernmental Grant System: An Assessment and Proposed Policies.* Washington, DC: U.S. Government Printing Office.

Alexander, Jennifer. (1999). A new ethics of the budgetary process. *Administration and Society* 34(4):542–565.

Ascher, William. (1978). *Forecasting: An Appraisal for Policy-Makers and Planners.* Baltimore: Johns Hopkins University Press.

Astley, W. Graham. (1985). Administrative science as socially constructed truth. *Administrative Science Quarterly* 30:497–513.

Berger, Peter L., and Thomas Luckmann. (1966). *The Social Construction of Reality: A Treatise in the Sociology of Knowledge.* New York: Doubleday.

Brunsson, N. (1989). *The Organization of Hypocrisy.* Chicester, UK: John Wiley.

Buchanan, James M. (1977). Why does government grow? In *Budgets and Bureaucrats: The Sources of Government Growth*, ed. Thomas E. Borcherding, 3–18. Raleigh, NC: Duke University Press.

Burchell, Stuart, Colin Clubb, Anthony Hopwood, John Hughes, and Janine Nahapiet. (1980). The roles of accounting in organizations and society. *Accounting, Organizations and Society* 5(1):5–27.

Chapman, Jeffrey I. (1996). The challenge of entrepreneurship: An Orange County case study. *Municipal Finance Journal* 17(2):16–32.

Cohen, Michael D., James G. March, and Johan P. Olsen. (1972). A garbage can model of organizational choice. *Administrative Science Quarterly* 17: 1–25.

Crecine, John P. (1969). *Government Problem Solving.* Chicago: Rand McNally.

Czarniawska, Barbara, and Pasquale Gagliardi. (2003). *Narratives We Organize By.* Philadelphia: John Benjamins.

Denison, Dwight V. (2002). How conservative are municipal investment practices in large U.S. cities? *Municipal Finance Journal* 23(1):35–51.

Downs, Anthony. (1959–1960). Why the government budget is too small in a democracy. *World Politics* 12:541–563.

Edwards, J. David. Managerial influences in public administration. Unpublished paper. available online at http://www.utc.edu/~mpa/managerialism.htm (accessed June 30, 2001).

Feldman, Martha S., and James G. March. (1981). Information in organizations as signal and symbol. *Administrative Science Quarterly* 26(2):171–186.

Forrester, John P., and Guy B. Adams. (1997). Budgetary reform through organizational learning: Toward an organizational theory of budgeting. *Administration and Society* 28(4):466–488.

Golembiewski, Robert T. (1999). Shortfalls of public administration as empirical science. *Public Administration Quarterly* 23(1):3–17.

Golembiewski, Robert T., and Gerald J. Miller. (1981). Small groups in political science. In *Handbook of Political Behavior*, ed. Samuel Long, 1 71. Vol. 2. New York: Plenum.

Grafstein, Robert. (1988). A realist foundation for essentially contested political concepts. *Western Political Quarterly* 41(1):9–28.

Greider, William. (1987). *Secrets of the Temple: How the Federal Reserve Runs the Country.* New York: Simon and Schuster.

Hammond, Thomas H. (1986). Agenda control, organizational structure, and bureaucratic politics. *American Journal of Political Science* 30(2):379–420.

Jones, Bryan D., Tracy Sulkin, and Heather A. Larsen. (2003). Policy punctuations in American political institutions. *American Political Science Review* 97(1):151–169.

Jordan, Meagan M. (2003). Punctuations and agendas: A new look at local government budget expenditures. *Journal of Policy Analysis and Management* 22(3):345–360.

Kamlet, Mark S., David C. Mowery, and Tsai-Tsu Su. (1987). Whom do you trust? An analysis of executive and congressional economic forecasts. *Journal of Policy Analysis and Management* 6(3):365–384.

Kant, Immanuel. (1992). *Perpetual Peace: a Philosophical Essay*, trans. M. Campbell Smith. Bristol, England: Thoemmes Press.

Kettl, Donald F. (1986). *Leadership at the Fed.* New Haven, CT: Yale University Press.

Kingdon, John W. (1984). *Agendas, Alternatives, and Public Policies.* Boston: Little, Brown.

Klay, William Earle. (1983). Revenue forecasting: An administrative perspective. In *Handbook of Public Budgeting and Financial Management*, ed. Jack Rabin and Thomas D. Lynch, 287–316. New York: Marcel Dekker.

Klay, William Earle. (1985). The organizational dimension of budgetary forecasting: Suggestions from revenue forecasting in the states. *International Journal of Public Administration* 7(3):241–265.

Klay, William Earle, and Joseph A. Vonasek. (2008). Consensus forecasting for budgeting in theory and practice. In *Government Budget Forecasting*, ed. Jinping Sun and Thomas D. Lynch, 379–392. Boca Raton, FL: Taylor & Francis.

Lehan, Edward Anthony. (1991). Organization of the finance function. In *Local Government Finance: Concepts and Practices*, ed. John E. Petersen and Dennis R. Strachota, 29–43. Chicago: Government Finance Officers Association.

Lexington (2000). The age of fiscal socialism. *The Economist*, April 13. http://www.economist.com/node/302225?story_id=E1_PDNNNV

Lowery, David, and Lee Sigelman. (1981). Understanding the tax revolt: Eight explanations. *American Political Science Review* 75:963–974.

March, James G. (1994). *A Primer on Decision Making: How Decisions Happen.* New York: Free Press.

March, James G., and Johan P. Olsen. (1976). *Ambiguity and Choice in Organizations.* Bergen, Norway: Universitetsforlaget.

March, James G., and Johan P. Olsen. (1986). Garbage can models of decision making in organizations. In *Ambiguity and Command: Organizational Perspectives on Military Decision Making*, ed. James G. March and Roger Weissinger-Baylon, 11–35. Marshfield, MA: Pitman.

March, James G., and Johan P. Olsen. (1989). *Rediscovering Institutions: The Organizational Basis of Politics.* New York: Basic Books.

March, James G., and Guje Sevon. (1984). Gossip, information and decision making. In *Advances in Information Processing in Organizations*, ed. L. S. Sproull and J. P. Crecine, 95–107. Vol. 1. Greenwich, CT: JAI Press.

March, James G., and Roger Weissinger-Baylon. (1986). *Ambiguity and Command: Organizational Perspectives on Military Decision Making.* Marshfield, MA: Pitman.

Martin, Rex. (2002). Right answers: Dworkin's jurisprudence. In *Is There a Single Right Interpretation?* ed. Michael Krausz, 251–263. University Park: Pennsylvania State University Press.

Martinez-Vazques, Jorge. (2001). *The Impact of Budgets on the Poor: Tax and Benefit Incidence.* Working Paper 01-10. Atlanta, GA: Andrew Young School of Policy Studies, Georgia State University.

Mattson, Kyle, Merl Hackbart, and James Ramsey. (1990). State and corporate cash management: A comparison. *Public Budgeting and Finance* 10(4):18–27.

McCaffery, Jerry L., and L. R. Jones. (2001). *Budgeting and Financial Management in the Federal Government.* Greenwich, CT: Information Age Publishing.

McCamy, J. (1947). Analysis of the process of decision making. *Public Administration Review* 7:41–48.

McCue, Clifford P. (2000). The risk-return paradox in local government investing. *Public Budgeting and Finance* 20(3):80–101.

Meltsner, Arnold J. (1971). *The Politics of City Revenue.* Berkeley: University of California Press.

Merton, Robert K. (1936). The unanticipated consequences of purposive social action. *American Sociological Review* 1:894–904.

Merton, Robert K. (1957). Bureaucratic structure and personality. In *Social Theory and Social Structure,* ed. Robert K. Merton, 195–206. 2nd ed. Glencoe, IL: Free Press.

Meyers, Roy T. (1994). *Strategic Budgeting.* Ann Arbor: University of Michigan Press.

Miller, Gerald J. (1998). Accreditation of budget and finance offices in New Jersey. Paper presented at the annual meeting of the Association for Public Budgeting and Financial Management, Washington, DC.

Miller, Gerald J. (1991). *Government Financial Management Theory.* New York: Dekker.

Miller, Gerald J., and Lyn Evers. (2002). Budget structures and citizen participation. *Journal of Public Budgeting, Accounting and Financial Management* 14(2):205–246.

Miller, Gerald J., W. Bartley Hildreth, and Jack Rabin. (2001). *Performance-Based Budgeting.* Boulder, CO: Westview.

Olsen, Johan P. (1970). Local budgeting: Decision-making or a ritual act? *Scandinavian Political Studies* 5:85–118.

Olsen, Johan P. (2003). Citizens, public administration and the search for theoretical foundations. Paper presented at 17th Annual John Gaus Lecture, American Political Science Association, Philadelphia, PA. Excerpted in *APSA Public Administration Section's Electronic Newsletter* 2(2):1–4. Available at http://www.h-net.org/~pubadmin/ (accessed October 7, 2003).

Padgett, John F. (1980). Managing garbage can hierarchies. *Administrative Science Quarterly* 25:583–604.

Phillips, Kevin. (1990). *The Politics of Rich and Poor.* New York: Random House.

Pierce, Lawrence D. (1971). *The Politics of Fiscal Policy Formation.* Pacific Palisades, CA: Goodyear.

Plott, Charles R. (1976). Axiomatic social choice theory: An overview and interpretation. *American Journal of Political Science* 22(3):511–596.

Roe, Emery. (1994). *Narrative Policy Analysis.* Durham, NC: Duke University Press.

Rubin, Irene S. (1998). *Class, tax, and power.* Chatham, NJ: Chatham House.

Saaty, Thomas L. (1980). *The Analytic Hierarchy Process: Planning, Priority Setting, Resource Allocation.* New York: McGraw Hill.

Schick, Allen. (1988). An inquiry into the possibility of a budgetary theory. In *New Directions in Budget Theory,* ed. I. Rubin, 59–69. Albany: State University of New York Press.

Schneider, Anne Larson, and Helen Ingram. (1997). *Policy Design for Democracy.* Lawrence. University of Kansas Press.

Scott, W. Richard. (2001). *Institutions and Organizations.* 2nd ed. Thousand Oaks, CA: Sage.

Searle, John R. (1995). *The Construction of Social Reality.* New York: Free Press.

Selznick, Philip. (1957). *Leadership in Administration.* Evanston, IL: Row, Peterson.

Sherif, Muzafer. (1935). A study of some social factors in perception. *Archives of Psychology* 23, monograph 187.

Silverman, David. (1971). *The Theory of Organizations*. New York: Basic Books.

Simon, Herbert A. (1947). *Administrative Behavior*. New York: Free Press.

Smith, Adam. (1991). *The Wealth of Nations*. New York: Knopf/Random House/Everyman's Library.

Sun, Jinping, and Thomas D. Lynch. (2008). *Government Budget Forecasting*. Boca Raton, FL: Taylor & Francis.

Thompson, Fred, and L. R. Jones. (1986). Controllership in the public sector. *Journal of Policy Analysis and Management* 5(3):547–571.

Thompson, James D. (1967). *Organizations in Action*. New York: McGraw-Hill.

Thompson, James D., and Arthur Tuden. (1959). Strategies, structures, and processes of organizational decision. In *Comparative Studies in Administration*, ed. James D. Thompson, Peter B. Hammond, Robert W. Hawkes, Buford H. Junker, and Arthur Tuden, 195–216. Pittsburgh: University of Pittsburgh Press.

Thurmaier, Kurt, and Katherine G. Willoughby. (2001). *Policy and Politics in State Budgeting*. Armonk, NY: M. E. Sharpe.

Tversky, Amos, and Daniel Kahneman. (2000). Rational choice and the framing of decisions. In *Choices, Values, and Frames*, ed. Daniel Kahneman and Amos Tversky, 209–223. Cambridge: Cambridge University Press.

Wildavsky, Aaron (1964). *The Politics of the Budgetary Process*. Boston: Little Brown.

Wildavsky, Aaron. (2001). The budget as a new social contract. In *Budgeting and Governing: Aaron Wildavsky*, ed. Brendon Swedlow, 259–275. Piscataway, NJ: Transaction.

Wright, George, and Peter Ayton. (1987). *Judgmental forecasting*. Chichester, England: Wiley.

Zucker, Lynne G. (1991). Institutionalization and cultural persistence. In *The New Institutionalism in Organizational Analysis*, ed. Walter W. Powell and Paul J. DiMaggio, 83-1–83-7. Chicago: University of Chicago Press.

Chapter 4

Fiscal Policy Impacts in Public Finance[1]

Introduction

Fiscal policies embody the optimizing logic financial officials use to interpret ambiguous phenomena. The research on fiscal policy impacts substantiates this logic beyond the liquidity, cost, and investment concerns that dominate the work financial officials do. Fiscal policies create incentives, distribute burdens and benefits, and trigger effects. Policy makers hope that intentions shape consequences. With the first-best or second-best alternatives in mind, this survey explores the origins and intentions of fiscal policies, the tools leaders choose to apply them, and the policy consequences found among seven policy impacts: incidence, work and leisure, savings and consumption, investment, portfolio choice, risk taking, and innovation-productivity relationships. We look at fiscal policies as government interventions in the economy—limiting or expanding liberty—for either pro-positive government or pro-business reasons resulting in either progress or leviathan.

Fiscal policy designs do have an impact. Public finance research shows the compelling force that variations in conventional and nonconventional tax and expenditure legislation can have for people at all levels of the economy (Keynes, 1964; Blinder and Solow, 1974; Auerbach, 2003). This survey also asks whether expected or unexpected impacts of fiscal policy designs have dominated findings from research.

To guide intentions to appropriate designs and tools, decision makers need analysis, and analysts need methods. Analysis helps predict the possible effects and outcomes of alternative policies. Positive research methods strengthen the analysis, as Musgrave and Musgrave illustrate. They describe the scope and method of fiscal policy analysis in a classic economic approach based on "if ..., then ...":

> If the merits of a corporation profits tax or of a sales tax are to be judged, one must know who will bear the final burden, the answer to which in turn depends on how the private sector responds to the imposition of such taxes.... [Such answers come from] the type of economic analysis which deals with predicting, on the basis of empirical analysis, how firms and consumers will respond to economic changes and with testing such predictions empirically. (1984, p. 4)

This review covers the analyses that have predicted policies' incidence and their impact on individuals, firms, governments, and the economy.

Economists, political scientists, and public administrators have found the traditional analytical public finance task a complicated one. Fiscal policy may not have the impact economic planners desire because monetary policy designs also exist to neutralize, mitigate, or intensify the effects fiscal policies have. Moreover, short- and long-term impacts may differ. Policy targets also vary considerably in the reception they give the designs. Efficiency goals may compete with intentions to increase fairness. Trade-offs confront analysts and policy makers, especially when the traditional ones involve saving and consumption, work and leisure, as well as investment risk and return. Policies must account for normative inclinations, and analysis must predict the consequences of various trade-offs and inform the choice of second-best policy designs and tools. Analysts must also take into account how likely it is that normative compromises, competing institutions, distorted policy designs, vaguely understood policy tools, and clumsy execution will frustrate policy intentions. Analysis must be sophisticated.

Analysis begs the question of why leaders and the dubious, skeptical, and hard-to-convince people they influence want fiscal policies. Griefer (2002) argues that fiscal policies formalize the goals of the executives and legislators. By such formalization, fiscal policies establish a method for determining and expressing leaders' economic, tax, debt, and budget policies to the public, business planners, investors, market analysts, credit underwriters, and central bankers. Fiscal policies clearly demonstrate that a systematic analysis of problems and solutions has taken place. Fiscal policies provide guidance and help steady expectations others have. Such guidance and expectations can help ensure suitable and expeditious execution of policy by stating the outcomes or results wanted and by which all executors may be judged. Finally, fiscal policies establish a standard and focus attention on evidence of performance or lack of performance, giving legislators, government executives, business managers and executives, market participants, and central bankers a sense of attempts, successes, and failures by policy makers to influence important behaviors, such as saving, investment, consumption, economic growth, employment, price-level stability, and innovation.

Whatever policies leaders pursue, governments and public authorities in the United States allocate the burden of paying for numerous responsibilities in distinctive ways. The federal government taxes incomes and payrolls primarily. States depend on intergovernmental revenues as well as consumption taxes (sales, excise, and gross receipts taxes) and income taxes. All local governments receive a large proportion of revenue from other governments, but they also levy most property taxes and charges or fees for services they provide. In fact, the largest amount of property taxes levied goes to school districts, followed by municipal and township governments and counties. States and municipalities both receive the largest proportions of charges and fees for services. Consumption taxes go primarily to states. Income taxes, estate and gift taxes, and payroll taxes flow substantially to the federal government.

The responsibilities of governments vary as well. The federal government is the major provider of social services and income maintenance in the form of payments (transfers) to individuals. State governments also provide social services and income maintenance, but are major spenders on education services, as are school districts. County governments provide some education services, but these governments' expenditures are even more likely to be social services and income maintenance related. Both counties and municipal-township governments spend substantial funds on public safety and administration of justice activities, such as the courts and corrections.

The scale of government differs substantially. The federal government collects approximately 43% of all tax revenue received by U.S. governments. This proportion is smaller than all Organization for Economic Cooperation and Development (OECD) member countries, except for Germany, Switzerland, and Japan (OECD, 2009). U.S. state governments are next proportionately, with over one-fourth of tax revenues collected, with localities having about one-sixth of them.

Government scale may also appear from a comparison of government outlays and then receipts with the total output of the economy, gross domestic product (GDP). The Organization for Economic Cooperation and Development (2009) publishes comparisons across nations with the largest, most highly developed economies. The OECD's databases show that the governments in the United States collect and spend approximately one-third of total U.S. GDP. That proportion has remained relatively constant for the last decade. In contrast, total government outlays and receipts in European nations are over 40% larger.

Whatever the burdens allocated, responsibilities assumed, or scale of outlays and receipts relative to other large national economies, fiscal policies have enormous influence in the United States. The tools with which government leaders influence behavior include numerous forms of spending and taxation, loans, loan guarantees, insurance, and regulation. When looking solely at the scope or magnitude of activity involving these tools, the metaphorical "reach" of U.S. federal, state, and local governments' decisions almost equals U.S. gross domestic product (Miller, 2005, p. 432).

The estimate reflects a large impact, but any educated guess should be viewed with caution. Many researchers have approached the size of government question in contrasting ways to the method here (Auerbach, 2004; Bozeman, 1987; Taylor, 1983). The estimate may include some double counting, some unrealistic assumptions about factual and counterfactual estimates—what happened or what might have happened without the policy tool, and an inapt comparison to gross domestic product. However, the actual impact fiscal policies have exceeds the size portrayed when government size equates to total government outlays or receipts as a percentage of gross domestic product revealed in the comparison across large economies above. The major characteristic of the impact is the "largely hidden," "complex networks that merge the activities of ... governments and ... private organizations in increasingly inventive ways" (Light, 1999, 2003; Salamon, 2002, p. vii). Fiscal policy makers' intentions and policy impacts under the new form of governance have an extremely intricate, perhaps tenuous relationship.

However, government leaders persuade individuals, groups, organizations, and firms to do much. These governmental actions may influence nongovernmental actors to do what nongovernmental actors wanted to be persuaded to do. The policy tools may subsidize actions already planned. In such cases, policy tools may have the impact of reducing risk, stifling innovation, and rewarding some and penalizing others inappropriately. The issue with policy tools becomes one of control of government rather than control or influence of the governed, an issue for discussion at the end of this chapter.

Fiscal Policy Tools

Although there are many different policy tools, this review concentrates on three basic ones. The public finance literature gives taxes the most attention, an emphasis followed here. Spending and debt have prompted a large amount of normative analysis in public economics, but these tools have less importance than taxes. This review gives spending and debt less emphasis also.

Taxes and Distribution Policies

When public economists speak of taxes, they often conceptualize them into lump-sum (head or poll), consumption, and means taxes. Some of these names may sound strange, but they correspond to understandable, existing forms. A lump-sum tax is most often a levy on every individual, perhaps graduated by income or some other meaningful category, sometimes not. A consumption tax is most often a tax on specific items purchased, and are most commonly known as sales taxes.

The sales tax may vary in scope, at one extreme being general and broad based in the sense that it applies to every item or service available for purchase (a value-added tax) or very narrow, as in taxes specifically on fuel, motor equipment, tobacco, alcohol, or luxury goods. A means tax may be just what the name suggests, the means to gaining a livelihood, but means may be taxed in the form of corporate income, individual income as wages, individual income as nonwage or capital income, or income from all these sources. The means tax base may also vary according to all income but investment earnings, all wages paid by an employer, or all wealth or assets held at the date of the tax levy, such as a property tax on residences or an inheritance tax paid at death.

Taxation is a major form of distribution policy, particularly when viewed as the distribution of the burden of government provision of goods and services. Although there are other facets to distribution policies on the spending and debt sides, the tax policy variation of distribution has become the greatest concern decision makers have.

There is a normative logic behind the raising of revenue to pay for government activities. Mikesell states the orthodox public economics approach as "avoidance of inequitable and inefficient revenue devices" (1978, p. 513). What does he mean? First, the basis for spending is theoretically and practically separate from the basis for taxing. Second, the taxing decision is based on the optimal combination of several criteria, particularly equity and efficiency.

All criteria for tax systems have roots in thinking by Adam Smith (1776) and have developed from the experience of every tax policy maker ever to face the question of what good government entails. Smith urges equity and efficiency, but he also suggests three basic criteria that apply to tax administration and the administrator's relationship to a government and a taxpayer: adequacy, collectability, and transparency. The identification of the latter three criteria follows immediately below, with more detailed discussion of equity and efficiency afterward.

First, the tax must be adequate to fund the government programs decided in budgeting. A tax is merely a nuisance for both government and taxpayer if it fails to generate sufficient revenue at rates falling within a zone of indifference felt by everyone participating in politics. The concept of adequacy has complex implications, especially as the nominal accounting differs from the actual behavior of taxpayers. Nominally, a tax will yield more the higher the rate. Actually, taxpayers may respond to higher rates by changing their behavior to avoid higher tax payments, and tax payments may actually decline as tax rates increase. Adequacy also encourages a view that spending drives revenue raising when, thinking realistically, we find the relationship much more complex. A high-needs jurisdiction may have an economic base and a tax base that do not yield the revenue to meet high needs. Bases that do not grow as quickly as spending have a bigger revenue adequacy problem than do those jurisdictions whose economic and tax bases grow more quickly than spending. The tax chosen in high-needs jurisdictions may have severe problems yielding adequate revenue, provoking a substantial and different reaction among policy makers, and then individuals, households, and firms. The search for revenues in other places and for means to stimulate economies to expand more rapidly will create incentives for local and foreign taxpayers to shift and share, and the outcomes for the high-needs jurisdiction are far from certain.

Second, government tax collectors must be able to do their work in an efficient way. As Smith says, "Every tax ought to be so contrived as both to take out and to keep out of the pockets of the people as little as possible over and above what it brings into the public treasury of the state" (1776, p. 655). Efficiency also suggests that collection costs provide no real economic benefit to society and certainly no political benefit to policy makers.

Third, the revenue system must have transparency. In a democracy, taxes—perhaps all policies—should be understandable in what they intend, in the process used to adopt them, in their administration, in what they require to comply, in the amounts to be paid, and the impact they can have (Finkelstein, 2000, pp. 1–9). These virtues may sum to clarity or simplicity (Institute on Taxation and Economic Policy, 2004). The taxpayers who face a revenue system that lacks either clarity or simplicity will take taxation's power to destroy as a fact about the motives of policy makers. Confused, angry taxpayers will view the system as one decided through favoritism and corrupt efforts to influence the system. Little transparency can lead to a widespread lack of understanding, or even outright fiscal illusion, about the real amounts levied and the uses to which they are put (Buchanan, 1970, 1977; Downs, 1960; Goetz, 1977).

The two other criteria for evaluating tax systems reveal conflicts between norms and actual behavior in government policy making, between equity and efficiency, and between allocation and distribution. First, the fundamental norm of fiscal policy is equity. Citizens should pay for government spending, goods, services, and institutions, Adam Smith (1776, p. 654) said, "in proportion to their respective abilities; that is, in proportion to the revenue which they respectively enjoy under the protection of the state." Smith might have implied in *some* proportion because different views exist on what equity or proportionality mean. Ability-to-pay (or egalitarian) norms and benefits-received (or utilitarian) norms both are accepted as reasonable in judging tax systems. Policy makers avoid regressive fiscal policies and especially regressive tax systems. For a comparison of different degrees of equity in tax systems, see Table 4.1.

An analyst may define a tax system's equity by contrasting the effective tax rates of the three taxpayers who appear in Table 4.1. In a regressive system, the effective rate declines as income increases, a situation in which those richest pay the least proportion of income among the three groups of taxpayers. The regressive system, generally criticized as unfair, does have some support when the point of view changes, especially in changing the point of view from an analyst to the taxpayers themselves. In general, analysts might view fairness as dictating some relationship between burdens and benefits of government fiscal policies, with the poor receiving fewer benefits than the rich and being entitled to a lower burden of paying for the

Table 4.1   Tax Equity under Three Different Systems

Taxpayer Income $	Regressive System		Proportional System		Progressive System	
	Net Tax Paid $	Effective Tax Rate %	Net Tax Paid $	Effective Tax Rate %	Net Tax Paid $	Effective Tax Rate %
20,000	3,000	15.0%	2,000	10.0%	1,000	5.0%
40,000	3,000	7.5%	4,000	10.0%	3,000	7.5%
60,000	3,000	5.0%	6,000	10.0%	9,000	15.0%

benefits. However, if we take into account the marginal utility of income—how taxpayers value the last dollars of their income—we might find the richest taxpayer always valuing the last dollars more than the poorest taxpayer, everyone valuing the last dollar the same, or the poor valuing the last dollar of income more. Each case would justify a different tax or fiscal system.

Proposed rules for determining the fairest distribution of tax burdens come from various sources, few of whom agree. Moreover, the experts providing these rules may not agree with eachother, although careful thought may bar pure expediency or one group's exploitation of others (Buchanan, 1970, pp. 102–104). The rules rely on specification of a base for determining burden—income, consumption, or wealth—and a principle for distributing burdens—ability to pay or benefit.

Equity and the Tax Base

The base for determining burden must conform to the equity idea that individuals in similar circumstances be treated equally (a horizontal equity principle) and individuals with greater resources be treated differently and bear a greater burden (a vertical equity principle). By defining a base comprehensively, one individual with habits different from another should get the same treatment in determining burden. The most comprehensive measure of ability to pay may be either income or consumption. When viewing taxation over a period of time or lifetime, income may be taxed more than once when the definition of income includes interest earned from saving, as Musgrave and Musgrave (1984, pp. 234–236) have argued. Therefore, the consumption tax usually wins a fairness argument, but the difficulties related to complexity, efficiency, and even adequacy raise more problems, returning the attention tax system designers pay to the income tax (Musgrave and Musgrave, 1984, pp. 236–237). Nevertheless, many argue the equivalence of a consumption tax and an income tax excluding savings from the income tax base. The income tax might then fall solely on earned income, excluding savings when defined as interest and capital income. Such a definition may run afoul of traditional beliefs that earned income be favored over unearned income. Tax-preferred savings may raise the prospect of a wealth tax as a fairer alternative. Such a tax policy, those who oppose it say, ignores that fact that wealth has as high a visibility as wage income and consumption. Moreover, they say, wealth includes gifts and bequests, windfalls or luck, certainly unearned, making a wealth tax a popular alternative to an earned income tax or a consumption tax.

Horizontal Equity

The horizontal equity problem grows as analysis moves to other substitutes, and reforms take place. The tax system design goal remains the same: to treat equals equally. Musgrave and Musgrave describe the issues (1984, pp. 238–239):

> … excluding the satisfaction of holding wealth, favors the saver and is not neutral. To treat people with equal options equally, a supplementary tax on "holding utility" would be needed…. While this shows the consumption tax to be defective, it also improves the rating of the income tax [because it taxes holding utility].

The Musgraves suggest that a consumption tax and an income tax are complements in creating horizontal equity in a tax system.

Decisions weighing horizontal equity against adequacy, collectability, and transparency are difficult to make. Tax policy is an art rather than science, according to the Musgraves, and can approach equity only by degree and never absolutely.

Vertical Equity

Once they choose a base combining income, consumption, and wealth to reach the goal of horizontal equity, tax policy makers confront the vertical equity problem. The principle of vertical equity lies in treating unequals unequally. Vertical equity analysts can apply the ability-to-pay principle among unequals, vertically among incomes, by treating them differently when making the rich individual pay more than the poor one.

The rules defining such a burden differ between a proportional and a progressive burden, and as a whole, the arguments make the case for progressive taxation "uneasy" (Blum and Kalven, 1953). The case for progression rests on several foundations: economic stability, benefit, sacrifice, economic inequality, and degression.

First, progressive taxes (particularly income taxes) contribute to economic stability. The effective rate of an income tax increases in periods when economic activity rises. A growing economy provides more income to individuals, and the progressive rates on income dampen the inflation growth that might take place by taking money from the economy and allowing governments to have surpluses. An economy with decelerating growth may need a stimulus, and progressive rates provide it. As deceleration takes place, incomes decrease, and progressive rates allow for lower taxes as individuals move down the income scale. Losing income taxes, governments borrow, providing the stimulus to the economy by maintaining spending levels as well as triggering automatic stabilizers.

A second defense of progressive tax rates exists in benefit theories. The benefit ideas come in two basic forms: benefits to property and benefits to the well-being of individuals. In the property sense, benefit proponents argue that without government services, such as police, fire protection, and the military, holding property would be risky. The government services reduce risks, and those who own large amounts of property should pay for the services in larger amounts than those who do not own property.

The well-being argument is far broader and is based on the idea that well-being springs substantially from the existence of government. Well-being may be measured in terms of income or wealth; therefore those receiving the largest amount of well-being must pay for it by taxes on income or wealth. Beyond the proportional increase in either the benefits of government services or the well-being individuals enjoy, proponents argue that benefits increase progressively so that increases in benefits more than exceed increases in income or wealth and increases in the effective tax rates levied to pay for benefits.

A third defense of progressive tax rates comes from sacrifice theory. Taxes are sacrifices individuals make, and decision makers must apportion the sacrifice equitably, according to this view. The sacrifice argument takes at least one of four forms: equal sacrifice, proportionate sacrifice (both of which flow from a declining utility of money idea), ability to pay, and social differences in spending preferences.

The equal and proportionate sacrifice arguments derive from the sense that the same amount of money has greater value to a poor person than a rich person. In other words, the utility of money declines as income increases. A reduction of income through taxes will matter less to the rich taxpayer than the poor one unless the tax has progressive rates. A proportional reduction in income will amount to equal sacrifice, but a progressive reduction more closely relates to declining utility, so that the rich taxpayer gives up the same utility of income as the poor. As Blum and Kalven (1953, p. 41) say, "[Equality of sacrifice] can mean that the quantity of sacrifice, that is, the loss of units of utility, demanded of each individual be equal (*equal sacrifice*), or it can mean that each should be required to give up an equal percentage of his total utility derived from money (*proportionate sacrifice*)."

Both a proportional and a progressive reduction result from progressive tax rates. Bentham (2000) and Mill's ideas of minimum sacrifice (1899) and Pigou's argument that the utility of income may come from one person's comparisons of utility to his or her economic and social rivals (1928) support the idea. All stress that either equal sacrifice or proportional sacrifice equate to minimum sacrifice. According to Bentham (2000), law should bring about the greatest quantity of total satisfaction, the greatest good for the greatest number. Mill (1899, p. 308) argued that government should require taxpayers to bear burdens in such a way that the "least sacrifice is occasioned on the whole." According to Blum and Kalven (1953), the example might be one in which taking a dollar from a person with the larger income involves less sacrifice than taking a dollar from a person with the smaller income. If required, a second dollar might still entail less sacrifice from the person with the higher income than the person with lower income if after the second dollar the higher-income person were still richer than the other person. Pigou (1928) argues that, logically, the procedure requires taking from the top of the highest incomes first until government needs are met, and if needs are not met, continuing to take from the top and middle incomes as well, at the same time providing income to the poorest. Such a procedure would follow from the definition of minimum sacrifice.

A contrast to sacrifice theory has survived in the form of the ability-to-pay principle of taxation. Blum and Kalven argue that the principle leads to the logically consistent choice of a tax base as well as the progressive rate structures on the base. For example, the income tax most often represents the "best test of the ability of the taxpayer to pay taxes" (1953, p. 64). As for the progressive structure of rates, Blum and Kalven argue that such a use of ability really means that ability increases more rapidly than income. They quote Seligman (1908, pp. 291–292) as a defender:

> The more [a wealthy person] has, the easier it is for him to acquire still more.... Hence ... the ... production faculty [increases] more rapidly than fortune or income. This element of taxable capacity [encourages] a more than proportionate rate of taxation.

Therefore, Seligman changes the emphasis from sacrifice to the ease of earning additional income or wealth and the corresponding capacity to pay taxes. Hobson (1919) defines the ability to pay as the extent of the person's ability to create a surplus above the cost of producing income. The ability to gain a surplus through a person's superior economic opportunities makes the ability to bear taxation fair.

Still another variant of sacrifice theory is the defense of progressive taxation on the basis of norms related to spending. In the use of income, some argue that household spending to meet survival needs has more importance in society or even the economy than any spending above those needs. Any income that exists above the money needed to satisfy survival needs might rightfully be taxed, these sacrifice theorists argue. Blum and Kalven classify Chapman (1913) among the leading surplus spending tax proponents. Chapman (1913, p. 23) argued:

> [The] poorer a man is, the more likely is some [taxation] of income to cause him deprivation of [some of the social value of his life] ... the richer he is, the more likely [taxation comes] at the expense of luxuries which add little [social value] as commonly understood.

Chapman's idea develops both minimum sacrifice theory and ability-to-pay theory into a shared norm affecting the taxation of important vs. trivial consumption.

Although applied to progressive income taxes by implication, Chapman's idea has served as the basis for degressive income tax rates or rates reduced by gradual amounts, sales tax expenditures, and property tax variations.

A fourth major defense of progressive taxes changes the focus from internal tax system dynamics to external ones, with the idea that the tax system always should redistribute wealth or income. The belief that the tax system should be equalitarian becomes the major reason for adoption of progressive tax rates. Blum and Kalven see no reason to adopt progressive tax systems without acknowledging the primary reason for doing so. They point out (1953, p. 71): "If one is persuaded that the society should reduce economic inequalities there are no real problems [with] the use of progression to accomplish that result." In fact, they say (p. 72), efficiency may result. Should public finance be used for redistribution and nothing else, the market decision makers may determine relative values and allocate resources via prices, leaving little for government decision makers to do, thereby preserving relatively unimpaired freedom for individuals.

Why reduce economic inequalities? One major reason relates to minimum sacrifice theory: maximum economic welfare comes along with tax systems that allow the wealthy to sacrifice a share of their income with less loss of welfare than the poor will gain in getting what the wealthy sacrifice. Another major reason relates to economic and political stability. The argument depends on the power of fiscal policy to stabilize the economy (Auerbach, 2002a). The political stability idea assumes that economic inequality threatens democratic deliberation, decision, and the balance of political power, that the rich man can vote more than once (Blum and Kalven, 1953, p. 77). Bound up in economic inequality are forces related to wealth, such as inheritance, social position, and the professional prestige and expertise of those people the wealthy are able to hire to assist them. However, the greater threat to political stability may lie in the lack of economic opportunity and the justice of rewards, say Blum and Kalven (1953, p. 85). In the economic opportunity case, fewer equalitarians argue for progressive income taxes than for progressive inheritance taxes. Reducing windfalls directly affects the inheritance of economic and cultural opportunities by future generations, equalitarians say, and utilitarians agree. Work incentives, savings incentives, higher standards of living, general well-being, and positive self-regard all derive from the equalitarian and utilitarian views, strangely enough, and form a part of the argument both groups use to increase or decrease inheritance taxes. In the case of justice of rewards, equalitarian theorists argue that economic achievement is not the whole of human accomplishment. Some methods must exist to balance economic achievement with other measures, to blunt the finality of the market's rating of people. A progressive tax system may be able to blunt finality and recognize other achievements, although this may be done primarily through spending—education, health care—rather than through tax expenditures.

The final major defense of the progressive system of tax rates is less theoretical than instrumental. In a way, degressive taxation looms as a means that suits the ends of progressive and proportional tax proponents (Blum and Kalven, 1953, pp. 94–100). Degressive taxation refers to the exemption from taxes of a minimum income with a scale of slowly increasing rates. For example, the tax base will exclude a certain amount of income for all taxpayers, and tax rates will then progress from the minimum to the maximum rate as a gradual rather than abrupt marginal increase above the exemption. The major difference in the graduated rates found in a degressive tax system and those found in a progressive tax system is the fixed curve found in the graduation of the tax rates from the exemption to the flat rate in a degressive system. Given the simplicity of decision making in determining what the exemption level will be, conservatives, both utilitarian and libertarian, embrace degressive taxes. Moreover, by assuming the exemption will never move lower but always higher, the degressive system imposes considerable pressure to increase the flat tax rate and the graduated system above the exemption as government revenue requirements increase.

Those opposed to progressive rates on a tax base that permits no shifting of burdens to others have strong arguments also. The arguments dismiss some supporting assumptions quickly and focus instead on the corruption of politicized tax policy decisions. On the quick dismissal of the value of government spending, Buchanan simply notes, "Public expenditures are considered to constitute always net drains on the private economy" (1970, pp. 103–104). He then moves to the least-sacrifice principle and attacks the concept of utility and specifically the marginal utility of income. He notes that in economics research and theory, individual utility is not measurable or comparable among individuals; therefore the least-sacrifice principle has no realistic, testable basis. Buchanan defies any least-sacrifice theorist to say anything other than "incomes must be leveled down by taxation in order to meet fully this principle [and] the major portion of the tax bill must be placed on the high-income classes."

Buchanan does find grounds on which progressive taxation may stand more firmly. These grounds are economic efficiency and political acceptability. On efficiency, he notes (1970, p. 104):

> If the utility functions of individuals are such that marginal valuations of public goods tend to be directly and disproportionately related to income levels, a progressive rate structure would be required for full neutrality.... A slightly different defense of progression emerges when the tax structure is recognized as quasi permanent and when uncertainty about individual income levels is introduced. Here individuals may choose to pay taxes under a progressive structure in order to concentrate payments during periods when the marginal utility of income is relatively low.

The progressive taxation view has a neutral (not antiwealth) economic efficiency argument, he says, but a substantial economic stability rationale.

In the end, however, Buchanan argues a specific reason why progressive taxation exists. He says (1970, p. 104), "If neither of the [two] defenses for progression can be used, the widespread use of this rate structure can be explained only on political grounds. In this case, progression represents one part of a process through which gains are secured by one group at the expense of remaining groups." He predicts serial, political fights between the one group that will bear the tax burden under progressive rates and the many groups who are destined to benefit.

The case for progression based on equalizing incomes may be the surviving rationale, particularly the exemption of a certain amount of income from any tax. Blum and Kalven (1953) reviewed the case for progressive taxation based on benefit, sacrifice, ability to pay, and economic stability, and having found each insufficiently justifiable. They argue that "the case has stronger appeal when progressive taxation is viewed as a means of reducing economic inequalities" (p. 104). They further argue that much of the uneasiness in relating progressive taxation to the reduction of economic inequalities lies in the use of the tax code as the primary or sole means of gaining fairness, leaving radical change in the other fundamental institutions of society alone.

The idea of reducing income inequality appealed to Thurow, who argues for reduced inequality as a public good, that some better distribution may be recognizable as preferable on the economic arguments. He asks (1971, p. 327) whether policies can improve the initial distribution of income to achieve a Pareto optimum, where one person is better off and no one else is worse off, a net social welfare improvement. He argues that others' incomes are often important to individuals; therefore they may redistribute their income. Individuals may enjoy giving gifts. However, he argues, the problem may be

> the distribution of income itself.... Preventing crime and creating social or political stability may depend on [income equality]. Alternatively, individuals may simply want to live in societies with particular distributions of ... economic power. There may be [individuals who have] an aesthetic taste for equality ... similar in nature to a taste for paintings.

Thurow leaves the matter at a philosophical point, a "way of life" argument, related to what is beautiful rather than efficient, stable, or broadly tolerable.

In forcing the argument to a philosophy of the senses, Thurow might accept the biblical relationship between the beautiful and the just. If so, the relationship leads to consideration of Rawls' arguments in favor of just political systems (1971), ones in which the "maximin" criterion of income distribution prevails, where social welfare increases no more than increases in the welfare of the poorest individual (1999, p. 65).

Beyond equity, the efficiency of the tax system, and eventually the entire fiscal policy system, rises in concern. The efficiency principle rests on eliminating economic distortions or making tax systems *neutral* in their economic effects, neither encouraging nor discouraging changes in behavior.

Neutrality

Neutrality suggests efficiency to public economists. Practically, all fiscal systems encourage economic actors to behave in specific ways, intentionally and unintentionally. Fiscal systems create excess burdens or "deadweight losses" on top of their nominal impact. For example, almost all people pay tax on the income they receive for the work they do in their jobs. Deadweight losses suggest an additional loss yielded on top of the income tax when netted against the gains from government services.

How do deadweight losses occur? Diewert, Lawrence, and Thompson explain (1998, p. 136):

> Consider taxes on income from labor. These taxes adversely affect incentives to work. When they increase, some people work fewer hours …; others work less intensively or undertake more do-it-yourself work; and a few shift into occupations offering relatively larger nonpecuniary benefits. The point is that in the absence of taxes people would have done things differently, which is to say that taxes have made them worse off, not only by the amount of the taxes they must pay, but also by causing them to shift away from the preferred patterns of work and leisure.

Taxpayers, facing higher taxes, respond with substitutions for what they were doing when they were taxed less. With higher income taxes on the work they are paid to do, taxpayers work less and vacation or stay away from work. They work less intensely, producing less. They do work for barter in the shadow economy that the tax authorities cannot track. They work less and do more in occupations with large benefits not related to money. They also search for tax loopholes, using part of their remaining assets to find and pay advisors. In sum, taxpayers substitute efforts that they do not prefer for efforts they prefer, reducing their "utility" and, by some measure more often than not, reducing the productivity of the economy (Goulder and Williams, 1999; Ballard and Fullerton, 1992; Hausman, 1981; Auerbach and Rosen, 1980). Behavior changes, taxable income changes, revenue collections fall below that predicted, and tax rates must increase, creating a spiral downwards (Rosen, 1985, pp. 276–277).

In contrast to neutrality, another view argues for intervention on grounds that taxes should have *favorable* economic effects: the outcome from market operations can be improved by using tax incentives to alter private behavior. Many policy makers argue that they could intentionally design fiscal systems to bring about economic and social health. For example, the earned income tax credit (EITC) has become a major incentive to replace lump-sum cash grants to the poor based on family size. The EITC is a cash grant representing the difference between work income and the base amount on which payroll and income tax are levied. The effort to synchronize all fiscal policy tools assumes that tax, spending, and debt systems should not work at cross-purposes. Then the question becomes an analytical or positive one in choosing the configuration of policy tools that will achieve the efficiency, effectiveness, or equity goal with the least effort (Miller and Illiash, 2001).

Expenditures and Allocation Policies

While fiscal policy deals with an important but specific subset of all government policies and often signifies tax policy, an allocation policy component exists. Eckstein (1973, p. 97) has defined fiscal policy as one of several short-run matters pursued by government decision makers: "the influence of government on total purchasing power, the use of the budget to fight recession and inflation … [c]hanges in taxes and expenditures that aim at the short run goals of full employment and price-level stability." Fiscal policy therefore often signifies budgetary allocations and the implicit choice between public and private sector provision of goods and services.

The shorthand meaning of different policies should be clear. Many economists use *allocation* to mean the policy toward tax system design grounded in a concern for greater efficiency and less waste. By *distribution policies*, they mean the distribution of the burdens and benefits of taxes and spending in efforts to achieve greater equity. Stabilization policies aim at credit expansion or tightening, inflation or price-level management, and ultimately economic growth and full employment. There is another meaning. *Allocation* may refer to the allocation of production of goods and services to the private and public sectors so that taxes may be put to their highest and best use. To simplify matters, this survey uses *allocation* to refer to political and economic choices between public and private sector resources to meet the demand for goods and services.

An economic logic toward allocation, or government spending, begins with a laissez-faire, individualistic point of view. Assuming that residents want a good or service, whatever that might be, they will demand it and someone will step forward to produce it. However, this willingness does not always lead to market provision of whatever residents demand. The welfare of society demands some goods or services the market will not provide, and thus market failure occurs.

In the market of firms, proprietors will not provide those goods that cannot be exhausted by use or that two or more residents may consume jointly. "Public" goods may include epidemiology and perhaps inoculation against the spread of a communicable disease, reduction of noise pollution and street crime at the local level, and antiterrorism efforts at the national and international levels. The social benefits of knowledge about a given communicable health condition and the action, inoculation, that takes place to deal with the condition actually grow in usefulness without congestion with the number of users. Moreover, worldwide antiterrorism efforts may solve problems more effectively the greater the number of beneficiaries, and one beneficiary's use does not ordinarily compete with another's use.

In a different view of public goods, pricing may indicate whether a good is relatively public or private. Levying a price in exchange for a good rations the good. The question making the good a public one is the degree to which society wants to discourage use or discriminate on some basis against potential users. As Musso argues, "Whether a good is [a public one] depends on legal frameworks, technology, costs, and social and professional norms" (1998, p. 352). In the latter case, norms construct a sense of deservingness that allows for the production of public goods. The larger the pool of deserving individuals, perhaps even the degree of deservingness of a small group that society constructs, the more likely the good will come from public provision as a matter of public policy.

Society can determine efficiently what public or other goods government should be responsible for and how much should be produced by making choices on the basis of two efficiency criteria. First, a Pareto optimal decision of what goods government should make available, and in what quantities, amounts to an efficiency improvement. If a choice is the "best that could be achieved without disadvantaging at least one group," or "the community becomes better off if one individual becomes better off and none worse off" with a choice, the community has made an efficient choice. The principle comes from the economist Vilfredo Pareto, who stated (1906, p. 261):

> We will say that the members of a collectivity enjoy maximum [optimality or his word] "ophelimity" in a certain position when it is impossible to find a way of moving from that position very slightly in such a manner that the [optimality] enjoyed by each of the individuals of that collectivity increases or decreases. That is to say, any small displacement in departing from that position necessarily has the effect of increasing the [optimality] which certain individuals enjoy, and decreasing that which others enjoy, of being agreeable to some, and disagreeable to others.

Determining an entire population's "optimality" is ridiculously difficult. Such difficulty results in trade-offs over voting systems and fundamental constitutions (Buchanan and Tullock, 1962). Therefore, another criterion has replaced the Pareto criterion in use, a criterion named for two economists, Nicholas Kaldor (1939) and John R. Hicks (1940). The Kaldor–Hicks variation on Pareto holds that, for a change in policy or policy regime to be viewed as beneficial, the gainers should be able to compensate the losers and still be better off. No compensation need actually be paid, which, if it did, would make this same as the Pareto criterion. With no compensation required, the Kaldor–Hicks criterion forms one of the key analytical bases for cost-benefit analysis, the technical and administrative features of which Miller and Robbins have discussed at greater length (2004).

The determination of how much of a good government might take responsibility for producing poses substantial difficulties for decision makers as well. A great deal of thought on what amount to produce comes from the concept of marginal utility, and thought about the concept stretches from Clark (1899), Marshall (1890), and Wicksteed (1910) to Pigou (1928). Based on Pigou, Lewis (2001) identified three factors in determining the level and type of public goods furnished. First, he argued in favor of the calculation of relative value. Whether to spend on more battleships or more relief for the poor cannot be resolved without relating the two in some way, he said. Lewis stated that relationship as opportunity cost, that the cost of anything is simply the amount that would have been realized had the resources been used for some other purpose. In other words, the opportunity cost of a choice reflects the real consequences a decision maker faces in making a particular decision. This cost is usually the difference between the magnitude of the consequences of the first and second choices.

Second, Lewis (2001) argued that decision makers use incremental comparisons, comparing value or cost at the margin. Knowing that value diminishes with quantity consumed—"four tires on a car are essential, a fifth tire is less essential but is handy to have, whereas a sixth tire just gets in the way" (p. 44)—consumers and decision makers can choose the fifth tire or something else, and certainly something else instead of a sixth tire. For governments, the number of poor needing relief will diminish as relief becomes available. Moreover, at some point, more of a given weapon will exhaust the ability of those who will use it. At the margin, decision makers can assess the relative value of more units of a given weapon or more units of a given type of relief.

Third, and most difficult of all, decision makers have aid in making marginal decisions if they have a standard for determining the relative effectiveness of alternative objects of expenditure. Political leaders set goals in reference to which subordinate executive and administrative policy analysts can make relative value and incremental comparisons. Political leaders change these goals as events unfold.

Expenditures and Stabilization

Spending has a stabilization meaning as well as an allocation one. Stabilizing economic growth through the budget has moved through both a pre-Keynesian and a post-Keynesian stage, suggesting the immense impact Keynes has had on stabilization for four generations of economists and policy makers. The pre-Keynes era, according to Musgrave (1985, pp. 44–45), relied on Say's law (1855)—that the economy could manage itself since "supply creates its own demand" (Keynes, 1964, p. 18; James Mill, 1992; J. S. Mill, 1899, vol. I, pp. 65–67 and vol. II, pp. 75–82; Ricardo, 1951). Musgrave disputes the beginning Say made against fiscal policy in stabilization by pointing out Steuart's ideas about government debt as an addition to the nation's income (1767, Book 4, Part 2, Chapters 1–2, and Part 4, Chapter 8). Even during Say's time, Malthus (1964) wrote about the distress brought about by excessive saving to the detriment of consumption, arguing that Ricardo and Say were wrong, at least in the short run (MacLachlan, 1999).

The unemployment depression of the 1930s provoked the Keynes revolution. Rather than supply creating its own demand, supply could contract as saving stood pat. In fact, the supply of savings could expand out of fear of loss or hope for eventual gain rather than hope of gain in a risk-return inverse relationship. Savings growth could produce a liquidity trap.

At the heart of Keynes's theory, three concepts formed fiscal policy's strength in stabilizing the economy between boom and bust (1964; Eckstein, 1973). First, demand for goods and services drive the economy. Total or aggregate demand, a macroeconomic idea, responds to budget policies that provide an incentive to consume rather than save. Second, consumption may have multiple if not quite compound effects as money works through the economy. The consumer spends; the retail firm owner pays salaries of employees, expands the business with profits, saves, and invests in other business expansions; and the government receives additional tax revenue. Whether the multiplier reflects a full compounding or simply the tendency of any person or organization to spend most but not all of what income they gain, the multiplier's stimulus to economic growth exists. Third, many expansions and contractions in the economy have less extreme limits due to the automatic stabilizers that exist in budget policies. Beyond the discretion to run deficits and borrow in contractions, policy makers find that the contractions move toward an end as the base for supply, capital equipment, wears out and gets replaced. The turn in demand from negative to positive automatically triggers the spending multiplier and turns contractions into expansions, job layoffs into rehiring, and government deficits into surpluses and debt repayment.

From the basic ideas that formed from Keynes's original insight, two major fiscal policy concepts came into being. The measurement of the economy as gross national product—the sum of consumption, saving, net exports or imports, and government spending—became a formal practice through the National Income and Product Accounts (Bureau of Economic Analysis, 1985). Fiscal policy, macroeconomics, and econometrics became intertwined. Also, budgeting for full employment grew in use as the discretionary component of fiscal policy. Full-employment gross national product (GNP), or the difference between current, nominal, and full-employment GNP, acted as the gap that fiscal policy incentives or disincentives could fill. An economy with capacity for growth demanded incentives to ensure growth. The incentives included combinations of tax reductions and spending increases. An economy exceeding full-employment GNP required policy makers to dampen the same incentives. The incentives came from the budget, and the budget came from the discretionary decisions by policy makers added to the already expected effect of automatic stabilizers.

The problems with Keynesian fiscal policy became points of contention among supporters and opponents of government intervention in the economy. Contending views surround the multiplier's actual effects, time lags, and deficit financing. First, all tax changes differ. Permanent tax changes have a higher multiplier than temporary ones (Carroll, 2001; Friedman, 1957). Higher-income individuals and two-earner families respond differently to tax rate changes than do middle- and lower-income individuals and one-earner families (Goolsbee, 2000; Feldstein and Feenberg, 1995). Consumption and corporate income taxes have uncertain effects, differ from period to period, and require analysis of shifting and incidence to understand fully (Feldstein, 2002; Eckstein, 1973).

Second, time lags bedevil effective application of fiscal policies to economic stabilization. Recognition by policy analysts lags behind the actual appearance of an economic contraction or expansion. Decisions about actions to take lag behind recognition. The full economic impact certainly lags behind the decisions made and the execution of those decisions (Eckstein, 1973). Correct forecasts, certainly dynamic forecasting, relying on rigorous economic models, can reduce the lags (Altig et al., 2001; Auerbach, 1996, 2002a, 2002b, 2003; Auerbach and Kotlikoff, 1987). However, forecasts require artfulness, and dynamic forecasting has gained political acceptance only recently and with partisan rancor (Barry, 2002; Lizza, 2003; Krugman, 2003; Stevenson, 2002).

Third, the government budget deficits that may emerge from fiscal policy stabilization actions may create offsetting destabilization. Government borrowing to finance the deficit may create competition in capital markets, leading to interest rate changes that can reduce private investment. Feldstein argues that discretionary fiscal policy can play a constructive role only in a lengthy economic contraction when both aggregate demand and interest rates are low and prices have tended to fall (Feldstein, 2002). At such a point, and only then, Feldstein says, stimulus may have an effect without increasing budget deficits by providing incentives for increased private spending (Feldstein, 2002).

The practice of discretionary fiscal policy stabilization has lost respect among many bankers and economists. In fact, at a Federal Reserve Bank of Kansas City symposium, most of the invited speakers called discretionary fiscal policy into question (2002). Research on decisions made by monetary policy authorities, what the researchers called the Berkeley story, suggests that stabilization has returned as the primary goal of monetary policy makers rather than fiscal policy makers, and that inflation is the key problem to solve rather than unemployment (Sargent, 1999, 2002; DeLong, 1997). The period of Keynesian fiscal policy stabilization efforts included a depression, three major wars, a period between wars with strong and sustained government spending on defense, long periods of economic growth without inflation, and one major period of oil supply shocks. The period ended with extremely persistent stagflation and, at the end, intense inflation. The ending of the long period when Keynesian fiscal policy dominated stabilization, with stagflation and then high inflation, led to a succession of monetary policy leaders bent on challenging inflation and letting economic retrenchment take its toll.

The succession, the monetary policy changes, and their success encouraged doubt about any effectiveness fiscal policy might have to stabilize the economy and to stimulate economic growth without inflation. Many have argued that fiscal policies have only blunt, unpredictable multipliers and lags. Fiscal policy stabilizers require monetary policy makers to ratify deficit-borrowing decisions with "an easy money policy" of readily available funds for financing private investment at moderate interest cost. Imprecise tools and impacts doomed fiscal policy. Much of the time, policy makers aimed fiscal policies at the wrong target (Eckstein, 1973; Auerbach, 2002a, p. 144).

The opponents object most to "discretion" in fiscal policy, but they laud automatic stabilizers (Auerbach, 2002a, pp. 120–127). Those who favor discretionary fiscal policy as a stabilization device see the same evidence to suggest large countercyclical effects in the last two decades of the twentieth century. They point to research that shows few long-term effects from temporary tax cuts and stimulus packages, at least in comparison to virtually permanent policies (Blinder, 2002; Friedman, 1948). Remaining supporters do sense the value fiscal policy has for stabilizing the economy, probably because fiscal policy lies within the responsibilities, and especially the opportunities, of political leaders. Political leaders have ambition and electoral accountability, giving them credit for initiative and a certain amount of legitimacy in defining economic problems and finding solutions. The legitimacy may outrank and the actions create less rancor than actions by more indirectly accountable monetary policy makers. The role for fiscal policy in stabilization hinges on the balance among accountability, representativeness, political responsiveness, leadership, and expertise sensed as right by decision makers at all levels of energy and vigor (Kaufman, 1956).

Spending may take place in a number of different ways as well: conventional and unconventional, on budget and off budget, with credible or not so credible commitments. We associate conventional spending with budget requests to legislative bodies on behalf of continuing operation of government departments or the institution of new programs. Unconventional spending may take place, not using direct spending by legislatures on government departments in which government employees or government contractors work, but through the incentive structures toward firms inherent in loans, loan guarantees, insurance, and regulation. In all nonconventional forms, legislatures have chosen nongovernmental organizations to carry out effective programs on behalf of government objectives. Finally, legislatures make credible commitments to target groups when they entitle the groups to transfer payments and make these entitlements a permanent appropriation subject only to changes in the basic authorization rather than appropriations law.

Distribution, allocation, and stabilization—fiscal functions—require tax and spending tools. The goals of fiscal policy vary and conflict. Distribution of burdens in a fair way may rival neutrality or efficient distribution, allocation, or stabilization. Above all, social values, politically expressed, may vie with positive analysis and force the choice of second-best fiscal policy designs and tools.

Fiscal Policy Impacts

Government leaders can choose fiscal policies and tools to avoid distorting economic behavior, to promote government neutrality regarding economic transactions, and to gain macroeconomic efficiency. The choices may also take a more interventionist slant. The choices may promote certain economic behaviors, and they may make specific guesses about whose costs and benefits will lead to preferred economic changes. The neutrality position may have its adherents (Ventry, 2002, pp. 45–52), but both the high, universalist spending and low-tax, high-savings groups offer competing policies that favor intervention (Lindert, 2004, pp. 302–306). The choice may involve a neutral tax and government delivery of narrowly defined public goods. The choice may also involve universal government-provided benefits with a progressive income tax. Finally, the choice may involve a consumption tax and narrowly targeted, highly policed, means-tested public programs.

Fiscal policies have favored a second-best, interventionist approach. Despite the first choice of economists—limited government, policies neutral in economic matters, and lump-sum taxation—these parts of Adam Smith's logic (1776) fell from favor in the early twentieth century as Goldscheid (1958) and Schumpeter presented and argued a new "fiscal sociology" (1954). Contextualizing fiscal policies, both economists disputed the first-choice fiscal policies—neutrality in the form of lump-sum taxation and limited government. Both pointed out that first-best policies had failed to satisfy policy makers' constituents.

The change from Smith's logic to the views of fiscal sociologists came from three pre-World War I sources. Bell (1974, pp. 37–40) suggests that the first source materialized from the policy maker's need to encourage capital accumulation in an industrial age. The second source, he said, was policy makers' compelling need to promote social harmony by satisfying newly middle-class (bourgeois), acquisitive individuals with "goods [that] are not 'needs' but wants" (Bell, 1974, p. 31). The third source of change arose from the necessity to find revenue to pay for wants without reducing capital accumulation (Bell, 1974; O'Connor, 1973). Needing more than a change in the power centers and individual tastes in capitalist society, leaders could find no method or policy to meet demands for change with a neutral, lump-sum tax. The fiscal support of the state, the incentive to accumulate capital, and the satisfaction of the members of the consumer class required thinking beyond neutrality.

Neutrality, adequacy, incentives to save and to spend—a hard enough set of conditions to meet—also clashed with the norm of fairness. The taxpayer reaction to the violation of any of the ideas, except neutrality, became severe enough in Goldscheid and Schumpeter's time to force considerable rethinking of the role of government and the role of fiscal policy. Why? Equity demands of distribution policy a relationship between taxpayers' wealth or income and the revenues they are responsible for providing to support government activity. Recall Adam Smith's way of stating the principle of tax equity (1776, p. 654):

> The subjects of every state ought to contribute to the support of the government, as nearly as possible, in proportion to their respective abilities; that is, in proportion to the revenue which they respectively enjoy under the protection of the state. The expense of government to the individuals of a great nation is like the expense of management to the joint tenants of a great estate, who are all obliged to contribute in proportion to their respective interests in the estate.

Fiscal policy neutrality failed to deal with the problems of the time, Goldscheid and Schumpeter said. Moreover, neutrality may not be fair. A flat-rate, lump-sum tax, the equivalent of what economists think of as neutral taxation, creates a proportional tax, given a wide tax base and generally inelastic demand or supply of income, goods and services, or assets. While possible, proportionality of ability, obligation, and enjoyment may not be probable.

History suggests that a neutral, proportional tax failed to provide adequate revenue, effective incentives, or fair burdens. The United Kingdom offers one history lesson, in a poll tax, levied three times in the fourteenth century, once in the seventeenth century, and then once more in the late twentieth century. The last poll tax was an attempt by Prime Minister Margaret Thatcher to make common sense of local revenue systems and intergovernmental formula transfers (Butler, Adonis, and Travers, 1994).

The neutral lump-sum tax in Great Britain has notoriety. The earliest poll tax had a rate of four pence (often one shilling) per capita among adults (Oman, 1906; Dobson, 1970). Differences in rate came about by action of the local notable paying all or some of the tax for the people indebted to him. The adult head tax had no progression according to wealth and appeared grossly unfair (McKisack, 1959, pp. 406–407). Tax collection took place without a census of the adult population, although it became one and included questions about personal circumstances asked by tax officials. McKisack (1959, p. 407) described the upshot of it all as "evasion on a large scale," with the poll tax payments/census of adults revealing "a fall of one third in the adult population between 1377 and 1381."

Already indelicate methods deteriorated in subsequent efforts to improve the collection rate. McKisack (1959, pp. 406–407) and Butler, Adonis, and Travers (1994, p. 12) give an example that they call typical:

> The age exemption for children worked on the principle that girls were exempt if they were virgin. A certain [tax collector] insisted on ascertaining this by physical examinations conducted in public.

All the researchers state that the collection rate remained terrible despite the methods used. They argue that the poll tax system, coming on the heels of the Black Death of 1349, contributed to the Peasant Revolt of 1381. The Black Death decimated the labor population, driving wages up and motivating employers to force the tax on wage earners. The revolt gave rise to one of England's most popular figures and folk heroes, Wat Tyler, who killed a tax collector after his fifteen-year-old daughter became the object of a tax collector's efforts. The Wat Tyler myth, based on a short, intense insurrection, inspired Thomas Paine's *Rights of Man* and efforts to end serfdom in England as well as to import the French Revolution.

Ultimately the revolt and the Wat Tyler myth teach how closely tax policy changes resemble the swings of a pendulum. The subsequent efforts in England to

levy a poll tax materialized in 1641 and 1987–1990. In 1641, the tax had grada-
tions, but collection occurred without a census or a register of taxpayers. Designers
thought that a graduated assessment would tax snobbery, the more willing rich
revealing their social status through their tax rates and payments. However, the
1641 tax "fell short of expectations" as people undervalued their status, pushing
social climbing to a lower standing than tax dodging (Butler, Adonis, and Travers,
1994, p. 13). In 1987, Prime Minister Margaret Thatcher proposed and Parliament
passed a poll tax for Scotland. She and the members of the Conservative Party won
the general election of 1987 proposing a poll tax for England and Wales as well.
The poll tax for the entire country passed through Parliament, with the House of
Lords approving it overwhelmingly during the highest turnout of lords in living
memory to that point (Butler, Adonis, and Travers, 1994, p. 124). The tax created
a fiscal emergency for local governments, requiring them to spend much more
than anyone anticipated to collect the tax. The taxpayers saw the tax, once implemented, as unfair, tried to avoid it, and finally rioted to protest it (Butler, Adonis,
and Travers, pp. 149–153). The opposition to the tax led to the Conservative
Party's loss of a by-election, the rise of opposition within the party to the prime
minister, Prime Minister Thatcher's resignation, and the abolition of the poll tax.

The lump-sum tax has led to the punishment of British policy leaders who
pushed it into law. Taxing to avoid distorting the economy with the most neutral
tax, by widely held norms, has gained the summary status as optimal tax policy
(Gentry, 1999). If a lump-sum tax is the least distorting, as some say, the British
example shows that care has to be taken because more economic efficiency may
lead to less equity. More equity may lead to less economic efficiency, less revenue
collected, a more complicated tax system, and higher tax administration costs.
Balancing numerous factors, leaders usually take the second best or third best
(Lipsey and Lancaster, 1956–1957; Meade, 1955; Corlett and Hague, 1953–1954;
Little, 1951; Ng, 1983; Greenwald and Stiglitz, 1986; Hoff, 1994; Hoff and Lyon,
1995; Bhagwati and Ramaswami, 1963). Sandmo (1985, p. 265) reveals the complex trade-offs required to produce efficient tax systems:

> If alternative tax systems can lead to different rates of private saving,
> then the choice between them should take into account the short-run
> effects on employment and inflation, the medium-term effects on the
> rate of growth, and the long-term effect on the capital intensity of the
> economy. These are basically issues of the efficiency of resource alloca-
> tion, but distributional policy is also involved. A tax policy designed to
> encourage saving may transfer income from "workers" to "capitalists"
> and from the present to future generations. Evidently, there are all sorts
> of tradeoffs to consider in policy design.

Tax analysis presents a difficult set of problems, to say the least.

Generalizing from the UK experience, the most neutral and least distorting tax may be the most unpopular. The second- or third-best tax, on neutrality grounds, may become a better tax on the political merits and prospects.

Should policy leaders move from a lump-sum tax to a lump-sum, flat-rate tax, and on to graduated-rate taxes, they have several choices beyond raising money for government operations. The policy leaders will face the consequences of their acts in lost tax neutrality. What second-best consequences they might choose may be a matter of socioeconomic and political debate.

The choice of the second-best alternative tends to follow two different courses. The first course emerges as a matter of incidence and the answers found when the analysis concerns who bears the burden and who receives the benefit of fiscal policies. A review of the incidence literature follows below. A second course influencing the second-best alternative to a lump-sum tax and a neutral fiscal policy comes from the analysis of behavioral reactions to tax policies, primarily those reactions found in work, saving, investment, portfolio choice, risk taking, and innovation and productivity. These behavioral reactions follow the discussion of incidence.

Incidence

Discussion of the market reaction to government fiscal policy decisions starts with some brief mention of incidence. Musgrave (1953a, 1953b) gets the greatest credit in focusing attention on "the changes brought about by a given public finance instrument in the distribution of real income available for private use," a definition Break uses (1974, p. 123) in recognition of Musgrave's work. Incidence studies (Mieszkowski, 1969; McIntyre et al., 2002) distinguish between those taxpayers statutorily directed to comply with or be entitled to benefit from the fiscal policy design (nominal incidence) and individuals who ultimately bear the burden or receive the benefit after all shifting of burdens and benefits takes place (economic incidence).

Incidence models also differ in the way economists choose to study the impact policy instruments have. The static incidence model characterizes much of the theory and empirical research in public finance in contrast to the more realistic dynamic incidence idea. Static incidence refers to the first shift in one tax bill from the check writer to the individual whose purchasing power and income decline as a result. Dynamic incidence refers to the rates of change in taxes and incomes and then the behaviors—saving, investment, consumption, and labor supply, for example—that are sensitive to changes in taxes and incomes (Krzyzaniak, 1972; Feldstein, 1974a, 1974b; Break, 1974). With effort, research with a dynamic incidence model can reveal not only current but lifetime income and current and multiperiod effects on the economy, taking into account individual and aggregate reactions.

Analyzing fiscal instrument effects by limiting study to a single tax or the substitution of one tax for another is artificial. More realism might come from studying the simultaneous effects of changes in several taxes, spending, and debt (Martinez-Vazquez, 2001). However, realism may be an unattainable goal. Any policy prescription based on dynamic and simultaneous effects may overwhelm the understanding and motivation of policy makers to take action. For example, Shoup (1969, p. 14) described the difficulty policy makers might face:

> If there are eight goals to be achieved, by the public finance system, eight public finance instruments will normally be required, with a unique set of eight rates or values. If the value for one of these goals is to be changed, as when the distribution of disposable income is to be made less unequal, while the values of each of the other seven goals are to be unchanged, the values of all eight of the public finance instruments must normally be changed. All eight are changed, just to alter one of the goal values.

Dynamic incidence and simultaneous effects may signal the direction for research, but the policy recommendations may have limited appeal to policy makers due to the complexity of execution.

While incidence refers to fiscal policy instruments and their effects on groups of individuals, researchers and policy makers often have a narrower focus. Researchers ask how much of the fiscal burden of a tax falls on the poorest and richest segments of the population. Policy makers ask about tax incidence by business sectors, between industry and labor, by geographic region or state, and by domestic or foreign beneficiaries. New estimates of generational incidence now exist (Auerbach, Kotlikoff, and Leibfritz, 1999; Fullerton and Rogers, 1993; Kotlikoff, 1992).

Incidence studies begin with the point that individuals ultimately bear the burden of any tax. Nominally, a firm may write the check for taxes, but then shifts take place. The tax reduces some individual's income in the end. Galambos and Schreiber illustrate (1978, p. 115):

> [Suppose] that local government officials are planning to increase the property tax rate. Who will bear the burden of this tax increase? ... The apartment owner may be able to shift the increase in property taxes to the renter through higher rents. Similarly, a business firm may shift all or part of the increase in taxes to consumers of its products through higher prices, or to its employees through lower wages.... Ultimately, a person or a household bears the burden of all taxes.

Many researchers agree on the incidence of specific taxes and tax bases. These agreed-upon shifts to final bearers of the tax burden appear in Table 4.2.

Galambos and Schreiber point out that many factors provoke the reaction to a tax change (1978, p. 116). The factors include market price competition in which the greater the competition, the less likely the tax may be passed on as higher

Table 4.2 Major Local Taxes and Incidence

Form of Tax	Nature of the Shift in Incidence
Sales taxes	Paid directly by the consumer or shifted forward to the consumer as higher prices
Personal income taxes	The income earner pays the tax
Property Taxes	
For owner-occupied housing	All owners of capital or property[a]
Property taxes on renter-occupied housing	Either the renter or the landlord[b]
Increase in the property tax on nonresidential property	Consumers pay through higher prices that owners shift to them, or owners do not shift but take reduced profits or returns on investment, depending on the degree of competition in markets, the ability of producers to switch to the production of other commodities, and the ability of consumers to buy other products or the same products in other jurisdictions where the products are not taxed in the same way

Source: Adapted from Galambos, E. C., and Schreiber, A. F., *Making Sense out of Dollars: Economic Analysis for Local Government*, National League of Cities, Washington, DC, 1978, p. 116; Aaron, H. J., *Who Pays the Property Tax?* Brookings, Washington, DC, 1975; Gaffney, M. M., in *Proceedings of the Sixty-Fourth Annual Conference on Taxation Sponsored by the National Tax Association*, 1971, pp. 408–426. Retrieved May 8, 2004, from http://www.schalkenbach.org/library/progressivet.pdf.

[a] The owner of the house is also the tenant in the case of owner-occupied housing. The owner has a portfolio with one asset, but the owner finds the tax capitalized into the property. Capital being mobile, higher property taxes force values of property after tax downward, as the higher property taxes force down wages and land values, when compared to lower taxing localities. The capitalization reduces the amount available for further investment, affecting all uses of capital.

[b] Some but not all tax policy analysts assume that an increase in property taxes is paid by the renter as higher rents. Some but not all analysts believe that renters pay only the portion of the property tax above that common to all jurisdictions.

prices. Also, the longer-term effects include finding substitutes. That is, producers can switch their work to untaxed products, and consumers can find other similar, untaxed products or can buy the same product in another, nontaxing jurisdiction.

In the broader context of state and federal taxes, incidence accounts for the impacts fiscal policy instruments have on both incomes and prices or the sources and uses of income. For example, an increase in the size of a tax expenditure (such as a tax credit) rather than deductibility of municipal bond interest from income might increase after-tax income. The tax credit may benefit more than the highest-income classes, since the credit might benefit all income classes that have a tax liability. The tax credit might lead middle-income households to either consume or save the increased amount of income at their disposal. Should the consumption choice be buying a new car, car prices may rise in the short run, but car manufacturing may increase in the longer term, with succeeding increases in either capital invested in car manufacturing or workers hired. A tax credit rather than a deduction from income for municipal bond interest may also reduce the cost of borrowing faced by state and local governments. Lower costs may convince state and local leaders to increase their capital investment. Results from increased investment may convince state and local officials to pass the productivity increases on to state and local taxpayers through general or targeted tax rebates, rate reductions, or a more stable fiscal system. Rebates and rate reductions will increase household and corporate income, provoking another round of short-run price increases, capital investments long run, and employment increases.

The price elasticity of demand and supply tends to be the major factor determining who bears the burden of a tax. Elasticity refers to the degree to which demand changes as prices change. Likewise, as prices change, a supplier's incentives change. Ultimately, the less the elasticity, the more likely those demanding or those supplying bear the burden of a tax.

As an example, take the market for automobiles in the United States. Car buyers and car sellers are probably sensitive to the price of a red Mercedes. Both car buyers and car sellers can find substitutes as prices of the red Mercedes rise. If a tax increase prompts a rise in the price, both buyer and seller will find some other car color to market, and the tax can be thought to have destroyed the market for the red Mercedes.

For a market dealing in any color Mercedes, more likely a market for all imports or all luxury cars, one might find the demand relatively insensitive to price. A buyer will absorb a tax on all Mercedes models.

For a market dealing in any car in Manhattan in New York City, the demand may change radically as prices change, due to a general new automobile tax. Substitutes may be found in taxis, limousines, phone cars, buses, jitneys, and the subway. The tax levied on cars in Manhattan will force an increase in prices, perhaps, but more likely, the seller will absorb the tax increase. Even more likely, the fares of every form of transportation from taxis to the subways will increase, reducing transportation substitutes.

Finally, the market for cars is relatively insensitive to price on both the demand and supply sides in the United States. Both car buyers and car sellers will share any new tax, although substitutes may exist for the car's financing. Just as likely, the tax will prove so unpopular that both buyers and sellers will organize an effort to reduce the tax.

In the longer sequence of effects caused by the levy of a tax, buyers and sellers, those demanding and those supplying, form a different set of actors in the households whose sources and uses of income change with the tax. In the red Mercedes case, both consumers and car dealers avoid the tax, preferring that their uses of income go to some other good, perhaps a blue Mercedes. Hardly anyone's sources of income change. In the case of the Mercedes per se, the consumer absorbs the tax, reducing that household's income. That consumer, as an income producer, finds his or her real buying power reduced. That consumer buys less, and his or her uses of income change. In the case of a car buyer and seller in Manhattan and a general automobile tax, both the buyer and seller's uses of income change, the buyer's toward substitute transportation and the seller's toward supply of something in addition to cars for sale. The income of the buyer, labor, does not change, but the income of the seller, capital, does. Rates of return to investors in car sales companies fall, and investment capital moves to sources of higher rates of return. Finally, in the car market in the United States generally, both consumers and sellers share the tax. Consumers find their uses of income affected, and so do investors in car sales. Certainly, the car suppliers, the owners of capital, find their sources of income reduced.

In the case of equity, the incidence of the tax on everything from a red Mercedes to a car generally has a possibility of being progressive or regressive. The red Mercedes has a neutral effect, but the Mercedes of whatever color appeals to an exclusive, perhaps high-income, group of buyers, in which case the car tax becomes a progressive tax. Should the product be salt rather than a Mercedes, a necessity instead of a luxury, the tax would fall inordinately on the lowest-income group for which the cost of salt is a bigger proportion of income than for the wealthier. The tax on the car in Manhattan, falling as it does far more on capital than labor, on car sellers rather than buyers, probably has a progressive tax impact. Finally, the car tax throughout the United States has the chance to be proportional, if car buyers tend to use a fixed percentage of their income on a car.

Incidence studies employ measures gauged before and after fiscal policy changes take place. The research question relates to distributional changes in income among groups. The analysis yields the conclusion that the fiscal system has become more regressive, proportional, or progressive. The illustration in Table 4.1 at the beginning of this review distinguished these systems on the basis of taxes alone, although the combination of all fiscal policy instruments may be characterized in the same way if the offsetting burdens and benefits can be calculated to produce a net effect. The incidence analysis employs various statistical measures of distribution to determine the nature of the before-change incidence, the after-change incidence, and the difference between the two, including the Lorenz curve, the Gini coefficient, the Suits index, newer, weighted Atkinson measures, and finally, a variety of measures of welfare dominance, concentration curves, and statistical testing surveyed and described by Martinez-Vazquez (2001; Pechman, 1985, p. 5, n. 10, p. 44, n. 3; Suits, 1977; Atkinson, 1983; Yitzhaki and Slemrod, 1991; Keifer, 1984; Musgrave and Thin, 1948; Younger et al., 1999; Davidson and Duclos, 1997).

To picture incidence, consider the relationship of a capital income tax and a wage income tax, following an approach called differential incidence. The substitution of a tax on capital with a tax on wages has different outcomes, as the assumptions about the factors of production and savings rates change.

First, the labor supply and the supply of capital may not respond (may not be elastic) to different rates of return, and rates of return on both tax bases (capital and labor) may be the same. In this case, the substitution of a capital tax for a wage tax shifts the burden to capital, and nothing else changes.

Second, should labor supply alone be responsive to rates of return, a different dynamic occurs. Lowering taxes on wages and increasing them on capital income leads to higher wage rates, and more people willing to work, with more people bidding the wage rate downward. As the wage rate declines, the rate of return on capital, despite the tax, increases. Lower wage rates and higher rates of return to capital mean that employees would share the burden of the tax on capital income.

In the long run, the shifts move the tax from labor to capital and back again and cancel out any real change. The real source of change in the long run is the growth of the population. With population growth, labor supply increases, setting the long-term wage rate. Long-run growth can assume that the savings habits and practices of wage earners and capital owners do not change, and there is no change in the amount of capital invested either. What is the result in this case, in the long run? The tax substitution (wage to capital) transfers the burden of the tax from labor to capital.

Changing the assumption to a supply of investment income (capital income) responsive to rates of return, the substitution of capital income taxes for wage labor taxes changes the outcome. The long-run complexion of the economy changes with the capital income tax. Although wage rates respond to the growth of population—more workers, less wages—the capital income tax will reduce the supply of capital as well. Again, the tax on capital shifts so that wages from labor share part of the tax burden.

In another situation where both wages and capital income reflect rates of return (i.e., where both are elastic), the shift from a wages tax to a capital tax duplicates the previous situation in which employees share the capital tax burden rather than enjoy a full tax reduction in the shift. As wages increase with the reduction of the tax on wages, the supply of labor increases and employer demand for workers decreases. Capital income tax increases lead to decreases in net or after-tax capital income. Investors reduce the supply of capital to the organizations and instruments taxed, while users of capital demand more, raising the cost of capital. Then, wages decrease and capital income increases. Labor shares the capital income tax because of the complex series of turns made among policy makers, wage earners, firms needing capital, and investors.

Consider finally the situation in which both labor and capital do not respond; i.e., both are inelastic or insensitive to the rate of return. A reduced rate of capital formation results. Again, the nominal tax on capital income shifts to become a tax on income generally, a tax shared by labor and capital. Overall, through long periods, at least the largest portion of the burden of a capital income tax shifts to labor to bear. For policy purposes, however, a shorter-term version might make more sense.

What other fiscal policy tools have incidence effects? Consider tax expenditures and conventional expenditures, both of which are negative taxes. Many, but not all, tax expenditures are broad based, such as the mortgage interest deduction for homebuyers and the corporate income tax deduction for health insurance and other related care provided to corporate employees as part of wages. These tax expenditures might have a neutral economic impact. Some economists classify conventional expenditures as either neutral in impact or pro-poor (Martinez-Vazquez, 2001; Musgrave and Musgrave, 1989). Loans and loan guarantees, insurance, procurement and contracts, and grants have an uncertain impact and have generally eluded incidence studies. Income transfers by definition are pro-poor. Debt, being delayed taxation, may also reduce the growth of the economy by reducing the investment capital otherwise available to the private sector through higher demand and fixed supply conditions in capital markets (Laubach, 2003; Federal Reserve Bank of St. Louis, 2004). The "crowding out" effect of government borrowing, however, may be offset entirely by the infrastructure and other investment for which government policy makers decide to use government borrowing.

Nonresidents of states and localities, more than those of the nation as a whole, pay all or a portion of some taxes. When nonresidents pay a tax levied on people or transactions locally, incidence analysts describe the tax burden as an export. Tax exports reduce the local tax burden and, unsurprisingly, are popular. Examples provided by Galambos and Schreiber include (1978, p. 116):

1. A visitor-paid tax on hotel rooms
2. A central city's payroll tax paid by commuters from the suburbs
3. A local property tax on manufacturing plants that sell all goods outside the locality, if product competition is weak enough to allow passing the tax on through higher prices

Analysts estimate the exported portion of nonresidential property taxes (that shifted forward to consumers) through economic base studies (to calculate total economic exports) and especially location quotient studies (Hildreth and Miller, 2002; Hayter, 1997; Galambos and Schreiber, 1978, pp. 13–47).

Work and Leisure

Policies may stress rewards of work over leisure. The choices involve deciding to favor one commodity or product over another. Incentives may favor future over present consumption. Tax and budget policy can prefer land to improvements to land. A variety of fiscal actions may encourage risky investments to promote innovation and increase productivity. These basic choices are explored here as fiscal policy impacts.

Leaders may also try to promote income equality and faster economic growth. Moreover, because a society needs a government, members must pay for that government in some way. Therefore, among all incentives, members of society must tax or choose not to tax but still pay for preferred government action. Other incentives flow from or exist beside the taxing decision. From the taxing decision, other decisions on trade-offs emerge simultaneously among spending tools and policies. Public agency provision of goods or services may result and may increase transfer payments, grants, and contracts. Loan funds, loan guarantees, and insurance programs spring to life. Nevertheless, the tax decision—what to tax, what to spend by not taxing, what to refund without taxing—sits at the heart of fiscal policy.

The trade-off consideration requires different analytical approaches. Sandmo (1985) characterizes the forms of analysis required as positive and normative. Both types of analysis must be used to minimize distortions created by a tax as well as to meet the expectations of taxpayers about a preferable tax, he says. Positive analysis is one in which policy makers question whether an expenditure tax will lead to a higher or lower level of saving than an income tax, for example. A normative analysis introduces a more fundamental question of criteria. Sandmo points out, "It is only when we introduce criteria for social welfare or efficiency that we can begin to consider the normative question of the desirability of an expenditure tax" (1985, p. 265). If considering the taxpayer reaction triggered by fiscal policies as saving, investment, portfolio choice, risk taking, productivity, innovation, adequate income in retirement, and stable economic expansion, analysts must follow both the positive and normative forms. Analysts may first compare several taxes in empirical or positive research terms and in terms of various goals, and then limit the discussion to the normative question of what constitutes equitable fiscal policy.

On efficiency grounds alone, what tax is second best? Using a head, lump-sum, poll tax as the reference point, consider the effects of the second best on a dozen sets of competing goals, following the consensus about effects and the logic of their materialization in Rosen (1985), Stiglitz (2000), Bruce (2001), Blinder and Solow (1974), Aaron and Boskin (1980), Bradford (2000), Aaron and Pechman (1981), Musgrave and Musgrave (1984), Eckstein (1973), Sandmo (1985), Bernheim (2002), Poterba (2002), and Hassett and Hubbard (2002).

While public economists consider a lump-sum tax the benchmark for financing public goods and maintaining economic efficiency, the tax creates equity problems. Everyone pays the same tax. No economic distortions occur. Equity becomes the chief issue, however, and the head tax provokes immediate and sometimes severe changes in taxpayers' behavior.

Nevertheless, consider first the trade-off between taxing all commodities or some commodities. The result of taxing all commodities is little distortion of taxpayers' consumption habits when compared to taxing a specific commodity. The exception is the case of demand for a taxed product that is so necessary that the same amount will be purchased whatever the cost added by the tax.

Table 4.3 Labor, Consumption, Work, and Future-Orientedness Effects of Taxes

Concentration	Trade-Offs			
	Consumption −	Work −	Labor +	Present-oriented +
Policy tool	Sales tax	Income tax	Property tax	Debt
	Saving +	Leisure +	Capital −	Future-oriented −
Focus of impact	Retirement, investment	Early retirement vs. later retirement	Investment, risk taking, later retirement	Consumption now if taxes are higher *later*; saving now if taxes are higher *now*
Alternative policy tools	Flat tax (Slemrod, 1997), value-added tax (Slemrod, 1997), or head tax (Butler, Adonis, and Travers, 1994)	Head tax	Tax on immobile factors	Progressive income tax or tax deferral in anticipation of lower future earnings or income

Next, consider a commodity tax and its impact on the trade-off between consumption and saving. If imposed, the commodity tax makes goods more expensive but allows saving to occur tax-free. The saving preference in the tax also pushes consumption out of the present and into a future period, making the fiscal system encourage future over present consumption. The commodity tax also leads a taxpayer to prefer the purchase of assets not taxed, such as property (or capital).

In contrast to a commodity tax, consider an income tax on wages from labor. The immediate impact of the income from a tax on wages is probably the increase in work hours to produce more income to make up for that taken by the tax. As probable, the impact of the income tax may be a reduction in work hours with the substitution of leisure or the substitution of one kind of work for another that is not taxed. The income tax, if levied on wages alone, favors both saving and the accumulation of nontaxed assets such as property. Both saving and accumulation of property or capital suggest a fiscal system preference for delayed consumption, a preference for future consumption over present consumption. Such delayed consumption may include retirement savings.

Finally, consider a wealth tax, a tax on all assets the taxpayer owns rather than the commodities the taxpayer consumes or the work done for wages. The wealth tax may be a property tax on the taxpayer's home. In this case, the fiscal system favors consumption over the accumulation of property, favoring risk-averse renting instead of what becomes a risky investment in capital. A property tax on land alone corresponds to the consumption tax on a commodity, the demand of which will never change no matter what the price. Since there is a fixed amount of land, the land tax will have no effect on decisions about owning land; the land tax will have no effect on any other economic decision either.

The property or capital tax—a tax on accumulated wealth, bequests, or the investment returns from stocks and bonds—favors labor income as well as consumption. The property or capital tax penalizes investment, unless the investment is in a risky effort to invent some new, unimagined, and thus far untaxed good or service. In such a case, the property or capital tax on one investment portfolio might actually promote another portfolio, one involving risk taking, and innovation. The property or capital tax penalizes productivity among business firms relying on investment. The property or capital tax promotes present consumption over future consumption.

By comparing possible tax targets, the great winners and losers in basic fiscal policy come into view. The immediate and long-term impacts of tax portfolios also appear. See Table 4.4 for the comparison. If a simple sum of the rows and then the columns in Table 4.4 were done, two striking phenomena would appear.

Table 4.4 Cross-Criteria Effects of Taxes

Tax Effect On	Tax On			
	Property	Sales/ Commodity	Income/ Wages	Lump Sum
Labor	+	+	−	+
Capital	−	+	+	+
Consumption	+	−	+	+
Savings	−	+	+	+
Work	+	+	−	+
Leisure	+	+	+	+
Present	+	−	−	+
Future	−	+	+	+

Note: + incentive; − disincentive.

Leisure (for some and more work for others) appears the best alternative when an assessor levies a tax on any target. The strategy for the taxpayer may not be "don't do anything" but instead "don't do anything the tax collector can see." Tax evasion, expatriation, and underground economic transactions may be what actually take place.

The best tax is a lump-sum tax. In the British examples of head taxes, however, simple lump-sum taxes fail the smell test of equity, leading tax policy makers to do something else, graduating the lump-sum tax rates in some way to make the lump-sum tax a tax on property, consumption, or income. Of these remaining taxes, none gain superiority for the same reasons. The tax on property supports wage laborers and consumption in the present rather than later, and undermines saving, investment, and owners of capital. The consumption, sales, or commodity tax favors wage laborers and capital owners, their saving, and future consumption over present consumption. The income or wage tax, simply defined to exclude no source of current income, penalizes wage laborers, their saving and work, as well as future consumption. The tax on wages rewards owners of capital and present-day consumption by all. What norm should prevail and what departure from fiscal policy neutrality should the policy maker pursue? Specific goals for policy tend to capitalize on different combinations of norms. To help clarify the goals and norms, the research on saving, investment, portfolio choice, risk taking, productivity, and expansion follows in the sections below.

Saving

A tax policy maker may intend to encourage saving. An individual's efforts to save vary according to disposable income: the higher the income, the greater the savings. However, the average propensity to save, which higher disposable income suggests, in fact does not reflect the even more basic marginal propensity. The marginal propensity does not vary greatly by income (Musgrave and Musgrave, 1989, p. 304). Interest rates, the amount willingly saved by everyone, the point in one's life cycle, and one's estimate of permanent income influence the marginal propensity to save (Modigliani and Brumberg, 1954; Friedman, 1957). The rate of return a saver might receive after paying an income tax might persuade the person to save, particularly when that person was at the point in his or her life cycle when retirement loomed and savings were important (Tin, 2000).

Savings incentives have become the traditional point of positive analysis, and positive analysis helps in understanding the results of normative analytical arguments (Sandmo, 1985; Boskin, 1988; Holcombe, 1998). A tax rate reduction or the elimination of a tax altogether, encouraging savings, will burden those reporting labor income or wages and will benefit those reporting interest earnings, dividends, and capital gains. The tax could encourage later consumption in retirement rather than current consumption. However, Sandmo (1985) and to a greater degree Stiglitz (2000, pp. 532–535) doubt the simple idea that lowering taxes on savings and capital promotes more of both. The more technical precision involved in the savings incentive analysis comes from Sandmo (1985, p. 271), who argues that if the tax rate on all income, both labor and capital, is assumed to be constant over time, the income tax works like a combination of a lump-sum tax and a special tax on interest income. Analysis of the effects on consumption reveals that the indirect or special tax has little effect on consumption, present or future, and that it becomes the equivalent of a lump-sum tax levied on labor income. Sandmo's analysis reveals (p. 272): "A general indirect tax at a rate which is constant over time is equivalent to a tax on labor income alone, leaving the relative price of present and future consumption unaffected.... Indirect taxation is accordingly also equivalent to a lump-sum tax being levied on all consumers in proportion to their labor income." Sandmo suggests that there may be income or substitution effects for income for the tax on labor income (working more or working less at the taxed activity), but the savings rate remains more or less the same. Stiglitz (2000) also notes that the broad-based tax on labor and capital income, from all empirical estimates, has a small though negative effect on savings. He concludes that any negative effect may reduce savings, but he also argues that any effort to add incentives by reducing taxes on interest earnings and other capital income will have very little impact (2000, p. 534).

Problems abound when research attempts the leap from discovering what influences an individual's saving to what influences the savings behavior of an aggregation of individuals. These problems include the assumption of a common reaction to changes in fiscal policy, a common price, good by good, for consumers, and a single interest rate, for every savings maturity, which all individual savers may exploit.

Economists agree that there is a small "significant negative substitution effect," a noticeable interest elasticity of consumption. That is, the rate of interest varies inversely with present consumption. Moreover, as fiscal policy favors decreasing marginal rates of income taxes, interest rates rise, saving increases, and present consumption falls (Sandmo, 1985, pp. 280–283).

Despite measurement problems, however, Denison's "law" (1958) appears to hold steady, as indicated by the fact that the savings rate in the United States remains at 16% of gross national product and has done so since 1929 over tax regimes that had low rates and were barely progressive and ones that were "onerous" (David and Scadding, 1974; Glennon, 1985). Glennon (1985) attributes the steady rate to an extremely large number of factors that have the effect of offsetting each other.

Briefly summarizing the research, economic theory predicts that household consumption depends on the household income available after taxes, the household's disposable income. The delay in consumption by saving part of that disposable income might be related to the level of taxation as well as the type of tax, one based on income or consumption. The delay in consumption may also depend on the level of wealth. Wealthier individuals have higher average savings rates than do poorer individuals, although the marginal propensity to save differs less so (Musgrave and Musgrave, 1984). Expectations about future income may have some effect on savings (Fisher, 1930; Modigliani and Brumberg, 1954). Expecting that in retirement income will fall, an individual may save more presently. However, the taxes on all forms of income have more of an effect on labor than savings, and any negative effect on savings comes about on relatively small savings magnitudes in the United States.

The more practical fiscal problems related to saving actually get greater attention from policy makers than abstract general problems. For example, policy makers ask whether a public retirement plan such as social security (Social Security Old-Age, Survivors, and Disability Insurance (OASDI) programs) displaces private saving? Perhaps. If government fiscal policies force saving, assuming the government investment manager had the same rate of return as private savers, theory predicts displacement. However, Feldstein (1976) argues that the government's policy toward retirement age, or the age at which an individual may begin drawing social security, may affect private saving. Should the government policy be fixed, one can begin drawing at least part of the social security payments to which he or she may be entitled at a fixed age, the policy induces individuals to retire earlier and to save more during the period they work so that they will have income over a longer period. Government policy therefore creates a replacement effect. The displacement and replacement effects offset each other, creating a result in which social security has a small, negative effect on saving.

Tax policy encouraging private saving for retirement through individual retirement accounts (IRAs) and 401(k) plans might also have some effects. In an IRA, the individual may accumulate a limited amount of savings free of tax until retirement drawdowns. The 401(k) plans are established by employers, have higher tax-deductible contribution limits than IRAs, and may include an employer match for individual contributions. Much of the research literature on tax-advantaged, pension-related savings plans such as these suggests that these plans merely displace what saving might have occurred anyway (Bernheim, 1997). Gale (1997, p. 327) concludes that while savings incentive accounts accumulated exceptionally large amounts in the recent past, personal saving actually fell over the same period.

Considerable thought and work have taken place to understand as much as possible about when and why people increase savings. Bernheim (2002) has summarized the classes of research as the life cycle approach, variations on the life cycle, and behavioral theories. This review looks more deeply at them here.

First, the life cycle hypothesis can help understand saving. Modigliani and Brumberg (1954) argued that over lifetimes, individuals' incomes vary. In addition, over lifetimes, individuals save and consume with different goals in mind. When young, an individual typically has large consumption obligations for housing, education, and child care. As an individual ages, these obligations diminish, altering consumption and allowing more saving at the same time that the individual enters a period of peak income. The individual also faces retirement and the prospect of not working and a smaller income. Therefore, savings not only may rise, but must rise in the peak earnings years. In retirement, the individual lives off the income from government benefits and savings, increasing consumption.

Three instances may affect the consumption-saving trade-off over a person's life. First, a person may have a strong desire to bequeath income. The desire may come from any number of motives, including altruism or selfishness toward individual heirs, patrimony as a cherished value, estate size maximization, and the agreement within a family about gifts from one generation to another (Bernheim, Skinner, and Weinberg, 2001; Kotlikoff, 1979, 1988). Saving may also relate to interest rates (Bernheim, 1997; Gale, 1997; Boskin, 1978). Individuals may save, in the life cycle sense, because they are uncertain about future government benefits, the nature of insurance contracts they may own, or simply their precautionary reaction to life expectancy (Engen and Gale, 1996).

Bounded rationality and self-control have entered the conceptual debate over the life cycle hypothesis and the saving-consumption trade-off more generally (Bernheim, 1997, 2002). Without large amounts of information or the intellectual wherewithal to analyze them, an individual seeks heuristic aids, especially about how much to save. Among these aids are repetition of behavior for learning's sake, imitation of peers, and advice of sophisticated professionals. Bernheim (2002, p. 1201) dismissed each of these possibilities. He argues that it is not easy for people to retire more than once (repetition and learning). Vicarious observation is "incomplete or of questionable relevance" given the difference between thirty-year-olds without knowledge and ninety-year-olds with it. And most people have difficulty evaluating the quality of advice even if sophisticated advisors use more than rules of thumb themselves.

Self-control intrigues Bernheim and others (2002, p. 1202; Thaler and Shefrin, 1981). If people are both savers and consumers over their lives, a "farsighted, patient 'planner' and a shortsighted, impatient 'doer,'" the people seek an efficient bargain between the two selves. The bargain is one over deferred gratification. Willingness to defer declines as the period promising self-gratification nears (Laibson, 1998). The individual constantly bargains mentally over self-control, reaching different states of satisfaction at different points in life.

Business saving is an important aspect of the entire savings phenomenon. Business firms must build new and maintain the existing capital stock—buildings and machinery—through capital investment. With savings that come from depreciation, retained earnings, and unpaid dividends, the firm may be able to finance large amounts of capital stock. Taxes on business income directly threaten savings, although taxes may be shifted to workers in the form of lower wages, to shareholders in the form of lower capital gains and dividends, and to customers in the form of higher prices. Firms might not be able to shift taxes. In fact, in highly competitive industries, the taxes on business profits may not shift at all. In the latter case, the reduction in profits by the amount of taxes also reduces the firm's savings (Musgrave and Musgrave, 1989, pp. 305–306).

Government saving comes in the form of surpluses. Government surpluses, as a form of saving, can increase the total resources available for private capital formation, reduce current consumption, or increase current consumption through public capital formation. The alternative outcomes are unpredictable and require analysis (Musgrave and Musgrave, 1989, pp. 534–537). Whether eliminating debt quickly or slowly with surpluses helps the economy is an open question.

Modern observers of government policy makers and their behavior tend to view surpluses as a constituency building resource (Buchanan, 1970, pp. 113–116, 312–317). Many take a demand-side view and advocate fulfilling unmet socioeconomic needs through expanded government spending. Others take surpluses to be a supply-side resource useful to reduce tax distortions and provide incentives for provision of goods and services outside the public sector. On the demand side, surpluses allow for greater consumption, employment, and investment through transfers, grants, subsidies, credit, and insurance. On the supply side, surpluses create the opportunity to cut tax rates and rebate prior tax payments. In either case, the government surplus falls, and, in theory at least, individual and business firm savings increase.

Investment

Investment takes place because of capital available at low cost, making the expected rate of return on the capital higher. Investment is a function of the supply of savings from individuals, households, firms, and governments. Taxes on saving might reduce the pool of capital available by forcing a trade-off between saving and consumption among individuals and households. Taxes may help reduce business saving directly through less favorable policies for retained earnings, unpaid dividends, or depreciation, and a firm's pool of internal capital available for investment without borrowing. Business saving may fall when the supply of savings from individuals and governments falls, forcing interest rates to rise.

However, the interrelationships among individual, household, firm, and government savings on the one hand and taxes on the other are complex. Many have shown that declines in any one savings sector tend to be offset by increases in another. Should governments run deficits, firms tend to increase savings.

Following Stiglitz (2000), when an economy is closed to outside investment, savings equal investment. Should savings increase, investment increases. Should savings decline because of a tax on savings returns, investment will decline as well. The tax on savings returns, however, can increase government revenue, reducing a government deficit or actually creating a surplus. The government saving will offset the decline in other savings and the decline in investment.

Should a wage or consumption tax replace a tax on savings, total savings and investment might increase. According to Stiglitz (2000, p. 503), wage taxes and consumption taxes are made equivalent through tax policies. In the wage tax case, tax policy calls for levying a tax on all wage income, exempting all interest, dividend, and other returns on capital. In a consumption tax case, policy levies a tax on total individual income less total savings. A reduction in either wages or consumption through a tax does not alter the budget preferences of the individual. The savings side of the trade-off against consumption grows stronger, and the government gains increased revenue, creating government savings.

Opening the economy to outside investment alters the domestic savings part of the theory. Since increasing amounts of investment capital come to the United States from abroad, Stiglitz argues, the supply of foreign investment has become inelastic, influenced little by the level of interest rates or the returns found more generally (2000, p. 587). If so, the supply of foreign investment acts to reduce domestic savings, increase taxes, or increase government deficits. The dynamics among foreign investment, domestic savings, taxes, and government savings may be very different, depending on the assumptions about the motives of private investors.

The role of taxes in distorting the picture has powerful adherents and opponents, as does the role of tax policies in providing incentives to savers (Bernheim, 2002, pp. 1182–1195; Bernheim, 1997). Fiscal policy impacts on business investment remain a research area as hotly debated on the normative analysis side as it is murky on the positive analysis side.

Portfolio Choice

Portfolio choice involves the amount of risk an investor may be willing to take. In concrete terms, fiscal policies provide incentives aimed toward encouraging and dampening investment risk-taking both generally and in the choices of specific assets. This review covers the general risk-taking/risk aversion balance fiscal policies may encourage. Recent research reported by Poterba (2004) outlines fiscal policies and their effects on the rate of return households earn on different and specific assets. The principles of economics and psychology have provided the basic tenets of portfolio choice. In the economic vein, an investor will prefer the greatest return for a given level of risk, the return a function of the probability of the return. In the psychology or behavioral economics vein (Rabin, 1998), portfolio choice may depend on a much more complex set of considerations. Four major factors affect portfolio choice and risk taking. First, individuals and business managers act in terms of how the risks and returns are framed, as large risks relative to small returns, large risks and large returns, or small risks and large returns (Tversky and Kahneman, 1981). Investors carefully select and use representative risk estimates; that is, they generalize a small amount of experience to a large class of events. Third, an initial estimate of the probability of an outcome has an anchoring effect—that initial estimates will define for an individual a psychological range into which subsequent estimates will fall even though they may differ radically from statistical estimates of actual experience (Tversky and Kahneman, 1974). Finally, individuals and managers act when past or vicariously experienced failure or success comes to mind easily (Tversky and Kahneman, 1974).

For economic efficiency, portfolios have more importance than does saving and investment, the total amount available. Sandmo, advocating the importance of portfolio composition, relates the important effects fiscal policies may have (1985, pp. 293–294). He states:

The classic argument for a systematic effect of taxation on portfolio choice runs in terms of risk-taking behavior. The popular view has traditionally been that the taxation of income from assets discriminates against risk taking through its lowering of the expected rates of return.

Since high risk and high return are related, lower returns reduce the willingness to undertake projects with high risks.

Many intuitively agree with fiscal policy's reach in dampening risk taking. Subsidies, tax incentives, insurance, insurance guarantees, and regulation appear to work against risk taking. Yet, fiscal policy has a risk-taking incentive, a risk-sharing dimension. Sandmo credits Domar and Musgrave (1944) with the government risk-sharing view. Fiscal policy serves to reduce both risk and return such that they offset each other. Sandmo points out that (1985, p. 294)

> perfect loss offset provisions [give] the government ... the same share of a possible loss as it takes in a gain. If individuals ascribed a sufficiently large weight to the loss sharing property of the tax, the direction of the tax discrimination could possibly go in the opposite direction.

Perhaps the loss-sharing provisions of fiscal policies would appear to be political control of the economy, government policy makers' choices of winners and losers among technologies, and an anti-innovation and change proviso for social change.

A modern variant of the risk-sharing argument comes from Mossin (1968) and Stiglitz (1969). The portfolio composition individuals prefer comes from their preferences for risk. A risky asset and a less risky asset, taxed at the same rate, will result in the investor preferring the riskiest asset, if risk and return do vary directly. If the risky asset carries a government subsidy, the return will exceed what existed without the subsidy and will make the risky asset irresistible as a part of a portfolio.

Risk Taking

The availability of capital affects risk taking as well. Higher business profits create an alternative source of capital. This source of capital, with relatively lower tax rates applied, yields a pool of available capital with a relatively lower imputed interest cost than credit. Such lower imputed interest makes more risky investments worthwhile.

The tax on business profits creates a trade-off. Firms may borrow some or all of the funds needed for capital projects or the business may pay for its capital projects wholly or in part out of profits. The basic trade-off requires a firm's managers to balance risk and return. The capital projects financed out of the business's own profits may have a risk level and rate of return equal to the bank financing. Should a tax incentive be added to subsidize bank financing, the return on the capital project increases.

The risk-taking incentive can appear an even simpler decision. Stiglitz presents the case (2000, pp. 589–590):

Assume that an individual has to decide between two assets: a safe asset yielding no return, and a risky asset.... [On which, the] average return is positive.... The individual is conservative and so allocates a fraction of his wealth to the safe asset and the remainder to the risky asset. We now impose a tax on the return to capital, but we allow a full deduction against income for losses. The safe asset is unaffected. The risky asset has its return reduced by half, but the losses are also reduced by half.... The tax has left him completely unaffected.

Again, as Domor and Musgrave point out (1944), the government shares the risks with the individual and acts as a silent partner. Perhaps, as Stiglitz argues (1969), in sharing the risk, the individual resists the framing, representative risk, anchoring, and memory effects of the typical, less than rational individual portrayed by Tversky and Kahneman (1974, 1981) and becomes much more willing to increase his or her risk taking (Rabin, 2000). However, if the fiscal policy favors one form of investment, such as municipal bonds over equities, the government policy makers substitute their judgment about risk taking for the investor's judgment. If the tax favors one investment, such as oil royalties or oil depletion allowances, over another, the policy makers may face criticism of cronyism. If the tax favors no form of investment or project for investment, the policy makers may still face criticism for indulging so many harebrained schemes or schemers.

Innovation and Productivity

Since British Prime Minster Margaret Thatcher's experiments with lump-sum taxation in the last decade of the twentieth century (described above), strong editorials and much argument have regretted the end of a just era in fiscal policy making. After the prime minister's poll tax experiment began, major "right turns" in developed countries' tax policies seemed to occur. Stroking the rich became a dominant theme in fiscal policy debate. Tax rates fell. The object of taxation became consumption. The number, type, and amount of unconventional fiscal policy tools increased. Together corporate welfare, tax injustice, and the end of the welfare state illustrated how far economic efficiency had gained influence as a fiscal policy goal at the expense of social equity.

The latest research confounds these views. It suggests that second- and third-best taxes do little, and little harm, as long as their designers also reduce distortions. Such a claim is made for consumption taxes. The surveys of countries belonging to the Organization for Economic Cooperation and Development (OECD) (Swank and Steinmo, 2002; Heady and van den Noord, 2001) and the European Union (Joumard, 2001) reveal a strong trend toward taxes that are second best but have broader bases and flatter rates. These countries are called high economic growth countries (Lindert, 2004). They are also called countries with low administrative and incentive costs (Bassanini, Scarpetta, and Hemmings, 2001). In either the administrative or incentive cost sense, "cost" signifies government policing, means testing, or regulating, whether of the poor, those with pensions, or business firms. Social spending has not decreased but instead has become more universal, making "people's basic guarantees [health, retirement, education, work, income] independent of their specific life choices" (Lindert, 2004, p. 302), those subject to government policing. These economies have grown, innovated, and become more productive, Lindert argues. Advances in technology, the force behind innovation and productivity, require investment in education and training, generally at government expense, Musgrave and Musgrave argued (1989, p. 311). Large investments in public infrastructure may have substantial positive effects on productivity, especially in the case of highway spending, where private sector inventory and logistics costs fall as a result (Shirley and Winston, 2004; Postrel, 2004). Therefore good reasons exist to believe that high-growth, highly productive economies thrive on universalist fiscal policies. These policies are more uniform, less costly to administer, fairer, and more transparent (Lindert, 2004, p. 302). These policies do not reduce or enlarge the size of the public sector but extend its reach without distorting individual choices.

Summary and Discussion

This literature review on fiscal policy impacts questioned whether intentions shape consequences. The review probed the possibility that intentions and consequences may closely relate. The study also considered the alternative that policy intentions may be largely frustrated by normative compromises, competing institutions, contradictory policies, distorted policy designs, vaguely understood policy tools, poor execution, and unintended effects.

A somewhat different answer appeared through the examination. Intentions, first of all, encompass processes as well as impacts. Government economic functions can provide frames of reference that leaders use in fiscal policy to influence what domestic and foreign individuals, business firms, and governments do. The frame of reference may be one dictating action to ensure economic growth, productivity, or innovation. However, the frame of reference may also be limiting government action and enabling action from individuals and organizations outside government. The latter frame emphasizes private and nonprofit organization capacity building to strengthen allocation, distribution, and stabilization efforts through tax incentives, including abatements, deductions, credits, refundable credits, and rebates. Fiscal policies can be implemented through direct government spending on government, whether on government agency operations, on the output of nonprofit or for-profit production of goods and services, on the purchase of products such as crops from farmers in order to maintain price levels, or on the direct transfer or payment of money to individuals. Fiscal policies also encompass grants-in-aid, loan guarantees, insurance, and debt. Intentions have led to the invention and more sophisticated use of numerous policy tools and designs.

If intentions shape consequences, the argument might lead to the discovery of what combination of function, policy, and policy tool has what impact on private consumption, saving, and investment. However, the attribution of control and choice to the policy maker should observe limits, the review suggests. These limits include the factors that have shaped fiscal institutions and policy tools and range widely to include historical, political, and social factors. The policy maker participates in fiscal institutions that have a definite shape due to past decisions, large and small, the historical preferences of those who will bear burdens and gain benefits, the balance of forces that exist at a given time, and the values developed within the institutions themselves. The policy maker never has complete control and limitless choice. The survey revealed that intentions may never emerge as a result of free individual choice. Policy makers may shape but cannot fully control either the tools used or the consequences of fiscal policy, policy designs, or policy tools.

In this research review, the allocation, distribution, and stabilization functions of government have appeared in their present guises. As discussed here, distribution has become a matter of the justice of net taxes or spending when all shifts take place. Allocation has favored sharper distinctions between public and other goods, with government provision becoming simply another, alternative way of making sure goods and services provided meet demand. Stabilization has settled into a minor function of fiscal policy, giving way to monetary policy.

The impacts these functional policies appear to have are much more benign than once thought. Specific impacts made by tax policies and their execution, through both conventional and unconventional fiscal tools, have fewer distortions than at first thought. Aggregate saving has not changed for almost a century; therefore fiscal policies, which have changed, seem to have at most a small negative impact on the savings rate. In any case, savings among individuals, business firms, and government have a compensating character; as one falls, one of the others rises. Investment policies, research suggests, have the least impact when they exist within an open economy. Foreign investor incentives outweigh incentives for domestic investors. Finally, portfolio choices and risk-taking behavior react favorably to fiscal policies that allow risk sharing among entrepreneurs, investors, governments, and the taxpayers generally. Innovation and productivity do relate to stable, broad-based, and flat, rather than decreasing levels of taxes and spending.

Fiscal policies can have a benign effect. In the long run, fiscal policy extremes offset each other. Relatively big government budgets, stable fiscal policies, and policy reach without distortions have a positive and salutary effect on the economy. The political economy of OECD member fiscal policies suggests variations that have tightened around the roughly equal weight given efficiency, growth, and fairness.

There are numerous policy tools and policy designs that policy leaders aim at problems. Policy leaders aim to intervene rather than remain neutral in economic affairs. Policy leaders respond to demands for capital accumulation, satisfaction of wants and needs, and adequate revenue, reach, or influence to improve economic performance. Yet, in the United States, the need for these fiscal policies vies with traditional doubt, suspicion, or cynicism for government institutions, policy designs, and policy tools, the theme Chapter 6 discusses at length.

The earliest debates over the U.S. Constitution reveal both a need for government and a deeply embedded distrust of government action. James Madison, in Federalist Paper 51, wrote (Hamilton, Madison, and Jay, 1978, p. 264):

> In framing a government which is to be administered by men over men, the great difficulty lies in this: you must first enable the government to control the governed; and in the next place oblige it to control itself.

The balancing of need and distrust can explain American politics. According to Wildavsky, "Those who made the American Revolution concluded from experience in Britain and the colonies that a free people had to keep its governors on a tight fiscal leash. From the earliest days of American government, [fiscal] decisions were treated as a struggle for power" (Wildavsky and Caiden, 2004, p. 25). One of the major controls over government was fiscal control, the control over the power to tax, to spend, to grant loans, to guarantee loans, to insure, and to finance regulation.

The Federalist perspective resonates in more modern times. The Federalist Papers provide the first interpretive dimension to fiscal policies. Policies represent both the government's ability to control the governed and its responsibility to control itself.

Unsurprisingly, some ideologues view control of the governed as a control at odds with liberty. The means of control, whether through taxes, conventional spending, regulation, credit, or insurance, whether control of the governed may come with good intentions, or whether control of the governed may take place on behalf of any one group against all others or not, violates the independence and need for self-reliance of individuals and organizations. Government control represents the naked meddling by those in power in the affairs and decisions of those they represent, ultimately permitting those in power to control for control's sake. Therefore, some policy makers and their followers, who view government power with distaste, call for limits on the use of fiscal policy tools, one of these limits being budget control.

At the same time, other government leaders sidestep traditional budget controls to solve problems and resort to different nonconventional spending tools, such as tax expenditures, credit, insurance, loans, and guarantees. What happens, as a result, is a "gradual shifting of programs and resources into less visible or accountable alternatives" (Heen, 2000, p. 762). These alternatives are usually parties outside government. They execute government policy, sometimes dutifully, most of the time without the constitutional limits or oversight institutions existing when government agencies implement policies. The use of unconventional policy tools, however, is growing faster, some say, than government leaders can control it, faster than efforts can be made to control government.

This distinction between government efforts through the budget to control government and government efforts through nonconventional means to control the governed has provoked wide comment, and two observers have provided insights. First, Wildavsky (1986, p. 350) has observed:

> The more government tries to affect citizen behavior, it appears, the less able it is to keep its own house in order. This new relationship between government and citizen may have many advantages, but control over spending is not one of them.

Schick (1981, pp. 349–350) is more forceful about the problem than Wildavsky. He detects in the growth of off-budget expenditure a "paradox of control." That is,

> off-budget expenditures have resulted from the transformation of the public sector from one in which spending was done within the government to one in which spending largely occurs outside government. Not the least of the reasons for this change has been the striving of government to strengthen its control of the economy, the distribution of income, investment policy, and the supply of goods and services. The paradox is that in its effort to extend its control over the private sector, the government has surrendered a good deal of its control over the public sector.

Therefore, reforms have attempted to bring nonconventional expenditures within the scope of the budgetary process (Schick, 1986) in order to increase government accountability.

Finding an appropriate role for government and restraining government power through analysis, progressive economists view nonconventional fiscal policy tools as just another form of intervention in society. Therefore, tax incentives, credit and insurance incentives, regulatory sanctions, and state and local government mandates are different values on the same dimension. These policy tools generally either induce or sanction. At bottom, there is no difference between inducement and sanction; both are means of influencing behavior by individuals, households, firms, and other governments.

Nonconventional spending therefore is a variation of intervention. Consider government intervention as a development of the policy tools approach (Vedung, 1998, pp. 22–25; Anderson, 1977).

This "tools" school of public policy analysis asks the question: When we face a public problem, what do we do about it? The answer is often: we leave it to the individual, the family, or household to decide. Sometimes the community, we think, should decide issues of import. Finally, some problems are matters "the market" should decide without government interference.

Where belief in government intervention exists, policy tends to be a matter of creating inducements and specifying sanctions or something in between.

Sometimes an indirect approach is taken, with education, moral suasion, the bully pulpit, propaganda, or other sermon-like approaches.

At other times, the conventional and nonconventional expenditure of effort—policy tools—represents the government end of the spectrum. What is more important than the distinction between government's direct and indirect efforts is that the budget can prioritize, allocate, economize, or control and otherwise "fit" the appropriate policy tool to the problem at hand. Control is exerted by forcing choices to be made among competing means for achieving some identifiable and sought-after end, maximizing the impact of government intervention.

Government intervention is not government neutrality, however, and the intentions-consequences connection does exist. Intentions and consequences may relate to two metaphors, leviathan and progress, and in relating, clarify the size and role of government in the economy. As progress, the fiscal policy serves as a collection of conventional and unconventional tools with which government intervenes in society, inducing, educating, or sanctioning behavior. Control is a means of selecting the most appropriate tool for intervention. The budget process aims through a form of logical positivism, open, informed, and representative, to gain progressive results.

As leviathan, through the more rationing, control of government arguments, a much different comprehension of fiscal policy exists. The dim view holds a different political and economic theory limiting government's size and role in society. Deadweight losses, unbalanced incentives, unfair penalties, heavy-handed efforts, ham-fisted action, and squandered wealth describe leviathan's fiscal policies. The unreformed decision chain advances through expedient means to produce destructive results.

Both metaphors, though, lead to a clear mandate to budget and thereby control. This traditional view in budgeting is also a matter of belief: Budget control usually means that someone somewhere can know what is being done, that they can know how much is being done with what effect, that they have good intentions, and that good intentions lead to positive consequences. Budget control also means that someone should limit and direct what is being done, at least to the extent of what a large, popular consensus demands, in the political economy through government or government sponsorship.

The issue of budget control is also a matter of research, as this review has revealed. What fiscal institutions—structures, procedures, laws, and organizations—do what with what result? The research cited and described here has provided many ways to define and measure institutions and results. Broadening the scope of budgeting and fiscal policy making beyond institutions to include norms, policy designs, and policy tools, and then to policy incidence, endurance, and impacts, has merit in understanding intentions and consequences.

The remaining question deals directly with intentions. Policy makers intend certain consequences. The very narrow range of fiscal policies reviewed here reveals that intentions bottom on work, thrift, business opportunity, sound economic growth, fairness, and wealth to be able to satisfy both needs and wants. Among all the intentions policy makers could have, why these?

In another, similar context, the question "Why these intentions?" takes a different form. Key (1940, p. 1138) roots a political theory of budgeting in the answer to the question, "On what basis shall it be decided to allocate x dollars to Activity A instead of Activity B?" He finds political philosophy to be the most likely place for the answer. His reliance on beliefs and faith in democratic processes and republican governance leave him with little doubt in letting allocation follow the dictates of representatives freely elected. He has no difficulty with the normative route to theory. However, this review assumes that government leaders have given Key's allocation question in large part to nongovernmental institutions. Moreover, political philosophy may do little to reveal intentions.

The answer to the question "Why these intentions?" may come from moral philosophy. Consider the following case in which Miller (1976, p. 28) illustrates the differences among three criteria for what he calls justifiable distributions of benefits and burdens. The case was one in which a homeowner engaged two small boys to clean windows, promising them £1 each for doing the job. After the task was finished, each of the boys had a right to £1, Miller argues. Yet, knowing that one boy did a much better job quicker than the other boy, one would recognize that the boy doing the better job deserved more and the other less than £1. Knowing even more, that one boy came from a well-to-do home with pocket money to spare and the other from a poverty-stricken home, one would also recognize that one boy needed more than £1and the rich boy less than £1.

What choice should the employer make, asks Miller, to avoid endorsing only one of three moral principles or to avoid appearing arbitrary in the selection of a mere preference for interpreting justice? Miller argues that the choice may be justified in terms of the view of society with which each interpretation is linked, however obvious such an interpretation may be to the employer.

Three views dominate thinking. First, some readers of the case could have a rights view. A view based on the existing order, rights refers to contracts: the boys should get what the contract called for. More broadly, political leaders should accede to rights of citizenship, such as voting, getting what the government promised, ability to own and transfer property, and mobility, for example, in fiscal policy making.

Second, Miller presents a deserts view. Such a view is based in measures of merit, in utilitarianism, based on rewarding some attribute of human effort. In the window washing job, one of the boys could claim, "I worked harder, I deserve higher pay," and he could provide the employer with a justification for a view other than contract. Similar cases may arise in fiscal policy making where merit and performance of the economy become synonyms for economic efficiency as a basis for fiscal policy designs.

Third, the case study may reveal the highest moral ground in "needs." The employer may decide that the neediest window cleaner may deserve the greater share of the pay. Needs-based allocations relate to the necessity of remedying a deficiency or supplying a basic requirement for survival or prosperity. Need may refer to the imperative to provide justice according to the moral order. The moral order may require decency and responsibility. The order demands that everyone be able to realize a good life whatever his or her condition. The neediest may have the view, "I am not responsible for what happened to me; the entire community is responsible or at least should help." In fiscal policy making, redistribution from rich to poor or from one section of a nation to another illustrates the dominance of the needs view.

Seldom do fiscal policy choices appear as clear moral imperatives as the employer dilemma illustrates. Rights and deserts can form a potent combination. One boy could say, "I must have the pay to survive; if I don't get paid, moreover, I'll never be able to get the training to get a job to allow me to stand on my own, to show merit and self-reliance." Rights often derive from needs. The moral rights based on the decency the community shows toward everyone, making sure that everyone has basic food and water, decent housing, reasonable access to health care, and a full education, often come from the paucity of socioeconomic system distribution. Finally, deserts and even rights may originate in a definition of the community or government as insurer of last resort. Rights or deserts can relate to government provision of protection or help in events for which the individual has no responsibility, such as disasters; inherited or innate characteristics such as physical disabilities, gender, and race; or comparative disadvantage due to endowment, bequest, inheritance, or birth, on the other hand.

What are the consequences or reactions of citizens, taxpayers, and leaders of organizations and institutions to fiscal policies? From an efficiency standpoint, a government spending program may alter choices among goods (Stiglitz, 2000, pp. 254–258). Should a program subsidize the price of one good rather than all goods, an individual will certainly choose the cheaper good (i.e., the subsidized good) rather than any unsubsidized one. The subsidy alters choices. The subsidy may come in the form of crop supports for farmers, making domestic farm goods the choice over imported farm goods. The program consequently transforms production of domestic farm goods. In contrast, the spending program may provide an income transfer from the treasury to an individual. The program may not change the prices of competing goods, but the increased income may lead the individual to react with a change in consumption. The individual may prefer imported French butter or Italian pasta to domestic varieties. The subsidized prices, the change of farm production, and the increased income of the consumer may have a beneficial effect with a larger food supply and lower prices, or leaders may view the entire government allocation decision as inefficient. That is, either the farm goods producers or importers may raise their prices and no increase in farm production may take place, canceling out any beneficial effects, as food consumers pay the entire transfer payment to farm good producers.

In both the beneficent and inefficient prediction of the consequences of allocation decisions, the distribution of benefits may have dominated policy maker thinking about fiscal policy. The subsidy for food prices may be aimed at consumers, and the income transfer may have targeted people who cannot afford to sustain themselves nutritionally. However, the pessimistic, inefficient distribution may appear as food exporters, rather than farmers, pocket the entire amount of the crop subsidy and the income transfer (Chapin and Williams-Derry, 2002; Egan, 2000; Browne et al., 1992).

The allocation and distribution consequences point to the reactions to fiscal policies by a broad group of individuals. In allocation, efficiency dominates norms. Policy makers desire Pareto optimal outcomes and prefer the use of cost-benefit analysis with or without contingent valuation, a Lindahl, or any other preference revelation technique (Lindahl, 1958; Ciriacy-Wantrup, 1947, 1955; Cummings, Brookshire, and Schulze, 1986; Samuelson, 1937). However, even Lindahl (1958) assumed agreement on the composition of public services, the willingness to tell the truth, and related to truthfulness, the even distribution of political power. With the distribution of political power, normative fiscal policy confronts the distribution of the burdens and gains from economic power. The allocation decision takes place simultaneously with the distribution decision over the long term. In fact, the changing support of those who have power for the just treatment of those who do not determines political power, and "views about what is just in [fiscal policy] determine its actual shaping" (Lindahl, 1958, p. 176).

On the other hand, some normative economists do not agree that acceptance of economic and political entitlements or rights under a given property order comes before the efficient allocation of social goods, however generous or yielding the entitled may be (Okun, 1975). Rather, the policy analyst, an "omniscient budget planner," must determine the allocation and distribution aspects of budget policy simultaneously in a general equilibrium system (Musgrave and Musgrave, 1989, p. 71). Reality confronts this policy analyst with a persuasive need to get along socially, producing a frame of mind that favors giving the political process credit for revealing preferences for social goods, but only within the context of whatever distribution of economic and political entitlements or rights exists (Traub, 1999; Miller, 1991; Musgrave and Musgrave, 1989; Kahneman and Tversky, 1979; Goffman, 1974; O'Connor, 1973). Allocation and distribution decisions, intentions, and consequences occur simultaneously, but they occur in their own practical way, reflecting some comprehension of the consequences a balance between efficiency and justice might have.

Intentions and consequences have the same coincidence as general equilibrium analysis suggests. Only basic norms guide action, as frames of reference, not as the complete control some suggest policy makers might or must have to make fiscal policies work. The dominance of certain norms can change as the revelation of the consequences of old norm combinations demands. Openness to change may yield budget control and give comfort to people who have needs to be met, as well as those who demand privacy and control over their own welfare, and those who view governmental institutions with a mixture of necessity and wariness.

Endnote

1 This chapter was adapted from Government fiscal policay impacts, in Donijo Robbins, ed., *Handbook of Public Sector Economics,* 425–521. Boca Raton, FL: Taylor & Francis, 2005. With permission of ABC-CLIO, LLC.

References

Aaron, H. J. (1975). *Who Pays the Property Tax?* Washington, DC: Brookings.

Aaron, H. J., and Boskin, M. J. (1980). *The Economics of Taxation.* Washington, DC: Brookings.

Aaron, H. J., and Pechman, J. A. (1981). *How Taxes Affect Economic Behavior.* Washington, DC: Brookings.

Altig, D., Auerbach, A. J., Kotlikoff, L. J., Smetters, K. A., and Walliser, J. (2001). Simulating fundamental tax reform in the United States. *American Economic Review* 91(3):574–595.

Anderson, C. W. (1977). *Statecraft: An Introduction to Political Choice and Judgment.* New York: John Wiley & Sons.

Anthony, R. N., and Young, D. W. (2003). *Management Control in Nonprofit Organizations.* 7th ed. Boston: McGraw-Hill Irwin.

Atkinson, A. B. (1983). *Social Justice and Public Policy.* Cambridge, MA: MIT Press.

Auerbach, A. J. (1996). Dynamic revenue estimation. *Journal of Economic Perspectives* 10(1):141–157.

Auerbach, A. J. (2002a). Is there a role for discretionary fiscal policy? In *Rethinking Stabilization Policy,* ed. Federal Reserve Bank of Kansas City, 109–150. Kansas City, MO: Federal Reserve Bank.

Auerbach, A. J. (2002b). The Bush tax cut and national saving. *National Tax Journal* 55(3):387–407.

Auerbach, A. J. (2003). *Fiscal Policy, Past and Present.* Working Paper 10023. Cambridge, MA: National Bureau of Economic Research. Retrieved October 18, 2003, from www.nber.org/papers/w10023.

Auerbach, Alan J. (2004). *How Much Equity Does the Government Hold?* Working Paper W10291. Cambridge, MA: National Bureau of Economic Research. Retrieved May 30, 2004 from http://www.nber.org/papers/w10291.

Auerbach, A. J., and Kotlikoff, L. J. (1987). *Dynamic Fiscal Policy.* Cambridge: Cambridge University Press.

Auerbach, A. J., Kotlikoff, L. J., and Leibfritz, W. (1999). *Generational Accounting Around the World.* Chicago: University of Chicago Press.

Auerbach, A. J., and Rosen, H. S. (1980). *Will the Real Excess Burden Please Stand Up? (Or, Seven Measures in Search of a Concept).* National Bureau of Economic Research Working Paper w0495. Retrieved January 19, 2004, from http://www.nber.org/papers/w0495.

Ballard, C. L., and Fullerton, D. (1992). Distortionary taxes and the provision of public goods. *Journal of Economic Perspectives* 6:117–131.

Barry, J. S. (2002, January). *Fiscal Forecasting: A Perilous Task.* Special Report 108. Retrieved January 5, 2004, from http://taxfoundation.org/sr108.pdf.

Bassanini, A., Scarpetta, S., and Hemmings, P. (2001). *Economic Growth: The Role of Policies and Institutions. Panel Data Evidence from OECD Countries.* Economics Department Working Paper 283. Paris: Organization for Economic Cooperation and Development. Retrieved November 12, 2003, from http://www.oecd.org/dataoecd/29/29/1891403.pdf.

Bell, D. (1974). The public household—on fiscal sociology and the liberal society. *Public Interest* 37:29–68.

Bentham, J. (2000). An introduction to the principles of morals and legislation. Retrieved January 21, 2004, from http://www.ecn.bris.ac.uk/het/bentham/morals.pdf.

Bernheim, B. D. (1997). Rethinking savings incentives. In *Fiscal Policy: Lessons from Economic Research*, ed. A. J. Auerbach, 259–311. Cambridge, MA: MIT Press.

Bernheim, B. D. (2002). Taxation and saving. In *Handbook of Public Economics*, ed. A. J. Auerbach and M. Feldstein, 1173–1249. New York: Elsevier Science.

Bernheim, B. D., Skinner, J., and Weinberg, S. (2001). What accounts for the variation in retirement wealth among U.S. households? *American Economic Review* 91(4):832–857.

Bhagwati, J. N., and Ramaswami, V. K. (1963). Domestic distortions, tariffs and the theory of optimal subsidy. *Journal of Political Economy* 71(1):44–50.

Blinder, A. S. (2002). Commentary: Should the European Central Bank and the Federal Reserve be concerned about fiscal policy? In *Rethinking Stabilization Policy*, ed. Federal Reserve Bank of Kansas City, 391–403. Kansas City, MO: Federal Reserve Bank.

Blinder, A. S., and Solow, R. M. (1974). Analytical foundations of fiscal policy. In *The Economics of Public Finance*, ed. A. S. Blinder, R. M. Solow, G. F. Break, P. O. Steiner, and D. Netzer, 3–115. Washington, DC: Brookings.

Blum, W. J., and Kalven, H., Jr. (1953). *The Uneasy Case for Progressive Taxation*. Chicago: University of Chicago Press.

Boskin, M. J. (1978). Taxation, saving and the rate of interest. *Journal of Political Economy* 86(2):S3–S27.

Boskin, M. J. (1988). What do we know about consumption and saving, and what are the implications for fiscal policy? *AEA Papers and Proceedings* 78(2):401–407.

Bozeman, B. (1987). *All Organizations Are Public: Bridging Public and Private Organizational Theories*. San Francisco: Jossey-Bass.

Bradford, D. F. (2000). *Taxation, Wealth, and Saving*. Cambridge, MA: MIT Press.

Break, G. F. (1974). The incidence and economic effects of taxation. In *The Economics of Public Finance*, ed. A. S. Blinder, R. M. Solow, G. F. Break, P. O. Steiner, and D. Netzer, 119–237. Washington, DC: Brookings.

Browne, W. P., Skees, J. R., Swanson, L. E., Thompson, P. B., and Unnevehr, L. J. (1992). *Sacred Cows and Hot Potatoes: Agrarian Myths in Agricultural Policy*. Boulder, CO: Westview.

Bruce, N. (2001). *Public Finance and the American Economy*. Boston: Addison Wesley.

Buchanan, J. M. (1970). *The Public Finances*. Homewood, IL: Richard D. Irwin, Inc.

Buchanan, J. M. (1977). Why does government grow? In *Budgets and Bureaucrats: The Sources of Government Growth*, ed. T. E. Borcherding, 3–18. Durham, NC: Duke University Press.

Buchanan, J. M., and Tullock, G. (1962). *The Calculus of Consent: Logical Foundations of Constitutional Democracy*. Ann Arbor: University of Michigan Press.

Bureau of Economic Analysis. (1985). *An Introduction to National Economic Accounting*. Springfield, VA: National Technical Information Service, U.S. Department of Commerce. Retrieved April 24, 2004, from http://www.bea.gov/bea/ARTICLES/NATIONAL/NIPA/Methpap/methpap1.pdf.

Butler, D., Adonis, A., and Travers, T. (1994). *Failure in British Government: The Politics of the Poll Tax*. Oxford: Oxford University Press.

Carroll, C. D. (2001). *A Theory of the Consumption Function, with and without Liquidity Constraints*. Expanded version, Working Paper 8387. Cambridge, MA: National Bureau of Economic Research. Retrieved September 22, 2003, from http://www.nber.org/papers/w8387.

Chapin, L. K., and Williams-Derry, C. (2002). *Green Acre$, How Taxpayers Are Subsidizing the Demise of the Family Farm*. Washington, DC: Environmental Working Group. Retrieved December 20, 2002, from http://www.ewg.org/reports/greenacres/exec. html.

Chapman, S. J. (1913). The utility of income and progressive taxation. *Economic Journal* 23(89):25–35.

Ciriacy-Wantrup, S. V. (1947). Capital returns from soil conservation practices. *Journal of Farm Economics* 29(4):1181–1196.

Ciriacy-Wantrup, S. V. (1955). Benefit-cost analysis and public resource development. *Journal of Farm Economics* 37(4):676–680.

Clark, J. B. (1899). *The Distribution of Wealth: A Theory of Wages, Interest, and Profits*. New York: The Macmillan Company.

Corlett, W. J., and Hague, D. C. (1953–1954). Complementarity and the excess burden of taxation. *Review of Economic Studies* 21(1):21–30.

Cummings, R. G., Brookshire, D. S., and Schulze, W. D. (1986). *Valuing Environmental Goods: An Assessment of the Contingent Valuation Method*. Totowa, NJ: Rowman & Allanheld.

David, P. A., and Scadding, J. L. (1974). Private savings: Ultrarationality, aggregation and "Denison's law." *Journal of Political Economy* 82:225–249.

Davidson, R., and Duclos, J.-Y. (1997). Statistical inference for the measurement of the incidence of taxes and transfers. *Econometrica* 65(6):1453–1465.

DeLong, J. B. (1997). America's only peacetime inflation: The 1970s. In *Reducing Inflation: Motivation and Strategy*, ed. C. Romer and D. Romer, 247–276. Chicago: University of Chicago Press and National Bureau of Economic Research.

Denison, E. F. (1958). A note on private saving. *Review of Economics and Statistics* 40:261–267.

Diewert, W. E., Lawrence, D. A., and Thompson, F. (1998). *Handbook of Public Finance*. New York: Dekker.

Dobson, R. B. (1970). *The Peasant's Revolt of 1381*. New York: St. Martin's Press.

Domar, E. D., and Musgrave R. A. (1944). Proportional income taxation and risk-taking. *Quarterly Journal of Economics* 58(3):388–422.

Downs, A. (1960). Why the government budget is too small in a democracy. *World Politics* 12(4):541–563.

Eckstein, O. (1973). *Public Finance*. 3rd ed. Englewood Cliffs, NJ: Prentice-Hall.

Egan, T. (2000). Failing farmers learn to profit from federal aid. *New York Times*, December 24, p. 1.

Engen, E. M., and Gale, W. G. (1996). Taxation and saving: The role of uncertainty. Washington, DC: Board of Governors of the Federal Reserve System.

Federal Reserve Bank of Kansas City. (2002). *Rethinking Stabilization Policy*. Kansas City, MO: Federal Reserve Bank.

Federal Reserve Bank of St. Louis. (2004). Budget deficits and interest rates. *Monetary Trends*, March, p. 1.

Feldstein, M. (1974a). Incidence of a capital income tax in a growing economy with variable savings rates. *Review of Economic Studies* 41(4):505–513.

Feldstein, M. (1974b). Tax incidence in a growing economy with variable factor supply. *Quarterly Journal of Economics* 88(4):551–573.

Feldstein, M. (1976). Social security and saving: The extended life cycle theory. *American Economic Review* 66(Papers and Proceedings):77–86.

Feldstein, M. (2002). Commentary. In *Rethinking Stabilization Policy*, ed. Federal Reserve Bank of Kansas City, 151–162. Kansas City, MO: Federal Reserve Bank.

Feldstein, M., and Feenberg, D. (1995). *The Taxation of Two Earner Families.* National Bureau of Economic Research Working Paper W5155. Washington, DC: National Bureau of Economic Research. Retrieved February 10, 2004, from http://papers.nber.org/papers/w5155.

Finkelstein, N. D. (2000). *Transparency in Public Policy.* Houndsmills, Basingstoke, Hampshire, UK: MacMillan.

Fisher, I. (1930). *The Theory of Interest.* London: MacMillan.

Friedman, M. (1948). A monetary and fiscal framework for economic stability. *American Economic Review* 38(3):245–264.

Friedman, M. (1957). *A Theory of the Consumption Function.* Princeton, NJ: Princeton University Press.

Fullerton, D., and Rogers, D. L. (1993). *Who Bears the Lifetime Tax Burden?* Washington, DC: Brookings.

Gaffney, M. M. (1971). The property tax is a progressive tax. In *Proceedings of the Sixty-Fourth Annual Conference on Taxation Sponsored by the National Tax Association*, 408–426. Retrieved May 8, 2004, from http://www.schalkenbach.org/library/progressivet.pdf.

Galambos, E. C., and Schreiber, A. F. (1978). *Making Sense Out of Dollars: Economic Analysis for Local Government.* Washington, DC: National League of Cities.

Gale, W. G. (1997). Comment. In *Fiscal Policy: Lessons from Economic Research*, ed. A. J. Auerbach, 313–330. Cambridge, MA: MIT Press.

Gentry, W. M. (1999). Optimal taxation. In *The Encyclopedia of Taxation and Tax Policy*, ed. J. J. Cordes, R. D. Ebel, and J. G. Gravelle. Washington, DC: Urban Institute Press. Retrieved November 13, 2003, from http://www.taxpolicycenter.org/research/Topic.cfm?PubID=100539.

Glennon, D. (1985). An examination of the stability of the gross private saving rate. *Quarterly Journal of Business and Economics* 24(4):44–54.

Goetz, C. J. (1977). Fiscal illusion in state and local finance. In *Budgets and Bureaucrats: The Sources of Government Growth*, ed. T. E. Borcherding, 176–187. Durham, NC: Duke University Press.

Goffman, E. (1974). *Frame Analysis: An Essay on the Organization of Experience.* New York: Harper & Row.

Goldscheid, R. (1958). A sociological approach to problems of public finance (E. Henderson, trans.). In *Classics in the Theory of Public Finance*, ed. R. A. Musgrave and A. T. Peacock, 202–213. New York: MacMillan.

Goolsbee, A. (2000). What happens when you tax the rich? Evidence from executive compensation. *Journal of Political Economy* 108(2):352–378.

Goulder, L. H., and Williams, R. C., III. (1999). *The Usual Excess-Burden Approximation Usually Doesn't Come Close.* National Bureau of Economic Research Working Paper W7034. Cambridge, MA: National Bureau of Economic Research. Retrieved January 19, 2004, from http://www.nber.org/papers/w7034.

Government Accounting Standards Board. (1999). GASB Statement No. 34: Basic Financial Statements—and Management's Discussion and Analysis—for State and Local Governments. Norwalk, C.T.: Government Accounting Standards Board.

Greenwald, B. C., and Stiglitz, J. E. (1986). Externalities in economies with imperfect information and incomplete markets. *Quarterly Journal of Economics* 101:229–264.

Griefer, N. (2002). Pension investment policies: The state of the art. *Government Finance Review* 18(1):36–40.

Hamilton, A., Madison, J., and Jay, J. (1978). *The Federalist or, the New Constitution*. New York: Dutton, Everyman's Library.

Hassett, K. A., and Hubbard, R. G. (2002). Tax policy and business investment. In *Handbook of Public Economics*, ed. A. J. Auerbach and M. Feldstein, 1293–1343. Vol. 3. New York: Elsevier Science.

Hausman, J. A. (1981). Exact consumer's surplus and deadweight loss. *American Economic Review* 71(4):662–676.

Hayter, R. (1997). *The Dynamics of Industrial Location*. New York: Wiley.

Heady, C., and van den Noord, P. (2001). *Tax and the Economy: A Comparative Assessment of OECD Countries*. OECD Tax Policy Studies 6. Paris: Organization for Economic Cooperation and Development.

Heen, M. L. (2000). Reinventing tax expenditure reform: Improving program oversight under the Government Performance and Results Act. *Wake Forest Law Review* 35(4):751–826.

Hicks, J. R. (1940). The valuation of the social income. *Economica* 7:105–124.

Hildreth, W. B., and Miller, G. J. 2002. Debt and the local economy: Problems in benchmarking local government debt affordability. *Public Budgeting and Finance* 22(4):99–113.

Hobson, J. A. (1919). *Taxation in the New State*. London: Methuen.

Hoff, K. (1994). The second theorem of the second best. *Journal of Public Economics* 54(2):223–242.

Hoff, K., and Lyon, A. (1995). Non-leaky buckets: Optimal redistributive taxation and agency costs. *Journal of Public Economics* 58(3):365–390.

Holcombe, R. (1998). The foundations of normative public finance. In *Handbook of Public Finance*, ed. F. Thompson and M. Green, 1–42. New York: Dekker.

Institute on Taxation and Economic Policy. (2004). *Tax Principles: Building Blocks of a Sound Tax System*. Policy Brief 9. Retrieved May 5, 2004, from http://www.itepnet.org/pb9princ.pdf.

Joumard, I. (2001). *Tax Systems in European Union Countries*. Economics Department Working Paper 301. Paris: Organization for Economic Cooperation and Development. Retrieved November 12, 2003, from http://www.olis.oecd.org/olis/2001doc.nsf/linkto/eco-wkp(2001)27.

Kahneman, D., and Tversky, A. (1979). Prospect theory: An analysis of decisions under risk. *Econometrica* 47(2):263–292.

Kaldor, N. (1939). Welfare propositions of economics and interpersonal comparisons of utility. *The Economic Journal* 49(195):549–552.

Kaufman, H. (1956). Emerging conflicts in the doctrines of public administration. *American Political Science Review* 50(4):1057–1073.

Keifer, D. W. (1984). Distributional tax progressivity indexes. *National Tax Journal* 37(4):497–513.

Key, V. O. (1940). The lack of a budgetary theory. *American Political Science Review* 34(6):1137–1140.

Keynes, J. M. (1964). *The General Theory of Employment, Interest, and Money*. New York: Harcourt, Brace Jovanovich.

Kotlikoff, L. J. (1979). Testing the theory of social security and life cycle accumulation. *American Economic Review* 69(3):396–410.

Kotlikoff, L. J. (1988). Intergenerational transfers and savings. *Journal of Economic Perspectives* 2(2):41–58.

Kotlikoff, L. J. (1992). *Generational Accounting: Knowing Who Pays, and When, for What We Spend*. New York: Free Press.

Krugman, P. (2003). Off the wagon. *New York Times*, January 17, p. A27.

Krzyzaniak, M. (1972). The differential incidence of taxes on profits and on factor incomes. *Finanzarchiv* 30(3):464–488.

Laibson, D. I. (1998). Life-cycle consumption and hyperbolic discount functions. *European Economic Review* 42(3–5):861–871.

Laubach, T. (2003). *New Evidence on the Interest Rate Effects of Budget Deficits and Debt.* Finance and Economics Discussion Series Paper 2003-12. Washington, DC: Board of Governors of the Federal Reserve System.

Lewis, V. B. (2001). Toward a theory of budgeting. In *Performance-Based Budgeting*, ed. G. J. Miller, W. B. Hildreth, and J. Rabin, 19–38. Boulder, CO: Westview.

Light, P. C. (1999). *The True Size of Government.* Washington, DC: Brookings.

Light, P. C. (2003). *Fact Sheet on the New True Size of Government.* Washington, DC: Brookings. Retrieved April 29, 2004, from http://www.brook.edu/gs/cps/light20030905.htm.

Lindahl, E. (1958). Just taxation—A positive solution. In *Classics in the Theory of Public Finance*, ed. R. A. Musgrave and A. T. Peacock, 168–176. New York: MacMillan.

Lindert, P. H. (2004). *Growing Public: Social Spending and Economic Growth Since the Eighteenth Century.* Cambridge: Cambridge University Press.

Lipsey, R. G., and Lancaster, K. (1956–1957). The general theory of second best. *Review of Economic Studies* 24(1):11–32.

Little, I. M. D. (1951). Direct versus indirect taxes. *The Economic Journal* 61(243):577–584.

Lizza, R. (2003). The nation. Reform? Republicans reconsider. *New York Times*, January 12, sect. 4:4.

Malthus, T. R. (1964). *Principles of Political Economy, Considered with a View to Their Practical Application.* 2nd ed. New York: A. M. Kelly.

March, James G. (1987). Ambiguity and accounting: The elusive link between information and decision making. In *Accounting and culture,* ed. Barry E. Cushing, 31–49. New York: American Accounting Association.

Marshall, A. (1890). *Principles of Economics.* London: The Macmillan Company.

Martinez-Vazquez, J. (2001, August). *The Impact of Budgets on the Poor: Tax and Benefit Incidence.* Working Paper 01-10. International Studies Program, Andrew Young School of Policy Studies, Georgia State University. Retrieved October 4, 2003, from http://isp-aysps.gsu.edu/papers/ispwp0110.html.

McIntyre, R., Denk, R., Francis, N., Gardner, M., Gomaa, W., Hsu, F., and Simms, R. (2002). *Who Pays? A Distributional Analysis of the Tax Systems in all 50 States.* 2nd ed. Washington, DC: Institute on Taxation and Economic Policy.

McKisack, M. (1959). *The Fourteenth Century, 1307–1399.* Oxford: Clarendon Press.

MacLachlan, F. C. (1999). The Ricardo-Malthus debate on underconsumption: A case study in economic conversation. *History of Political Economy* 31(3):563–574. Retrieved April 25, 2004, from http://muse.jhu.edu/journals/history_of_political_economy/v031/31.3maclachlan.html.

Meade, J. E. (1955). *Trade and Welfare.* London: Oxford University Press.

Mieszkowski, Peter. (1969). Tax incidence theory: The effects of taxes on the distribution of income. *Journal of Economic Literature* 7: 1103–1124.

Mikesell, J. L. (1978). Government decisions in budgeting and taxing: The economic logic. *Public Administration Review* 38(6):511–513.

Mill, J. (1992). *Elements of Political Economy.* London: Routledge Thoemmes.

Mill, J. S. (1899). *Principles of Political Economy.* Rev. ed., 2 vols. New York: Colonial Press.

Miller, D. (1976). *Social Justice.* Oxford: Clarendon Press.

Miller, G. J. (1991). *Government Financial Management Theory*. New York: Dekker.

Miller, Gerald J. (2005). Government fiscal policy impacts. In *Handbook of Public Sector Economics*, Donijo Robbins, ed., 425–521. Boca Raton, FL: Taylor & Francis.

Miller, G. J., and Illiash, I. (2001). Interpreting budgets and budgeting interpretations. Paper delivered at the American Society for Public Administration Conference, Newark, NJ, March 13, 2001.

Miller, G. J., and Robbins, D. (2004). Benefit cost analysis. In *Public Productivity Handbook*, ed. M. Holzer and S.-H. Lee, 405–430. 2nd ed. New York: Dekker.

Modigliani, F., and Brumberg, R. (1954). Utility analysis and the consumption function: An interpretation of cross-section data. In *Post Keynesian Economics*, ed. K. K. Kurihara, 388–436. New Brunswick, NJ: Rutgers University Press.

Mossin, J. (1968). Taxation and risk-taking: An expected utility approach. *Economica* 35(137):74–82.

Murray, Charles A. (1984). *Losing ground: American Social Policy, 1950–1980*. New York: Basic Books.

Musgrave, R. A. (1953a). General equilibrium aspects of incidence theory. *American Economic Review* 43(2, Papers and Proceedings):504–517.

Musgrave, R. A. (1953b). On incidence. *Journal of Political Economy* 61(4):306–323.

Musgrave, R. A. (1985). A brief history of fiscal doctrine. In *Handbook of Public Economics*, ed. A. J. Auerbach and M. Feldstein, 1–59. Vol. 1. New York: Elsevier North-Holland.

Musgrave, R. A., and Musgrave, P. B. (1989). *Public Finance in Theory and Practice*. New York: McGraw Hill.

Musgrave, R. A., and Musgrave, P. B. (1984). *Public Finance in Theory and Practice*. New York: McGraw Hill.

Musgrave, R. A., and Thin, T. (1948). Income tax progression, 1929–48. *Journal of Political Economy* 56(6):498–514.

Musso, J. A. (1998). Fiscal federalism as a framework for government reform. In *Handbook of Public Finance*, ed. F. Thompson and M. Green, 347–396. New York: Dekker.

Ng, Y.-K. (1983). *Welfare Economics*. London: MacMillan.

O'Connor, J. (1973). *The Fiscal Crisis of the State*. New York: St. Martin's Press.

Okun, A. M. (1975). *Equality and Efficiency: The Big Tradeoff*. Washington, DC: Brookings.

Oman, C. (1906). *The Great Revolt of 1381*. Oxford: Clarendon Press.

Organization for Economic Cooperation and Development (OECD). (2009). *Evolutions in Budgetary Practice: Allen Schick and the OECD Senior Budget Officials*. Paris, France: OECD Publishing.

Organization for Economic Cooperation and Development (OECD). (2009). *Revenue Statistics 1965–2008*. Paris: OECD. Retrieved December 13, 2010, from http://dx.doi.org/10.1787/724430327878.

Pareto, V. (1906). *Manual of Political Economy*. 1971 trans. of 1927 ed. New York: Augustus M. Kelley.

Pechman, J. A. (1985). *Who Paid the Taxes, 1966–1985?* Washington, DC: Brookings.

Pigou, A. C. (1928). *The Study of Public Finance*. London: MacMillan.

Postrel, V. (2004). Economic scene: High spending is meant to be a public investment in the nation's infrastructure that pays off for everyone. Does it? *New York Times*, May 20, p. C2.

Poterba, J. M. (2002). Taxation, risk-taking, and household portfolio behavior. In *Handbook of Public Economics*, ed. A. J. Auerbach and M. Feldstein, 1109–1171. Vol. 3. New York: Elsevier Science.

Poterba, J. M. (2004). Taxation and household portfolio behavior. *NBER Reporter*, Spring, pp. 18–20. Retrieved May 29, 2004, from http://www.nber.org/reporter/spring04/poterba.html.

Rabin, J., Miller, G. J., and Hildreth, W. B. (2000). Introduction. In *Handbook of Strategic Management*, ed. J. Rabin, G. J. Miller, and W. B. Hildreth, i–x. 2nd ed. New York: Dekker.

Rabin, M. (1998). Psychology and economics. *Journal of Economic Literature* 36(1):11–46.

Rabin, M. (2000). Diminishing marginal utility of wealth cannot explain risk aversion. In *Choices, Values, and Frames*, ed. D. Kahneman and A. Tversky, 202–208. Cambridge: Cambridge University Press.

Rawls, J. (1971). *A Theory of Justice*. Cambridge, MA: Harvard University Press.

Rawls, J. (1999). *A Theory of Justice*. Rev. ed. Cambridge, MA: Harvard University Press.

Ricardo, D. (1951). *Works and Correspondence: Notes on Malthus's Principles of Political Economy*, ed. Pierro Sraffa with collaboration of M. H. Dobb. Vol. 2. Cambridge: Cambridge University Press and Royal Economic Society.

Romer, C. D., and Romer, D. H. (2002). The evolution of economic understanding and postwar stabilization policy. In *Rethinking Stabilization Policy*, ed. Federal Reserve Bank of Kansas City, 11–78. Kansas City, MO: Federal Reserve Bank.

Rosen, H. S. (1985). *Public Finance*. Homewood, IL: Irwin.

Salamon, L. M., ed. (2002). *The Tools of Government*. Oxford: Oxford University Press.

Samuelson, P. A. (1937). A note on measurement of utility. *Review of Economic Studies* 4(2):155–161.

Sandmo, A. (1985). The effects of taxation on savings and risk taking. In *Handbook of Public Economics*, ed. A. J. Auerbach and M. Feldstein, 265–311. Vol. 1. New York: Elsevier Science.

Sargent, T. J. (1999). *The Conquest of American Inflation*. Princeton, NJ: Princeton University Press.

Sargent, T. J. (2002). Commentary: The evolution of economic understanding and post-war stabilization policy. In *Rethinking Stabilization Policy*, ed. Federal Reserve Bank of Kansas City, 79–94. Kansas City, MO: Federal Reserve Bank.

Say, J.-B. (1855). *A Treatise on Political Economy*, trans. C. R. Prinsep. Philadelphia: Lippincott, Grambo & Co. Retrieved April 25, 2004, from http://www.econlib.org/library/Say/sayT0.html.

Schick, A. (1981). Off-budget expenditure: An economic and political framework. Paper prepared for the Organization for Economic Cooperation and Development, Paris. Quoted in A. Wildavsky (1986), *Budgeting: A Comparative Theory of Budgetary Processes*, 349–350. 2nd rev. ed. New Brunswick, NJ: Transaction Books.

Schick, A. (1986). Controlling nonconventional expenditure: Tax expenditures and loans. *Public Budgeting and Finance* 6(1):3–20.

Schumpeter, J. A. (1954). The crisis of the tax state, trans. W. F. Stolper and R. A. Musgrave. *International Economic Papers* 4:5–38.

Seligman, E. R. A. (1908). Progressive taxation in theory and practice. *American Economic Association Quarterly* 9(4):1–334.

Shirley, Chad, and Winston, C. (2004). Firm inventory behavior and the returns from highway infrastructure investments. *Journal of Urban Economics* 55(2):398–415.

Shoup, C. (1969). *Public Finance*. Chicago: Aldine.

Slemrod, J. (1997). Deconstructing the income tax. *American Economic Review* 87(2, Papers and Proceedings):151–155.

Smith, A. (1776). *An Inquiry into the Nature and Causes of the Wealth of Nations*. London: Ward, Lock & Co., Ltd.

Steuart, J. D. (1767). *An Inquiry into the Principle of Political Economy*. Retrieved January 4, 200, from http://socserv2.socsci.mcmaster.ca/~econ/ugcm/3ll3/steuart/prin.html.

Stevenson, R. W. (2002). Group may estimate effects of tax cuts. *New York Times*, September 17, p. A26.

Stiglitz, J. E. (1969). The effects of income, wealth and capital gains taxation on risk-taking. *Quarterly Journal of Economics* 83(2):262–283.

Stiglitz, J. E. (2000). *Economics of the Public Sector*. 3rd ed. New York: W. W. Norton.

Suits, D. B. (1977). Measurement of tax progressivity. *American Economic Review* 67(4):747–752.

Swank, D., and Steinmo, S. (2002). The new political economy of taxation in advanced capitalist democracies. *American Journal of Political Science* 46(3):642–655.

Taylor, C. L., ed. (1983). *Why Governments Grow: Measuring Public Sector Size*. Beverly Hills, CA: Sage.

Thaler, R. H., and Shefrin, H. M. (1981). An economic theory of self-control. *Journal of Political Economy* 89(2):392–406.

Thurow, L. C. (1971). The income distribution as a pure public good. *Quarterly Journal of Economics* 85(2):327–336.

Tin, J. (2000). Life-cycle hypothesis, propensities to save, and demand for financial assets. *Journal of Economics and Finance* 24(2):110–121.

Traub, S. (1999). *Framing Effects in Taxation: An Empirical Study Using the German Income Tax Schedule*. New York: Physica-Verlag.

Tversky, A., and Kahneman, D. (1974). Judgment under uncertainty: Heuristics and biases. *Science* 185(4157):1124–1131.

Tversky, A., and Kahneman, D. (1981). The framing of decisions and the psychology of choice. *Science* 211(4481):453–458.

U. S. General Accounting Office. (2001). Information on payroll taxes and earned income tax credit noncompliance: Statement of Michael Brostek before the Committee on Finance, U. S. Senate (GAO–01–487T). Washington, DC: GAO.

Vedung, E. (1998). Policy instruments: Typologies and theories. In *Carrots, Sticks and Sermons: Policy Instruments and Their Evaluation*, ed. M.-L. Bemelmans-Videc, R. C. Rist, and E. Vedung, 21–58. New Brunswick, NJ: Transaction Publishers.

Ventry, D. J. (2002). Equity versus efficiency and the U.S. tax system in historical perspective. In *Tax Justice*, ed. J. J. Thorndike and D. J. Ventry, 25–70. Washington, DC: Urban Institute Press.

Wicksteed, P. H. (1910). *The Common Sense of Political Economy, Including a Study of the Human Basis of Economic Law*. London: Macmillan.

Wildavsky, A. (1986). *Budgeting: A Comparative Theory of the Budgetary Process*. 2nd rev. ed. New Brunswick, NJ: Transaction.

Wildavsky, A., and Caiden, N. (2004). *The New Politics of the Budgetary Process*. 5th ed. New York: Pearson Longman.

Yitzhaki, S., and Slemrod, J. (1991). Welfare dominance: An application to commodity taxation. *American Economic Review* 81(3):480–496.

Younger, S. D., Sahn, D. E., Haggblade, S., and Dorosh, P. A. (1999). Tax incidence in Madagascar: An analysis using household data. *World Bank Review* 13(2):303–331.

Chapter 5

Conventional Budgeting with Targets, Incentives, and Performance[1]

Gerald J. Miller, Donijo Robbins, and Jaeduk Keum

The incentive vs. targets trade-off in conventional budgeting is a variation on an economizing logic finance officials use—one trading off budget results with budget control. The issue has interested everyone in government budgeting and finance, from researchers to practitioners to, especially, students. For example, the International Public Management Network recently published a symposium on out-year savings (Jones, 2005). The symposium arose from the question, "Does anyone know of any academic research (either empirical or policy proposal-type) on the issue of what happens to government agency budgets at time $t + 1$ if they achieve costs savings (for example, efficiency savings) at time t?" (Kelman, 2005, p. 139). The blog conversation revealed that little research or experience existed, however tight the logic of savings. The published symposium related a well-known counterlogic—that budget reviewers routinely penalize savings.

The savings incentive problem comes from several sources. Reflecting one of the oldest stories students tell teachers about their experience with government budgets, Barrett and Greene (2002, p. 74) point out: "When a state or local agency has money left at the end of the year, a spendthrift mentality tends to take over." They tell the story of purchases of goods and overtime for employees not already budgeted. Long experience must drive behavior to avoid the budgetary consequences of agency cost savings.

Yet budget theory suggests the incentive for a spendthrift mentality. Since empirical research began to accumulate, some have warned budgeters to "avoid too good results" (Wildavsky, 1964, p. 93). The support for the warning about the reaction to unspent funds by political leaders is not hard to find. Wildavsky quotes a typical budget reviewer as saying, "Since you are doing so well, as we have heard for fifteen minutes, you surely do not need [a bigger budget]" (p. 93). Warren's empirical test (1975) confirms Wildavsky's view. Other budget behavior observers, such as Schick (1978, p. 179), have agreed, pointing out that the "budget process conventionally confronts managers with the uncomfortable risk of a loss of funds if they try to purge inefficiencies from their agencies."

The fact that an agency performs well does not inform the decision maker about the need for additional resources: "Should it be provided with more resources to do an even better job, or should it be cut back on the grounds that its purpose has been achieved and it is no longer needed? ... If a program is doing badly, and showing few results, does this mean it should be terminated, or provided with more resources to do a better job?" (Caiden, 1998, p. 44).

Perhaps the fault lies in poor performance measurement or the believability of performance measures that suggest success, failure, progress, or stagnation. In broader issues of resource allocation, Caiden finds performance somewhat irrelevant in deciding "whether a given sum of money is too little, too much, or just right to preserve a species, operate a system of trauma centers, or monitor or control contagious diseases" (1998, p. 44). Political popularity and the necessity of balancing budgets often become the sole reasons for budget decisions.

Incentives to save can give way to top-down directives to adjust to targets, or a ceiling, for spending. When a professor described target base budgeting, a student reacted, "The politicians are financing the pork barrel!" Students realized that the soft version of a savings incentive could collide with the hard, target version in real-life budgeting. Why would a set of policy makers choose one reform over the other? Thus, the implicit subject of this research is the reason for choice of a retained savings policy over a target base budget discretionary reserve policy.

Current reform efforts strive to strengthen government accountability by tightening the link between budget decisions and government performance. The belief in tightening the link, widely held, rests on the idea that the public, recognizing and understanding the performance-funding linkage and the success professionals in the public sector have in achieving results, will see the public sector, and public managers, as a productive, necessary, and important part of society.

The current performance-based reforms hail from some obvious places. Critics constantly beset governments with the complaint "Why can't you operate like a business?" Many have rebutted the notion behind the question: by the very nature of their work, government leaders aim for efficiency as only one goal among several. The fact remains that taxpayers, even politicians and managers, need a bottom line to tell them quickly whether their decisions are probably right or probably wrong, and whether they are succeeding in their efforts to do their jobs well.

We recognize one major response to much of the taxpayer revolt in the message delivered by the "price of government" wing of the "reinventing government" movement both led by David Osborne. He argues that the movement he leads stems from the public servants' extreme discomfort when they think traditionally and, finding that they do not know how to communicate how well or how poorly their work serves the public, face latent opposition at best and either incipient or fully developed revolt at worst (Osborne and Hutchinson, 2004, pp. 41–61).

One definition of the current problem—no one in government knows how to communicate how well they are doing what they think the citizens want them to do—reflects an insider view. As many have observed, the citizen often is very far away from the issue of concern, and the manager and elected official somewhere between citizen and issue (King, Feltey, and Susel, 1998).

As tax revolts and citizen complaints have mounted, the issues that most citizens, managers, and officials are alarmed about have surfaced in the budget. The budget directly or indirectly reflects every issue, with a power to force action in the direction citizens' desire. Therefore, a second definition of the current problem emerges and reflects an outsider view: Does the budget instill trust and confidence in how leaders spend citizens' money? How well has budgeting not only met professional standards of accountability, but also achieved government's broader obligations?

The present performance-based reforms have focused attention more than ever on allocating discretion in budgeting. Sharing information about what governments do well, through performance measurement and reporting, can go a long way in reducing cynicism (Berman, 1997). Broader and deeper participation in trading off various goals and means to achieve them, as well as in measuring progress made as principals allocate resources, will yield better decisions and a sharing of risks among citizens, public managers, and elected officials. It is not surprising, however, that many, if not most, decision makers find it difficult to gain and even more difficult to analyze and apply as they want performance and efficiency savings information.

It is reasonable to assume, therefore, that each reform promises decision makers productivity increases and actual dollar savings. Given this assumption, this study seeks to answer a central research question: Which of these reforms does a seasoned public manager use and why? To do so, we begin by providing the impetus for the research, the performance reforms, and the model in its entirety.

Movements toward the Performance-Based Reforms

The current reform efforts in the United States reflect similar concerns in the private sector. The private sector model of budgeting takes a definite input-output-outcome form (Lazere, 1998; Churchill, 1984; Hax and Majluf, 1984; Knight, 1981; Trapani, 1982). A similar picture develops in the operation of the Government Performance and Results Act of 1993 (Radin, 1998). With these performance plans, "Congress intended … to establish a direct annual link between plans and budgets" (GAO,

1999, p. 3) and to capture the long-range implication of choices and decisions with new methods of recognizing and measuring transactions in the budget (GAO, 2000; see also GASB, 1999).

Reforms have emerged through state and local government reforms in the National Advisory Council on State and Local Budgeting (1997). According to their last major review, a budget should clearly define policy direction, translate taxes and revenues received into concrete levels of service, show consequences of increases or decreases in service and communicate this to stakeholders, facilitate control over expenditures, motivate and give feedback to employees, and evaluate employee and organization performance and make adjustments.

Other reform stories have appeared in the literature as expenditure control budgets or the so-called entrepreneurial budgets found in Schick's research in British Commonwealth and Scandinavian countries (1997).

These private and public sector examples serve as models. The models lead to a synthesis expressed in our own model. What the models may be interpreted to mean is either a mixture of different reforms or a muddle of piecemeal reforms titled with a vivid metaphor, performance budgeting. Given the history of reform movements in the United States at all levels of government, we may ask: How is this reform similar to the past?

Larkey and Devereux (1999, p. 167) categorize past reforms in five different ways. Budget process reforms, with their emphasis on economic analysis of costs and benefits or marginal utility, especially the Planning, Programming, and Budgeting System (PPBS) and zero-based budgeting (ZBB), belong to the rationalizing reforms category. Additional elements include techniques related to planning, relative value comparisons, and productivity analysis. Ad hoc norms—budget balance, comprehensiveness, and annularity—among performance-based reforms arise from what Larkey and Devereux call decisional efficiency, primarily the savings in time and effort that come with decentralization, and feasible comparisons, the stimulation of competition or cooperation, as appropriate, among agencies in solving particular problems. Democratizing reforms like freedom of information and sunshine laws come from the wider scope of accountability problems the reforms try to tackle to yield greater stakeholder and citizen participation and involvement. The line item veto is one of a number of reforms to shift power. These reforms entail broad decentralization of power over budgets, implicit incentives to reallocate funds from lower- to higher-priority programs, and the retention of savings when improvements in efficiency provide them. Finally, performance-based reforms produce a reversal of the traditional reform emphasis on increasing input controls to provide greater output controls. Thus, performance-based reforms clearly signal a massive effort to reform government, to become more rational, professional, democratic, authoritative, and honest.

The present concern for results or performance is not a muddle, we argue. Performance builds on the past while contributing something new. According to Cothran (2001, p. 158), later reforms kept parts of earlier reforms, with the later ones containing "performance measures from performance budgeting, functional categories from program budgeting, negotiation of objectives from management by objectives, and ranking of objectives from zero-base budgeting." Later reforms, Cothran said, "are generally simpler, more streamlined, and require less paperwork and analysis." More line manager discretion and greater emphasis on accountability also mark the new contribution by later reforms. The new budgeting culture stresses more manager initiative and less bureaucratic reaction or inertia. Cothran observes centralized authority being traded for results.

True to our own view as well as that observed by Schick among Scandinavian and Commonwealth national governments (2001a) and related in a general, comparative context by Pollitt and Bouckaert (2000), Cothran reports reforms as trading details for outcomes and often for control of aggregate resources. To put it more simply, leaders want results and control over spending totals. Results justify spending levels, but control over spending totals also permits control of the politics related to both broad spending priorities and tax regimes. Leaders may be willing to trade micromanagement of work methods and program choices for control of the totals. Work methods and program choices leave lower-level managers responsible for the results leaders know less about how to achieve. The decision: control the totals; delegate the choices of means to get results.

Interrelations among Incentives, Certification, and Targets

The review of movements toward performance-based reforms reveals three major budget reforms that have competed over the last two decades in using or ignoring performance information: an incentives approach, a certification approach, and a spending target approach. All three have tried to connect budgeting with larger efforts called either managing for results or expenditure control. The model we try to understand comes from "trade the details for the totals" scheme based on these three approaches.

Because roots for aggregate control lie in target base budgeting (TBB), that form of budgeting, one that may have come into being as early as 1929 in Berkeley, California, may work as precedent (Buck, 1929; Rubin, 1998, pp. 57–59). We call this the spending target approach. In Cincinnati, Ohio, for example, the target approach gave the legislative body a significant role in allocating, initially 10% of the revenue estimates for the coming fiscal year among competing proposals from departments for new programs. The approach forced reallocation of the remaining 90% among existing programs (Wenz and Nolan, 1982). Forced savings in Cincinnati led to innovation.

A management-oriented incentive system based on retained savings or even greater discretion lies at the other end of a continuum based on decentralization. In the event of retained savings, agencies would be allowed to keep their savings rather than returning it to the general fund. The savings retained could be used for bonuses for management and employees, training, technology upgrades, or other general services conducted by the agency.

Greater discretion has a different appeal. Klay argues: "In addition to recommending retained savings, [some have] recommended greater degrees of freedom from restrictive controls (that is, awarding lump-sum appropriations) to reward well-managed agencies. Their proposal deserves close attention, as it may be more politically feasible than the retained-savings strategy" (2001, pp. 221–222). Savings, according to Klay, leads to efficiency and effectiveness.

The hinge lies in the measurement of performance, the trade made by central agency staff with subordinate bureau managers. The certification approach designed by Maricopa County, Arizona, for example, required the Internal Audit Department (IAD) to perform ongoing independent evaluations of departmental performance measure collection methods, accuracy, and reporting. Upon completing these evaluations, the IAD assigns certification ratings and reports whether performance measures are relevant, timely, reliable, understandable, and verifiable (Tate, 2003, pp. 6–8). The certification approach leads to accountability, higher-quality communication to stakeholders, and perhaps greater trust in government. Budget decision makers reading the performance information that accompanied budget requests might have greater confidence in the veracity of what they read.

Perhaps the dynamic is some connection between performance levels and the decision about targets, as below:

TBB → performance measures (PM) → rewards based on measures

The system connects by linking all three:

TBB → funding based on level of service → measured by PM
→ linked to rewards and future budget targets

The latter concept's funding-service connection may be implicit in many ideas, but the connection seldom gets the attention and technical explanation needed to understand how anyone connects the two.

Feit (2003) confirms the existence of such a dynamic at least in part. He summarizes the State of Minnesota's transportation department (MnDOT) transition to performance measures and its attempt to link performance management (PM) to funding. The department followed four key criteria for a PM system. Feit (2003, p. 39) describes the requirements:

1. It must be clear from the start that the objective is to improve performance.
2. All top-level managers must give the implementation strong initial and constant support.
3. Funding must be tied to level of service by service type.
4. The reward system must be tied to performance results based on objective evidence.

In Minnesota the "objective [is] to measure, track and evaluate whether customer needs and public goals are being met throughout the state with the most efficient use of resources," according to Feit (2003, p. 40). Furthermore, the Minnesota transportation managers ask themselves, "Why we are doing this?" The answer came in the form of a list (Feit, 2003, p. 40):

1. Provide information on which to base key investment decisions;
2. Enable customers and stakeholders to communicate with Mn/DOT about their choices and priorities;
3. Guide employees and partners in focusing on resources, time, energy, and creativity, on the most important work—the focus of our measures;
4. Use performance measures to identify and define gaps between customer/stakeholder expectations and actual Mn/DOT performance; and
5. Target process improvement areas for better product and service delivery.

The result? Feit reported that the department managers found it difficult to get agreement on the measures. Therefore, the department hired a consultant who created "performance dashboards." Simple and easy for everyone to understand, the 45 dashboards were red, amber, and green—but also blue, representing "too much performance"—and 100 performance measures replaced the standard data tables. The dashboard display provided a comment section where the department managers explained the variances or why the department had not achieved the goals. The dashboard idea got top-level management support.

The budget managers next tried to fund services based on the level of need. Need came from customers; therefore Mn/DOT managers conducted market research that "identified the following key customer segments: commuters; carriers, shippers, emergency vehicle operators, farmers, personal travelers, community and neighborhood groups" (Feit, 2003, p. 42). Market research revealed that customers had a long-range view as well as immediate needs. In the long view, customers valued "improving heavily traveled routes between cities; providing funds for local governments; developing a long-range, 20-year, transportation plan; and [the lack of information] about safety related issues." The near-term issues and services of concern to customers were "plowing, sanding, and salting; maintaining roads and bridges; building roads and bridges; removing debris from roadways; posting signs; maintaining lighting, guard rails, and pavement striping; and communicating road and traffic conditions" (Feit, 2003, p. 43). Not rocket science: the market research gave a sense of focus to activities by forcing priorities among a laundry list of needs.

The dashboards underlie decisions on service levels. Service levels connect to funding. The entire set of connections, backward or forward looking as the case may be, are service levels → workload levels → staffing levels → support levels associated with staffing (materials, equipment, services, support staff, overhead) → rewards → budget funding. Despite these linkages in Minnesota, a last issue

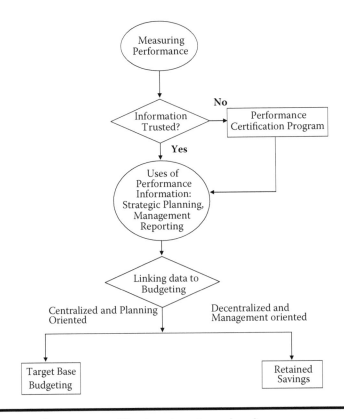

Figure 5.1 Performance certification, targets, and savings.

remained at the time of Feit's 2003 article—linking the reward system to performance results based on objective evidence.

The conceptual links we draw and the Minnesota case results led us to a general model. The diagram in Figure 5.1 illustrates the interrelationships among four components of managing for a results system: (1) performance measures, (2) the quality of data collected, (3) multiple uses of performance information, and (4) balance between centralized control over goals and decentralized incentives.

Performance-based resource allocations must require the identification of performance measures and performance indicators. Generally, the following types of performance measures are suggested: input, workload, outputs, outcomes, efficiency, and effectiveness. In addition, these types of measures must be converted into discrete indicators supporting data collected on a regular basis.

Once performance measures are identified and data for these measures are collected, the focus moves to the quality control issue. It is important to note that performance information is worthy only if decision makers trust the quality of the data (Tate, 2003). Although program managers are principally responsible for the control over the quality of performance data, there is always a possibility that the data might be manipulated, exaggerated, or intentionally concealed. Thus, mechanisms are needed to ensure the quality of performance data collected (Hatry, 1999, p. 216). In practice, however, this is often overlooked (Tate, 2003).

In addition to the issue of quality control over performance data, the use of performance measures is another critical issue. According to Schick (1990), performance measures may be more easily applied if the uses of performance measures are not limited to resource allocation but extended to internal management, strategic plans, and accountability. Indeed, these measures may be more valuable if they are used as a tool for evaluating the extent to which government operates efficiently, how fully the objectives of government programs and activities are achieved, and whether individuals in government are held accountable for the results of their work.

Finally, recent budgetary reforms, trying to link performance information to resource allocation, have employed two devices in order to make government accountable for results: central control of goals and decentralization of means. Policy makers in government want to control total expenditures, and priorities for public services they provide. In order to succeed, policy makers demand that departmental objectives be listed and ranked as well as specific indicators developed to measure the achievement of such objectives. Once policy makers have made such decisions, they seek to attain those ends through decentralized means. The decentralized means intend to motivate public managers by giving them considerably more discretion over how they spend their money. Such incentives include setting and transferring priorities among expenditure items within departments or transferring money from operations to capital expenditures, sharing or carrying over year-end surpluses, and even paying employees for the work with gain sharing. Cothran argues, "Centralization and decentralization can go together" (p. 158).

Our primary research question focuses on the model's portrayal of a choice between targets and incentives, both aimed toward savings. We also want to know the role of performance measures, their certification, and their impact on the targets vs. incentives choice. Therefore, our questions were

1. Do performance measure certification, targets, and incentives exist in any budget system?
2. If some elements appear, how do they relate?

The Research

Research to find answers to the research questions rested on a series of focus groups and instrumented interviews of seasoned public managers and decision makers. Our major focus of this research is to confirm the existence of our model further and to answer a central research question: Which of these reforms does a seasoned public manager use and why?

Investigating these questions involved a three-step process. First, a focus group was convened involving twenty-eight seasoned public managers from state government in New Jersey who provided the insiders' view on targets, performance reforms, and retained savings. Second, we analyzed department responses to a survey administered by the State of Washington's Office of Financial Management on its retained savings program. Finally, using the information we gathered from the focus groups and the Washington survey, we created our own survey, the survey on local government financial management tools. The survey consisted of twenty-four questions focusing on target base budgeting, retained savings, and performance measures and certification.

The survey was distributed via email using an interactive form where respondents could simply check the appropriate box or type their responses. We developed a population of fifty-four U.S. cities by determining which cities have developed citizen-driven or comparative performance measurement programs, expenditure control budgeting reform programs or retained savings programs. Of the fifty-four cities, eight responded and formed the pilot study group, a group neither too large nor too small to help ground research questions and refocus the research project to fruitful questions. In addition to the survey, we conducted two phone interviews to probe more deeply. Although the number of responses is low, the qualitative data collected through all the steps—the focus group, state survey, and local government survey—are robust.

Research Findings

The answers to the research questions appeared in each venue we searched, the focus group, the Washington State government reports, and the local government survey. The findings appear in that order below.

The Focus Group

In a focus group of twenty-eight seasoned managers from state and local governments in New Jersey, we asked whether their organizations had a retained savings program. Specifically, we asked whether "retained savings already exists in [your] organization in various forms, from formally accounted for reserves to information overestimates of spending." About 40% of the group did recognize that their organization pursued retained savings. Then, we asked whether the retained savings required certification informally or formally. Almost three-fourths of those with organization retained savings said budget authorities required proof, and almost two-thirds of the entire focus group said evidence should be required. Said one person, "The agency should be able to show how it delivered its program economically, thereby resulting in the savings." Another noted, "Retained savings does, indeed, depend on the ability of the agency to account for the incurred savings [and] occurs because the budgeting consists of ... performance targets [including] indicators [that] are identified and analyzed."

When asked about the necessity of merit pay, individual sharing in these retained savings, the group turned negative. Of those having retained savings programs, only about one-eighth thought individual shares necessary to gain savings. In the focus group as a whole, one-fourth thought individual shares were required as an incentive. One individual noted, "Government retained savings should never be used to award monetary bonuses. Public administrators are evaluated on their ability to appropriately develop and spend what they have budgeted."

We probed the role of certified performance information in producing savings, asking whether high-performing organizations, certified or not, were those that produced savings. Only two of the twenty-eight members of the group thought performance led inevitably to savings. In fact, one-half of the group thought the performance information "could actually provide the rationale for increased spending." One focus group member argued, "If data are accurate and all systems are working well, then there may be a 'comfort' level with allowing increased spending, ... [but] there must be a level of openness and trust among the players with everyone's goal being the same."

The discussion in the group focused on where the three reforms—incentives, certification, and targets—would lead. We wanted to know what reform would allocate discretion in a decisive way toward achieving control of aggregate spending and whether any were helpful in regaining public trust. Targets, the group said, give top decision makers more control. Moreover, targets hold the greatest power to control aggregate spending. However, performance measure certification and the retained savings incentive seemed most likely or preferable in building trust in government, participants said.

The Washington State Government Case

The state government of Washington, an exemplar of an intelligent approach to budgeting in a time of distrust of government and tax revolts (Osborne and Hutchinson, 2004), provides us with evidence on retained savings. The authors' conceptual overview of budgeting included four provisions. The first was an analysis of revenue levels of a group of similar governments, city, county, school, or state. Taxpayer analysis followed, and budgeters tried to find the level at which taxpayer resistance might occur within the comparative analysis. The second provision required the budget managers to determine what goods and services citizens wanted and at what level of intensity. The service priorities, third, got funding down to the level of taxpayer resistance. Finally, Osborne and Hutchinson described methods of purchasing and contracting to gain the most efficient services at the "price citizens are willing to pay" (p. 13).

We looked at the state Office of Financial Management's *Report of Fiscal Year 2005 Savings Incentive Account Expenditures*. This study reported a survey of department participants in the state's savings program. The survey responses supplement our other work to gain a deeper understanding of the retained savings incentive idea as applied in Washington State government (State of Washington, 2005).

The Washington retained savings plan grew from Governor Locke's "initiative to promote efficiency in agency spending and to help support public schools," an initiative beginning in 1997. In that plan, "agencies are credited with one half of all state general fund state (GF-S) savings not related to entitlement or other targeted spending authority." The savings that remain after the credit "are directed to the Education Savings Account, 10% of which is transferred to Higher Education for distinguished professorships, the graduate fellowship trust fund, and the college faculty award trust fund." The remaining Education Savings Account transfer "may be appropriated for common school construction and educational technology." The legislature could not further reappropriate the credits in a future fiscal year. The savings over the seven years following the plan were $34.4 million, and by FY2005, "agencies had used $21.1 million of the $34.3 million." The ground rules for the plan called for the funds to be used for "one-time activities that improve the quality, efficiency, and effectiveness of customer service in agencies [and not] to create new or expanded services or to incur ongoing obligations."

Their findings suggest that the incentive effects were imperceptible. According to the report, "Most agencies indicated that the existence of the [plan] had no direct effect on end-of-fiscal-year spending patterns, although it was recognized as a useful management tool" (p. 4). Of the 62 agencies surveyed, 48 (77%) said the plan had no effect and 14 (23%) said that the plan did have an effect (pp. 20–25).

Of those who said yes, the claims varied. For example, the Columbia River Gorge Commission respondents reported, "Throughout the year, we have managed our spending with the savings incentive fund in mind. We have slowly built a 'bank' of savings that we intend to use for training, technology improvements, and work process improvements that have not been funded in our agency budget. The bank is a result of the ongoing efforts of staff to implement cost-saving measures" (p. 20).

The Washington Department of Ecology reported, "Our focus was on carrying out the purpose and objectives of the funded programs, rather than on saving money. But as the end of the biennium was nearing, we had the ability in some activities to spend federal funds, dedicated funds, or [plan funds]. Although the potential for rebates did not cause a reduction in activity, nor did it cause a net savings, it did give us an incentive in some cases to spend federal or dedicated funds rather than [savings credited to the Department]" (p. 21).

The military department commented that the savings reinforced strategic plan provisions. The survey response stated, "The ability to make one-time quality improvements and/or provide incentives to staff with … savings is very beneficial to a small agency like the military department. The opportunity to carry the unspent savings account forward for multiple years gives us a chance to have sufficient dollars to take on a significant one-time expense that promotes the key part of our strategic plan" (p. 23).

Emergencies prompted some uses in small agencies, such as the Public Disclosure Commission (PDC). The commission reported that, having "very limited fiscal flexibility, [savings] rebates are critical to the agency's ability to manage unanticipated expenses. Having a Savings Incentive Account means the PDC has the wherewithal to fund prudent technology improvements, replace failed equipment, and pay for performance-related employee training beyond the modest amount allotted in the operating budget.... PDC staff intentionally left nearly $40,000 unspent in fiscal year 2005 in order that the rebate would be available for additional technology services in fiscal year 2006, if necessary" (pp. 23–24).

Despite the Public Disclosure Commission's admission of altered spending patterns, the report found little widespread alteration. The report found, "Actual fiscal year GF-S expenditures (by month) for the nine years of the program's existence do not demonstrate any expenditure patterns that can be solely attributed to the Savings Incentive Program" (p. 4).

The Washington practice on retained savings found greater impacts among small agencies. The findings also suggest a gain in financial flexibility, leading perhaps to greater risk taking and innovation.

A Survey of U.S. City Budget Officials

Finally, our survey and instrumented interviews of city finance officials, usually budget officers, followed. The eight cities varied in size from Los Angeles to Sandy, Oregon. The group represented the three major governing structures found in the United States. Table 5.1 presents the descriptions of the responding cities.

The interviews showed us that no city in our group uses all three budget reforms as a single formal system. From this set of interviews, we can conclude that the elements of the model exist, but not in the tandem way we portray. Two cities rely on both retained savings and targets: Boise, Idaho, and Sandy, Oregon. Formal reliance on performance measures, certified or not, does exist, but seems to be the option when neither retained savings nor targets are used.

As Table 5.2 portrays, where there is TBB, there are performance measures (PMs) as often as not. No one would say for certain that PMs are linked directly to allocations. The weak, if existing, linkage may explain why TBB exists to begin with; PM may seem to legitimate the TBB process. Budgeters could use the PM as a way to reduce the targets—observing that departments do not live up to potential; department heads could use PM to advocate for more money. In the end, it does not matter, the target will prevail. Also, exemptions from the target are common.

Table 5.1 City Descriptions, Instrumented Interviews on Retained Savings, Performance Measures, and Targets in Budgeting for Selected U.S. Cities

City (Reputation)	Form of Government	Net Assets	Current Year Revenue	Number of Departments	Number of Employees	Population
Austin, Texas (CITISTAT)	Council—manager	$3.8 billion	$2.0 billion	26	11,380	672,001
Boise, Idaho (RS)	Mayor—council	$892 million	$300 million	12	1,515	190,117
Dixon, California (ECB)	Council—manager	$158 million	$33.6 million	10	92	20,100
Lake Forest, Illinois (TBB)	Council—manager	$232 million	$54 million	10	214	20,057
Los Angeles, California (RS)	Strong mayor—council[a]	$1.9 billion	$5.95 billion	39	38,500	3,819,915
Salina, Kansas (TBB)	Council—manager	$101 million	$60.0 million	13	502	45,833
Sandy, Oregon (RS)	Council—manager	$20.8 million	$13.0 million	7	48	5,385
Urbandale, Iowa (CDGP)	Weak mayor—council[b]	$85 million	$28.5 million	15	250	31,868

[a] Mayor is elected chief executive, department heads report to the mayor, and mayor proposes budget.

[b] City manager by ordinance.

Note: All cities have full-service governments. CDGP, citizen-driven government performance; CITISTAT, acronym for management systems using strategic planning, results measurement, and intense, weekly monitoring of agency performance; ECB, expenditure control budgeting; RS, retained savings; TBB, target base budgeting.

Table 5.2 Interview Results on Retained Savings, Performance Measures, and Target Base Budgeting for Selected U.S. Cities

City	Use Retained Savings	Use Performance Measures	Use Target Base Budget
Austin, Texas	Depends on the department and its fund location. Used for bonuses, one-time expenses.	Always. Sometimes used to assess savings; sometimes measures are audited. Allocations seem to be less dependent on measures.	Never.
Boise, Idaho	Yes. Savings divided: portions go back to the general fund, bonuses for all city employees, or department keeps a portion. Combination depends on overall financial position of the general fund.	Sometimes, but never used to assess savings and never audited. Not tied to allocations.	Sometimes the council sets aside a designated dollar amount but departments are never tied to a proportion of the budget. The target is determined by program type, revenue elasticity, and department performance. Exempt items include collectively bargained amounts and mandated expenditures.
Lake Forest, Illinois	No. Savings that occur are lost and go to either a rainy day fund or the general fund.	Never.	Always. Council designates amounts and departments receive a proportion of total budget. Target is determined by last year's budget and judgment on amount needed for exempt items. Exempt items include fixed costs, grant funded expenditures, and mandated expenditures.

Table 5.2 (Continued) Interview Results on Retained Savings, Performance Measures, and Target Base Budgeting for Selected U.S. Cities

Los Angeles, California	No. In the general fund, saving that does occur is lost and goes to either a rainy day fund or unrestricted fund balance. However, most are transferred to departments with shortfalls. Departments with savings during the year in other funds, particularly capital projects, can request to spend those monies during the following year.	Sometimes used, although the new mayor plans to focus more on measures. Currently, they are sometimes used to assess savings and are sometimes audited. Allocations less dependent on measures. Workload measures are used for staffing purposes.	Always. Council designates amounts but departments never receive a proportion of total budget. Target is determined by last year's budget and judgment about amount needed to cover all amounts not connected to grants. Performance is also a factor, but not specifically for fee-supported departments. Exempt items include collectively bargained amounts, mandated expenditures, and off-budget grants.
Salina, Kansas	No. Saving that does occur is lost and goes to the general fund.	Never.	Sometimes the council sets aside a designated dollar amount, but departments are never tied to a proportion of the budget. The target is determined by last year's budget and the judgment about the amount needed to cover all amounts but mandated expenditures.

Sandy, Oregon	Yes. Whole amount goes back to the department for out-year, one-time expenditures.	Sometimes. City never requires an audit of measures, but sometimes uses them to assess savings. Allocations seem less dependent on performance.	Always used a targeted proportion of the total budget, but council never sets aside a designated amount. The target depends on last year's budget and judgment on amount needed to cover exempt items, such as fixed costs, unions, grants, mandated expenditures, and inflation.
Urbandale, Iowa	No. Saving is lost and goes to the general fund. The whole amount may go to the department for out-year special purchases as long as the agency does not suffer a reduction in service, and the savings must not be due to the deferral of legitimate expenditure obligations.	Always requires departments to use performance measures, used to assess savings, and are sometimes audited. Department performance is always linked to next year's allocations. Increased (decreased) performance does not imply an automatic increase (decrease) in next year's allocations.	Never.
Dixon, California	Calls budget and expenditure control budget with lump-sum allocations. Transfers allowed among line items (for example, salaries and others) within fiscal year.	Never.	Informal use of targets, always basing a department allocation on a previous proportion of the budget, but only sometimes allowing the council to set aside a designated dollar amount to appropriate for new programs.

However, as the size of government grows, TBB fits less well. For example, if personnel costs take up 70% of the budget and most of this is mandated from collective bargaining—unions, contracts, the proportion of health care and pension costs—there is little room for TBB to make a difference. If they use TBB, the cities seem less likely to use retained savings (RS), although we have to be careful not to make leaping associations with such a small number in our group. Sandy, Oregon, is the exception here—they use TBB to set the proportion of the budget but do not designate additional amounts above the targets for innovation projects, if the above target amounts appear in revenues collected. Perhaps, this light touch with targets explains why the city uses RS: any additional funding will have to depend on the department's ability to save.

The City of Austin provides a generalizable treatment of savings. According to the city's respondent:

> What happens to year-end savings depends on whether or not the department [operates as an] enterprise fund [or is part of the general fund]. Savings for enterprise funds, such as aviation, convention center, water and electric utilities, drainage, and solid waste services, drop into their funds' ending balances. [The fund balances] can be re-appropriated the next year [based on proposals from the enterprise]. Some of these enterprise funds also distribute part of the savings to their departmental employees as end of year bonuses. Sometimes, prior year savings in enterprise funds can offset the need for future increases in service fees. For the general fund, savings [follow fund balance policies]. In FY 2006, all city employees received a one-time two percent bonus with [surplus] funding, but this [did not relate to] departmental savings within the general fund.

The Austin general fund savings policy comes in two provisions. The first provision states that "unreserved fund balances in excess of required amount shall normally be used to fund capital items in the operating and capital budget. However, if projected revenue in future years is not sufficient to support projected requirements, an unreserved ending balance may be budgeted to achieve structural balance." The structural balance might be a transfer to cover an account that has grown beyond normally forecast general revenue allocations.

The default provision, covering all instances, whether capital and structural imbalance needs exist or not, is the permanent fund balance. Austin's policy states that "at the end of each fiscal year, any excess revenue received in that year and any unspent appropriations at the end of that year will be deposited into the budget stabilization reserve. The reserve may be appropriated to fund capital or other one-time costs, but such appropriation will not normally exceed one-third of the total amount of the reserve, with the other two-thirds reserved for budget stabilization in future years." The Austin policy reflects a consensus among all but two cities in the group we interviewed.

Discussion and Conclusions

Our original research question asked whether a certification-target-incentive system appears in states and localities in the United States and, if so or not, what parts of the system seasoned public managers preferred to achieve various goals. Our findings reveal that parts of the system have appeared. Our expectation was a convergence among budget reform trajectories (Pollitt and Bouckaert, 2000, pp. 64–71). We did not find a convergence but a choice. Five cities used targets with no carryover (savers). Two cities had targets with carryover (block budgets). One city used block budgeting with benchmarked performance measures (performance informed). One city used performance measures and retained savings but no targets. One city centers all effort on performance measurement, employs no targets, and allows no retained savings.

In no case, however, did we find the system our original reading of reform behavior led us to think possible, one linking targets, performance measurement, and retained savings. We expected to find a locality in which targets represented performance measured in money. Instead we found a major divide in classifying budget systems. On one side we found those aimed toward savings in different ways. On the other side of the divide, we found performance management systems that seemed to drive budgeting, those budget systems in Austin, Texas, and Urbandale, Iowa.

Performance management systems benefit from the traditions in pro-positive government normative thought. However, a substantial group in our small sample used savings-oriented budget systems, suggesting the pro-business train of thought among government budget and finance norms. We found savings as forced savings programs—line item budget ceilings—or savings related to both decentralized decision making about the employment of funds and narrow and well-defined targets. Savings, then, had two meanings. In an incentives sense, savings means motivation to reallocate. Reallocation in mild forms takes place in our eight locality groups and in the State of Washington. These savings, however, are budget process reforms in which loosened financial control leads to strategic use of savings and strengthened administrator discretion. The agencies often reported using organization savings as a strategic organization and management aid in the use of funds to keep key employees and to fund capital projects. Little evidence exists that agencies use savings as an incentive to build slack into their management systems or to pay bonuses to employees. We found actual resistance among managers to pay for performance; "Doing one's job is not a reason for paying a bonus," one focus group member argued. This resistance may arise because experience tells managers that performance means only average achievement or work performance that did not fall below expectations. Defining performance in a way to signify excellence, innovation, merit, or effort beyond expectations may yield more clarity or insight. Common sense leads to opposed views and normative theories provide no guidance; in fact, two normative ideas, one pro-positive government and one pro-business, clash. The normative and descriptive theories connecting job performance and pay confuse easily rather than guide human resources research, much less budgeting research.

In the narrower sense of savings as a protection of the tax rate, we found wide use of top-down expense targets. In no case did we find top-down targets used in conjunction with certification of performance. We wondered why because targets unconnected to measurable efforts have little use in managing performance. The most common meaning of budget targets, in fact, refers to contracts for performance in which some effort is made to develop a cost for a preferred level of goods and services agencies will provide, resembling health care cost accounting or "output-purchase budgeting" (Serritzlew, 2006). The budget becomes a contract, and both budgeting and management include considerable effort to monitor performance and apply progressive pressure toward reaching targets (Scheps, 2000).

This research reveals the opinions public managers have about integrating budgeting with management. First, a board of directors model may allow a stronger role for budgets, one we called the protection of the tax rate model above. This radical model invests ultimate accountability in the governing board. The board has a strong incentive to control budgets and management through resource control—the tax rate—approximating target base budgeting: establishment of ceilings, restricting within-fiscal-year transfers without board approval, and creating board institutions for monitoring and auditing costs rather than performance auditing. A variation on the board of directors model is the adoption of market-type or business-like mechanisms: strategic planning, transaction cost analysis of implementation of strategies by comparing public and private service delivery, asset sales, and government downsizing. In our small pilot group sample, we found no evidence of this radical, market-type model's adoption.

Second, a checks and balances system may allow budget decisions to check and balance management decisions, and top managers allow the two systems to exist side by side. The best example is one in which managers and budgeters have competing interests and incentives. The traditional hierarchical organization strengthens competition between management and budget concerns (Golembiewski, 1964). This centralized organization forces a comprehensive integration at the top manager level at the end rather than the beginning of budget formulation, and it forces substantial efforts to monitor and compel corrective action during the work year. The scorecard question—"Am I doing well or badly?"—displaces problem solving and work to connect outputs with results.

Third, a management system may integrate budgeting with other resource systems such as personnel and technology in employing and allocating resources. This decentralized, responsibility center model of performance budgeting requires strong, decentralized management, and a top manager who prefers to yield integration of staff at the organization apex to the location of staff expertise in the unit having the responsibility for producing some output. Each responsibility center manager has control over the organization resource elements and expertise necessary to produce the output demanded.

Only in the responsibility center model of management and budget do we find a meaningful role for management information in budgets. That is, the new "targets" or performance contracts have more management than financial content—risk sharing, relationship building, feedback, progressive pressure, trust, and goodwill. The model assumes stable resources, a strategic approach to resource employment, and a diminished role for managers in finding constituent and governing board allies to support an increase in budget share. Central control consists of strategy, work plan milestones, and progressive pressure to reach or exceed the milestones.

Our findings suggest that state and locality performance budgeting falls between the traditional checks and balances system and the responsibility center, the second and third clusters described above. Decentralization of means and centralization of control over the totals in budgets have occurred in important but still minor ways. Guarding against the "take the money and run" behavior of agencies receiving devolved functions can define budget office behavior. Investment in performance management systems is the vanguard, rather than the commonplace. Moreover, state and local governments that use performance budgeting do not dismiss both line item budgeting and the nature of negotiation in the formation of budget among legislative body, executive branch, and others. Among our focal localities, there are a number of exempt items that do not belong to performance targets. These exempt items are still monitored and negotiable. In this sense of items inside or outside the target, the localities depend on the contractual nature of their budgeting.

Commonplace budgeting following the traditional approach we describe above does have a savings focus and has developed in some places as a complement rather than competitor in management decision making. Targets, probably loose ones, often yield savings or fund balances. Financial policies and organization strategy guide the use of these fund balances. The general fund, because its size is a function of the tax rate, gets the most severe scrutiny and control. Enterprise and capital funds policies give managers flexibility in comparison to the general fund. The flexibility comes with less scrutiny and a tighter connection among revenues, spending, and management.

Which savings approach is helpful in satisfying the norms of budgeting? We use the norms suggested by Wildavsky (2001, pp. 96–97) and Schick (1997). According to Wildavsky, budgeting serves norms that include accountability, control, continuity for planning, flexibility for the economy, and change for policy evaluation. He argues that no budgetary process can satisfy all norms simultaneously. Schick's new functions of budgeting include fiscal discipline, allocative efficiency, and technical efficiency (Schick, 1997). Table 5.3 plots the traditional management-budget integration against the responsibility center version and the findings from our pilot sample of localities.

Our findings support the synthesis that most seasoned public budgeters have two major normative criteria for the allocation of public resources. One norm holds that leaders should allocate public resources in light of the achievement of the missions or purposes that they are intended to further. This we think represents the pro-positive government view. The other criterion holds that these resources must

Table 5.3 Budget Found in Traditional Practice: Responsibility Centers and Practices Found in This Research Compared by Normative Criteria for Budgets

Purposes	*Traditional*	*Responsibility Center*	*Reality from Research Findings*
Accountability	Linking expenditure to activities	Linking expenditure to activities and results	Linking expenditure to activities
Control	Control over the details for the designated activities	Control over the total and the results	Control over both the details and the total; control over the results does not get as much attention as we expected
Flexibility for the economy	Annual, cash basis	Annual, cash basis	Annual, cash basis
Continuity for planning	Emphasized control; keep continuity through tax expenditures and mandatory entitlements	Emphasized planning	Emphasized planning
The capacity to make and support decisions	Incremental calculation	Increased efficiency and effectiveness through the decentralization of means and centralization of control	Incremental calculation, somewhat increased savings through the flexible budgetary process
Fiscal discipline	Ineffective control—budget maximizers	Effective control over total	Effective control over total
Allocative efficiency	Does not reflect priorities but preferences	Reflects priorities	Reflects priorities

Table 5.3 (*Continued*) **Budget Found in Traditional Practice: Responsibility Centers and Practices Found in This Research Compared by Normative Criteria for Budgets**

Operational efficiency	No self-efforts to reduce cost	Discretionary power leads managers to find out some ways for cost savings	Very limited discretionary power; there are little incentives for managers to save

Source: Adapted from Wildavsky, A., *Public Administration Review*, 38(6), 501–509, 2001; Schick, A., *Modern Budgeting*, Organization for Economic Cooperation and Development, Paris, 1997; authors.

be spent efficiently and effectively, in our opinion, the pro-business view. However, the organization interpretation responsibilities to satisfy such criteria are dispersed to both central budget officers and line managers: allocation responsibility belongs to the budgeter, and the efficient and effective employment of resources to the department manager. Linkages may exist through traditional hierarchies or decentralized responsibility centers.[2]

Endnotes

1. Earlier versions of this chapter were published in *Public Performance and Management Review* (30(4): 469–495, 2007), presented at the Performing Public Sector conference in Leuven, Belgium (June 3, 2006) and the Association for Budgeting and Financial Management conference in Atlanta, Georgia (October 20, 2006). (Copyright by M. E. Sharpe, Inc. Used by permission.) The authors thank two anonymous journal reviewers, the editors of the journal symposium, and Johan De Kruijf of the University of Twente, the Netherlands, our commentator at the Leuven conference, for their insight, comments, and help.

2. Our findings come from a pilot study, however. The focal localities appear to fall within the bounds of traditional and responsibility center budgeting, but the forty-six other budget reform localities in our population could point reform toward the market-like mechanisms we did not see. The research also does not suggest how to characterize the distance between traditional and responsibility center budgeting and where the eight focal localities, much less the forty-six others in the population, fall within that space. Future comparisons among a larger number of reform localities can help determine the fate of market-like mechanisms at the locality level in the United States, as well as provide more detail about the traditional responsibility center dimensions.

   Three other ideas limit our findings. First, our research is budget-centric, especially performance budget-centric. Like Schick (2001b, p. 58), we believe that reformers have the view that "budgeting drives management; if the budget is oriented to performance, managers will drive their organizations to perform." However narrow the view, reform gains more leverage by focusing on budgeting first, then on management. Many contest the view that budgeting drives management. For instance, our model's supposition that performance measure certification precedes allocation ignores the independent function certification serves for both accountability and transparency. We thank an anonymous reviewer for reminding us. Certification is a good idea, even a necessity, and is used by Maricopa County, Arizona, for many purposes along with budgeting.

Second, retained savings or carryovers clash with basic beliefs held by people in the United States and other countries about how government should reward efficiency. Our focus group suggested that government efficiency should confer communal benefits rather than individual benefits. The consensus about who should gain from efficiency deserves more scrutiny across industrialized countries and then across the world.

Third, the decentralization vs. centralization issue concerns not only managers and budgeters but also policy designers. Whether a responsibility center can best implement a program design or not, the responsibility center does not drive the decision about program design, and neither does a budget. The program, management system, budgeting, and financing of a results-oriented effort are mutually contingent matters, all of which the socioeconomic and political environments frame (Salamon, 2002, pp. 9–37).

In terms of methods, future studies could go deeper with verification of claims in documents and in some interviews in the eight cities especially. Other studies in the future can provide comprehensive data on consequences of the presence or absence of certification, target, and incentive schemes.

References

Barrett, K., and Greene, R. (2002). You can't bank on it. *Governing* 15(12):74.

Berman, E. (1997). Dealing with cynical citizens. *Public Administration Review* 57(2):105–112.

Buck, A. E. (1929). *Public Budgeting.* New York: Harper.

Caiden, N. (1998). Public service professionalism for performance measurement and evaluation. *Public Budgeting and Finance* 18(2):35–52.

Churchill, N. C. (1984). Budget choice: Planning vs. control. *Harvard Business Review* 62(4):150–164.

Cothran, D. A. (2001). Entrepreneurial budgeting: An emerging reform? In *Performance Based Budgeting*, ed. G. J. Miller, W. B. Hildreth, and J. Rabin, 147–167. Boulder, CO: Westview.

Feit, D. (2003). Measuring performance in the public sector. *Journal of Cost Management* (March/April):39–45.

General Accounting Office (GAO). (1999, July). *Performance Budgeting: Initial Agency Experiences Provide a Foundation to Assess Future Directions.* GAOIT-AIMDGGD-99-216. Washington, DC: General Accounting Office.

General Accounting Office (GAO). (2000, February). *Accrual Budgeting: Experiences of Other Nations and Implications for the United States.* GAOIAIMD-00-57. Washington, DC: General Accounting Office.

Golembiewski, R. T. (1964). Accountancy as a function of organization theory. *The Accounting Review* 39(2):333-341.

Government Accounting Standards Board (GASB). (1999). *Statement no. 34: Basic financial statements—and management's discussion and analysis—for state and local governments.* Norwalk, CT: GASB.

Hatry, H. (1999). *Performance Measurement: Getting Results*. Washington, DC: Urban Institute.

Hax, A. C., and Majluf, N. S. (1984). The corporate strategic planning process. *Interfaces* 14(1):47–60.

Jones, L. R. (2005). Outyear budgetary consequences of agency cost savings: International Public Management Network Symposium. *International Public Management Review* 6(1):139–168. http://www.ipmr.net (link live October 29, 2006).

Kelman, S. (2005). The dialogue. *International Public Management Review* 6(1):139. http://www.ipmr.net (link live October 29, 2006).

King, C. S., Feltey, K. M., and Susel, B. (1998). The question of participation: Toward authentic public participation in public administration. *Public Administration Review* 58(4):317–326.

Klay, E. (2001). Management through budgetary incentives. In *Performance Based Budgeting*, ed. G. J. Miller, W. B. Hildreth, and J. Rabin, 215–227. Boulder, CO: Westview.

Knight, H. C. (1981). Budgeting: A contrast of preaching and practice. *Cost and Management* 55(6):42–46.

Larkey, P. D., and Devereux, E. A. (1999). Good budgetary decision processes. In *Public Management Reform and Innovation: Research, Theory, and Application*, ed. H. G. Frederickson and J. M. Johnston, 166–188. Tuscaloosa: University of Alabama Press.

Lazere, C. (1998). All together now: Why you must link budgeting and forecasting to planning and performance. *CFO* 14(2):28–36.

National Advisory Council on State and Local Budgeting. (1997). *A Framework for Improved State and Local Government Budgeting and Recommended Budget Practices*. Chicago: Government Finance Officers Association.

Osborne, D., and Hutchinson, P. (2004). *The Price of Government*. New York: Basic Books.

Pollitt, C., and Bouckaert, G. (2000). *Public Management Reform*. New York: Oxford University Press.

Radin, B. A. (1998). The Government Performance and Results Act (GPRA): Hydra-headed monster or flexible management tool? *Public Administration Review* 58(4):307–315.

Rubin, I. (1998). *Class, Tax & Power*. Chatham, NJ: Chatham House.

Salamon, L. M. (2002). The new governance and the tools of public action: An introduction. In *The Tools of Government*, ed. L. M. Salamon, 1–47. New York: Oxford University Press.

Scheps, P. B. (2000). Linking performance measures to resource allocation. *Government Finance Review* (June):11–15.

Schick, A. (1978). The road from ZBB. *Public Administration Review* 38(2):177–180.

Schick, A. (1990). Budgeting for results: Recent developments in five industrialized countries. *Public Administration Review* 50(1):26–34.

Schick, A. (1997). *Modern Budgeting*. Paris: Organization for Economic Cooperation and Development.

Schick, A. (2001a). Budgeting for results: Recent developments in five industrialized countries. In *Performance Based Budgeting*, ed. G. J. Miller, W. B. Hildreth, and J. Rabin, 129–146. Boulder, CO: Westview.

Schick, A. (2001b). Getting performance measures to measure up. In *Quicker, Better, Cheaper? Managing Performance in American Government*, ed. D. Forsythe, 39–60. Albany: State University of New York Press.

Serritzlew, S. (2006). Linking budgets to activity: A test of the effect of output-purchase budgeting. *Public Budgeting and Finance* 26(2),101–120.

State of Washington, Office of Financial Management, Budget Division. (2005). *Report of fiscal year 2005 savings incentive account expenditures*. RCW 43.79.460. Olympia: State of Washington, Office of Financial Management, Budget Division.

Tate, R. L. (2003). Performance measure certification in Maricopa County. *Government Finance Review*, February, pp. 6–9.

Trapani, C. S. (1982). Six critical areas in the budgeting process. *Management Accounting* 64(5):52–56.

Warren, R. S. (1975). Bureaucratic performance and budgetary reward. *Public Choice* 24(5):1–57.

Wenz, T. W., and Nolan, A. P. (1982). Budgeting for the future: Target base budgeting. *Public Budgeting and Finance* 2:88–91.

Wildavsky, A. (1964). *The Politics of the Budgetary Process*. Boston: Little, Brown.

Wildavsky, A. (2001). A budget for all seasons? Why the traditional budget lasts. *Public Administration Review* 38(6):501–509. In G. J. Miller, W. B. Hildreth, and J. Rabin, eds. *Performance Based Budgeting*, 95–112. Boulder, CO: Westview.

Chapter 6

Budgeting for Nonconventional Expenditures[1]

Gerald J. Miller and Iryna Illiash

> Budgeting is all about ... the interplay of people and their ideas and goals.... Budgets are the result of a compromise amongst alternative views of the desirable size and composition of government activities.
>
> **—Allen Schick, OECD, p. 28, 2009.**

The context in which governments operate has changed dramatically over the last twenty years. Under the sweeping forces of globalization and the reform efforts of the new public management (NPM) movement, government in the United States has been undergoing a significant transformation, involving the devolution of traditionally federal programs to the states, localities, and private parties, privatization of government functions, and contracting out with for-profit and nonprofit agencies—all with the view to increase the efficiency of service delivery and its responsiveness to customer needs and, most importantly, to put an end to the era of big government. And yet, as Schick (2009, p. 219) indicates, the size and scope of government during the same period "has been remarkably stable.... National governments have neither rolled back the boundaries of the modern state, nor have they expanded it."

How can this be possible? This chapter explores a trend that counters Schick's view. Gradually, the federal government agency officials are carrying out their functions as a "service provider or financier" (Schick, 2009, p. 219) through an elaborate network of indirect administrative tools, such as intergovernmental grants, tax expenditures, loans and loan guarantees, insurance, mandates, and regulations (Kettl, 2000; Salamon, 1989). How could the scope of government not increase? More important, this gradual increase in government reach could be a pro-positive government one or a pro-business one, and given the right turn in electoral politics in the United States, the pro-business one seems likely. The question remains, however: How has influence among the original reform coalition moved? What effect has the shift in influence had on finance officials' sense of appropriate logics—more economizing than responding, or what?

The main political attraction of these indirect tools of public policy making is that they allow "government to increase its reach without increasing its size" (Kettl, 2000, p. 493). Their invisibility and absence from conventional budgets led some scholars to dub them as "hidden spending" (Ippolito, 1984; Bennett and DiLorenzo, 1983) or "the hidden welfare state" (Howard, 1997). We call them (after Schick, 1986, 2007)[2] nonconventional spending, as opposed to conventional, or direct, spending. Weakened (or altogether nonexistent) accountability for nonconventional spending helps conceal not only areas of government growth but also areas of government inefficiency in cases when scarce public resources are channeled to less efficient or equitable alternatives.

Our task in this chapter is twofold: to address the problem of nonconventional spending control and to examine the trade-off among different forms of conventional and nonconventional spending. We recall from Chapter 4 the problem of budget control and the way partisans have interpreted it in budget discourse. Then we analyze the problem of trade-off criteria and demonstrate with the welfare reform case how the process of trading off different policy tools permits a particular policy to develop.

The lack of control over indirect spending has resulted in calls for new types of budgets. In governments across the world, we find not only a long-standing call for a separate capital budget, but also cries for a tax expenditure budget, a mandate budget, a regulatory budget, a credit budget, and an insurance budget. These calls have occurred at all levels of government and in many different countries, but perhaps most loudly at the federal level in the United States. We assume calls for other budgets will emerge as observers reveal additional areas of "hidden spending."

A proposal for a "superbudget"—a comprehensive budget containing subordinate budgets for nonconventional and conventional expenditures (President's Commission on Budget Concepts, 1967; Litan and Nordhaus, 1983)—has existed for some time as well.

A superbudget could complicate the decision about what criterion to use for allocation among competing purposes and goals. A finance official has an ambiguity problem as a result. Which view shall prevail? The responding logic is arguably the typical interpretation by finance officials. The question of what or who to respond to then arises—political masters who have a majority of votes or the political culture that bonds both political majorities and minorities? Then, there is the question of what cultural value appropriately fits the budget control problem. This chapter investigates alternative responding logics as it explores the idea of a superbudget and the cultural values vying to control superbudget allocations.

The Budget Problem

The reason why we have these calls for budgets in areas of growth, however measured, is probably because we traditionally interpret budgets primarily as a means of control. Having a budget means asserting control in areas some think are growing beyond restraint by forcing them into broad daylight, often to cap their growth. Control suggests that we give extra strength to the guardians in the budget formulation process or to those budget actors who have played a "conserving" role in budget formulation (Schick, 1988, pp. 64–67), opposing that of the "claiming role" or advocates of spending increases.

Having a budget also can mean allocating available resources to their highest and best use. The Government Performance and Results Act of 1993 forced performance-based budgeting into the lexicon once more and has focused attention on the performance of not only agencies but of government efforts through third parties (Heen, 2000) and through conventional and nonconventional spending. Within this framework, the call for scrutiny of nonconventional spending has immediate appeal as well.

Lastly, having a budget can mean engaging the principles of distributive justice. As inherently normative enterprises, budgets engage these principles and incorporate political values and moral norms of that political system whose purposes they serve. In the context of the United States, this involves balancing two distinct perspectives on budgeting as a means of control: progressives' efforts to reveal cost-effective government intervention in society and conservatives' efforts to stem government influence.

Conservative Interpretation of Control: Controlling Government Instead of Controlling the Governed

Conservatives view with distaste expansion in the exercise of government power. They believe that government, through the group of nonconventional spending tools as a whole, acts to control the governed.

Budgets serve as a brake on the ability of the government to control the governed; in a sense, they serve the second great responsibility of government—to control itself.

The distinction comes from James Madison himself in Federalist Paper 51. He wrote (1978, p. 264):

> In framing a government which is to be administered by men over men, the great difficulty lies in this: you must first enable the government to control the governed; and in the next place oblige it to control itself.

Through this interpretation of budget control, we find calls to limit the use of power.

This presents the first interpretive dimension to conceptualize budgets. The Federalist perspective echoes in more modern times. The distinction between government efforts through the budget to control itself and government efforts through nonconventional means to control the governed has provoked wide comment. It seems that the use of different techniques, at first glance only a means of evading traditional budget controls, is growing faster, some say, than government can control their use, faster than efforts can be made to control government. In this regard, two students of budgeting deserve mention. First, Wildavsky (2002, p. 350) has observed:

> The more government tries to affect citizen behavior, it appears, the less able it is to keep its own house in order. This new relationship between government and citizen may have many advantages, but control over spending is not one of them.

Schick (1981, pp. 349–350) is more forceful about the problem than Wildavsky. He detects in the growth of off-budget expenditure a "paradox of control." That is, off-budget spending has converted government spending to "spending largely … outside government." Serving the worthy goals of managing economic growth and gaining a fairer distribution of incomes, government positive and negative incentives for private sector spending have extended government control. According to Schick, "The paradox is that in its effort to extend its control over the private sector, the government has surrendered a good deal of its control over the public sector."

The control of the governed presents a problem of liberty. Government control represents the naked meddling by those in power in the affairs and decisions of those they represent, ultimately allowing those in power to control for control's sake.

Progressive Interpretation of Control: Intervention in Society

Finding an appropriate role for government and using analysis to restrain government power, the progressives view nonconventional spending as just another form of intervention in society. Therefore, tax incentives, credit and insurance incentives, regulatory sanctions, and state and local government mandates are different values on the same dimension. These policy tools generally either induce or sanction. At bottom, there is no difference between inducement and sanction; both are means of the government's intervening in society.

Nonconventional spending therefore is a variation of intervention. Consider government intervention from the policy tools perspective (Vedung, 1998, pp. 22–25; Anderson, 1977).

This school of thought asks the question: When we face a public problem, what do we do about it? The answer: Often we leave it to the individual, the family, or household to decide. Sometimes the community, we think, should decide issues of import. Finally, some problems are matters "the market" should decide without government interference.

When we do believe in government intervention, it tends to be a matter of creating inducements and specifying sanctions or something in between. Sometimes an indirect approach is taken, with education, moral suasion, the bully pulpit, propaganda, or other sermon-like approaches.

Adding the element of scarcity can also exert budget control. Intervention as a whole must be allowed to cost no more than x, in other words. To maximize intervention, advocates would either limit the cost or set a goal on the amount of intervention it will take to achieve a just and productive society.

Interpreting Control Today: Cost Control of Nonconventional Spending

Where do we stand now between the conservative and progressive views of nonconventional spending? So far, each of the areas of nonconventional or otherwise seemingly uncontrolled expenditure has yielded somewhat to control through budget devices as we presently know and use them. Consider the U.S. federal government experience. Budget rules in several pieces of legislation, starting most forcefully with the Budget Enforcement Act of 1990 have tried to constrain direct spending, tax expenditures, and entitlements. Administrative and legislative efforts have focused on trade-offs among direct government operations, contracts, and grants in the name of privatization. Credit reform has forced into the traditional budget process the direct costs of interest subsidies and the discounted future costs of loan defaults. Insurance reform, particularly that related to bank deposits, has led to considerable legislative scrutiny and new proposals for budget treatment of losses— the difference between discounted future outlays and expected insurance premium receipts. Gradually, many different nonconventional financial techniques are being forced to take on the characteristics of cash transactions that must submit to the limits placed by cash budgets.[3]

Missing here are the areas of mandates and regulation. So far only mild efforts have been made. The "point of order rule" requirements for mandates, (Thompson, 1997; Litan and Nordhaus, 1983) proposals to cost out the financial burden of regulation on individuals and organizations (Thompson, 1997, p. 91), and proposals to monetize mandates and regulation are part of these efforts.

They, too, illustrate the possibility to control government nonconventional budgets through the element of cost.

The efforts to control nonconventional spending have taken place piecemeal. We now subject each tool of government action to control or at least, at this stage, special scrutiny. This comes in the form of either relatively sophisticated or primitive budgets for each area of activity that we perceive as "hidden spending." As a result, we now have or soon will have elementary tax expenditure budgets, credit budgets, insurance budgets, and regulatory budgets.

Interpreting Control: A Matter of Substitutable Policy Tools

The progressive view of direct and indirect policy tools as different ways of doing the same thing suggests that efforts to control them should focus not only on their cost but also on their substitutability.

Therefore, budget control is also a matter of the analysis of alternative policy tools and the choice of the appropriate one based on its fitness in the context in which it is examined. According to Surrey and McDaniel (1985, p. 3):

> Whenever government decides to grant monetary assistance to an activity or group, it may choose from a wide range of methods, such as a direct government grant or subsidy; a government loan, perhaps at a below-market interest rate; or a private loan guaranteed by the government. Or the government may use the tax system and reduce the tax liability otherwise applicable by adopting a special exclusion, deduction, or the like for the favored activity or group.

A tax credit may work similarly to a government grant, the tax credit having some administrative advantages perhaps, and the government grant distributional advantages. Nevertheless, analysis, many argue, should focus on the trade-off over many dimensions of policy tools, selecting the one tool that suits the purpose the best. And this brings us to the issue of criteria.

Trade-Off Criteria

This need for analysis of trade-offs probably appears regularly in legislative and administrative bodies as in the following testimony in Congress. In this instance (Salamon and Lund, 1989, p. 23), one member asked the budget director and staff:

> [Where are] governmental loans ... an effective policy instrument and where ... not? ... Loan guarantees...? ... We are looking at these in relation to other tools that the government has to operate.... Have there been any studies...?

The budget director and staff concluded, "We are unaware of any such literature, Mr. Chairman." Chairman Blanchard's frustration may be understandable, as the policy tools approach seems so practical, so rational. The unified budget, far from an ivory tower construction, fulfills a felt need of decision makers.

In policy argument, budget theory, and practical affairs, many call for placing all government action in one or *the* budget. With unified budgets given some credence for managing, even maximizing, government intervention or minimizing government control, we might ask what such a budget might entail. Some see the super-budget's scope as merely nonconventional and conventional dollar spending. Others include mandates and regulation. Beyond, but in this same spirit, others would include all social regulation and its coercive effects (Schattschneider, 1975, p. 106).

Unification permits scrutiny, analysis, and wise choice. On the basis of great purposes that are served, budgeteers can search for various, alternative policy tools, calculate the costs and benefits of each, and determine the appropriate tool given limited resources budgeted to achieve these purposes.

The Problem of Criteria

The centrality of criteria in budgeting can hardly be disputed. And yet, we have only the vaguest ideas about the trade-off criteria.

We assume the nature of the budget control system will also condition the choice of whether we choose direct spending, tax preferences, loans, or other tools, such as regulation. For example, a criterion related to expenditure control might strictly define costs and stringently limit budget totals. This criterion would lead budget controllers to choose those programs that minimized government growth or influence (Niskanen, 1988; Koven, 1999, pp. 63–72). Another criterion might be economic efficiency—for the given level of expenditure, decision makers would choose those programs using those tools that minimize the use of economic resources or maximize economic growth (Feldstein, 1980). On the other hand, economic growth might yield different measures of cost and totals and might yield a criterion suggesting cost-effectiveness, which we define as the expenditure needed to achieve a given level of, say, employment (Harris, 1955). Still another criterion might be the distribution of costs and benefits or even the distribution of income. Therefore, a worthwhile project, high on the priority list within the limits of scarcity, would be one in which all income strata of society received the same proportional or appropriate benefit (see Rosen, 1985, pp. 70–97). The possible criteria are many, and in short, they serve as the fundamental purpose of the government and its budget.

Criteria are sometimes relatively easy to establish, as where there is a consensus, gained for a variety of reasons, on the basis for comparison of alternative means. According to Schneider and Ingram (1997, p. 78), research by analysts and advisors implicitly seeks to reveal or suggest the appropriateness of various budgetary and policy tools under different conditions.

Where consensus does not exist, either broadly in society or narrowly as with deference to expertise, the criterion becomes the flashpoint for contending forces.

According to Fainstein (1987, p. 233), "The conflict over criteria often boils down to a dispute over efficiency versus equity."

In such cases, the contention over a single criterion is often rooted among institutional values. One institution's preferred portfolio of spending tools that is geared toward helping the homeless, for example, is not easily compared with an institution the aim of which is to control them (perhaps a mental health agency or a public housing agency), or with an institution that wants homeless people to make up their own minds (an authority that guarantees housing developers' loans) (Schon and Rein, 1994, pp. 129–161; March and Olsen, 1989).

Rist (1998, p. 151) argues that the political and organizational contexts in which decisions are made influence the choice of a policy instrument. In particular, the way in which a policy problem is defined and addressed, the probable behavior of the targets of the policy, and the unique implementation costs and benefits of the various candidate tools will sway choice of the trade-off criterion.

Drawing heavily on ambiguity theory, which centers on the disconnectedness of ends and means and the vagueness of ends themselves, researchers argue that much of life in organizations involves unknown or contradictory goals and technologies as well as individuals who may differ in their levels of participation over time. That is

> Intention does not control behavior precisely. Participation is not a stable consequence of properties of the choice situation or individual preferences. Outcomes are not a direct consequence of process. Environmental response is not always attributable to organizational action. Belief is not always a result of experience. (March and Olsen, 1976, p. 21)

In such pervasive situations, choice, according to March and Olsen, comes with difficulty. The actors may seldom realize their preferences until they have made choices. Or, as Weick has put it (1980, p. 19), "How can I know what I think until I see what I say."

Simply stated, this alternative approach to budget control criteria discussed here holds that interpretation drives out ambiguity; that is, the greater the number of different, constructed realities, the greater the ambiguity that exists within and among people, organizations, or governments. For practical problems of management, the greater the ambiguity, the less likely prescriptions, such as economic criteria for budget control decisions, have any real applicability. Not agreeing about what a criterion means, to what set of values it relates, if at all, decision makers employ procedures that are "loosely coupled" to any one view of reality (Weick, 1976). As a result, the greater the compounding of differences among views in a group of individuals having some collective interest, such as an organization or a government, the greater the influence of randomness—in terms of events and specific people shaping meaning—and the larger the amount of interpretation needed by members to make sense and to act in a concerted way (Weick, 1979).

Focusing on the social construction of reality (Berger and Luckmann, 1966; Goffman, 1961, 1974; Schon and Rein, 1994), researchers also emphasizes the relativity of meaning. This field argues that every organization, being in essence a social assemblage somewhere between transience and permanence, embodies a set of shared views of the world that give meaning to what they do. These views or "interpretations of reality" build and gain legitimacy through an interaction among individuals. Moreover, the existence of interpretations belies the notion that there exists an objective reality shared by all organizations or people.

A contextual school of thought involved with microbudgeting holds that an imperative, sometimes political, sometimes a social or economic problem, sometimes the experience gained from living with an existing program as it develops through implementation, provides a frame of reference or context within which to view the economic or technical imperatives demanded by budgets (Thurmaier, 1995; Forester, 1984; McCaffery and Baker, 1990).

Assuming a trade-off criterion emerges from context, the decision-making context that helps resolve the ambiguity by constructing the reality underlying the choice of the policy tool. Each scientific community and its particular interests provide a context within which such experts draw deference; their assertion of the appropriate criterion dominates. Powerful groups dictate or force attention on problems, and the criterion emerges. Institutions control the criterion when given responsibility for dealing with a public problem.

Salamon (1989), on the other hand, argues that a context exists around the policy tool, not around a problem or area of scientific theory and expertise. That is, each tool—from tax expenditures to loan guarantees—has grown out of a different environment of executive departments, legislative committees, and beneficiaries. Salamon (1989, p. 8) observes: "Each instrument has its own distinctive procedures, its own network of organizational relationships, its own skill requirements— in short, its own 'political economy.'"

The politics of budgeting argues for criteria based on political power. As Fainstein (1987, p. 233) argues:

> [Economic efficiency and] growth with equity solutions are difficult to achieve because those favoring equity measures are usually relatively powerless. Nowhere are the relations among evaluative criteria, group power, and political outcomes more evident.

Group power, then, says all.

The context, it would seem, is the area within which a given set of public problems, budget tools, group power, and institutions exists. Within these contexts, budget controllers enforce the criterion; they intend that advocates justify their proposals on meaningful grounds and intend that advocates' proposals stand judgment by objective and systematic means. Even if final decisions in the budget process seem to take on the image of horse trading, there is a need to ensure that the horse trading is within the bounds of acceptability to the horse traders' constituents, other participants in the process, and the larger public. As Schneider and Ingram (1997, p. 111) point out:

> To maintain credible arguments about policy effectiveness, [public officials] need to have a believable causal logic connecting the various aspects of the policy design to desired outcomes.... They also must take into account the tendency of the American public to believe in fairness and justice. Government should not give anyone more than they deserve, nor should government contribute to unfairness or injustice.

Budgeting Interpretations: The Social Construction Approach

Another view of the criterion problem comes from those who take the social construction/interpretive approach in public policy. To them, criteria affecting trade-offs are not based solely on how much the particular tool will stimulate or dampen economic growth or remedy market failure or restore balance in the distribution of income or some other variation on the theme of making domestic progress. Criteria are not based solely on political variables either: Does the spending tool maximize what some constituents get or some others do not get?

Criteria are also, and mostly, they argue, based on human nature. In this view, as humans, we classify groups targeted for government intervention through our social constructions of them. Groups are targeted as deserving or undeserving, or even groups to be rewarded and punished. We tend to think that the context within which claiming and conserving functions meet develops out of a social construction of people and their problems or the problems they cause. From context emerges a criterion that makes a particular tool appropriate. Therefore, any analysis of the trade-offs among tools will be affected by this fit between our social constructions and the tool. Said in another way, the tool chosen will be based on its relationship to the construction of the target population, and not on its cost-effectiveness, cost efficiency, or political constituency reward potential.

Policy Design and Social Construction

The application of the social construction approach has proceeded quickly over the last two decades, most notably in the work in policy design by Schneider and Ingram (1990, 1993, 1994, 2005). However, adaptations could serve to make a case for this research in the discussion of the criteria for trading off direct and indirect policy tools.

According to Ingram and Schneider (2005, p. 5), "Public policy is the primary tool through which governments act to exploit, inscribe, entrench, institutionalize, perpetuate or change social constructions." And though the role of government policies is smaller in social construction than the combined influence of market advertisements, popular culture, religion, and historical tradition, "remarkable durability" of policies makes it extremely hard (but not impossible) to change the direction of social construction of a group or idea once the course has been set (Ingram and Schneider, 2005, p. 5).

Therefore, in policy design, it is an important distinction whether those who will receive the benefit or bear the burden of the policy—target populations—are perceived in a positive or negative light. What is a target population? Schneider and Ingram, who came up with the term, define it as "persons and groups whose behavior and well-being [affect] and are affected by public policy" and in the case here, the budget (1993, p. 334).

They go on to characterize their view of the social construction of target populations as referring to "1) the recognition of the shared characteristics that distinguish a target population as socially meaningful, and 2) the attribution of specific, valence-oriented values, symbols, and images to the characteristics. Social constructions are stereotypes about particular groups of people that have been created by politics, culture, socialization, history, the media, literature, religion, and the like" (p. 335). The characterization or social construction of the various target populations tends to be negative or positive, given the conditions under which it occurs—rewarding or punishing through public policy. This tendency toward negative or positive social constructions "depends partly on the power of the target population itself (construed as votes, wealth, and propensity of the group to mobilize for action) but also on the extent to which others will approve or disapprove of the policy's being directed toward a particular target" (p. 335).

Policy design, Schneider and Ingram say, follows these social constructions. Policy design, as an "inherently ... purposeful and normative enterprise," one used "to serve particular values, purposes, and interests" (Schneider and Ingram, 1997, p. 3), follows these social constructions. Target populations' problems (or the problems with certain target populations) are the country's (state's, locality's) problems: what is good (bad) for them is good (bad) for the country. Solutions designed to benefit them or punish them are designed. The justification is then found to convince the public. Such a process is illustrated below.

Government decision makers

↓

Reflect the social construction of target groups for government action and consider the electoral impact of their decision (Donovan, 2001)

↓

Budget by rewarding the deserving and punishing the undeserving

↓

Which they rationalize (justify after the fact) in terms of values

---

First, government decision makers socially construct target populations and then design policy tools to act on these social constructions. Finally, they rationalize these tools as appropriate to a given problem.

Such a construct, budget, and rationalized sequence is consistent with March's view. He says (1987, p. 38) that "most information in organizations is collected and recorded not primarily to aid decision making directly but as a basis for interpretations that allow coherent histories to be told. As a structure of meaning evolves from the information and from the process of decision making, specific decisions are fitted into it."

If budgets contain the major policy tools we want to use, we can readily choose the appropriate mechanisms for dealing with different, constructed, target populations. Thus, we have budgets for taxes, budgets for spending, budgets for regulation, budgets for insurance, budgets for credit, and budgets for mandates, all of which follow on the already constructed context of target populations. We select the policy tool that best fits the deserving or undeserving target population's needs or threats.

We tend to think that the tool ought to fit the context appropriately, and the context derives from the social construction of the target group. Therefore, any analysis of the trade-offs among the policy tools—the choice of what criterion to use—should be affected by this fit between our social constructions and what we want to do for or against target groups we have defined. Said in another way, the tool chosen will be based on its appropriateness to the construction of the target population as well as, if not instead of, its cost-effectiveness, cost efficiency, or reward potential for a political constituency.

Deserving and Undeserving Target Populations

Ingram and Schneider (2005) warn that the policy-making dynamics based on social constructions of target populations is not without pitfalls. As it happens, "government does not treat all people equally, but instead falls into a pattern of allocating benefits mainly to the advantaged populations and punishments to the deviants" (p. 17). As a result, differences between deserving and undeserving become amplified, legitimized, and institutionalized "into permanent lines of social, economic, and political cleavage" (p. 5). At the same time, in democracies, "where legitimacy is a constant concern," policies are justified either on logical grounds—as contributing to some important end—or as promoting fairness and justice (p. 17).

The basic criterion on which constructions rest and on which the interpretive approach to budget tool trade-offs may shed light, the division of the deserving from the undeserving, has a rich history, especially that related to need, "desert (merit)," and rights.

Miller (1999) argues that people stand in different relationships to one another and make demands of justice on each other depending on the particular nature of the relationship involved. Although in reality human relationships are complex and multifaceted, he says that it is possible to reduce them to a small number of basic modes: solidaristic communities, instrumental associations, and citizenship.

In solidaristic communities, the most typical of which is the family, people share a common identity and see themselves as bound by common beliefs, culture, and kinship. Here the primary distributive principle is need, which, at the societal level, is understood as a "baseline below which no one should be allowed to fall" (Miller, 1999, p. 91). Solidaristic community was the predominant mode of association for all premodern societies, in the form of village and feudal communities.

In instrumental associations, typical of capitalist societies, people relate to one another in a utilitarian manner, trying to realize their personal needs and purposes through collaboration with others. Economic relations are dominant in this mode. The primary distributive principle here is that of desert.

As for the third mode of human relationship, specific to modern liberal democracies, people relate to each other not only through their communities and instrumental associations, but also as fellow citizens. A full member of a democratic society is viewed as a bearer of a set of rights and responsibilities that together define the status of citizen (Miller, 1999, p. 30). Jordan (1998, p. 13) agrees, arguing that citizenship is "full membership of a political community" and

> implies a closed, exclusive system of cooperation, [with members contributing] to the common good and [refraining] from mutually harmful conflict. The [traditional republican] ideal ... polity ... is made up of active citizens, sharing a commitment to a high quality of life, within institutions that bind them to common interests and purposes. In this tradition, issues of justice arise between members only in a context of shared resources, mutual benefits and agreed goals. The exclusivity of such an association is closely linked with the principles of contribution and collective responsibility.

The main principle of justice in citizenship association is equality: each citizen enjoys the same set of liberties and rights, including rights to various services that the political community provides for all of its members (Miller, 1999, p. 30). Yet, as Jordan states, the rights are subject to the citizen's willingness to contribute to the common good and to take responsibility for collective well-being.

Returning to a budget context and to V. O. Key's fundamental, criterion-related question for budgeting,[4] we now argue that the basis for a superbudget allocation decision would depend on the context, the dominant mode of human relationship, in which this decision is being made; if the context and mode of relationship change, so does the criterion for allocation. Change becomes especially evident if we analyze historically evolved patterns of social assistance and the criteria that underlie past and present welfare policies.

Trade-Off Criteria, the Poor, and Welfare Policy

Schneider and Ingram (1990, p. 523) warn us to watch for the evolution of policy. Evolution produces changes in behavioral assumptions. They also want to watch for changes in the policy tools that officials favor, toward tools that assume different roles for government, motivations for people, and ideas about how far government policy tools should be allowed to manipulate people.

What insights does the evolution of social welfare policy toward the poor offer us? As Ron Haskins (2001, p. 103) observes, "The poor are the perennial focus of national concern. We are concerned about their income, their work, their use of welfare, their child rearing, their sexual behavior, and their values." How do we deal with them? Oftentimes, this is "a major criterion by which the success of government programs [is] judged" (Haskins, 2001, p. 103). In large part, policy prescriptions depend on our perceptions of the poor. And here controversies abound. Haskins (2001) points out some of them: "The poor have bad genes; no, they have bad environments. The poor are shiftless; no, they are unfortunate victims of society. The poor are retarded; no, they are poorly educated. The poor should be given decent provision; no, they should be required to work for what they get. The poor have illegitimate children they cannot support; no, they have nonmarital births because their choices are constricted by an indifferent society" (p. 103).

Historically, as social institutions have developed, a directly related poverty policy has also materialized. These poverty policies have moved from the "poor laws" that held sway for centuries during feudalism to other policies that arose along with capitalism and the problems of political order and economic management, new institutions, and the ideologies that framed explanations of poverty.

Punctuated development characterizes the changes in society and the materialization of social institutions and poverty policy. Golding and Middleton (1982) argue that the central ideas about the poor have "fed into the mainstream of popular consciousness at key periods of economic and social development" (p. 6). Two key relationships mark the punctuated development, the relationship between the individual and the labor market and the relationship between the individual and the state, in other words, between economic and political control.

The relationship between the individual and the labor market has two features. The first facet encompasses the issues of labor control, work discipline, and motivation of the workforce. The second aspect concerns the problem of social order outside the labor force, namely, "the control of those beyond labor discipline and the consequent criminalisation of certain forms of pauperism, most notably those that threaten the good order of the work force or exploit systems of income maintenance or subsistence provided by society for an impoverished minority" (Golding and Middleton, 1982, p. 7).

The evolving relationship between the individual and the state reveals two features as well. The first one, conditional citizenship, refers to the political rights, such as voting, of the propertyless and those dependent on the charity of society. The other issue has a more modern ring, the right balance between state provision of help to the poor and individual self-help.

Society's first attempts to deal with these problems can be traced back to feudal times.

Then social assistance to indigents was need based. Through church charity, alms giving, and the monastic hospitality of solidaristic communities, assistance to the poor provided benefits to certain people whose incomes fell below a defined level (Jordan, 1998, p. 60). With the development of capitalist relations and the growing crisis in the feudal economy, the solidaristic community gradually disintegrated and need-based help gave way to the repressive and selective attitudes associated with utilitarianism (Golding and Middleton, 1982).

Typically, the birth of public welfare is associated with the dissolution of the British feudal system (Cammisa, 1998, p. 26). The Statutes of Laborers of 1349–57 are regarded to be the first welfare legislation. The law was said to respond to labor supply shortages and rising wages. The statutes, according to one view, "produced a pre-industrial, property-less and disciplined working class." More important, however, is the fact that for the first time the distinction between "god's poor and the devil's"—the poor and the paupers or the deserving and undeserving poor—was introduced into public policy making (Golding and Middleton, 1982, pp. 8–10).

Bureaucratic organization of the state's relationship to the poor emerged and developed with predictable consequences. Classifications came into being, and categorization distinguished the necessarily from the voluntarily indigent. The voluntarily indigent became stigmatized. Finally, stigma led to action, and both in England and colonial America, "rehabilitation of the poor" became the ultimate goal of welfare (Cammisa, 1998, p. 30).

As capitalism matured, intolerance of the poor would also grow. Society became concerned with the costs required for the correction of the idle poor: "The unemployed were now viewed as a burden, a drain on hard-won wealth, rather than simply as unused potential" (Golding and Middleton, 1982, p. 13).

After the publication of Smith's *Wealth of Nations* in 1776, poverty was denounced as an unnatural condition, contradicting the laws of supply and demand, and the intervention of the state was justified as necessary to solving the poverty problem as harmful to the economic system (Golding and Middleton, 1982, p. 13; Mencher, 1966, p. 39). Poor relief to the able-bodied was declared unnecessary, and in the Poor Law Amendment Act of 1834, the English government aimed to keep the able-bodied workers off relief and in the labor market (Mencher, 1966, p. 40).

The Poor Law Amendment Act centralized authority for poverty management in the national government and established stringent tests for eligibility of aid and penalties when the aid was bestowed. First, the act provided for less eligibility of the unemployed worker, as compared with the independent laborer, for poor relief. The law justified such action with the thought that "every penny bestowed that tends to render the condition of the pauper more eligible than that of the independent laborer, is a bounty on indolence and vice" (The Poor Law Report of 1834, 1966, p. 53). Thus, the law reinforced the principle that able-bodied people on welfare should always be worse off than those who worked (Winston, 2002, p. 24). By making work more desirable than idleness, this principle therefore was viewed as an inducement for the poor to remain employed or accept employment (Mencher,

1966, p. 40). Second, the act enforced the workhouse test. The workhouse was viewed as "the major institutional means of containing the idle and instilling the work ethic" (Golding and Middleton, 1982, p. 12). It was assumed that no one who could obtain employment would prefer to live in a workhouse instead.

According to some, the act of 1834 vindicated the political expediencies of a maturing capitalism in the language of moral theory that, aided by the press, quickly and easily became embedded in the system of values and beliefs of the civil society (Golding and Middleton, 1982, p. 29). The desert criterion of the instrumental association and utilitarian views of the community firmly took root in the poverty policy arena.

Between the early colonial period and the nineteenth century, American society's attitudes toward the poor were influenced by the British welfare policies. Public assistance, at that time available mostly exclusively at the local level, was limited and reflected the view where poverty was attributed to individual shortcomings rather than to economic, social, and political causes (Winston, 2002, p. 24). The belief of moral fallibility of the poor was so strong that some towns could go as far in their righteousness as to take away children from destitute parents and make the latter leave town borders (Winston, 2002, p. 24). As the most extreme expression of this view, a strand of social Darwinism lived shortly in the mid-1800s. Regarding poverty as a sign of unfitness, its advocates argued that helping the poor was dangerous, as their survival would weaken the species (Winston, 2002, p. 24).

The state involvement in providing aid came in the form of institutions borrowed from Great Britain—poorhouses and workhouses—and at first on a small scale. Subsequently they multiplied and improved, becoming more competent and professional. By 1929, twenty-five states had established public welfare agencies (Winston, 2002, pp. 24–25).

The first attempts of the federal government to make welfare policy occurred during the Civil War, when Congress established the Bureau of Refugees, Freedmen, and Abandoned Lands under the auspices of the U.S. War Department. As "the nation's first welfare agency," the bureau's purpose was to facilitate the transition of slaves to freedom during and immediately after the war (Winston, 2002, p. 24). Although its long-term impact on public and private welfare policies was insignificant, the bureau demonstrated the federal government's capacity to alleviate poverty where subnational governments and private charities either could not or would not (Winston, 2002, p. 24). Also, it signified the birth of a new approach to poverty, the one that was not purely based on desert.

With the extension of the franchise in the second half of the nineteenth century, the third mode of relationship—citizenship—began influencing allocation decisions about social assistance. Along with the acceptance of political equality, of rights and responsibilities of citizens as the guarantee of human prosperity, there emerged recognition that people could not become fully equal citizens if they lacked the resources necessary to play their roles in a political community (Miller, 1999, p. 31). This recognition drew attention to the existence of economic and social causes of poverty (Winston, 2002, p. 25), which led to the explosion of reform effort in the first decade of the twentieth century that laid the foundation for the welfare state.

Miller's crucial argument is that in citizenship, along with the principle of equality, other principles of justice have valid claims. Political equality calls for social equality to be realized through the satisfaction of the fundamental needs of the citizens, such as medical aid, housing, and income support (1999, p. 31). However, in the rights version of social justice, society does not distribute goods and services on the basis of need per se; rather, society distributes to enable a citizen to have and exercise rights.

Likewise, the principle of desert may take precedent over need and equality. Under even rights-based welfare policies, for example, many consider it unjust if A, who has searched for a job and now holds it, receives only the same income as B, who is unemployed but could have had a similar job if he tried enough (Miller, 1999, p. 36).

Why? The fact that the distinction between the deserving and undeserving poor has been made means that the distributive claims of need or equality are no stronger than those of desert. The distinction indicates that people must prove themselves to be sufficiently deserving before their needs or rights are recognized as valid from the point of view of justice (Miller, 1999, p. 76).

Recent experience suggests that leaders increasingly reflect their followers and articulate the rights and responsibilities of citizens in terms of citizens' limitations and duties, especially on the part of those who receive public services (Jordan, 1998, p. 15).

In the United States, the word *responsibility* has captured the definition of rights as limited and duty-bound. It has repeatedly surfaced in policy and budget discourse over welfare, and has emphasized deservingness, independence, and the need to reduce the number of families on welfare (Jordan, 1998, p. 76). In fact, Solow (1998) has characterized the redefinition of the American welfare system as one based on two criteria, work and personal responsibility. He said that the American welfare model is guided by two explicit aims: "one, to increase self-reliance among those citizens who are now on welfare, and two, to decrease the need for altruism among those citizens who now pay for welfare" (pp. vii–ix).

This suggests that new welfare reform, like the old ones, is still based on the principle of desert rather than any other.

What do budget trade-offs entail? These trade-offs require a criterion on which to rest social judgment about what budget tools—direct expenditures, tax incentives, regulation, credit, and loans—might work best. Social justice offers three criteria: need, desert, and rights. Research suggests that the tool used should fit the context appropriately, and the context derives from the social construction of the target group. The social construction of the target group, in each context, follows the appropriate criterion of social justice. Therefore, any analysis of the trade-offs among the policy tools—the choice of what criterion to use—should be affected by this fit between our social constructions and what we want to do for or against target groups we have defined on a plane of need, desert, or rights.

The problem then is budget arguments over who is deserving and who is undeserving. The budget therefore could be thought of as two budgets, one for the deserving and one for the undeserving/punishable. In each, the incentive budget and the sanctions budget, the total of action is capped, then allocated among strategic initiatives, and the particular tools proposed to achieve these initiatives are traded off against each other. The tool chosen is the one that provides the appropriate measure of cost-benefit, cost-effectiveness, or incidence in achieving the strategic initiative.

A Case Study: The Earned Income Tax Credit and Aid to Families with Dependent Children

A particularly relevant case of the trading off of policy tools between the deserving and the undeserving exists in the development of U.S. federal budget policy toward the poor in the period from the 1930s to the present, and specifically between President Johnson's War on Poverty in the 1960s and the so-called welfare reform era ending in 1996. In the case, we can see a battle fought over who was deserving and who was undeserving. In addition, we can see a trade-off emerge between direct spending and tax expenditures (Howard, 1997). In fact, the growth of the earned income tax credit—a tax expenditure with large direct costs—and the entirely direct expenditure found in the Aid to Families with Dependent Children can illustrate some of the prominent features involved in this trade-off.

Certainly, the trade-off had features that economic analysis helped highlight (Ventry, 2000). However, another reading of the historic development of budgeted welfare policy sheds light on the development of the concept of the poor and the relationship the development produced in the classification of those who were and are deserving and undeserving among the public.[5]

The ultimate event that crystallized the deservingness of certain poor people, as well as their counterparts, the undeserving, was the passage of welfare reform in 1996. Recall some of the facts that had developed by that watershed date.

The 1930s were the time when the citizenship mode of relationship gained momentum in the national policy-making arena. Destitution caused by the Great Depression was of such tremendous scope that it required the most decisive measures on the part of the American government. As pinpointed by Winston (2002), "The sheer scale of poverty during the Great Depression challenged, for a time, the concept that poor people themselves were to blame for their situations" (p. 27). Even if briefly, the poor were regarded as a group of citizens with legitimate political claims; however, the manner in which these claims were addressed depended on the social construction to which they belonged.

Thus, the problem of massive unemployment caused by the depression of the 1930s and primarily affecting able-bodied male workers was resolved by a series of work relief measures consisting of a number of publicly supported jobs. Here, as in 1834, the work requirement became the main prerequisite of help, the proof and the test of one's need. Moreover, "federal direct involvement with employment programs and the labor market more generally was treated as a temporary, emergency activity ... [that] eventually faded away with the passing of the depression and the onset of World War II" (Heclo, 2001, p. 171).

On the other hand, the deservingness of those "who enjoyed a stable full-time attachment to the work force" (Heclo, 2001, p. 171) was rewarded with the Social Security Act of 1935. Through a system of contributory social insurance, the act guaranteed financial security to the families of working men against future loss of income due to old age, unemployment, widowhood, and disability.[6] The existence of this singularly successful policy of the federal government has never ever been challenged, even in recent years, amidst heated debates about its future insolvency. This is truly the case when rights to welfare have entered into the definition of citizenship.

The third bunch of legislative measures was aimed at those needy persons who, although unemployed, were perceived as nevertheless deserving of public assistance. Single mothers with children, along with the destitute elderly and the blind, were among such categories. With breadwinning being a responsibility most exclusively attributed to the man in the traditional delineation of duties within the family, the woman—including a single (usually widowed) mother—was perceived as a keeper of the family entrusted with the functions of child rearing, care giving, and family maintenance. This helped protect her for some time against the stigma of undeservingness. What became known as the Aid to Families with Dependent Children (AFDC),[7] according to Heclo (2001), was designed to provide cash benefits—"mothers' pensions"—to impoverished, deserving widows so that they could "remain at home caring for their children rather than be forced to enter a Dickensian job market or send their children to work (and thus undermine state compulsory public education laws that were becoming more prominent in the early twentieth century)" (p. 171). The key feature of this program was "a de facto separation of the welfare income transfer ... from the world of work and labor market policies" (Heclo, 2001, p. 173). In other words, AFDC legitimized the entitlement of needy families to cash assistance. Ironically, it is this same feature that will become the focus of later welfare reform efforts, when the attitudes toward nonworking women start to change.

Interestingly, President Franklin Roosevelt, the acknowledged creator of the American welfare state, voiced his concern about cash benefits for single mothers from the very beginning, in his message to Congress following his 1935 proposal:

> The lessons of history, confirmed by the evidence immediately before me, show conclusively that continued dependence upon relief induces a spiritual and moral disintegration fundamentally destructive to the national fiber. To dole out relief in this way is to administer a narcotic, a subtle destroyer of the human spirit. It is inimical to the dictates of sound policy. It is in violation of the traditions of America. Work must be found for able-bodied but destitute workers. (Haskins, 2001, p. 104)

Thus before it even started, Roosevelt had urged that the government "must and shall quit this business of relief" (Haskins, 2001, p. 104).

It was not going to happen for another sixty years, however. As Mead (2001) indicates, in its early decades, AFDC was protected not only by "a powerful ideology of entitlement" (p. 210), but also by just as powerful congressional tax committees under the control of which it fell (p. 211).

With time, though, constructions of deservingness may change, and this change can precipitate change in public policy (Ingram and Schneider, 2005, p. 8). After all, "a program that stays the same while the society around it is changing can actually amount to a transformed policy" (Heclo, 2001, p. 173). That's exactly what happened with AFDC.

Among the social changes that influenced the shift in attitudes toward nonworking women, two were of especially far-reaching consequences. One was the gradual replacement of widowed mothers[8] with expanding rolls of divorced, deserted, and young unmarried mothers that took place in the AFDC system by the 1960s (Heclo, 2001, p. 173). Among those, many were African American. Daniel Patrick Moynihan's 1965 report on "a collapsing black family structure associated with illegitimacy and desertion" helped shape the view of welfare as a problem with black people (Heclo, 2001, p. 173).

Another important change was the dissolution of the "male breadwinner" model of income security under the influence of an emerging "feminist consciousness" that drove increasing numbers of women, including those with children, to join the workforce. The number of mothers and children joining AFDC also grew significantly, from 701,000 in 1945 to 3 million in 1960, as did the average monthly benefits, which increased by 77% (Winston, 2002, p. 24). Combined with such statistics, these social changes eroded public support for AFDC (Heclo, 2001, p. 173). The mood that settled in was: something had to be done to curb this permissive welfare spending.

The success of the civil rights movement in the 1960s brought the racial politics of welfare into the open. Heclo (2001) called this decade a watershed at which "the political meaning of welfare policy became explicitly infused with issues of race" (p. 174).

The 1960s also were the time of the second "big bang" of welfare legislating. The Economic Opportunity Act of 1964 "declared" war on poverty with a swarm of educational, employment, and social service programs for the poor, followed by signing Medicare and Medicaid into law. The expansion of the welfare state was "couched in terms of work and personal responsibility" (Haskins, 2001, p. 104). The claim for "welfare rights" of the poor became the cornerstone of Lyndon Johnson's War on Poverty, seeking to attack the structural causes of poverty and unequal opportunity. For the second time in history the debate on poverty was framed in terms of citizenship. Unfortunately, "such social engineering was rife with unintended consequences" (Heclo, 2001, p. 175), the most damaging of which was the depiction of wide-specter programs such as Head Start, community action, education grants, and Model Cities projects as mere income maintenance to the poor, thus further reinforcing negative perceptions toward the federal welfare program (Heclo, 2001, p. 175).

A new emphasis inside and outside government, largely attributable to University of Wisconsin economist Robert Lampman (e.g., Lampman, 1954), helped redefine welfare problems as a matter of income poverty. Having focused on the measurement of poverty as an expression of an officially designated level of income, social policy experts attempted to fill what was termed the poverty gap, or the income deficiency between a family's income level and a specified poverty level (Heclo, 2001, p. 176).

The period after President Johnson's War on Poverty narrowed the definition of deservingness when applied to the poor. Rooted to some degree in Johnson's own aversion to cash relief rather than work relief, social policy became linked to morality and especially the morality Johnson's Council of Economic Advisors advocated, namely, enabling those who were in need of income to earn it in order to "escape poverty" (Council of Economic Advisors, 1964; Ventry, 2000). This aversion to cash relief led to the failure of numerous versions of a guaranteed annual income, and especially any version of a negative income tax that resembled a guaranteed annual income.

By the end of the 1960s, the disillusionment with AFDC peaked. However, the survival of the program was ensured, first of all, by the fact that welfare was perceived as a chronic rather than an acute problem (Mead, 2001, p. 209) and, secondly, by its political profitability to both left and right political forces. The conservative right used it "as a marker of the excesses of liberalism," while for the left it was "a foil for charges of racism and hostility toward the poor" (Heclo, 2001, p. 177). By Heclo's admission, "AFDC was becoming a program that some people wanted but no one really believed in" (p. 177).

Thus by default, by 1970, the number of people receiving payments through AFDC grew to 7.5 million recipients from 3.1 million in 1960 (U.S. Congress, 1998, Table 7.2). Welfare dependency became a catchphrase characterizing the poor as both a deserving segment of the population and increasingly as a dependent one. During the period after President Johnson, President Nixon and Patrick Moynihan's Family Assistance Plan (FAP) lived shortly as a proposal for reforming the welfare system. Proposed as a bottom or floor for incomes for working or dependent families, FAP was not to be thought of as a guaranteed income, but rather a family assistance plan that increased the incentive to work. Essentially, the plan reduced the income tax on earnings up to a breakeven point of $4,000. FAP failed, however, primarily because it could not be shown conclusively through the now-famous New Jersey Graduated Work Incentive (or negative income tax) Experiment (Pechman and Timpane, 1975) that the negative tax encouraged work and discouraged dependence on welfare government support.

The true definition of the deserving poor as the working poor came through the efforts of Senator Russell Long (R-La.), the chair of the Senate Finance Committee at the time. His most famous utterance on the subject was a remark reported by Moynihan that Long objected to "paying people not to work," to encouraging them to "lay about all day making love and producing illegitimate babies," and to welfare mothers becoming nothing more than "brood mares" (Ventry, 2000, fn. 30; Moynihan, 1973, pp. 519, 523).

What motivated the senator, however, was the effort to supplement the income of the working poor through the Internal Revenue Service. His major insight was offsetting the social security tax paid by the employee, as well as the social security tax paid by the employer for the employee, through a tax credit he called a work bonus. It differed from guaranteed annual income plans, negative income tax plans, and of course, the welfare grant, in that the tax credit required the recipient to work. In this distinction in policy, Long reflected what had become the political gospel by this time: welfare is indolence, a way of life; poverty implies hard luck, a temporary condition (Moynihan, 1973).

Out of all this, a political awareness was born that the federal welfare system was oriented to nonworkers, leaving the working poor to fend for themselves (Heclo, 2001, p. 179). To overcome this flaw, it was suggested that the solution should be "to promote work from within the welfare system, rather than substitute work for aid" (Mead, 2001, p. 210). In the 1960s and 1970s, liberal social scientists believed that this could be accomplished with work incentives. When they did not produce the desired effect, the interest of both liberal and conservative researchers turned to welfare work programs. In the evaluation studies spanning two decades they established that "mandatory work requirements had a potential to square the welfare circle" (Mead, 2001, p. 210).

What became the first earned income tax credit came about in a rather complicated context. In 1975, President Ford, with typical Republican budgetary restraint and also with the pledge to stimulate a flagging economy, backed what became the Tax Reduction Act of 1975. In this act, taxpayers with incomes below $6,000 could receive a refundable tax credit equaling 10% of the first $4,000 of all earnings. The tax credit, however, was regarded as income if one were still receiving a welfare grant. Nevertheless, the earned income tax credit was given life for three reasons: the promotion of the interests of the "deserving, working poor," budget constraint—it didn't cost much—and economic stimulus. In the economic stimulus idea, however, there were clearly those who believed that some of the poor were able to help stimulate the economy and some of the poor were not.

Three major efforts to increase the prominence and importance of the earned income tax credit followed. First, in 1978, Congress allowed those eligible to receive an advance payment instead of a year-end, lump-sum payment. In this same year, Congress made the credit a permanent part of the tax code.

Second, the Reagan administration's Tax Reform Act of 1986 enlarged the credit. The reason for the enlargement at this time was multifaceted. The Reagan administration wanted to remove the poor from the tax rolls (Conlan, Wrightson, and Beam, 1990). In addition, inflation had eroded the value of the credit, and payroll taxes had increased to 14%, shifting the burden for these taxes considerably toward the poor. Most important, however, the Reagan administration's criteria for tax reform required distributional neutrality; that is, no income group could benefit by tax rate reduction any more than any other. Clearly, the poor would receive the least benefit by any ordinary tax rate reduction; therefore their benefit came in the form of an increase in the earned income tax credit.

The third major step up in the magnitude of the earned income tax credit came in 1993. The Omnibus Budget Reconciliation Act of 1993 led to increases in the credit's maximum benefit and other features such that it tripled in nominal size from $6.9 billion in 1990 to $19.6 billion in 1994. Although by that time welfare spending had doubled from 1980, the nominal size of the earned income tax credit exceeded the size of the federal contribution to the Aid to Families with Dependent Children program—the welfare grant program. The number of families receiving tax credit benefits was several million greater than the number receiving AFDC.

In the 1980s, direct policy tools continued to play a role in social welfare policy. Thus, the 1988 Family Support Act aimed to help welfare recipients in the transition to work by providing them with educational opportunities, job training, and medical and child care services. The act also stipulated mandatory work obligations. Most importantly, the act signaled a watershed turn in welfare policy: "Unlike welfare reform efforts of the Nixon and Carter years, there was now a growing agreement among national policymakers on the need to bring welfare recipients into the workforce" (Heclo, 2001, p. 179).

The 1990s, however, were shaped by the interplay of three political forces: conservative policy intellectuals, Republican resurgence in state governorships during a sharp recession, and electoral strategies at both the presidential and congressional levels. By Heclo's admission, "after the stunning Republican takeover of Congress in 1994, [the convergence of] these forces had ample strength to overturn a policy status quo that by then had essentially no effective political defenders" (2001, p. 180).

Charles Murray's *Losing Ground* (1984)—the landmark work on welfare policy—exemplifies the impact of conservative intellectuals on social constructions of target populations. The main argument of the book was that the entire system of welfare, instead of helping the poor, in reality was the major cause of their misery, and therefore should be abolished (Heclo, 2001, p. 182). The resonance of his message was such that it left even his staunchest opponents in doubt.

The book helped construct the image of the poor as undeserving of government aid. Such sentiments as "staying poor and not working is their choice" and "their benefits are unearned because they refuse to help themselves" were widespread (Mead, 2001, pp. 201, 206).

Thus, by the end of the 1980s, under the influence of the conservative intellectual elite, public criticism of welfare focused on behavioral norms and personal responsibility, or lack thereof, of those on public assistance and on the perceived abuses of the system that traditionally did not enforce work-oriented behavior. However, as Heclo (2001) indicates, those could have remained abstract battle lines, if recession and state budget stress did not provide "the opening for conservative policy ideas to assume concrete form in various parts of the federal system" (Heclo, 2001, p. 183). Mead (2001) characterizes the 1980s and 1990s as the conservative period, "when the agenda shifted to making welfare mothers work and restraining dependency" (p. 201). As a result, Republicans gained unprecedented credibility and political appeal as potential architects of welfare policy (Heclo, 2001, p. 182). They made radical conservative welfare reform a centerpiece of their Contract with America (Mead, 2001, p. 209). With "the stunning 1994 election results [that] gave Republicans control of the entire Congress for the first time in almost half a century" (Heclo, 2001, p. 191) and offset the Democratic party's influence "that had long blocked fundamental change from the right" (Mead, 2001, p. 209), the fate of AFDC was sealed. At the same time, quite surprisingly, it was Democrats who brought the welfare reform to the fore of the presidential campaign agenda. Heclo (2001) comments in this regard, "Never before had the politics of welfare reform been played out at this supremely high-stakes, electoral level" (Heclo, 2001, p. 185). On the one hand, "Republicans were refashioning themselves as compassionate in social policy" (Heclo, 2001, p. 186) by arguing that "true compassion lay in saving people from a demoralizing and dysfunctional federal program of welfare dependency" (Heclo, 2001, p. 182). On the other hand, for Democrats, "stunned into self-examination by defeats at the hands of Reagan and Bush" (Heclo, 2001, 186), welfare reform became a vehicle for repositioning their party on social issues (Mead, 2001, p. 209) by honing the "new Democrat" concept, requiring the abandonment of "traditional Democratic softness and permissiveness in social policy arena in favor of newly found toughness" (Heclo, 2001, p. 186). The new Democratic platform was found to be appealing to the public, as confirmed by the campaign polls showing a strongly favorable public response to the candidate Clinton's promise to "end welfare as we know it" (Heclo, 2001, p. 188).

Thus in intense partisan clashes, a consensus emerged that the new world of welfare should be based on two things: work requirements in exchange for welfare benefits and time limits on welfare assistance (Heclo, 2001, p. 191). In accordance with Donovan's (2001) model of public policy making in which elected officials consider the electoral impact of their decisions, "the final maneuver in legislating welfare reform, [as underscored by Heclo (2001)] flowed from the converging electoral interest between a Democratic president seeking a second term and congressional Republican leaders struggling to retain control of Congress after only two years at the helm" (Heclo, 2001, p. 193).

The passage of the Personal Responsibility and Work Opportunity Reconciliation Act (PRWORA) in 1996 was an outcome of intense intellectual and political partisan struggles that led to the welfare policy neither side had anticipated—with the work requirement at its core (Heclo, 2001, p. 197). As Heclo (2001) put it, "Long-standing rhetorical promises about making welfare a transition-to-work program were crystallized in the statutory language of federal law" (p. 169). Mead (2001) called PRWORA "the first truly radical welfare reform" (p. 202). For the first time the federal law actually required work as the prerequisite for help, and ended the entitlement to cash benefits.

The PWORA replaced the AFDC program with the Temporary Assistance for Needy Families (TANF) block grant, imposing a five-year time limit on the eligibility for benefits.

The legislation led to pervasive changes, the most significant of which was the influx of former welfare mothers into the workforce (Haskins, 2001, p. 105). The history made a full circle: the criterion of desert once again rose above need and rights in public policy making. Final crystallization of the poor into deserving and undeserving took place, with nonworking mothers now making up the undeserving group. As Haskins (2001) points out, "From the perspective of our brief historical overview, the 1996 welfare reform law was a return to the tradition of welfare that requires something of recipients or to the type of individual responsibility Roosevelt (1935) had in mind" (p. 104).

Table 6.1 compares welfare spending that appears in the column as Aid to Families with Dependent Children (AFDC) and in 1997 through 1999 as Personal Responsibility and Work Opportunity Reconciliation Act (PWORA) spending with the EITC.

Introduced as a means to offset payroll taxes, the EITC was available only to working parents (Michalopoulos and Berlin, 2001, pp. 271–272). The refundability of the credit means that the poorest workers, who owe no taxes, are actually paid money back (Blank et al., 2001, p. 86). Moreover, the credit increases with earnings up to a maximum amount (Michalopoulos and Berlin, 2001, pp. 271–272). It unequivocally increases work incentives in those who are out of the labor force, and, in combination with the minimum wage, in low earners (Blank et al., 2001, pp. 86–87). With a view to "further reward work and reduce poverty, the federal government significantly expanded the generosity of the EITC in 1990 and 1993" (Michalopoulos and Berlin, 2001, p. 272). Administrative data show that between 1993 and 1999 the number of families receiving the credit grew by approximately 30%, from 15.1 million to over 20 million, the average benefit increased from $1,028 to $1,541, and total spending on the EITC increased from $15.5 billion to $30.0 billion (Haskins, 2001, p. 122). By 1999, it increased the earnings of taxpayers with two or more children by up to 40%, to a maximum credit of $3,816—nearly three times the amount available in 1990. Although additional earnings would reduce the credit, some amount was nevertheless available to families earning as much as $30,000 per year. Moreover, fifteen states followed suit and began offering EITCs based on the federal credit (Michalopoulos and Berlin, 2001, p. 272).

The growth of the credit was not without controversy, however. There was a major backlash from those who thought the tax credit program had grown too big, too fast (Ventry, 2000). The fundamental bottom of the backlash was not only speed and size but also the character of the credit. The credit had grown, but had grown into a payment rather than just lost revenue receipts to the government. It resembled a negative income tax to many, and it provoked the ire of the class

**Table 6.1   Comparison of Federal Welfare and
Tax Credit Spending 1980–1999**

	AFDC and PWORA[a]	EITC[b]
1980	7.2	2.0
1981	7.8	1.9
1982	7.8	1.8
1983	8.2	1.8
1984	8.6	1.6
1985	8.7	2.1
1986	9.2	2.0
1987	10.0	3.9
1988	10.3	5.9
1989	10.6	6.6
1990	12.0	6.9
1991	13.2	10.6
1992	14.6	12.4
1993	14.8	13.2
1994	15.7	19.6
1995	16.2	22.8
1996	15.1	25.1
1997	12.5	29.7
1998	11.3	30.6
1999	11.3	31.2

Note: Years 1997–1999 PWORA data are not entirely equivalent to those under AFDC in that they do not include IV-A childcare administration (which accounted for 4% of 1996 administrative expense).

[a] U.S. Congress, House Committee on Ways and Means (2000), *2000 Green Book*. Washington, DC: U.S. Government Printing Office, Appendix A, p. A-10, Table A-3. Amounts in billions of current dollars. Years 1990–1999 prepared by the Congressional Research Service based on data from the U.S. Department of Health and Human Services.

[b] Years 1980–1996 from U.S. Congress, House Committee on Ways and Means (1994), *1994 Green Book*, pp. 389, 700; years 1997–1999 from U.S. General Accounting Office (2001), Table 2, p. 8. All numbers in billions of current dollars.

warriors who argued that the credit put the federal government back in the business of taxing the many on behalf of the few (Ventry, 2000). The distinction between the deserving, working poor and the dependent poor grew blurry.

Added to the problem of blurring was the additional problem of noncompliance. What looked like fraud to many bedeviled the program. In contrast to AFDC and food stamp overclaims, the earned income tax credit appeared to the Internal Revenue Service to have a considerably larger number of recipients who were not playing by the rules. Of all tax credits received, the IRS estimated that the amount of overclaims for 1995 and 1998 were 24 and 26%, respectively (U.S. General Accounting Office, 2001, p. 10). This part of the backlash led to considerable activity by the Internal Revenue Service that had also been accused recently of terrorizing taxpayers. Congress appropriated more money for audits of the poor. By 1999, audits of tax returns overall fell to a record low, to less than 2.5% of all tax returns. However, tax audits of the poor who had filed for the credit rose to be 44% of all IRS audits (Johnston, 2001). Interestingly, their effect on the number of fraud cases was rather ameliorative—intimidating to those who were seeking the tax credit but who were not working and rewarding to those of the working poor who had failed to apply (for a number of reasons) as law allowed them to do.

In the early and middle 1990s, budget deficit reduction had become an important issue. The federal deficit had increased from $74 billion in 1980 to $164 billion in 1995. Budget controllers or conservers in 1996 had a strong position to find and designate the undeserving among those receiving federal benefits. The hunt for the undeserving began, and among those found undeserving were tobacco interests (the Hatch-Kennedy bill to raise tobacco taxes by 43 cents to pay for uninsured children's health benefits) and welfare recipients (Palazzolo, 1999).

Public opinion, strengthening deficit reduction hawks or conservers, had moved to stereotype the nonworking poor and immigrants as undeserving. Gilens (1999) and Weaver (2000) track various polls and questions in which opinion in favor of forcing welfare beneficiaries to work for their benefits had grown from 1985 to 1996. At the same time, opposition to scuttling the earned income tax credit for the working poor also grew. Table 6.2 shows events and the interpretation model.

Choosing among direct spending, tax expenditures, loans, loan guarantees, or insurance seldom divides opinion and pushes citizens to the barricades. And yet, a trade-off between direct expenditures and tax expenditures did energize partisans and divide the country as change in social welfare policy toward the poor took place. The budget serves as a means by which government intervenes in society, inducing, educating, or sanctioning conduct and effort. Budget control is a means of selecting the most appropriate tool for maximizing the achievement of intervention. As this issue suggests, budgeting truly is a critical political and administrative battleground where it is decided who gets what, when, and how.

Table 6.2   Budgeting Interpretations in U.S. Welfare Policy

Government Decision Makers	Authorities in Charge of Taxing and Spending Policies—the Budget
↓	
Reflect the social construction of target groups for government action	Gilens (1999) and Weaver (2000) at least for welfare and the working poor
↓	
Budget by rewarding the deserving and punishing the undeserving	The apparent history of the EITC and TANF
↓	
Which they rationalize (justify after the fact) in terms of values	The counterattack and its blunting: fraud as imperfections in the law, not imperfections in values related to helping the working poor

Let's assume that Schneider and Ingram are correct. That is, the social construction of the target population as basically deserving or undeserving will dictate the fundamental criterion in any trade-off. Consider also the libertarian notion that growth in budgets, however translated through financial tools, only results in greater government control of the governed and less control of government. Budget control does seem contradictory. The greater the control, the more we tend to allow favored status for some and force punishment on the others. The less budget control, the greater the government control of the governed, although through multiple budget tools representing multiple perspectives, decentralization, and diverse, sometimes contradictory, even countervailing approaches.

Political leaders often reflect constituents and supporters whose social constructions are firm; thus the construction is followed by the choice of tool and then a rationalization of the suitability of tool to the context. These leaders, however, may also reflect views that are not firm, in which case, oftentimes, an objective criterion, stipulated by scientific observers knowledgeable in the particular field or professionals in budget control, leads to the choice of the policy tool.

The Context That We Force to Emerge, That We Enact, That We Socially Construct

While many view the program objectives in a budget arena as important in analysis, the interpretive approach, based on well-accepted notions of fact and value, might be easier to use in finding a solution to the budget control problem in a comprehensive budget. Advocating that objectives determine tools, Salamon (1989, pp. 261–262) predicts improvement in the capacity of government finance officials "to manage alternative tools and make choices among them." Recognition "that particular programs embody particular types of tools that may have distinctive consequences for the performance of the program" is very important, he goes on. Salamon argues that finance officials should notice their own willingness to sub-optimize their decision making. Officials do not choose tools in terms of goals, and "tool choices are often dictated by factors wholly unrelated to a program's purposes—such as a desire to avoid budgetary impact or escape governmental personnel ceilings." More explicit attention to optimizing tool choices will increase their effectiveness and their control, Salamon concludes.

The counter to this line of thinking digs deeper. An alternative approach asks: What is an objective and how is it established? If there is a problem, there is a mindset (enactment, social construct) that defines the problem in a particular way. That definition is not different from, fundamentally, the deserving/undeserving mindset that may characterize many, if not all, policies beyond the 1996 welfare policy intervention described here.

Thus, the problem definition is a problem of values in the Simon sense (1976). Values establish the problem, the context that is enacted or socially constructed. From these values, people are able to perform rationally in relating means to these ends.

So, how do we regenerate, rather than degenerate to deserving/undeserving, the establishment of values, ends, problems? How do we establish the context in other than a primitive and perhaps unhealthy way? Consider the approach Schattschneider's work (1975) suggests. The establishment of greater scarcity—with a comprehensive budget—will stimulate more conflict and more competition and more debate. In fact, he has faith that the greater the conflict and competition, the greater the participation in the process (pp. 126–139).

The basis of this debate would then be the budget. The budget, as it monetizes everything, becomes the substance of the whole governmental system.

How can this debate be held so that it does not end in stalemate? This might yield from the establishment, in the public's debate, of the possibility, but the unbelievably negative consequences of the possibility, of government shutdown and, more importantly, the absolute political downfall and removal of those leaders who let it happen.

Results are the commonsense criterion used in a system of popular sovereignty. Results are guaranteed when there is enough discussion of what problems there are (ends) and what means there are to solve them. Discussion, says Schattschneider (1975), comes from conflict, and that comes from competition. Conflict comes from the tension between government's role in coercion (sticks) and its role in promotion (carrots). Conflict comes from the tension between government intervention, and control of the governed, and government control of itself. According to Madison, competing decision arenas (Federalist 51) and competing interests or factions (Federalist 10) work to increase the number of different views that compete and prevent the dominance of any one view over all issues.

How can we guarantee competition and also prevent stalemate? Constraint breeds the effort to outwit it, as all lessons in budget control, and control generally, concede. Despite the problems this holds for most budget controllers, the wisdom of the constraint actually can show through. The effort to outwit the control is really a contribution to innovation. In the instances pointed out by Salamon (1989), new policy and budget tools have actually not expanded government control of the governed but have bred more public-private partnerships. These partnerships have blurred the line between what is government and what is private and have actually gained the consent of the governed in going beyond privatization of government action. Therefore, in a comprehensive budget, scarcity breeds the solution to problems with which all can live.

Endnotes

1. This chapter is adapted from Nonconventional Budgets, Gerald J. Miller, In Aman Kahn and W. Bartley Hildreth, eds., *Budget Theory in the Public Sector*, pp. 77–103. Westport, CT: Quorum Books, 2002. Used with permission of ABC-CLIO, LLC.
2. Schick's definition of nonconventional spending is narrower, as it only includes tax expenditures and direct or guaranteed loans.
3. At the U.S. state and local government levels, government accounting standards now prescribe the reporting of all financial and capital assets, liabilities, revenues, expenses, gains, and losses as one net total using an accrual basis of accounting (Governmental Accounting Standards Board, 1999).
4. "On what basis shall it be decided to allocate x dollars to Activity A instead of Activity B?" (Key, 1940, p. 1138).
5. Considerable work done by Ventry (2000) sheds light on the historic development of the earned income tax credit, and we give him credit specifically here, as we do the work of Heen (2000) and Cammisa (1998). However, we take a unique, revealing analytic tack.
6. Disability benefits were added to social security several years later.
7. Initially, the program was called Aid to Dependent Children (ADC). Its title was changed in 1950.
8. In the 1939 amendments to ADC, widows and children of workers who had been covered by Old Age Insurance were transferred to that program.

References

Anderson, Charles W. (1977). *Statecraft: An Introduction to Political Choice and Judgment.* New York: John Wiley & Sons.
Bennett, James T., and Thomas J. DiLorenzo. (1983). *Underground Government: The Off-Budget Public Sector.* Washington, DC: Cato Institute.
Berger, Peter L., and Thomas Luckmann. (1966). *The Social Construction of Reality: A Treatise in the Sociology of Knowledge.* New York: Doubleday.

Cammisa, Anne Marie. (1998). *From Rhetoric to Reform? Welfare Policy in American Politics.* Boulder, CO: Westview.

Conlan, Timothy J., Margaret T. Wrightson, and David R. Beam. (1990). *Taxing Choices: The Politics of Tax Reform.* Washington, DC: CQ Press.

Council of Economic Advisors. (1964). *Economic Report of the President.* Washington, DC: Government Printing Office.

Donovan, Mark C. (2001). *Taking Aim: Target Populations and the War on AIDS and Drugs.* Washington, DC: Georgetown University Press.

Fainstein, Susan S. (1987). The politics of criteria: Planning for the redevelopment of Times Square. In *Confronting Values in Policy Analysis: The Politics of Criteria,* 232–247. Newbury Park, CA: Sage.

Feldstein, Martin. (1980). A contribution to the theory of tax expenditures: The case of charitable giving. In *The Economics of Taxation,* 99–122. Washington, DC: Brookings Institution.

Forester, John. (1984). Bounded rationality and the politics of muddling through. *Public Administration Review* 44(1):23–31.

Gilens, Martin. (1999). *Why Americans Hate Welfare: Race, Media, and the Politics of Antipoverty Policy.* Chicago: University of Chicago Press.

Goffman, Erving. (1961). *Asylums.* Garden City: Doubleday.

Goffman, Erving. (1974). *Frame Analysis: An Essay on the Organization of Experience.* New York: Harper & Row.

Golding, Peter, and Sue Middleton. (1982). *Images of Welfare: Press and Public Attitudes to Poverty.* Oxford: Martin Robertson.

Harris, Seymour. (1955). *John Maynard Keynes: Economist and Policy Maker.* New York: Charles Scribner's.

Haskins, Ron. (2001). Effects of welfare reform on family income and poverty. In *The New World of Welfare,* 103–136. Washington, DC: Brookings Institution Press.

Heclo, Hugh. 2001. The politics of welfare reform. In *The New World of Welfare,* 169–200. Washington, DC: Brookings Institution Press.

Heen, Mary L. 2000. Reinventing tax expenditure reform: Improving program oversight under the Government Performance and Results Act. *Wake Forest Law Review* 35(4):751–826.

Howard, Christopher. 1997. *The Hidden Welfare State: Tax Expenditures and Social Policy in the United States.* Princeton, NJ: Princeton University Press.

Ingram, Helen M., and Anne L. Schneider. (2005). Introduction: Public policy and the social construction of deservingness. In *Deserving and Entitled: Social Constructions and Public Policy,* 1–33. Albany: State University of New York Press.

Ippolito, Dennis S. (1984). *Hidden Spending: The Politics of Federal Credit Programs.* Chapel Hill: University of North Carolina Press.

Johnston, David Cay. (2001). Rate of all I. R. S. audits falls: Poor face particular scrutiny. *New York Times,* February 16, pp. A1, C11.

Jordan, Bill. (1998). *The New Politics of Welfare.* Thousand Oaks, CA: Sage Publications.

Kettl, Donald F. (2000). The transformation of governance: Globalization, devolution, and the role of government. *Public Administration Review* 60(6):488–497.

Key, V. O. (1940). The lack of a budgetary theory. *American Political Science Review* 34:1137–1140.

Koven, Steven G. (1999). *Public Budgeting in the United States: The Cultural and Ideological Setting.* Washington, DC: Georgetown University Press.

Lampman, Robert J. (1954). Recent changes in income inequality reconsidered. *American Economic Review* 44(3):251–268.

Litan, Robert E., and William D. Nordhaus. (1983). *Reforming Federal Regulation.* New Haven, CT: Yale University Press.

Madison, James. (1978). The Federalist, No. 51, New York Packet, February 8, 1788. In *The Federalist or, the New Constitution,* 262–267. New York: Dutton.

March, James G., and Johan P. Olsen. (1976). *Ambiguity and Choice in Organizations.* Bergen, Norway: Universitetsforlaget.

March, James G., and Johan P. Olsen. (1989). *Rediscovering Institutions: The Organizational Basis of Politics.* New York: Free Press.

McCaffery, Jerry, and Keith G. Baker. (1990). Optimizing choice in resource decisions: Staying within the boundary of the comprehensive-rational method. *Public Administration Quarterly* 14:142–172.

Mead, Lawrence M. (2001). The politics of conservative welfare reform. In *The New World of Welfare,* 201–222. Washington, DC: Brookings Institution Press.

Mencher, Samuel. (1966). Introduction to the Poor Law Reports of 1834 and 1909. In *Social Welfare in Transition,* 37–44. Pittsburgh: University of Pittsburgh Press.

Michalopoulos, Charles, and Gordon Berlin. (2001). Financial work incentives for low-wage workers. In *The New World of Welfare,* 270–290. Washington, DC: Brookings Institution Press.

Miller, David. (1999). *Principles of Social Justice.* Cambridge, MA: Harvard University Press.

Moynihan, Daniel Patrick. (1973). *The Politics of a Guaranteed Income: The Nixon Administration and the Family Assistance Plan.* New York: Random House.

Niskanen, William. (1988). *Reaganomics: An Insider's Account of the Policies and the People.* New York: Oxford University Press.

Palazzolo, Daniel J. (1999). *Done Deal.* Chappaqua: Seven Bridges Press.

Pechman, Joseph A., and P. Michael Timpane, eds. (1975). *Work Incentives and Income Guarantees: The New Jersey Negative Income Tax Experiment.* Washington, DC: Brookings Institution.

The Poor Law Report of 1834. (1966). In *Social Welfare in Transition.* Pittsburgh, PA: University of Pittsburgh Press.

President's Commission on Budget Concepts. (1967). *Report and Staff Papers and Other Materials Reviewed by the President's Commission.* Washington, DC: Government Printing Office.

Rist, Ray C. (1998). Choosing the right policy instrument at the right time: The contextual challenges of selection and implementation. In *Carrots, Sticks and Sermons: Policy Instruments and Their Evaluation,* 149–163. New Brunswick, NJ: Transaction Books.

Rosen, Harvey S. (1985). *Public Finance.* Homewood, IL: Irwin.

Salamon, Lester M., ed. (1989). *Beyond Privatization: The Tools of Government Action.* Washington, DC: Urban Institute Press.

Salamon, Lester M., and Michael S. Lund. (1989). The tools approach: Basic analytics. In *Beyond Privatization: The Tools of Government Action,* 23–49. Washington, DC: Urban Institute Press.

Schattschneider, E. E. (1975). *The Semisovereign People.* Hinsdale, IL: Dryden Press.

Schick, Allen. (1986). Controlling nonconventional expenditure: Tax expenditures and loans. *Public Budgeting and Finance* 6(1):3–20.

Schick, Allen. (1988). An inquiry into the possibility of a budgetary theory. In *New Directions in Budget Theory,* 59–69. Albany: State University of New York Press.

Schick, Allen. (2007). Off-budget expenditure: An economic and political framework. *OECD Journal on Budgeting* 7(3):1–32.

Schick, Allen, and the OECD Senior Budget Officials. (2009). *Evolutions in Budgetary Practice*. Paris: OECD.

Schneider, Anne, and Helen Ingram. (1990). The behavioral assumptions of policy tools. *Journal of Politics* 52:511–529.

Schneider, Anne, and Helen Ingram. (1993). Social construction of target populations: Implications for politics and policy. *American Political Science Review* 87:334–347.

Schneider, Anne, and Helen Ingram. (1994). Social constructions and policy design: Implications for public administration. *Research in Public Administration* 3:137–173.

Schneider, Anne L., and Helen M. Ingram, eds. (2005). *Deserving and Entitled: Social Constructions and Public Policy*. Albany: State University of New York Press.

Schneider, Anne Larson, and Helen Ingram. (1997). *Policy Design for Democracy*. Lawrence: University of Kansas Press.

Schon, Donald A., and Martin Rein. (1994). *Frame Reflection: Toward the Resolution of Intractable Policy Controversies*. New York: Basic Books.

Simon, Herbert A. (1976). *Administrative Behavior*. 3rd ed. New York: Free Press.

Solow, Robert M. (1998). *Work and Welfare*. Princeton, NJ: Princeton University Press.

Surrey, Stanley S., and Paul R. McDaniel. (1985). *Tax Expenditures*. Cambridge, MA: Harvard University Press.

Thompson, Fred. (1997). Toward a regulatory budget. *Public Budgeting and Finance* 17(1):89–98.

Thurmaier, Kurt. (1995). Decisive decision making in the executive budget process: Analyzing the political and economic propensities of central budget bureau analysts. *Public Administration Review* 55(5):448–460.

U.S. Congress, House Committee on Ways and Means. (1998). *The 1998 Green Book: Background Material and Data on Programs within the Jurisdiction of the Committee on Ways and Means*. Washington, DC: Government Printing Office.

Vedung, Evert. (1998). Policy instruments: Typologies and theories. In *Carrots, Sticks and Sermons: Policy Instruments and Their Evaluation*, 21–58. New Brunswick, NJ: Transaction Publishers.

Ventry, Dennis J. (2000). The collision of tax and welfare politics: The political history of the earned income tax credit, 1969–1999. *National Tax Journal*, December, 983–1026.

Weaver, R. Kent. (2000). *Ending Welfare as We Know It*. Washington, DC: Brookings.

Weick, Karl. (1976). Educational organizations as loosely-coupled systems. *Administrative Science Quarterly* 21:1–19.

Weick, Karl. (1979). Cognitive processes in organizations. In *Research in Organizational Behavior*, 41–74. Greenwich: JAI Press.

Weick, Karl. (1980). The management of eloquence. *Executive* 6:18–21.

Wildavsky, Aaron. (2002). *Budgeting: A Comparative Theory of Budgetary Processes*. 4th ed. New Brunswick, NJ: Transaction Books.

Winston, Pamela. (2002). *Welfare Policymaking in the States: The Devil in Devolution*. Washington, DC: Georgetown University Press.

Chapter 7

Budgeting Structures and Citizen Participation

Gerald J. Miller and Lyn Evers

When asked why they chose their community, citizens answer: "Good schools and low taxes." Nearness to work and closeness to extended families are added factors. Government budgeting decisions enable these choices even though citizens may never have participated in them. So, why the concern with democratizing budgeting?

Government budgeting and finance decisions during periods of economic instability especially beg for citizen participation. Property values have a governmental and personal impact in the community, a threat to governments during downturns and individual homeowners during upturns. In a downturn such as the 2008–2010 period, tax appeals and declining home values hit government budgets hard. When resources are scarce, budgetary decisions need to be made that may have serious long-range implications on how well the community maintains its attractiveness to residents and business, property values, and ultimately its long-term economic vitality—all of which citizens care about.

Citizens have the right to know how serious the circumstances are and at least be given the opportunity to ask questions and provide input in the budget areas that affect them. Rational people understand the basics of budgeting in their own household and, given the current economic situation, would now, more likely than at any other time since the late 1980s, understand why financially the government cannot continue being all things to all people.

Some argue that most elected officials fear a long overdue discussion of what the government should be doing. However, those who argue so may be underestimating the average citizen. Unfortunately, delaying the discussion will only result in certain services being maintained when they should probably be cut, or supported by new user fees, especially if services would be delivered shoddily because of staff reductions. Discussions with citizens may reveal to finance officials that it is better to have a few unhappy citizens because of eliminated services or increased fees than a whole town angry because city managers cannot staff all services and deliver them any way other than poorly.

Dissatisfaction with government stems in part from government budgeting in good and bad economic times. Economic change has persisted for about four decades if we consider Vietnam wartime inflation and surtaxes in the late 1960s or the oil price increases in the 1970s as the start. Dissatisfaction at least partly borne of economic changes is a major feature of the right turn that has influenced government budgeting and finance officials over the last three decades. Citizen participation is also the democratizing logic finance officials say they sometimes use to interpret ambiguous events. Why finance officials rarely consider the citizen participation form of their democratizing logic an appropriate basis for interpretation is the subject of this chapter's discussion. Here, finance officials are budgeteers, since citizen participation[1] research focuses on taxing and spending issues that are at the center of government finance to citizens. Also, when we refer to budgeteers, as with finance officials, we include elected and appointed officials, political masters, and technicians.

Large "disconnections" between satisfaction with services and willingness to pay taxes have appeared regularly in surveys (e.g., Glaser and Hildreth, 1999). Finance officials often get the blame even though, on the whole, citizens value what they get for their taxes in their decisions to live where they live. What is the problem with budgeting? Are budgeteers' values misplaced? Have budgeteers lost important links to citizens?

As for aims or values, budgeteers express their ideals without reservation. City managers and finance officers, pressed hard to think through their reasons for joining their professions, say they devote their efforts to helping build the "city on the hill," the "city beautiful," or simply, a community.

As for the lost links to citizens, officials desire citizen involvement. The idea of citizen participation must, from a secure and enlightened manager's and governing body's perspective, be not only desirable but also essential for government to be truly representative and to identify, prioritize, and meet the most urgent needs of the community with ever more limited resources. Participation can certainly help deal with events, as citizens participate in providing more information to decision makers, taking part of the risk in complicated situations, and helping to integrate relatively different views of the world.

The positive view of citizen participation led to its early use. President Lyndon B. Johnson's "maximum feasible participation" executive orders for programs within his War on Poverty in the mid-1960s gave the movement a start. The tenor of the times was pro-positive government; thus participation was an unalloyed good.

If the history of citizen participation and public officials' values lead them to prize community, and common sense leads them to involve citizens, why today's concern? Why are "citizens angry with their political leaders, estranged from civic institutions, distrustful ..., pessimistic about the prospect for collective action to solve community problems" (Weeks, 2000, p. 360)?

Generally, the answer may lie in the divide between the ideal world of aspirations and the structures that exist in the real world of politics and government operations. In the political realm, citizens often have overdeveloped or unrealistic expectations of what government should do or be involved in. These expectations add to the challenge of budgeting. A "caretaker mentality," in which government is all things to all people, has gained wide acceptance, as federal officials have promoted it and it seeps into citizen thinking at all levels. Citizen participation, focused on what governments were created to do and going back to the basic premise that government should do only what will not or cannot be done by the private sector, would certainly make budgeting less complicated, however tantalizing a return to that thinking might be. Redefining government goals would potentially reduce competition for available resources. However, the sense of entitlement, often voiced by large segments of the population and often nurtured by politicians and special interest groups, will be difficult to curtail during the right turn in the U.S. Government managers, and particularly budget officials, observe that what many people forget is *they* are the government when it comes to funding, *they* need to realize the money almost always comes out of their or their neighbor's pocket. This concept may be more effectively pointed out to citizens during an economic downturn. However, the loss of personal resources may intensify citizen insistence that government should not divert from the caretaker role.

The primary subject of this chapter is not the political realm but the real world of government operations. Citizens often stand a large distance from the real world of budgeting. The high ideal of participation may underestimate the structural complexity in budgeting and understate the time and effort required for *anyone* to understand budget issues and processes.

Research can reveal how budgeting actually works in the year-in, year-out process that many call dreadful (Leo, 1998, p. 23), especially for meaningful citizen understanding and influence. This chapter presents evidence from existing research that sheds light on when and in what way participation can have an impact on budgeting. The first part of the chapter conceptualizes, through the literature, five facets of budgeting, each having both problems and solutions for citizen involvement—budget issues, publics, tools, officials, and procedures. The chapter emphasizes structures in which citizen participation can take place constructively and effectively. The second section of the chapter outlines intervention designs that have proved to be constructive in dealing with the larger problems connecting budgeting and citizen participation. The chapter therefore seeks to determine where participation in budgeting can have an impact on citizen anger, cynicism, distrust, and pessimism. This chapter suggests solutions to the real-world problems in budgeting.

Structures

Specifically, what are these complicated structures that pose obvious and subtle problems for broad public engagement? First, issues in budgeting intersect with other policy issues and political agendas in any year and over a number of years, and prior decisions limit discretion and make new challenges difficult to surmount. Following the money will often give a clear picture of the limiting impact of prior year decisions. Second, various publics wanting to get involved vary by type and composition; often, they breed suspicion and rivalry. Third, tools for engaging citizens have only recently emerged as tough and reliable. Fourth, budgeteers' roles and norms frequently seem to fixate on expertise or representation justifying sole discretion and fail to change or evolve to broad participation. And finally, those in the budget process itself bury their methods of decision making deep within their practice, often hiding the reason for making choices even from themselves. For each of these structures, budgeting research reveals problems bedeviling citizen participation. Yet, there are also in each of these structures facets that favor citizen involvement.

Issues

Budgeting encompasses a variety of issues, and the question immediately arises: Are they equally important to citizens and can citizen preferences have an impact on all of them? Important budget issues are those for which preference revelation is important to the community, and those for which risk sharing between citizens and officials can take place.

There are four classes of issues that pose problems yet provide opportunities for participation: uncontrollable issues, budget knots, planning issues, and non-negotiable issues. First, there are issues beyond citizens'—and even officials' and professionals'—immediate control. Budgeteers must clearly explain to citizens the issues that are beyond immediate control. These issues include the law, generally and especially tax and expenditure controls, budget process requirements, including deadlines; mandates for certain services, service levels, and service recipients; and tax sources, or what can and cannot be taxed.

Second, at a slightly different level, there are tight budget knots or issues that include choices and trade-offs with both foreseeable and unforeseeable consequences. The budget knots frequently confound understanding and prediction. Consider such a situation. A locality's citizens and officials, a broad consensus, may decide to provide affordable housing. The participation is genuine and the response immediate. The affordable housing, by necessity, must be a high-density land use. The population density eventually has a substantially greater impact on services, especially schools, than would have been the case with lower-density development. The higher service demand, of course, leads to higher property tax increases.

The affordable housing project may have displaced something else, levee construction and drainage improvements. Shortly after the locality's budgeteers respond to provide affordable housing, a flood may occur, creating an emergency situation. Capital spending must take place immediately without knowledge of whether federal and state aid will support it. The budget for the following year immediately goes up as the deficit for the present year balloons. The flood destroys property, reducing property tax revenues felt in the following year. Spending increases and revenue reductions squeeze other parts of the budget. The squeeze, in turn, may actually lead to layoffs and delays in still other projects. Layoffs and project delays will only increase costs due to inflation and the need to find and rehire the laid off experts or new experts who will demand higher salaries than the people laid off.

The series does not end. The responsible parties—in this case, the locality's budgeteers—may face intense opposition and even defeat and removal from office for not accurately portraying the trade-off among housing, greater demand on schools, and higher property tax payments. They may be punished for not accurately portraying the consequences of the decision on levee construction and drainage improvements. They may be punished for not accurately portraying the vagaries of nature.

Thus, we have a real effort by budgeteers to encourage participation and be responsive. From instinct and experience, many budgeteers could have warned of some or all of the series of events happening and probably do. Some of the events cannot be portrayed with more than probabilities even in a reasonably well-organized participation effort. Some officials would avoid being responsive, in the first place. Other officials, pained by the unfolding events, may never attempt citizen participation again.

Such a discretionary and meaningful issue as affordable housing and its consequences, of course, beg for planning, risk sharing, and understanding. Who could make such a decision without citizen *and* elected official *and* professional manager participation? The problem lies in ensuring that the effort to inform is a good faith one.

Third, besides budget knots, there are tractable issues relating to the future. There are four groups. First, there are capital budgets, since by law in most places they must deal with periods of up to a decade. Second, there are economic development strategies, especially as they bear on tax abatements. Third, there are, generally, policy or strategic plans, annual performance plans, and budgets into the near future, all of which help determine what problems to solve, what services citizens want, and how to find out. Finally, there are performance evaluations well suited to citizen involvement. Performance evaluation deals with what expectations citizens have for the performance of existing and new services, and can involve everyone in defining how well agencies perform now, how they should perform, how this performance should be measured, and how these measures and the performance itself should be evaluated.

All of these issues permit a planning process in which time exists to think through the problems and choices. All will sooner or later have large consequences for the operating budget.

A final group of issues causes even greater concern. These are often nonnegotiable issues, and they are a major problem. These issues involve equity and a very closely related, even overlapping one: the interest of the community as a whole.

The nonnegotiable issues are those we find budget officials holding for themselves. Budgeteers are often not willing to reveal them, and few people bother to probe for them or question them ahead of time. Making them nonnegotiable, even not discussable, gives the appearance that budget officials have set the agenda for decisions before citizens arrive.

Some of these ways of dealing with issues are very basic. They include questions about whether the budget should redistribute upward or downward among income groups. For example, when cuts take place, should officials cut social services or police, given the view that social services represent a distribution downward in support for the poor and police spending a distribution upward in social control of the poor?

Another, more immediate nonnegotiable issue lies in how tax burdens should be shared across existing, living generations. For example, should schools be paid for by parents and seniors or by parents only? How should burdens be spread across living and unborn generations? Should debt finance spending? Should deferred maintenance of infrastructure be permitted?

This group of nonnegotiable, community-wide interest set of issues is a major sticking point in budgeting. Delving deeply might be worthwhile in establishing what is a community-wide interest; who is able, where and when, to voice concern; and who ultimately should decide them.

On community-wide issues, we may find the greatest differences among professionals: What is the whole community's interest, officials and citizens? Who should define it? The debate over these issues can lead to even more fundamental questions about whether an election defines participation ultimately and finally. Does a professional owe the official a duty, since the official is the final decision maker and the person to whom professional expertise must serve? Is the official a trustee or a representative? If an official is a representative, whom does he or she serve for community-wide budget issues? With such issues, the conflict over who should play what role in budgeting becomes severe.

Advocates of citizen participation debate what issues participation can deal with effectively. Broad agreement favors planning issues. However, participation cannot affect uncontrollable issues, although understanding which issues are controllable and uncontrollable will influence the amount of cynicism budgeting generates. Beyond uncontrollables lie tricky budget knots that require long-term and deep immersion in trade-offs and efforts to foresee consequences, a requirement that may be beyond many citizens. Nevertheless, most individuals have a clear view of what risks are probably worth taking and which are not. Citizen participation can add valuable insights—and a willingness to share risks—that risk assessors may never contemplate. A real problem for citizen participation does remain. Nonnegotiable issues represent a standoff and require an initial and much deeper inquiry into theories and beliefs about government, particularly political representation and administrative delegation. These issues, too, require citizen deliberation, but this deliberation goes far beyond that normally contemplated among advocates. These issues require that both citizens and budgeteers understand the meaning of the words *of, by,* and *for* the people, a task of many dimensions, large time commitments, and steady concentration.

Publics

The citizen involvement literature does not provide the textured pictures of the public that budgeteers have to deal with. We find several publics: an attentive, partisan one, a group of volunteers, watchdog groups, and news media; the inattentive public; and a reachable public.

Most often budgeteers deal with attentive publics. That is, much of the time, budgets involve exhausting effort to deal with groups supporting a partisan agenda or present or potential elected officials. These groups have sufficient leverage to demand attention and get it. Yet, these people may be the cause of widespread cynicism among the broader public: in order to appease cronies and interest groups, officials "use smoke and mirrors ... to mislead the masses" (Berman, 1997, p. 106).

Just as important as attentive, outside publics, budgeting includes those who are inside, usually the volunteers on civic boards who officials appoint. What are these officials' motives, and what do budgeteers do to encourage and control them? Baker (1994) observes many reasons to serve as a volunteer on a municipal board or commission. His research indicates that most volunteers view service as a civic duty, and others serve because they need to be involved. These motives, he found, were joined by the desire to provide expertise as well as to respond to calls for help. Purposeful volunteers had a yen for problem solving. In each of these cases, cooperative participation appears to have a good possibility for success. Nevertheless, some volunteers also expect a future payoff in terms of jobs, money, or elected office, Baker said.

The research also pointed to other, potentially disruptive motives. Some volunteers, according to Baker, saw their efforts simply as the advancement of their political careers. He also found a more distrustful set of motives for volunteering, stating:

> A possible reason for volunteering was mistrust or pessimism about others' collective action. [Baker's survey respondents] thought they could do things better than their fellow citizens (expertise), or they did not trust others in terms of city policymaking. (Baker, 1994, p. 126)

Distrustful volunteers can resist participation, sabotage the efforts of those they mistrust, and eventually bring work in their area to a halt. In order to reduce the risk of distrustful volunteers disrupting efforts, it is not unheard of for an appointing body to check the political affiliation of a potential volunteer hoping to minimize the likelihood that a volunteer could break up the agenda being promoted by the incumbents.

If the motivations are varied, the efforts to keep these volunteers and make use of their contributions vary as well. One of the most compelling reasons to recruit, care, and feed volunteers is cost. The volunteer represents one less position to fill and pay for. Volunteers do not require the complex set of controls and oversight that coproduction with nonprofits or contracting out with private sector vendors entails. The volunteer becomes an educated citizen who often plays an advocacy role on behalf of policies the volunteer has had a hand in fashioning.

Finally, among attentive publics are watchdog groups (Callahan, 1997; Beinart, 1997) and the news media (Swoboda, 1995). In the latter case, especially, small local newspapers, using inexperienced reporters with very little or no knowledge about government, can increase cynicism by misreporting. Controversy sells newspapers, something local managers often learn the hard way by way of a misleading headline. Local government managers can educate the staff members of these media, but only temporarily, as reporters change jobs to newspapers and media outlets in larger localities. The cycle must start over again and again. In the cases of both watchdog groups and the news media, these groups can gain knowledge with government officials' help. The time required varies directly with the number and levels of knowledge of these groups. These groups are so varied that each requires its own style of attentiveness, and this attentiveness is perhaps the skill at which budgeteers are most adept.

In contrast to the attentive, there are publics who are not. First, hardened antigovernment partisans, some alienated, some not, comprise a no-win situation for most budgeteers. These groups are so convinced of their positions that little headway may be made in convincing them otherwise. The best one can do, one budgeteer noted, is to observe neutrality and permit a view by the rest of the world of them as gadflies. Second, there are transient residents or residents who are temporary residents in either mind or body.

Public opinion polling has revealed another group that is neither organized nor inattentive but is reachable in budget terms. Glaser and Hildreth (1999) questioned individuals through telephone interviews to determine their satisfaction with services provided by their locality and their willingness to pay for those services. They argued that budgeteers could conceivably disregard those individuals who expressed low satisfaction and an unwillingness to pay for services as unswayable antigovernment types.

However, they went on to explore the attitudes of the remaining groups. Glaser and Hildreth (1999, p. 57) found strong support among these individuals for paying increased taxes if (1) "I could see how my tax dollars are being spent," (2) "government made a greater effort to honor citizen's values and priorities," (3) "government reduced the cost of each service produced" or "I could be sure that government was spending my money wisely." The strongest reason for willingness to pay more taxes—rested efforts to convince publics of the value and wisdom of government spending.

The "public" combines many different groups. Each has a different reason for participating. Each citizen's participation has an impact on budgeting, in actual practice or by default. Citizen participation may have a very contextual and consequential meaning, depending upon how the word is defined and applied.

Tools for Engaging Citizens

Success in citizen participation comes readily with tractable issues and reachable publics through successful application of tools. What tools exist to engage citizens? Under what circumstances does what work? We find that numerous tools exist, but those that work tend to be those that reveal the budget in ways that allow citizens to deal with their concerns.

Two descriptive pieces deserve mention because of the number of tools they describe. Denhardt, Denhardt, and Glaser (2000) reviewed many citizen participation strategies in the context of strategic planning in local government. Their work, and the experience it reflects, provides a guide as to what change programs might work well under what conditions. Also, the International City/County Management Association has published a revealing Management Information Service Report called *Talking with Citizens about Money* (Jimno, 1997).

However, the analytical literature promises even more. The most important piece is that by Berman (1997), whose empirical research deals directly with "When does what work?" His premise (p. 107) is that cynicism arises when

> (1) citizens believe that local government is using its power against them or otherwise not helping them; (2) citizens do not feel part of local government, or they feel misunderstood or ignored; and (3) citizens find local government services and policies to be ineffective.

Berman attempts to explain low levels of cynicism in terms of specific strategies used to reduce it. First, there are education strategies that encourage awareness of government activities, and these activities further the individual citizen's purposes and aims. A second set of strategies incorporates citizen feedback into public decision making and includes hearings, citizen surveys, panels, and focus groups. A third set of strategies aims "to enhance the reputation of local government for competency and efficiency [with] good performance and effective communication of that performance" (Berman, 1997, p. 106).

The third strategy actually asks something of those in government—to get results—that is missed by the others.

The findings are straightforward; many strategies work. Many strategies work well in the eyes of Berman's respondents, city managers and chief administrative officers in 304 cities over 50,000 population, in being associated with less cynical populations. Several specific methods are especially powerful, as Berman (1997, p.

109) states: "Informational mailings about what government does, and the levels of service performance, the use of mailings to explain how government balances interests, the use of citizen panels and voter referenda, and media campaigns."

Berman observes that the most successful strategy depends on the level of cynicism. First he reported that "respondents in cities with low levels of cynicism identify the use of public hearings, public access broadcasts of council meetings, a few citizen advisory panels, annual reports, and sporadic surveys of citizen attitudes as important cynicism-reduction initiatives" (p. 108). Moreover, cities in which respondents reported low cynicism or high trust are more active. These cities are engaged in much less sporadic effort and much more of a sustained campaign with "dozens of citizen task forces and focus groups, ... strategies to respond immediately to citizen queries and complaints, ... surveys to identify citizen preferences (in addition to attitudes), ... regular meetings with neighborhood activists, ... newsletters, and [a consistent and sustained explanation of] what government does and how it meets citizen needs" (pp. 109–110).

The findings deal with citizen participation in the most obvious way—tools and techniques—but Berman's work does not deal with the issue of who decides budgets and in what way.

The research by O'Toole and Marshall (1988) offers some insight into the "what way" question. Their survey of finance officials delved into the budgeting mechanism itself and the use of other tools of citizen participation. They found that localities that went beyond simple line item budgets—decision making involving inputs—to budgets involving outputs and outcomes incorporated more citizen participation tools. These localities are "more likely to have citizen advisory groups/committees as one of their citizen input mechanisms ..., are also significantly more inclined to use both presentations before interested groups and budget summaries and other explanatory material ..., and are significantly more likely to include advisory groups/committees in the budget process" (O'Toole and Marshall, 1988, pp. 52–53).

The necessary emphasis on performance and the necessity to have citizen feedback on performance, perhaps even what to perform well on, seems unmistakable. Berman and O'Toole and Marshall together suggest that efforts in budgeting to encourage performance, and the work to communicate this performance, require more than a line item budget. The higher-level, more revealing forms of budgets allow citizens to understand performance, to sharpen perceptions of performance, and to help make choices about what to perform well at.

The Budgeteers Themselves

Having looked at issues over which citizen involvement may have some sway, as well as the definition of the attentive and reachable publics and the tools that have some use, consider the budgeteers on the inside—politicians, managers, and technicians—and their views and attitudes on budgeting in and with the public.

Balancing the budget is difficult. Given budget constraints—higher government mandates, collective bargaining agreements, tax and expenditure limitations and extreme pressure against raising taxes at all—demands by citizen participants often make budget balancing even more complicated and place pressure directly on the treasury controller. Budgeteers understandably reject all but very carefully planned interventions involving citizens.

Budgeteers have more disincentives for encouraging citizens to participate. In many states, localities must respond to the incentives posed by state supervisory officials. These officials can minutely scrutinize every facet of localities' budgets to ensure that they follow state laws. The controller is the person who must advise local officials on state finance laws, laws that often limit the responses officials can make to citizens.

Collective bargaining also discourages citizen participation directly. No citizen will participate in collective bargaining. Moreover, results from collective bargaining, and even more often the arbitration required when bargaining reaches stalemate, displace other possible programs and services.

State supervision and collective bargaining, however, can and often do become convenient scapegoats to use in resisting change or new ideas. Citizen cynicism grows as one hears "The state—or the unions—won't let us do it" or even worse "That's illegal" when such is not the case. The situation has to be explained. If not, the result is a citizen who feels badly informed and dangerous and who will not be likely to contribute again. Sooner or later, it can breed feelings of fatalism.

Another blamed source for controller resistance lies in the professional norms budgeteers have learned and practiced. These norms, while blamed as a source of resistance, actually can be a source of support, even if very lukewarm, as research reveals.

Jennifer Alexander (1999) focused on discretionary action by nonelected budgeting administrators in state and local governments in the midwestern United States. She compared the reaction of these officials to scenarios contrasting an "a-ethical" ethos of technocracy with a bargaining ethos in which particular interest groups and elected officials all believe that the invisible hand of competition will ensure the appropriate and best action win. These two norms of budgeteers then were contrasted with a democratic (citizen participation) ethos. She interviewed eighteen local budgeting administrators and budgeting analysts. According to Alexander, "They were provided with a brief description of [the] ethical codes … (bargaining, technocratic, and democratic), and asked if any of them pertained in their work" (p. 557). The budgeteers reported that they were responsive to citizen demands, often to the detriment of efficiency or the reelection interests of officials. The respondents reported themselves to anticipate citizen demands and act in citizen interests as well. Surprisingly, she found the interviews to reveal "several examples … of the technocratic ethos, the democratic, and occasions when both pertained. None of the administrators provided examples that conformed with the utility-maximizing norms of a bargaining ethos" (p. 560).

The research results provide support for citizen participation in different ways. The New Jersey focus group research by Miller (Chapter 3) suggests that local government finance officers (CFOs) value citizen participation, in the abstract, but they also value the representative function elected officials fulfill. While there was no conclusive support for representation as the preeminent norm, the discussion by CFOs led to the conclusion that they were unlikely to risk the consequences of citizen participation without elected officials sharing the risk. Despite legislators' willingness to delegate, CFOs are unwilling to risk the conflict they face in assuming the legislators' role as representative of the people. The solution? CFOs say that they should not be the formal initiators of citizen participation efforts. Once convinced of elected officials' sincerity about participation, as well as their practicality, CFOs seem more than willing.

How far finance officials are willing to go informally is another matter. The interviews of Midwestern state and local officials by Alexander reveal that budgeteers have acted to involve citizens much more than their norms would lead one to believe. Her interviewees reported being responsive to citizen concerns and often anticipating them. The respondents never mentioned abiding by the norm of loyalty to representatives.

Both pieces of research answer our initial question of whether budgeteers' values were misplaced and contributed to citizen distrust. As leaders in the movement for more citizen participation, CFOs are not secure. They are cross-pressured when citizen participation is added to the considerable number of factors with which they already contend. The first reaction may be to defer to elected officials. The second may be defensiveness and opposition since they bear so much of the responsibility for decisions, the consequences of which they foresee as threatening their ability to balance lower taxes with expanded services.

CFOs see their uppermost goal as gaining the respect of legislators so that their discretion expands. This discretion can expand so that the bulk of budgets constructed by financial officials become law, having been altered only marginally by legislators. Only then, feeling secure, do CFOs act as Alexander suggests, anticipating or responding to citizens.

How the Budget Processes Work

Beyond the issues, the publics, the techniques, and the officials lies the process of budgeting itself. In the explicit and implicit assumptions officials use, we find much of budgeting's mystery and major problems for effective citizen participation.

One extreme is that found by Meltsner (1971). He described the City of Oakland, California's, revenue decision makers as devoted to avoiding the public. They used anticipatory tactics by not raising taxes enough to give rise to opposition. They also resorted to indirect taxes to hide from the public the true size of tax payments. When they did raise taxes, Oakland decision makers negotiated them with "friends," such as those who were insiders, and would receive favorable attention in other matters.

O'Toole and Marshall (1988) had a more optimistic view of budgets. Their research suggested that the more information the budget contained, the more likely the governments used other citizen participation methods as well. These other methods included advisory groups and committees, presentations before interested groups, and special analyses for communications media.

Berman's (1997) research complements this finding. Methods to reduce cynicism about government that seemed to work for city managers and chief administrative officers, he found, involved budgeting in such a way that it reinforced the need for participation. Participation fed useful information into budgeting.

Participation, however, requires knowledge. Knowledge of complicated budgets is difficult and time-consuming. Also, knowledge comes with knowing how much discretion really exists and being able to see and use both explicit and implicit assumptions built into budgets.

First, discretion, or how much discretion there really is, has become a difficult phenomenon to communicate. Discretion ranges greatly across localities, we're sure, but the amount of discretion remains relatively small. Localities are at the bottom of the hierarchy among governments. As such, decisions on many costs and revenues are beyond local control. Pension costs, in New Jersey, for example, are controlled totally by the state pension system, although the basis—salaries paid—is still generally a local matter. Salaries paid are more often than not in New Jersey subject to collective bargaining backed by binding arbitration, resulting in the phenomenon that relatively low-ranked police officers and fire department personnel are the highest paid employees in local government. Inflation and technological change wreak havoc, as do insurance premiums demanded by commercial insurers bent on getting out of the government insurance business. Utilities also are beyond much organizational control. All of these costs come on top of budgets that have a New Jersey state law mandated expenditure cap (no more than an increase of 3.5%, with formal action of the governing body or the local urban price index). In addition, a recently enacted 2% tax levy cap, with its limited exemptions, further hamstrings local government budgeting. The revenue forecast, which enforces a balanced budget, may be no greater, generally, than the previous year's collections. As can be seen, there may be much less discretion—flexibility for change—than one might think. The lack of discretion prompts budgeteers to be leery of citizen participation. By its very nature, citizen participation inflates expectations about change. The realization that so little change may be possible often follows with discouragement and cynicism.

A second area for learning and insight exists in the explicit assumptions that guide budgeting. Explicit assumptions may be fairly easily found, often in budget policies that drive decision making. These policies can change, but knowing them helps understand budget choices and the likelihood of one fact, rather than another, being accepted. In fact, budgeteers adopt explicit assumptions to clear away some of the clutter from a complicated task of putting together a budget each year. As Barber (1966, pp. 44–45) observed, "By consciously devoting time early in the budget process to determining [budget policies], these matters are removed from the agenda of many meetings on specific budget items removing a source of frustration at constantly revisiting the same decisions in every department they review.... Such cross-cutting decisions on specific, clearly defined topics offer much better possibilities for [transparency and] improvement [in the overly complicated way budgets are often encountered] than vague discussions of general goals or theories of administration."

Implicit assumptions in budgets are much harder to force out into the open. Nevertheless, they exist and have a profound effect on budget decisions. One major assumption exists in the choice to question past courses of action. This is the problem of incrementalism, or not reexamining base budgets and dealing only with incremental increases in budgets afforded by incremental increases in revenue. The incremental budget and its reason for being are well documented; conservation of effort, reduction of conflict, and a stabilizing influence on the community all come to mind. Nevertheless, incrementalism may prompt as much cynicism as it provides utility. The program budget suffers just as much despite the contrast it provides incremental budgets. Program budgets are hard to sustain over the period that it takes to invest in certain policy goals, especially through changes in leadership. The program often breeds its own form of inertia in the sunk costs leaders face after following a course of action for a number of years. Few individuals, much less leaders, find a willingness to admit failure and chuck it all.

Another major assumption involves what will be traded off against what as proposals for spending exceed revenue available. Rubin (1997, p. 5) notes that budgeteers "may determine the relative importance of each category first, attaching a dollar level in proportion to the assigned importance, or they may allow [proposals to accumulate] in each area to go on independently, later reworking the choices until the balance between the parts is acceptable." Knowing the approach used may involve knowing priorities. In most local governments, policing is such a high priority that no policing matter will be traded off against anything else. Police spending in one area may be traded off only against police spending in another area.

Implicit in the budget may be decisions about trade-offs among larger matters. Some decision makers will allow trade-offs between capital and operating budgets. If no room exists in operating budgets for a proposal, the decision makers may decide to place it in the capital budget and finance it through borrowing. In all too familiar a case, the resort to deferred maintenance may have become an implied assumption; cuts in the operating budget come first in infrastructure maintenance, forcing future claims for repairs and replacement into the capital budget.

The implicit assumptions in the budget may involve the order of decisions and the trade-off between spending and taxes. Again Rubin (1997, p. 5) observes:

> The order of decisions is important.... I can determine how much money I am likely to have first and then set that as an absolute limit on expenditures, or I can determine what I must have, what I wish to have, and what I need to set aside for emergencies and then go out and try to find enough money to cover some or all of those expenditures. Especially in emergencies, such as accidents or other health emergencies, people are likely to obligate the money first and worry about where it will come from later. Governmental budgeting, too, may concentrate first on revenues and later on expenditures, or first on expenditures and later on income. Like individuals or families, during emergencies such as floods or hurricanes or wars, governments will commit the expenditures first and worry about where the money will come from later.

If not an explicit assumption, taxes may have an unwritten inviolability about them, a built-in assumption of stable rises in tax rates. If so, spending can increase to maximize performance at a given tax rate.

Budget decisions almost never apply to just the upcoming fiscal year, since many decisions represent commitments or obligations that stretch into the indefinite future. Capital projects and new services imply enough commitment to get them finished and maintained to ensure their full useful life. Hiring an employee usually implies enough commitment or obligation to see the person trained and performing well. Implicitly, however, budgeting hides many multiyear commitments. How long can these commitments be: one year, five years, twenty years?

Related to this multiyear commitment idea is the method of counting commitments. Accounting systems dictate formal means of counting, but budgeteers either do or do not take into account the long-run dollar value of their commitments in straightforward fashion. The pension and retiree health care commitments are well known. The budget fails to show how spending has encumbered the future revenue stream more often than not.

Another whole class of implicit assumptions emerges when one observes the simplification mechanisms officials use to make an extremely unruly intellectual process manageable. Barber's research (1966) points to six major simplification devices, all of which become implicit assumptions in the budget process. First, there is the question of controllability; if an expenditure such as one required by law appears and is deemed uncontrollable, it is given cursory attention. In another way, however, consensus may have developed that reviewing an item with change in mind is undesirable; "it can't be touched" (pp. 37–38). Second, officials who have less time than needed conserve energy and attention for large items and items that increase by large percentages from year to year. Implicit in large items and large increases is the idea of importance and the basis of comparison: last year vs. this year rather than Department A vs. Department B. Third, officials implicitly relate their choices to similar choices they have experienced in their work lives. When officials come from the business world, they tend to be familiar with budgets and the costs for familiar activities. What officials do not feel comfortable with, however, are less concrete, more policy-related and consequential questions underlying budgets and largely controlled by budgets. For example, what are alternative ways of achieving certain outcomes such as the health and welfare of children through recreational programs? In the absence of familiarity with such analytic processes, officials opt for the more concrete decision: How much should fencing the playground cost? Fourth, scarcity of time and comfort with dealing with the concrete issues in the "here and now" implicitly limit attention and focus. Immediacy confounds the long-range picture, the consequences of various courses of action, and the lessons of history. Fifth, implicit assumptions govern how to handle the uncertainty attached to such things as estimates of costs and revenues. Barber observes (p. 42), "At any given time the [budget officials] will a) not reconsider decisions about which [they] have been certain in the past, and b) make new decisions, without feeling entirely certain about them, only if such decisions can be taken tentatively and any ill effects … corrected later." Finally, implicit in budget deliberations is the idea that the dollars and cents are reality, that the arithmetic is more important and deserves more time—especially in balancing the budget—than the analysis of the underlying reality the dollars and cents represent. For example, "a decision to cut a request from one department by a certain amount may be treated as a precedent of sorts for cutting another department by the same amount. The forest is lost sight of as the trees fall all around" (p. 43).

In all, simplification and conservation of energy and attention force officials to make certain assumptions as a matter of course. Far from observable, except to a researcher in a laboratory and a content analysis of what is actually said over a period of time, these assumptions become implicit in the way a deliberative group works. Those who hold them may not even acknowledge such assumptions. They certainly bar citizens' understanding the budget and the process of deliberation. Explicit and implicit assumptions in budgets make understanding budgets difficult and participation all but impossible except for the truly driven. Any participation design or intervention or training session must educate as well as equip the citizens involved for analysis and what lies below the surface as well as above it.

What Works toward Citizen Participation?

Does anything favor citizen involvement in budgeting, one may ask after reading how complicated and involved the structures of budgeting have become? The literature and research offer distinct possibilities. First, issues vary in their ability to be controlled through citizen participation or even budgeting. A large number of tractable issues, those over which long-range planning will have an effect, can benefit from citizen participation.

Second, the "public" is a naive concept. There are many publics in budgeting. Research suggests that one of these, the reachable public, has a strong willingness to understand the services-taxes trade-off when they can see how money is spent, when government takes into account citizens' values and priorities, and when budgeteers make an honest effort to reduce the cost of services produced. Such a public does become a force for influence with the appropriate tools and techniques for involvement.

Third, among these tools and techniques, groups throughout the world have devised many interventions that evidence suggests will reduce cynicism and educate the public. Citizens codesigning performance goals and measures may be the most promising approach.

Fourth, norms of insider participants in the budget process may actually be less inflexible and more malleable than is customarily thought. Finance officers, surprisingly, are more open to citizen participants than is generally believed.

Finally, budget assumptions, embedded by officials often unwittingly, could easily be the greatest barriers to public understanding and participation. Implicit assumptions may be conscious efforts to hide real budget decisions, or they may be relatively unnoticed, so commonplace in group decision making and so necessary to smooth and ease arduous tasks in the budget process. Finding these implicit assumptions, examining them, and reworking them might be citizen participants' most difficult yet most valuable product.

Participation Designs for Budgeting

Given tractable issues, attentive but more important reachable publics, somewhat willing insiders, and a mysterious but knowable budget process, what larger designs for intervention might work? Here, we revisit three major unresolved issues in the citizen participation in budgeting debate: (1) the nonnegotiable issues or those issues in which the interest of the community as a whole is at stake, (2) the argument related to the complexity of budget issues and the need for expertise in solving them, and (3) the existence of implicit assumptions, almost unknowable to the inexperienced citizen participant. What combination of tools would provide either widespread involvement when it is needed? What same set of tools, at other times, will also allow intensive involvement of a few people who become deeply knowledgeable and then full-fledged participants in a process in which power is shared?

The Often Nonnegotiable, Interest of the Community as a Whole Problem

As we stated before, on some issues, particularly those related to equity, elected representatives claim to be the only legitimate decision makers. Some elected officials view their representative function as the essence of republican government, especially for deciding whether the budget will redistribute up or down the income ladder and how the budget will allocate financial responsibility and community patrimony over present and future generations. The official may actually not view informed citizens as having a legitimate role in identifying issues and solutions, as well as judging measures of effectiveness and evaluating performance. In such cases, officials see it their legitimate obligation as representative officials to take the risks of their decision for the whole community. They see their legitimate role as one greater than listening to vocal and outspoken groups or sharing risks with citizen participants.

In this area, we view the community visioning design as particularly apt, since it calls for broad participation, with the product being a sense of the community's views on just these sorts of issues communicated to officials. Community visioning comes from a national civic league's explanation of the strategic planning process. Epstein et al. (2000, p. 11) explain this broad and inclusive process:

> A community vision typically involves scanning major developments in the community's political, social, and economic environments, and polling citizens on their expectations for a desirable future. Focus groups and larger public meetings can yield valuable citizen input for focusing on the direction a community wants to take for the future. A community's leaders hear citizens articulate what is important and how a desirable future for their community should look. This can be a complex process involving many stakeholders, and many issues in relation to the expectations for public services, as part of the strategy to achieve a community vision.

Epstein et al. add that a community-generated vision can extend to broader community conditions and aspirations.

The problem in community visioning is a difference between opinion and judgment it reveals. Daniel Yankelovich (1991) concentrates on the difference and presents a method by which judgment can emerge. He defines opinion as value judgments expressed with some but not great amounts of information that probably contain many contradictions. The best example is: "I want this government to tax less and give us citizens more." Information, which may have come haphazardly, is collected in a framework predisposed to view some sources as valid and some as invalid. Clearly, questions about where the person really stands still exist, and they tend to let the individual be whipsawed among focal issues, first supporting, then opposing the same position.

Judgment, on the other hand, is a resolution of the value conflicts that lie in opinion. Part of the resolution comes with information. But a greater part of the resolution comes by wrestling with the values that conflict, deciding finally where the person really stands. This process of resolving value conflicts lies at the heart of Yankelovich's design.

Yankelovich proposes a three-stage design: consciousness raising, working through value conflicts, and finally resolution. Consciousness raising he finds to be a very easy process in the media-drenched communities in the United States. Simply, events occur or are brought out into the open by media of all sorts. In this stage, an individual begins to shape an event into an issue about which the individual has some opinion. The opinion has some basis in its cogency—something happened, not something might happen—and the applicability to one's self—"The event matters to me." Happily, Yankelovich says, many times our consciousness is raised, and at the same time, we receive and believe a given interpretation and choice of action to be credible. The stage is set to work through the issue without delay. In other, less happy circumstances, he says, "People do not understand what the possibilities for action are, or ... they are given insufficient and inadequate choices, or ... they do not grasp what the consequences of the various choices would be, or ... their attention is diverted away from the issue before they have a chance to come to grips with it or ... they are given contradictory information about it, or ... they believe those who propose the action are acting in bad faith" (pp. 84–85).

In the latter case, the road to judgment is made harder. Judgment comes about by working through the event and by confronting the need for action. For example, people now see many of the problems of society originating in the schools—events have occurred to raise consciousness, but no one's interpretation suggests so far a single, easy, credible solution. People "want the schools to do everything: teach the basics, prepare young people for jobs, help them be good citizens, impart moral values to them, introduce them to the arts, make them good drivers, teach them to be computer literate, engage them in sports, and help them cope with emotional difficulties" (Yankelovich, 1991, p. 167). At the same time, another of society's perceived ills intrudes with citizens objecting to the schools taxing them too much. The working-through process is one in which the individual confronts the value conflict, looks at the consequences of various alternative ways of resolving it, and finally sides with the most deeply felt value.

As the individual works through the event, interpretation, and value conflict, he or she engages in a resolution of cognitive, emotional, and moral stands. Cognitively, the person clears up fuzzy thinking, reconciles inconsistencies, and begins to see relationships where independencies once existed. Emotionally, the person confronts his or her own ambivalent feelings, becomes comfortable with reality, and overcomes procrastination. Finally, moral resolution requires people to put "doing the right thing" ahead of themselves and their own needs and desires. Once the individual has resolved the issue, judgment prevails.

In the real world, how does a community employ Yankelovich's design for "visioning?" In the context of a major issue, Yankelovich provides an application. The issue was one in which there seemed to be no judgment; there was waffling as new events occurred with no consistent way of dealing with the issue proposed or supported. The leaders in the application first consulted experts and knowledgeable individual citizens to propose four "futures," each of which was independent and inconsistent with the others. In our schools example, the choices might be a parsimonious, teach the basics future and several, more expensive variations built on the parsimonious one, each of which goes in a different direction—vocational, citizenship, and moral teaching.

The futures were simple enough to be intelligible to the nonexpert but not so simplistic as to be meaningless and irrelevant. A group of individuals, a cross section of the public, came together and first rated the futures; apparently an individual could vote twice when more than one of the futures seemed to be a part of his or her opinion. Then, the individuals became aware of the salient features of each of the four futures "and the costs, risks, and trade-offs associated with it" (p. 153). The individuals participated in a discussion moderated by "professors with a reputation as outstanding teachers … [who] were given intensive training" and who were not experts in the subject. After the discussion, the individuals voted again, giving their first, second, third, and fourth choices among the futures after being instructed to take into account the pros and cons of each future and the arguments and counterarguments that had been the main focus of the discussion. While the group did not reach a consensus, the change from the pretest to the posttest revealed a considerable amount of movement, and "they grew less prone to endorse incompatible futures and more likely to select realistically among them" (p. 155). The underlying values came to the surface; individuals were more likely to be able to argue a position not prone to internal contradiction.

In summary, the Yankelovich design promises a method by which individuals may see, first, several stark choices, then their own values, and finally the application of these values to the stark choices. The method does not allow or imply a one-way method of communication from the powerful or the expert to the less powerful or less expert. The method assumes genuine communication in which "all forms of domination—overt and hidden—have been removed" (p. 216). The genuineness of the result provides, he says, far greater guidance or proof of judgment than a phony consensus that is likely to change with the next event.

The Lack of Knowledge and Expertise Problem

The second charge we deal with is the argument that no citizen knows enough to get into and wisely advise on the knotty, interconnected budget problems only elected officials and especially professional budgeteers have become expert at. To this we say, everyone can learn.

Many localities have instituted mini-seminars to bring interested citizens into contact with the day-to-day and explicit limits on discretion officials and managers have. The mini-seminars provide information on everything from sewer construction to building streets to state controls on finance, environment, housing, and public safety. The mini-seminar approach reflects a proactive attitude, but it is also a reaction to those outside government who would try to rouse involvement with inaccurate information.

The citizen university model has also appeared in at least two places: Glendale, Arizona, and Cocoa Beach, Florida. In the Cocoa Beach instance, the citizen's academy seems to emphasize communicating efficiency and effectiveness information to citizens who attend (Miller, 2000). The academy lasts for twelve weeks. One of the areas included is the finance department. Managers and government employees, apparently, teach all classes. The Glendale version, operating since 1996, treats government processes at a greater distance. Professors from local colleges teach the classes. The information includes scenario building: "If citizens want a new program or don't want some project undertaken, they can learn how to follow the dollars and the decision-making process. They find out, for instance, how complicated—and expensive—it is to build a new street" (Lemov, 1997, p. 69).

The differences in the two approaches reflect very different philosophies and probabilities of understanding and participation. The Cocoa Beach insider alternative has the capacity for creating attentiveness among government insiders as they explain what they do and, we assume, why. The approach, however, has a built-in bias toward citizens as students, as passive acceptors of information and the assumptions built into those data. The approach might very well do little to change the manager-as-expert view of the world, although the approach does represent a reaching out to citizens and, perhaps, an effort to absorb other views of how to do their work.

The Glendale approach may have more depth and objectivity but involves learning at the price of immediate influence. We doubt whether local professors are insiders in the budget process. The information provided may have a high level of generality and objectivity; it may even provide needed perspective, particularly the rules of state supervision and laws that confine decision making. The intimacy with managers and decision makers, however, is not there. Relationships built between citizens and administrators are not part of the objectives of the Glendale approach. Perhaps they may come later.

Elected officials' and managers' fears of such structures as citizen's universities relate to their views on competition and the legitimacy of citizen participation. Many elected officials view citizen's universities as breeding grounds for political rivals. The budget manager may actually resent the need to explain financial control and "good financial management" since they are so much an implicit part of the right turn in politics. He or she may also resent the fact that citizens might expect to quickly and fully understand accounting systems and budget processes the financial manager has taken years and many certifications to achieve.

Therefore, the citizen's university idea raises questions about how public officials and managers view citizens. The view may relate to advertising. The view may actually require that citizens understand. However, the view may promote interaction, involvement, and acceptance of other rationalities.

The Implicit Assumptions in Budgeting Problems

The fact that there are alternative rationalities, that there is no one best way to solve problems, threatens those elected and those commissioned to be the experts. Implicit in budgeting, differing worldviews, norms and decisions that officials and professionals, often as a group have developed, often confuse decision making. The norms and decisions may have developed to simplify a very difficult and time-consuming budget adoption process. Or unwittingly, officials and professionals may have come to view avoiding the public as necessary and bred of a common fantasy, as in "angry constituents will mobilize to remove them from office if they vote 'incorrectly' on a controversial issue" (Vogelsang-Coombs, 1997, p. 492). Vogelsang-Coombs attributes avoidance to the rise of "groupthink" among decision makers. Simply, some groups, believing group members to have superior intellectual capacity and morality, stereotype outsiders as ignorant, quash dissent among themselves, falsely perceive group unanimity, suppress negative information and perceptions, and ultimately lead themselves into fiascoes (p. 492; Janis, 1972, p. 198).

Despite the avoidance behavior and the tendency to groupthink, the more important, perhaps root cause of the problem might actually be the common view of necessary budget actions that has developed among insiders without anyone's realizing it over several budget periods. These common views might include at least those implicit assumptions described earlier: how trade-offs will be handled, the order of decisions, the inviolability of tax rates, and the norm of maximizing performance at a given tax rate. Here, educating citizens is more than merely telling them how matters should be handled and accepting the implicit assumptions that exist as reasonable without question. What is needed is a reexamination of the assumptions.

Let's assume officials decide to go ahead with the citizen's university idea. They first balance the advantages and disadvantages of insider or outsider instructors. They decide to go beyond just providing information and to actually allowing some scenario building with the incentive that this scenario building might actually influence decisions. How is scenario building conducted?

Consider one design. Participation should expose assumptions underlying a proposed plan of action so that all can reconsider them. Participation should even suggest new and more relevant assumptions on which the planning process can proceed.

Thus many officials find useful the deployment of citizens to identify issues, search for options, then play through scenarios with each of the options, especially examining assumptions and forcing to the surface implicit assumptions that already exist, examining risks and consequences, and often trade off one option against another or against the status quo.

The examination of options can lead to revelations of goals and a commitment to goals rather than to various means, technologies, or programs. Bland and Rubin (1997, p. 50) recognize the potential and argue that "presenting and costing out options with this degree of clarity takes effort and creativity, but it facilitates decision making."

Open participation could force goals out into the open, but it should often force out into the open strategies to hide goals as well. They relate (p. 50) an illustration of a city choosing between a well and an aboveground storage tank for water:

> A citizen noted that the grant being used to fund the project required only a well and questioned why a tower should be built at four times the cost. A staff member answered angrily that this was a technical question and was therefore under the staff's jurisdiction; staff proceeded to deal with the issue on technical grounds. But the debate as framed—water tower versus well—obscured an underlying policy issue that ought to have been presented to citizens: namely, whether water services should be expanded to attract new business to that part of town.

Participation must deal with implicit assumptions in order to have any effect. Mason and Mitroff (1981, pp. 129–131) argue that to examine assumptions, options, and goals, the process must begin with looking at the present courses of action and the information from which it was derived. They pose the question to those involved: "Under what view of the world is this the optimal plan to follow?" The results are "a set of plausible and believable assumptions that underlie this plan, assumptions that serve to interpret the data so as to logically conclude that this plan is best for achieving the organization's goals" (p. 129). The most important step, however, is to identify "another plausible and believable alternative—the counter plan" to test existing assumptions and even surface new ones. The counterplan is another view of the world in which the group reaches the same goal, using the same data as the present course of action. Mason and Mitroff (1981, p. 130) advocate "structured debate … [in which] each side must interpret, in its entirety, the same organizational data bank" upon which both the plan and the counterplan were based. They predict that the observer will integrate the plan and counterplan in such a way that he or she forms a new and expanded worldview and a plan that supports it.

The Mason and Mitroff design aids in bringing to the surface implicit assumptions. In budgeting, these assumptions compound the difficulties for participation in an already complicated and time-consuming process. If allowed to exist unquestioned, implicit assumptions stymie any authentic effort at citizen involvement and influence over budget decisions. Implicit assumptions set the agenda ahead of any citizen contribution, and understandably lead to alienation and disgust.

Discussion and Summary

Our purpose in this chapter was to use existing research to reveal and suggest solutions to the real-world problem of citizen participation in budgeting. We operated on two levels at once.

At one level, we tried to determine whether structures distance budgeting from outsiders and, if so, why. We found high aspirations but clear reasons why officials resist all but extraordinary and isolated instances of true involvement. Our conversations with budgeteers led us to conclude that most officials believe in the value of building a community and a sense of belongingness to that community. They believe that education will help citizens have an impact. However, most officials believe that the republican ideal should still dictate which community-wide decisions are entrusted to them. Moreover, most officials see participation as a road to increased conflict. Budget participation rouses expectations for accomplishments, some of which are beyond reach. Participation, per se, often stands as a repudiation of officials' management skills and policy decisions and creates a defensiveness that seldom wanes. Most officials believe scarcity of revenues can defeat efforts to realize the work of citizen budget participants, and they see time pressure as an enemy of participation.

At another level, we wanted to know what works in the fullest sense of the word *participation* by asking what structural problems in budgeting stand in the way and whether or how they might be removed. Officials argued that citizen participation is a function of what citizens know. What citizens know is a function of what questions they know to ask. What they know to ask depends on the accessibility of the budget itself.

The budget's accessibility, we found, relates to the way the budget frames issues, too often only as inputs—salaries, supplies, and utilities—and too little of the time as goals to accomplish. Budgets often deliberately hide goals rather than display them in such a way that citizens can subject goals and methods to analysis.

The budget's accessibility often is linked to the amount of time officials are willing to take to involve citizens. The will to provide accessibility often correlates with the form of government and the amount of partisanship.

Finally, accessibility hinges on beliefs officials hold about equity issues and issues that have an impact on the whole community. Related to these issues is the question of who has the right to decide them: representatives who picture themselves as acting in the interest of the community and against particular interests *or* the particular interests, participating as citizens and competing with one another?

The literature and research discussed in this chapter have also revealed several misconceptions about budget structures and citizen participation. First, issues vary in their sensitivity to broad, inclusive deliberation. Second, the "public" is a naive concept. Third, among tools and techniques, codesigning "ex post" controls, such as performance goals and measures, may be the approach to involvement both citizens and budgeting officials find most effective. Fourth, norms of insider participants revealed, through the discussion and development of their norms, some openness to citizen involvement, but greater openness than is generally believed. Finally, budget assumptions, embedded by officials often unwittingly, could easily be the greatest barriers to public understanding and effective participation.

The debate about how budgets frame questions has settled at this moment on performance. Budgets and budget officials' attitudes have increasingly centered on the notion that we should seek the best performance for the same tax rate, year in, year out. If this is the case, budgeteers need citizens to define better performance and to guide its measurement. Budgeteers need answers to questions about what is important enough to perform well. Since performance is a fairly vague concept, citizens can help by participating. Budget officials' norms and attitudes make participation possible. Incentives are there for officials to share the risk of these decisions with the citizens who do participate.

Endnote

1. This chapter was adapted from "Budgeting Structures and Citizen Participation," *Journal of Public Budgeting, Accounting & Financial Management*, 14(2), 205–246, 2002. With permission.

References

Alexander, J. (1999). A new ethics of the budgetary process. *Administration and Society* 31(4):542–565.

Baker, J. R. (1994). Government in the twilight zone: Motivations of volunteers to small city boards and commissions. *State and Local Government Review* 26(2):119–128.

Barber, J. D. (1966). *Power in Committees: An Experiment in the Governmental Process*. New York: Rand McNally.

Beinart, P. (1997). The pride of the cities. *The New Republic* 216(26):16–24.

Berman, E. (1997). Dealing with cynical citizens. *Public Administration Review* 57(2): 105–112.

Bland, R. L., and Rubin, I. S. (1997). *Budgeting: A Guide for Local Governments*. Washington, DC: International City/County Management Association.

Callahan, D. (1997). Big apple bites liberalism. *The Nation* 265(9):16–20.

Denhardt, R. B., Denhardt, K. G., and Glaser, M. A. (2000). Citizen-driven strategic planning in local government: The case of Orange County, Florida In *Handbook of Strategic Management*, ed. Jack Rabin, Gerald J. Miller, and W. Bartley Hildreth, 709–720. 2nd ed. New York: Marcel Dekker.

Epstein, P., Wray, L., Marshall, M., and Grifel, S. (2002). Engaging citizens in achieving results that matter: A model for effective 21st century governance. In *Meeting the Challenges of Performance Oriented Government*, ed. K. Newcomer, E. T. Jennings Jr., C. Broom and A. Lomax, 125–160. Washington, DC: American Society for Public Administration, Center for Accountability and Performance.

Glaser, M. A., and Hildreth, W. B. (1999). Service delivery satisfaction and willingness to pay taxes: Citizen recognition of local government performance. *Public Productivity and Management Review* 23(1):48–67.

Janis, I. L. (1972). *Victims of Groupthink: A Psychological Study of Foreign Policy Decisions and Fiascoes*. Boston: Houghton-Mifflin.

Jimno, K. (1997). *Talking with Citizens about Money*. Washington, DC: International City/ County Management Association.

Lemov, P. (1997, September). Educating the elusive taxpayer. *Governing*, pp. 68–69.

Leo, J. P., and Roth, R. A. (1998). Budgeting for success. *The Bottom Line*, pp. 23–25.

Mason, Richard O., and Mitroff, Ian I. (1981). *Challenging Strategic Planning Assumptions*. New York: John Wiley & Sons.

Meltsner, A. J. (1971). *The Politics of City Revenue*. Berkeley: University of California Press.

Miller, J. (2000, March). Citizen's academy builds relationships. *PA Times* 23(3):1, 15.

O'Toole, D. E., and Marshall, J. (1988). Citizen participation through budgeting. *The Bureaucrat* 17(2):51–55.

Rubin, I. S. (1997). *The Politics of Public Budgeting: Getting and Spending, Borrowing and Balancing*. 3d ed. Chatham, NJ: Chatham House.

Swoboda, D. P. (1995). Accuracy and accountability in reporting local government budget activities: Evidence from the newsroom and from newsmakers. *Public Budgeting & Finance* 15(3):74–90.

Vogelsang-Coombs, V. (1997). Governance education: Helping city councils learn. *Public Administration Review*, 57(6):490–500.

Weeks, E. C. (2000). The practice of deliberative democracy: Results from four large-scale trials. *Public Administration Review* 60(4):360–372.

Yankelovich, D. (1991). *Coming to Public Judgment*. Syracuse, NY: Syracuse University Press.

Chapter 8

Revenue Regime Change and Tax Revolts

Before understanding what a tax revolt is and what may create conditions for one, most people blame high taxes. Yet, there have been no tax revolts in Canada despite high Canadian provincial tax levels. High taxes have not had the revolt-provoking effect that we attribute to them in the United States.

The comparison of Canadian provinces and U.S. states over tax revolts reveals two contrasting logics finance officials might use. Canadian finance officials could use agency logic, responding to parliamentary masters with pro-positive government and large amounts of intergovernmental aid. U.S. finance officials may live with a democratizing logic brought about by referendum-voted tax limits even if they did nothing to encourage them.

This chapter reports on a project that investigated the causes of "tax revolts." The popular assumption underlying the project predicts: "when the price of government gets too high, citizens let government know.... They oust incumbents, elect antitax candidates, and/or embrace antitax initiatives" (Osborne and Hutchinson, 2004, p. 42). U.S. tax revolts often do unfold as a process of popular complaint, effort to force a response, and creation of new tax regimes and government decision-making elites.

But, do burdensome taxes alone trigger revolts? This research tests that connection. Research on the tax revolts in two-thirds of the states suggests that revolts result from contagion, mimicry, or simply yardstick competition. So far, research has failed to find a direct connection between tax revolts and high tax burdens. Case study and anecdotal research concludes that many other factors must exist; yet high tax burdens become part of the narrative used by pro-tax-revolt stalwarts to recruit support.

The high tax burden idea motivated a comparison of states with Canadian provinces. Burdens are heavier in provinces, but revolts have not occurred. Why is the price of government high enough to provoke revolts in states but not high enough to provoke them in provinces? What role does price play in revolt?

This research tested a performance budget model in the subnational governments of the United States and Canada as the primary tax revolt predictor. The performance budget model includes four index-like categories of data: the explicit price of government, implicit price of government, openness of government decision making, and government performance incentives embedded in fiscal controls. The existence of a performance budget should predict taxpayer acceptance of current fiscal policies; the performance budget's absence should predict tax revolt.

This chapter presents first the general background of the project through discussion of the analytical bases for the four indices. Then the chapter explains how the research questions were answered. In the final sections, we reveal the project findings and interpret their meaning.

The Analytic Base and General Background

Government leaders make fiscal decisions that connect revenues and spending to citizen preferences. The devolution of fiscal decision making in federal governments complicates the efforts to bridge tax and spending policies in satisfying preferences of the people leaders represent. This research describes an approach that provides comparative information from federal states about efforts to bridge the revenue and spending decisions and meet citizen expectations. The project concentrates on efforts public administrators have made to overcome the argument that "the revenue process is a logically and pragmatically separate planning question from the expenditure process" (Mikesell, 1978, p. 512). The project approaches the separation by questioning a popular assumption: "when the price of government gets too high, citizens let government know" (Osborne and Hutchinson, 2004, p. 42). The message may take the form of exit or voice, as Hirschman frames decision making (1970). The reaction to a climbing price of government could be loyalty under some conditions. This project asks why some fiscal decisions create confusion, decrease citizen trust, and mobilize taxpayers to vote with their feet, recall elected officials, or petition for fiscal limitations. Why do other fiscal decisions unite taxing and spending decisions in an understandable way, a way that preserves citizen trust, deference, or indifference?

What Is a Tax Revolt?

A tax revolt institutes a statutory or constitutional control on fiscal policy making that limits tax increases, spending increases, or both. Revolt often occurs in U.S. states via a citizen initiative that leads to legislative action and perhaps a referendum

Table 8.1   Tax and Expenditure Limitation Characteristics

1. Initiated by citizens
2. Approved by voters via referendum
3. Have constitutional rather than statutory legal status
4. Applies to spending and revenues, broadly defined
5. Limits growth in government spending to inflation plus population growth
6. Includes state, municipality, and other locality spending and revenues
7. Requires mandatory tax refunds when surplus exceeds a prescribed limit
8. Comprehensive in coverage of government spending and revenue collection

Source: Adapted from Clemens, J. et al., *Tax and Expenditure Limitations,* The Fraser Institute, Vancouver, CA, 2003, pp. 17–20.

on changes to the status quo tax regime. Table 8.1 portrays the starkest picture of U.S. limits and the narrowest working definition of the dependent variable in this research, a tax revolt.

Popular opinion holds that high tax burdens breed revolt. High tax burdens in the tax revolt sense are state, provincial, and local government own source revenue as a relatively high proportion of personal income. Tax regime fiscal illusion complicates the high taxes picture and may neutralize popular opinion, especially where intergovernmental transfers or equalization exists.

Popular opinion also holds that tax revolts are mass movements rather than elite manipulation of popular opinion and action. Yet, little is known or understood about the nature and cultural foundation of citizen-initiated, direct democracy antitax movements. A comparative analysis of federalist systems should reveal how closely high taxes and tax revolts relate.

The General Predictors of a Tax Revolt

This research takes its cues from Osborne and Hutchinson's discussion in *The Price of Government* (2004). Before turning to the model these cues support, this chapter presents a review of the research done to find tax revolt predictors. Three sets of explanations help understand what the price of government predicts, rational ignorance and fiscal illusion, fiscal policy change and politics, and tax revolts specifics. These explanations roughly parallel those found in research by Temple (1996), Alm and Skidmore (1999), and Cutler, Elmendorf, and Zeckhauser (1999).

Fiscal Clarity and Fiscal Illusion

Downs theory of rational ignorance (1959–1960) answers Osborne and Hutchinson's idea that voters will know the price of government and will do what they need to do to control it. Downs answers that ignorance among voters causes government decision makers to enact budgets smaller than the ones they would enact if the electorate possessed complete information.

Ignorance is rational in that knowledge costs money and time to gain. There may be many things about which taxpayers have perfect knowledge. However, there are others in which they have only partial knowledge: voters may know all the actual or potential items in the budget but not all the benefits and costs attached to each. Then there are those about which they know nothing: voters may be ignorant of both the items in the budget and their benefits and costs.

Along with rationally ignorant voters, there are budget decision makers. A governing politician, looking over a budget's possible expenditures "tries to decide whether [voting for it] could gain more votes than financing it would lose," Downs observes (1959–1960, p. 542). The politician and the legislative body consider additional spending and taxes, trading off gains with losses until there is no net gain. At that point, they enact a budget. The upshot is the relationship: the more remote the benefit, the less support; the more immediate the tax, the less support. What are these benefits and costs? Remote benefits might be preventive measures such as economic aid to a distant nation, water purification, regulation of food and drugs, safety control of airways, or regulation of utility and transport prices. Also, few know the benefits as programs are launched.

Immediate costs, Downs says, are immediate because they are familiar to some degree and familiar enough to lead to opinions. For example, Downs says, every April 15 we have to pay taxes. Every paycheck shows the amount we would have received had there been no taxes. We have a facility for discussing taxes but hardly any to discuss any part of proposed spending in the budget that does not affect us directly. The result is far less public support for spending and far more public opposition to taxes.

In contrast to Downs, Buchanan (1977) asks whether political leaders mislead people into thinking that their taxes are low and that public spending benefits are high. Do they operate under a set of fiscal illusions, he asks? Buchanan explains that fiscal illusion does exist in a world in which government grew by 4,200% in real dollar terms from 1870 to 1970. The government demands 50% of the economy, he points out.

Buchanan asks what can explain it. He offers one set of pro-political leader explanations and then four antipolitical leader arguments. Population growth, income elasticity of demand, decline in public sector productivity, urbanization and congestion, and government responsiveness account for much but not all of the growth in the size of government.

The rest, he says, can be explained by a combination of

1. The illusion that we pay less in taxes than we actually do through the piecemeal nature of sales taxes, the withholding of income taxes, the hiding of property taxes in mortgage payments, and the windfall nature of grants.

2. Politicians don't have enough ways for their feet to be held to the fire; they tend to want to make taxes remote and spending benefits immediate.
3. Bureaucrats vote in contrast to many other voters.
4. Spending goes up because of the creative ways political leaders structure government, e.g., consolidated school districts that become monopolies and reward administrators with higher pay as they grow.

The Downs vs. Buchanan argument dwells in the remote and immediate senses of tax levels and spending. The question may be settled with more knowledge of fiscal operations and by assisting and motivating the rationally ignorant to become rationally well informed.

Fiscal Policy Change and Politics: Generational Change Explanations

A second set of explanations of what the price of government predicts lies in the tax reform and change literature. These explanations suggest that abrupt changes in taxes create their own consequences. Consider Berkman (1993) first. The state roots model of tax change appears in Figure 8.1.

1. Stagnant economic growth leaves winners and losers among states and localities.

2. What do local political leaders of winner states and localities attribute their economic power to? Local labor costs, available land, transportation facilities, well-trained labor force, lower taxes.

3. What policy changes can political leaders make to build economic power or competitiveness? Lower taxes mean higher profits of private firms and higher incomes for some households, making the area with lower taxes more attractive.

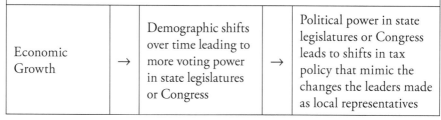

Source: Adapted from Berkman, M. G., *The State Roots of National Politics*, University of Pittsburgh Press, Pittsburgh, PA, 1993.

Figure 8.1   Berkman's state roots model (a generational succession model).

The state roots model translates change at the local level into changes at the national level. Whatever economic or political problems future national leaders had in the early stages of their careers, many of them took action with new tax policies. These policies may have related to economic development with tax incentives or reductions. These policies may also have led to leadership in tax revolts. Whatever the early career taught, the political leader carries the lesson up the career ladder. He or she applies the same approach to other problems at the state and national level, aided by the economic power and demographic shifts over time that give his or her district or state greater or lesser voting power in the state legislature or in Congress.

Fiscal Policy Change and Politics: Incrementalism and Nonincremental Change

A second facet of this tax change model comes from the career protection theme as well. Meltsner (1971) follows in the incrementalist tradition (Wildavsky, 1961; Lindblom, 1959; Witte, 1985), both in the study of Oakland (Pressman and Wildavsky, 1973) and by describing incrementalist revenue-raising practices.

Meltsner's data came from research done in Oakland, California. He found that in Oakland:

1. Taxes never are maximized (a rational model of firm behavior applied to the public sector) and neither are they cut to the bone.
2. Taxes are instituted and applied with a view to
   a. React as other cities did when they instituted such a tax (limitation)
   b. Calculate based on negotiation with the most important and attentive taxpayers
   c. Maintain consensus about the level of taxes by changing taxes only marginally from year to year
   d. Avoid letting the public focus on one tax increase—move rates upward in small increments across a broad number of revenues sources
   e. Underestimate revenues and overestimate spending to create a small surplus in the budget, both to justify small revenue increases and to cushion

The marginal changes over time constrict the area of possible movement, straitjacketing the system into one that bears no resemblance to an acceptable tax system normatively. The marginal changes mask the price of government, however. The price becomes evident only when a major catastrophe occurs, forcing tax increases and destroying the carefully built fiscal illusion of no change or quietly traded favors with friends in exchange for more than marginal tax changes.

Fiscal Policy Change and Politics: Cyclical Change

The third explanation comes from a journalist and a traditional idea of cyclical change. Phillips' idea (1990) is a cyclical model of taxation. Changes occur in the tax system just as a pendulum swings, he says. He explains that political leaders orient tax policy toward their long-term constituency interests and only incidentally toward the greater good or to achieve some normative ideal. Rather, all tax policies redistribute wealth, and at heart, all parties and political office holders want that to happen.

Phillips' history of tax policy changes shows that policies regarding the wealthy have a cyclical character in the United States, especially at the federal level. There is a cycle of distributing the tax burden up the income ladder, followed by a cycle of distributing it down, then up, then down, through history.

The cycles, Phillips argues, have occurred three times, and the result has always been a major cleavage in wealth (the richest getting much richer than the poorest) and a reaction that reduced that cleavage. Reagan–George W. Bush era tax policy making was the third of these eras, he says. In these cycles, especially those redistributing the tax burden down the income ladder from the rich, Phillips poses a particularly interesting paradox: the fairer the tax system, the less popular it is, and the less fair, the more popular. High aspirations for wealth and low taxes make anything other than a cut in taxes the rich pay very unpopular. The price of government is always too high. Only the hegemony of pro-rich tax policy makers leads to popular tax cuts. A high price of government might predict a coming election of pro-rich tax policy makers and the defeat of those favoring a traditionally "fairer" tax system.

Tax Revolt Specifics and Research

This chapter defines tax revolts as a specific unit of analysis in research on fiscal change. At this point, this research assumes that a tax revolt may occur as an event in the context of generational, incremental, nonincremental, or cyclical change. This research first focuses on the research literature that presents tax revolts as events rather than sociopolitical movements. Then, the focus shifts to a review of research that concentrates on states that have experienced tax revolts.

Specific Predictors of Tax Revolts: The Event Literature

A substantial literature has reported factors that might explain tax revolts. As Sigelman, Lowery, and Smith asked (1983, p. 30): "Why have some states adopted major limitations on government taxing and/or spending, while others have not?" This review examines an important part of this research and uses these studies to justify the selection and testing of variables here. The most remarkable finding from the predictive factor literature is the relative unpredictability of the tax revolts across all states and revolts. The relative unpredictability may lie in the fact that many studies, if not most, based prediction on individual-level variables in which the researchers tried to generalize from opinions individuals held and from facets of individual socioeconomic standing (Lowery and Sigelman, 1981).

Moreover, many studies, if not most, have dealt with local property tax or other limitations when a statewide ballot on a constitutional amendment or statute asked the question. Many, if not most, of these case studies in specific states dealt with California's Proposition 13 voted on in 1978. Two Proposition 13 reactions came from eminent fiscal policy authorities, Richard Musgrave and James Buchanan. These reactions typify the specific state case study literature. Musgrave argued (1979, p. 697) that California's situation leading up to the referendum was unique: "An unusually strong housing boom which, combined with an unusually efficient assessment procedure, resulted in a rapid rise of assessed values. While mill rates remained largely unchanged, property taxes increased sharply." Coupled with rising taxes was a state budget surplus, initially pledged to reduce property taxes, but then mired in political "wrangling over the pattern of relief" that delayed any action. Beyond their patience, California voters approved Proposition 13's property tax relief.

Musgrave questioned the inherent bias in state-local tax systems toward overexpansion of the public sector and argued for "removing or correcting features of our fiscal institutions that distort the decision process and thereby foreclose rational action" (p. 702). He argued for action to deal with the explicit price of government. Musgrave's arguments therefore can be read as a starting point for what became the Osborne and Hutchinson performance budget model.

Buchanan also commented on Proposition 13. He directly addressed the implicit price of government problem and its fiscal illusion. He argued (1979, pp. 692–693):

> If the benefits of public spending programs are concentrated and well-identified, either with respect to distinct groups of citizens that are geographically, functionally or otherwise defined, or with respect to distinct programs (e.g., education, health and highways), while the costs are diffused and generalized, we can predict that such programs will be undertaken in many circumstances without due regard to the costs. Conversely, if the costs of public spending (taxes) are concentrated and well-defined while [p. 693] the benefits are diffused and generalized, we can predict that in many circumstances governmental fiscal outcomes will reflect failure to take benefits sufficiently into account.

His rule to use to prevent tax revolts suggested that local and state taxes should support local and state spending, respectively and exclusively. Within those budgets, he said (p. 695), "General taxes should be levied to finance programs that yield general benefits." Otherwise, fiscal illusion grows, and leaders can more easily convince taxpayers that their taxes provide them no direct benefit or even redistribute their taxes to undeserving beneficiaries. Buchanan suggests that the seeds of tax revolt lie in the general taxes–general benefits principle, one stricter than Downs' direct taxes–indirect benefits idea.

Specific Predictors of a Tax Revolt: State-Centered Variables

The focal question for this research is a statewide vote or legislative decision on state rather than local taxing or spending (tax and expenditure limitations (TELs)), particularly the political and economic effort leading up to and since Colorado voters approved a taxpayer bill of rights (TABOR) in 1992.

The earliest state-centric study on limitation prediction came from Sigelman and his colleagues (1983). They tested for the power of eight variables to predict revolt. Their variables appear in Table 8.2. Their findings, using discriminant analysis, classified 74% of the states correctly.

Table 8.2 State-Centered Predictors of Tax Revolts in 1983

Predictor	Definition
Revolt	Radical tax-cutting proposals mandating cuts in either state or local taxes on a scale similar to Proposition 13's slashing of property taxes by nearly 50%; broad-based limitations imposing a cap on spending or taxing that is tied to some external measure of state fiscal capacity, such as total state income (dummy variable)
Tax level	State and local taxes as percent of total state personal income, 1977; percent change in per capita state and local taxes, 1973–1977
Tax distribution	Property taxes as percent of total state personal income, 1977; percent change in per capita property taxes, 1973–1977
Cost-benefit	Welfare spending as a percent of total state spending, 1977
Political ideology	Percent of presidential vote won by McGovern, 1972
Political participation	Percent of eligible voters voting for president, 1976
Political culture	Moralistic, individualistic, traditionalistic, percent of presidential vote won by the Progressive Party in 1912 (Elazar, 1972, as individual dummy variables)
Diffusion of innovations	Regionalism (dummy variables for Sharkansky's regions, 1970: Northeast, South, North Central, and Transplains)
Rules of the game	Initiative (dummy variable)

Source: Adapted from Sigelman, L. et al., *Western Political Quarterly*, 36(1), 30–51, 1983.

An indirect account of possible determining factors of a tax limitation comes from the tax innovation literature, particularly that by Berry and Berry (1992). This research tries to account for the adoption of taxes during the twentieth century, but it may be useful simply to account for tax innovation, whether adoption or limitation. Using probit analysis of factors relating to a set of adoption variables (adopt = 1, otherwise = 0), they found that states adopted gas taxes when highway use rose. For income tax adoption, they found that distance from a gubernatorial election, poor fiscal health, and adoption of taxes by neighboring states explained most of the variation in adoptions by states. They stated (p. 737) a distant election permitted tax increases, since a politician was less likely to be punished unless voters had good memories. Also, state economic trouble led voters to agree with raising taxes to permit efforts to stem contraction or encourage growth. Finally, neighboring states that have raised taxes give cover to a state's politicians to mimic their action. Would Berry and Berry's variables help understand tax limitation? Perhaps the nearness of an election, good fiscal health, and adoption of tax limitations by neighboring states might help predict the adoption of TELs.

Alm and Skidmore (1999) looked at the success and failure of statewide balloting during the period 1978–1990. They argued that (p. 490) "passage of these TELs [relates] to various economic, fiscal, political, and demographic factors of the state, as well as specific TEL features." They focused on what conditions might exist to persuade the median voter to support the ballot question. With ballot success or failure as the dependent variable, their quantitative analysis relied on the specification of multiple thresholds; a first set of threshold conditions must exist to get the TEL question on the ballot, a second set to gain the support of a majority of voters, and an estimate of the maximum likelihood that some or all threshold conditions and election success existed. Their independent variables (p. 504)—threshold conditions—appear in Table 8.3.

They found that property tax revenues and the growth in local revenues as a proportion of total state and local revenues were statistically significant estimators of the likelihood of TEL ballot question success. Rapid population growth, growing nonfederal tax payment amounts taxpayers could deduct from federal taxes, increasing federal transfers, existence of a previously enacted TEL, and total tax revenues—the price of government—emerged as statistically significant estimators of the likelihood of ballot failure.

Specific Predictors of a Tax Revolt: Survey Research

The most recent compilation of studies provides the opinion survey research (Mullins and Wallin, 2004, pp. 10–15; Mullins, 2003, pp. 107–114). The variables that appeared most often were voter preferences for smaller government size, lower taxes, greater government efficiency, and (satisfying self-interest in) reducing or shifting tax burdens, as well as general displeasure with taxes, overall frustration, and objections to particular types of spending.

Table 8.3   State-Centered Predictors of Tax and Expenditure Limitation Referendum Success, 1999

Percentage change in real state income over a 5-year period (income)
Percentage change in real intergovernmental transfers from federal government over a 5-year period (federal transfers)
Percentage change in ratio of itemized returns to total federal tax returns over a 3-year period (deductibility)
Percentage change in population over a 5-year period (population)
Percentage change in real property taxes over a 5-year period (property tax revenues)
Percentage change in real total tax revenues over a 5-year period (total tax revenues)
Percentage change in the ratio of local revenues to total state and local revenues over a 5-year period (local revenue share)
Percentage change in real welfare expenditures over a 5-year period (welfare expenditures)
Percentage change in population over the age of 65 over a 5-year period (aged)
Percentage change in population between the ages of 5 and 17 over a 5-year period (youth)
Dummy variable equal to 1 if the state government is controlled by Republicans and 0 otherwise (Republican control)
Dummy variable equal to 1 if the state government is controlled by Democrats and 0 otherwise (Democrat control)
Dummy variable equal to 1 if a tax and expenditure limitation (TEL) has already been imposed and 0 otherwise (TEL already imposed)

Source: Adapted from Alm, J., and Skidmore, M., *Public Finance Review*, 27(5), 481–510, 1999.

Research Connecting Individual and Aggregate Revolt Predictors

Tax regime change or reform requires a multilevel explanation. Individual-level opinion and position variables must have a complementary, aggregate, contextual explanation (Teske et al., 1993). The two levels must then find a connection in a mobilization of bias explanation—decisions and nondecisions (e.g., Bachrach and Baratz, 1962, 1975)—for institutions and procedures that bring opinions, status, and the circumstances into being.

The connectors for the individual- and aggregate-level studies appear as various hypotheses. The first, the so-called contextual hypothesis, explains that tax revolts occur as a result of events and interactions unique to the time and place (Levy, 1979). The second, a symbolic social movement hypothesis, derives from the long-standing opinion many taxpayers have, that taxes levied by distant governments are either too high or are misused. Tax limitation may occur to many who are unhappy about taxes, but taxpayers do not mobilize to express sentiments and act unless there is leadership. If leadership emerges, the mobilization can take place "almost literally overnight" (Lowery and Sigelmen, 1981, p. 972). The sentiment grows through the symbolic leadership of a major figure, leading to voting. The third hypothesis comes from the literature on the Tax Reform Act of 1986. Here an "ideational/entrepreneurial" approach to reform (Conlon, Wrightson, and Beam, 1990) unfolds. As Conlon and his colleagues argue (pp. 252–253), tax experts wanted reform, and policy entrepreneurs like Senator Bill Bradley and Representative Jack Kemp promoted it. The media strongly encouraged it. Good government groups lent support. Powerful members of Congress saw tax reform in their personal and committee's best political interest to move the legislation. Entrepreneurs wedded the experts' ideas to a snazzy concept the entrepreneurs had hawked already. Picked up by those people adept at attracting a media following, the reform finally attracted interest by leaders able to push the proposals through the labyrinth of legislative procedure.

Miller, Lin, and Xu (2006) investigated tax limitations across all states (the aggregate level). Like Sigelman and his colleagues, they asked whether the price of government helps explain "why ... some states adopted major limitations on government taxing and/or spending, while others have not." They tested six hypotheses:

1. The higher the tax-to-income ratio, the more likely a state will adopt TELs.
2. The faster state economic growth, the less likely a state will adopt TELs.
3. The larger the number of contiguous states that have adopted TELs, the more likely a state will adopt TELs (the diffusion theory).
4. The states that created TELs prior to 1980 will be more likely to be states that adopt more stringent TELs later.
5. The higher the electoral competitiveness, the less likely states will adopt TELs.
6. The more ideologically conservative the state, the more likely the state will adopt a TEL.

In contrast to Sigelman and his colleagues (1983), they did not test for either tax distribution (property taxes per se), cost-benefit as the proportion of spending on "welfare," or participation. They did look for the contribution of the rules of the game variable—the degree to which initiative played a part in tax revolt—in the examination of contiguous states.

Independent variables included the tax-to-income ratio, real gross state product growth rate, lagged real GSP growth rate (lagged by one year), number of contiguous states that adopted TELs prior to the observation, number of TELs adopted prior to 1980, district-level competitiveness, and ideology.

Their generalized, random effect logistic model used pooled time series cross-sectional data comprising twenty-two years for each of the forty-seven selected states (less Alaska, Hawaii, and Louisiana).

Their dependent variable in the analysis was a binary response, 1 for the years when a state adopts the TEL, 0 for other years. Thirty-one out of the fifty states adopted some form of tax and expenditure limits during the time period they analyzed.

They found no support for the price of government as a condition related to the existence of a TEL. In fact, the only hypothesis even partially supported was the faster state economic growth hypothesis, e.g., the faster state economic growth, the less likely the existence of a TEL.

Miller, Lin, and Xu (2006) also looked at the price of government in TEL states and compared it to that in states that had not imposed TELs. To gain the maximum possible distinction between TEL and no-TEL states, they added the states whose voters imposed term limits on legislators to the TEL states (event states).

The results of the comparison of event or tax revolt states and nonevent states appear in Table 8.4. Table 8.4 shows only the years in which most of the actions for either term limits or TELs occurred. No consistent differences emerge. Event states exceed nonevent states and the all-state average in both price of government measures in 1998. Event states exceed nonevent states in just one-quarter of the years.

Finally, they looked at the geographical dispersion of the event states (term limits and tax/expenditure limits). Mullins and Wallin (2004, p. 10) report that states having initiative powers as well as those having referendum powers tend to be located in the western United States disproportionately. This fact may account for the finding, shown in Table 8.5, that western states have adopted limits disproportionately.

Table 8.5 also shows that politics plays some role. Comparing the limits states with the states voting Democratic and Republican in the 2000 presidential election, on average, Republican states were more receptive to limits than Democratic Party-voting states.

In summary, Miller, Lin, and Xu found that lagged GSP growth helped explain the low likelihood of limitation legislation. The relationship, whether the limitation came about through initiative, referendum, constitutional amendment, or statute, was statistically significant.

The answer to the price of government–tax revolt relationship posed by Osborne and Hutchinson is clear. There is no evidence to support what they argued. Miller, Lin, and Xu also found evidence against the relationship in the relatively infrequent appearance of higher than peer prices of government and higher than peer rates of change in these prices among limits states.

The region and politics results have some face validity. Western, followed by southern states, chose limitations in disproportion to midwestern and eastern states. States voting Republican in the 2000 presidential election were more likely to have limitations than states voting Democratic.

Table 8.4 Price of Government and Rates of Change in Price of Government, United States, by Year of Term Limits or Tax/Expenditure Limits

Event year	1978	1979	1980	1985	1990	1991	1992	1993	1994	1995	1996	1998	1999	2000
Event states[a]	8	4	3	2	2	1	16	2	3	1	5	1	1	2

Price of Government (Above) or Below All States

	1978	1979	1980	1985	1990	1991	1992	1993	1994	1995	1996	1998	1999	2000
Event states[a]	0.000	0.000	0.008	0.000	0.009	0.013	0.004	(0.003)	0.004	0.004	0.012	(0.005)	0.006	0.006
Nonevent states	(0.001)	0.000	0.001	0.002	0.001	0.001	0.002	0.000	(0.001)	0.001	0.002	0.004	0.000	0.002

Rate of Change in Price of Government over Previous 5 Years

	1978	1979	1980	1985	1990	1991	1992	1993	1994	1995	1996	1998	1999	2000
Event states[a]	7.8%	5.4%	5.8%	4.4%	3.6%	5.6%	3.7%	3.7%	3.9%	0.2%	2.7%	2.9%	0.6%	0.9%
Nonevent states	5.4%	5.4%	7.0%	6.7%	4.0%	4.1%	3.9%	3.9%	3.1%	2.6%	2.1%	1.2%	0.8%	1.1%
All states	6.1%	6.4%	8.0%	6.3%	3.7%	4.0%	3.8%	3.8%	2.7%	2.7%	2.1%	1.8%	0.7%	1.1%

Source: Adapted from National Conference of State Legislatures, State Tax and Expenditure Limits—2005, www.ncsl.org/programs/fiscal/tels2005.htm; National Conference of State Legislatures, Tax and Expenditure Limits: The Latest, February 2006, www.ncsl.org/programs/fiscal/tels2006.htm, for events, nonevents, and states.

Note: For price of government: Numerator came from U.S. Bureau of Census, The 2010 Statistical Abstract, State and Local Governments—Revenue, by State and State and Local Governments—Expenditures and Debt, by State, 2010, http://www.census.gov/compendia/statab/cats/state_local_govt_finances_employment.html. Denominator came from U.S. Bureau of Economic Analysis, State Personal Income by State, 2009, http://bea.gov/regional/index.htm#state.

[a] States imposing the term limits or tax/expenditure limits.

Table 8.5   Region and Politics of Term and Tax/Expenditure Limitation

	States	*Actual Term and Tax/ Expenditure Limitations*	*Percent of States in Regions with Term/Tax/ Expenditure Limitations*
Region			
West	18	24	42.1%
South	13	15	26.3%
Midwest	8	9	15.8%
East	11	9	15.8%
	50	57	100.0%
Presidential Vote 2000			
Democratic	20	17	85.0%
Republican	30	40	133.3%

Source: Adapted from National Conference of State Legislatures, State Tax and Expenditure Limits—2005, www.ncsl.org/programs/fiscal/tels2005.htm; National Conference of State Legislatures, Tax and Expenditure Limits: The Latest, February 2006, www.ncsl.org/programs/fiscal/tels2006.htm, for actual term and tax/expenditure limitations; U.S. Census Bureau, *The 2010 Statistical Abstract*, Table 388. Electoral Vote Cast for President by Major Political Party—States, 2010, http://www.census.gov/compendia/statab/cats/elections.html.

Discussion and Summary of the Predictors of a Tax Revolt

Research has examined indirectly and directly the claim by Osborne and Hutchinson that the price of government might incite an antitax revolt when the price rose beyond some level apparent to voters and taxpayers. We found that the price did not directly relate to voter- or legislator-imposed tax and expenditure limitations. We believe that the same lesson applies to events that include both TELs and term limits.

If there is wisdom or insight or both in Osborne and Hutchinson's argument, what might the relationship between price of government and voter/taxpayer reaction be? For an answer, consider the tax revolt literature that explains public opinion about voting against taxes rather than the state-centric, aggregate socioeconomic information we used.

One study stands out. Lowery and Sigelman (1981) provide a classic example of a research design in which competing hypotheses clash. In doing so, they try to create an individual-level explanation for what the price of government predicts.

Lowery and Sigelman begin with eight hypotheses. We summarize them as follows:

1. Certain groups oppose (demographics) because of self-interest: "The individual's demand for government taxes and expenditures is seen as a function of self-interest," such as race, income or homeownership.
2. There is a prevailing view that government is too big and taxes are too high: The Buchanan "leviathan"—as opposed to the Downs rationally ignorant taxpayer.
3. There is a relative view that government now wastes too much money: Taxes are too high relative to benefits received.
4. Some feel that they are bearing more than their fair share of taxes—the war of the income classes.
5. Economic contraction—or the lack of economic progress felt in individual paychecks—makes people feel vulnerable and they fight back.
6. Ideological opposition to taxes exists: Some view the scope of government as excessive, and they gain ascendance, echoing Berkman (1993).
7. Researchers report a broadly felt loss of confidence in government found in surveys and interviews, as in "People like me don't have any say about what the government does" or "Sometimes politics and government seem so complicated that a person like me can't really understand what's going on."
8. A mobilization of the naïve occurs, as in "Only those who are grossly ill-informed about government in general and public finance in particular ... favor Proposition 13-style tax limitation."

The researchers used public opinion survey data from the American National Election Study of 1978 (National Election Studies, 1998). Of the eight variables, they found that loss of confidence was the best single explanation for supporting a vote to limit taxes. Reporting that they believed such statements as "People like me don't have any say about what the government does," voters feel it necessary to avoid fatalism and instead to express anger by voting to limit taxes. Second best was the "government is a leviathan" idea, one that the survey respondent relates to government leaders wasting much of the taxes paid. Finally, Lowery and Sigelman found that ideological conservatives opposed taxes! However, overall these variables did not say a lot about why people revolt.

The research could be summarized in three ways. First, each tax revolt is a product of its own context. Something happened in each instance that provoked the revolt. Revolts, in the aggregate, are coincidental unless we accept the next two summary statements. Second, taxing is a perennial political issue. Everyone hates paying taxes (so, Downs is right and Buchanan is wrong). Third, taxing is a latent political issue, a secondary or even third- or fourth-level issue in importance to most voters. Latency becomes manifest when an issue or a charismatic leader and a massive organizational effort force it. The charismatic leader strikes the match and ignites a wildfire.

If a symbolic issue, taxing should have brief duration. Does the self-imposed limitation by political leaders amount to a revolt of brief duration? Lowery and Sigelman use the simile of the child touching a burning stove top the first time and ask whether the child, even as an adult, ever touches a burning stove again. Does the child, even as an adult, avoid anything that burns to the touch? Do political leaders avoid any tax increase?

In basic terms, the price of government could rise or not rise beyond what voters and taxpayers prefer whatever their frame of reference. The issue of high taxes and wasteful spending, remote or immediate, remains present but latent until either an expert report or policy entrepreneur excites both the voters/taxpayers and those who can help stimulate and direct public opinion—bloggers, journalists, publicity-savvy interest groups. The issue will gain importance and resonance, and strong leaders will take over the shepherding of the issue through the legislative or electoral process. The antitax issue and all that follows may be a symbolic issue, as Fischel has shown in part. The dynamic, however, may follow the Lowery and Sigelman model (1981), one that Conlon, Wrightson, and Beam (1990) found in the 1986 Tax Reform Act, more closely than once thought.

How will we know? The future research to be done on our model involves five possible improvements to the variable and design we used. First, more experimentation with lags in the relationship between price and rate of change in prices relative to TELs may resolve the issue of the time from recognition of a tax problem to the election in which action takes place. Second, inflation may be a part of the variable definition of price or rate of change in price that relates more closely to action about the high price of government. Taking inflation into account will allow us to compare nominal dollars for all price measures in addition to constant dollars. Third, the similarity between voter intent in presidential elections and antitax/term limit political moves makes sense, especially in the period between the mid-1970s and the present, and further exploration might bring insight. Fourth, and related to politics, ideology and culture may be valid measures in some political contexts explored in research, but some better measures must exist or must be found to work in public finance research if these concepts have any worth. Finally, the peer effect hypotheses need attention, especially the degree to which the exit alternative—voting with your feet—influences public officials' decisions about the price of government. Identifying who peers or competitors are and applying appropriate deviation from the mean measures to comparisons among groups might yield greater insight as well.

The Performance Budget Indices and Tax Revolts

The mid-1990s U.S. Taxpayer Bill of Rights movement was the last tax revolt episode of its kind. In their book *The Price of Government*, David Osborne and Peter

Hutchinson argue the importance of one antecedent: "the price of government gets too high." Given Osborne's fame from his book *Reinventing Government*, whose thesis motivated and helped leaders defend major government management reforms in the 1990s, this research project takes his argument in *The Price of Government* seriously enough to test it. We ask first and foremost whether price, the sum of all taxes, fees, and charges collected directly by a given locality, divided by the locality's total economic resources (Osborne and Hutchinson's definition), actually predicts tax revolts.

This research tests the price of a government–tax revolt connection even further. The research hypothesized that tax revolts will occur in states:

- Where tax burdens are heaviest
- Where fiscal illusion is greatest
- Where citizen participation is least evident
- Where public governance emphasizes fiscal controls to prevent unlawful acts rather than to encourage program performance and results

In their positive form, these hypotheses are the equivalent of a performance budget. The research argued that performance budgeting within a context of fiscal policy change will lower the likelihood of a tax revolt.

As a review of research on what predicts tax revolts, the next section of this research report organizes the research to question whether the compound effect of fiscal illusion, insufficient citizen participation, and little yardstick competition among governments creates a veil that plants the seeds for tax revolts. Testing the claims made by Osborne and Hutchinson—the ability of the performance budget model to predict tax revolts—is the research task.

The Explicit Price of Government

The first independent variable in the research design follows directly from the price of government hypothesis. That is, the price of government is the actual tax burden borne by the individual taxpayer. The price of government measure appears here first as a static variable across time, the ratio of general own source revenues of a government to the total personal income of the locality. Then, the price or the tax burden appears as a dynamic measure, as its change over time.

Thus, if taxes in Canadian provinces are lower than those in the U.S. states, the absence of tax revolts in Canada gives face validity to the claim that high tax burdens predict tax revolts.

If taxes in Canadian provinces are higher or not significantly different from those in the U.S. states, why has there been no revolt as there has in the United States? Why no efforts to limit them? To explain why there have been no tax revolts in Canadian provinces, the project asks other questions about explicit conditions. Is tax autonomy the same in both countries (OECD, 1999; Rodden, 2004)? Is government responsibility the same (Citizens Budget Commission New

York, 2000)? These questions underlie a size of government argument as well as a value argument, implicitly, and the project develops these questions further in the next section.

The Implicit Price of Government

While the tax price a citizen actually pays may contribute to revolt, the veil covering tax regimes, fiscal illusion, hides an implicit price of government. An implicit price exists and describes the complex connections between government costs and their sources of financing easily ignored by responsible citizens given the indirect connection between taxes paid and benefits received by citizens, and much more important between tax and spending decisions.

What role does fiscal illusion play in motivating a tax revolt? The greater the fiscal illusion, says the performance budget model, the less obvious the link between taxing and spending, and the less likely a tax revolt. However, fiscal illusion increases the risk of a tax revolt, as events occur to reveal illusion. For example, the surplus-deficit problem appears in states where budgets do not shrink with the economy (Hill et al., 2006). Many forms of fiscal illusion exist, and most help form contexts in which U.S. tax revolts have occurred. Therefore the more obvious the link and balance between taxes and benefits, the less likely a tax revolt.

Fiscal illusion may provide a strong and direct set of tax revolt predictors. The rational ignorance and fiscal illusion among citizens become an interpretation of the price of government. As an interpretation of the price as being too high, the interpretation becomes an implicit price.

In addition to the fiscal illusion related to perception of immediacy of taxes and spending, other practices form part of the "confusion" basis for the implicit price of government. These practices include using debt rather than current revenues for financing spending and earmarking revenue for spending. Illusive and confusing practices also include nonconventional spending through tax incentives or tax expenditures, loans and loan guarantees, insurance, government corporations and authorities, regulation and mandates, and staff compensation through benefits rather than pay. The entire list of possible sources of citizen interpretation of a particular price of government, whether valid or not, represents an indexing of perception and relies on knowledge of these practices, a replica of which can be gained through both quantitative and qualitative analysis.

Openness of Government Decision Making

What role does citizen participation play? Citizen participation comes in many forms. This research defines active citizen participation as the voice variant of the exit-voice-loyalty model. Some of the definitions of citizen and voice come from direct observation in different political cultures. Consider those observations by Adams (2007) and Nevitte (1996) captured in Figure 8.2.

Traditional participation via Adams (2007):

1. Contact officials, both in writing and speaking

2. Organize other citizens

3. Speak/attend public meetings

4. Join organizations/committees

5. Attend/organize community meetings

6. Network

7. Contact media

8. Petition

9. Protest

Unconventional participation in protest potential of publics via Nevitte (1996) and Dalton (1988):

1. Vote (e.g., in tax limitation referenda)

2. Sign a petition

3. Join in boycotts

4. Attend unlawful demonstrations

5. Join unofficial strikes

6. Occupy buildings

Sources: Adams, B. E., *Citizen Lobbyists*, Temple University Press, Philadelphia, 2007, p. 135; Nevitte, N., *The Decline of Deference*, Broadview Press, Toronto, 1996, p. 78; Dalton, R. J., *Citizen Politics in Western Democracies*, Chatham House, Chatham, NJ, 1988, p. 65.

Figure 8.2 Provisional model of citizen participation in fiscal policy change.

In Nevitte's scheme signing a petition is the closest to citizen-initiated, direct democracy forms of tax revolts. In Adams, protest actually forms a category with the other eight categories describing many of the forms of participation found in accounts of tax revolts since California's Proposition 13 (Lo, 1990). Voting is a significant omission in both the Adams and Nevitte views. Voting to replace old with new elites, and voting in referenda on specific constitutional changes form the tax revolt definition used by Osborne and Hutchinson (2004) and Clemens and his colleagues (2003, pp. 17–20). This research report takes voting into account.

Citizen participation is a function of public officials' willingness to allow it. Citizen participation varies directly with the beliefs officials have in either democracy or representative government–republicanism. Likewise, citizens will participate when they believe more strongly in democratic than representative government. The question lies in political beliefs about legitimate ways to influence change in public policy, and especially fiscal policy. Related to legitimacy is experience with political institutions and the speed with which they have adjusted—these institutions being parliamentary majoritarian or separation of powers systems. Political culture influences citizen participation in fiscal policy changes. Fiscal policy changes should differ over cultures with individualistic political cultures associated with belief in individual action, mobilization of individual actions into social movements, and tax revolts as in the United States. Hierarchical political cultures define civic space with few interest groups, but groups that have more legitimacy than individuals in swaying public policy makers. Is the hierarchical culture associated with citizen deference to public leaders in fiscal policy making? If U.S. and Canadian political cultures differ, these differences can help explain resort to tax revolts only in the United States.

Incentives Embedded in Fiscal Controls

Incentives may or may not exist to motivate political leaders and public managers to reveal information on government performance and the value of programs and services to voters and taxpayers. The incentives to reveal performance and results information have emerged as important fiscal controls, called ex post controls, often complementary, strong controls beyond better known accounting, auditing, and line item budgeting controls, called ex ante controls. What is the effect of ex ante fiscal controls as opposed to ex post fiscal controls on the likelihood of a tax revolt?

Assuming that ex post controls motivate activity and action, are highly transparent, and involve citizens in a risk-sharing effort with leaders, the presence and performance of ex post controls would suggest the lower likelihood of a tax revolt. On the other hand, ex ante controls suggest a strong belief in the likelihood of official wrongdoing. Acting as preventive measures, ex ante rules might appear to a plurality of public officials as a signal to do nothing rather than face risk. Above that base instinct, the officials might find considered action, slowly undertaken, to be wise, leading to the citizen participation corollary that the public not knowing the rules need not be consulted or made knowledgeable of official action.

The ex post control system comes from the body of research called the economic theory of organization. Thompson and Jones (1986) track this theory back to Coase (1937). They argue the goal of a finance official is "getting the best bundle of goods and services purchased with public monies" (Thompson and Jones, 1986, p. 548). Under such a goal, they say, a control system design may apply to either an individual or an organization and force controls either before or after the subject acts, respectively ex ante and ex post controls. Ex ante controls are those preventing subjects from acting in opposition to the goal. The ex ante controls correspond to typical "internal" controls found everywhere and at all times—segregation of duties among fiscal actors, limited discretion to act, many levels of review and approval for decisions—and are also called red tape. Ex post controls create incentives to act to achieve a certain outcome; they exist to make subjects take responsibility for their actions and face the rewards or sanctions that come with the outcome. Typical ex post controls include organization goals and performance pay and, in the fiscal sphere, are central to the performance budget model tested here (Miller, Hildreth, and Rabin, 2001).

This research expects the use of ex post controls, rather than ex ante controls, might provide incentives to serve citizens' interests to the extent that serving citizens' interests prevents revolt. Therefore this research investigates whether the absence of ex post controls creates a greater likelihood of revolt. Comparatively, which federal states use these ex post controls? With what results do these federal states use ex post controls? What policy justifications emerge?

Therefore this research investigates the prevalence of ex post controls and the use of performance frameworks to replace the ex ante controls at provincial levels. This research seeks evidence of what provincial ex post controls are in use. Analysis of how far apart use and ideal levels of ex post controls lie should follow. The conclusions of the analysis may permit an assessment of the contribution these types of fiscal controls make to the likelihood of fiscal system change and of tax revolts.

Summary of Research Question

The existence of performance budgeting should predict taxpayer acceptance of current fiscal policies (in short, the fiscal regime); the performance budget's absence should predict tax revolt. Therefore the research question—"Why are there no tax revolts in Canada?"—leads to a test of a performance budget model in the subnational governments of the United States and Canada as the primary predictor. The performance budget model includes four index-like categories of data—the explicit price of government, implicit price of government, openness of government decision making, and incentives embedded in fiscal controls.

Answering the Research Question

Devising a research design to prove why an event did not occur challenged this project. Less convincing, indirect evidence dominated direct evidence. A comparison of legislative and constitutional procedures to enact tax and expenditure limitations accounted for much of the research on political structures. The U.S. National Conference of State Legislatures provided data on state tax and expenditure limitations. Reviews of current research and debate as well as statistical analysis of data from Statistics Canada, the Department of Finance in the Canadian federal government, the Organization for Economic Cooperation and Development (OECD), the International Monetary Fund (IMF), and the U.S. Bureau of the Census support the explicit and implicit price of government research. The closed or open system of decision-making research rested on opinion survey data—the World Values Survey—on citizen deference to authority over the period 1980–2000; these data included a strong battery of questions that help predict the likelihood of citizen protest in Canada and the United States. Inferential data on public leader willingness to share decision making came from existing surveys on budget transparency and public budget consultation. The information on ex ante and ex post fiscal controls came from existing provincial and state surveys of budgeting practices as well as judgments of professionals about the balance that exists between ex ante and ex post controls.

Findings

The findings appear here in seven parts: definition of *tax revolts*, specification of tax and expenditure limitations, state and province experience with revolts and limitations, the explicit price of government, the implicit price, openness of government decision making, and fiscal control system performance incentives.

1. This research incorporated a definition of a tax revolt used by Clemens and his colleagues (2003) at the Fraser Institute. In a revolt, the Clemens group specified a citizen initiative that results in legislative action and perhaps a referendum on changes to the existing tax regime. A citizen initiative requires a petition signed by a specific proportion of the voter population for a referendum on the question of a tax and expenditure limitation as specified in the petition; the petition process must follow the path specified in provisions of either a statute or a constitution. The referendum may require further action by a legislative body or may hold that the majority or supermajority vote for the petition-referendum question enacts the question as either a statute or constitutional amendment. Since many state limitations exist without petition and referendum, the definition produces an index-like variation—strong citizen initiation vs. strong legislative initiation. The research focused on events that occurred between 1976 and 2005.

   The most important finding dealt with political structures in provinces, specifically the initiative process, referendum, and constitutional amendment process. The referendum exists in provincial law. Only one province, British Columbia, allows initiative. Amending the constitution, the chief aim of state fiscal limitation supporters, is quite different in the provinces. Clemens and his colleagues (2003, p. 5) argue that "the Canadian constitutional system is vastly different from that in the United States." Entrenching provincial tax and expenditure limitations might require "assent" by both provincial and federal parliaments—a bilateral amendment—with federal assent to amending the Canadian Constitution of 1982 more likely after convincing popular support in the province through a referendum.

2. The definition of a limitation measure also came from Clemens and his colleagues (2003). The crucial part of the definition of an optimal limitation is one "initiated by citizens through a petition [a legal process called initiative and] approved by voters via referendum" (p. 6). An optimal limitation, they also said, has constitutional rather than statutory legal status, applies to spending and revenues broadly defined, limits growth in government spending to inflation plus population growth, includes state, municipality, and other locality spending and revenues, requires mandatory tax refunds when a surplus exceeds a prescribed limit, and covers all government spending and revenue collection. The types of limitations differ across the states. The definition produces an index-like variation—strong limit vs. no limit. The period for limitations studied was the same as for tax revolts.

3. The province and state experiences with limitations varied. Tax revolts occurred in Canada if a looser definition of revolts applies. MacKinnon (2003) and Boothe and Bradford (2001) found what they call tax revolts in Saskatchewan, Alberta, and British Columbia. The definition becomes very important when researchers base limitation measurement and statistical analysis on a dummy, dependent variable—where analysts assign a value of 1 to what they consider a tax revolt, or the existence of a limitation measure, and a 0 otherwise.

The tax revolt—when called such by MacKinnon (2003, p. 134)—may be limited to Saskatchewan, but a broader, fiscal responsibility movement has roots in Canada's prairie provinces: Alberta, Saskatchewan, and Manitoba in the early 1990s (Clemens et al., 2003, pp. 9–12). The Canadian fiscal responsibility movement and the U.S. balanced budget movement have remarkable similarities, says a major researcher in fiscal policy research (Smith, 2007).

Other events in Canadian provinces suggest tax limitation movements. A fiscal limitation named the Taxpayer Protection and Balanced Budget Act passed the Ontario Legislative Assembly on November 23, 1999, requiring a referendum for increasing taxes in the province. However, the next premier elected affirmed the law as a candidate but renounced the law in his first budget and gained a judicial decision supporting his retraction (*Canadian Taxpayers Federation v. Sorbara*, 2004). Also, there exists a tax and expenditure limitation in the form of the Alberta Advantage (Bergman, 2004). In Canadian history, grassroots protests appeared as the social credit movement that vied for power and prominence with a Co-operative Commonwealth Federation (CCF) movement. Both initially advocated a larger government role in national economic affairs to pursue social and economic reform, politically conservative social credit through provincial supremacy, and progressive CCF through both provincial and federal intervention (Mallory, 1976, pp. 161–163). These movements had their greatest electoral impact at the provincial level and developed as provincial movements.

As for the states, whatever the popular idea of widespread tax rebellion may be, the data in Table 8.6 reveal more modest accomplishments. Only a small number of limitations – of the thirty-six measures in thirty-one states— remain after applying the criteria the Clemens group (2003) prescribes.

While state referenda yielded constitutional amendments, far fewer resulted from initiatives and by referendum. The constitutional limitations had a far narrower application. At their broadest, the U.S. tax and expenditure limitation efforts succeeded—by optimal tax limitation standards—in only one state, Colorado. There the movement succeeded in enacting the Clemens group's optimal limitation as the Taxpayer Bill of Rights. California's limitations closely resemble those in Colorado, but California does not require mandatory tax refunds when surplus exceeds a prescribed limit.

4. The explicit price of provincial governments exceeds by over one-third the explicit price in states. The comparison measure is the median of total subnational own source revenue divided by personal income for the period 1989–2004, shown in Table 8.7.

However, government responsibility—defined as the proportion of taxes and spending at federal, provincial, and local levels—lies more heavily on provinces than states. Provincial governments had almost twice the tax responsibility of states, and more than twice the spending responsibility.

Table 8.6 Optimal Tax and Expenditure Limitation Characteristics with Number of States Enacting, 1978–2006

Characteristic, Number of States
1. Initiated by citizens, 5
2. Approved by voters via referendum, 17
3. Have constitutional rather than statutory legal status, 19
4. Applies to spending and revenues, broadly defined, 2
5. Limits growth in government spending to inflation plus population growth, 5
6. Includes state, municipality, and other locality spending and revenues, 2
7. Requires mandatory tax refunds when surplus exceeds a prescribed limit, 2
8. Comprehensive in coverage of government spending and revenue collection, 2

Source: Adapted from Clemens, J. et al., *Tax and Expenditure Limitations*, The Fraser Institute, Vancouver, CA, 2003, pp. 17–20; National Conference of State Legislatures, State Tax and Expenditure Limits—2005, www.ncsl.org/programs/fiscal/tels2005.htm; National Conference of State Legislatures, Tax and Expenditure Limits: The Latest, February 2006, www.ncsl.org/programs/fiscal/tels2006.htm.

Table 8.7 Tax Burdens Subnational Government Taxpayers, United States and Canada, 1989–2004

	1989	1990	1991	1992	1993	1994	1995	1996	1997	1998	1999	2000	2001	2002	2003	2004
United States Subnational Government Medians																
Total subnational revenue/personal income	0.212	0.212	0.218	0.223	0.227	0.232	0.231	0.232	0.238	0.239	0.240	0.239				0.248
Change 1989–2004																16.7%
Total subnational revenue from own sources/personal income	0.180	0.183	0.184	0.187	0.190	0.189	0.188	0.189	0.199	0.199	0.200	0.195				0.202
Change 1989–2004																12.2%
Canadian Subnational Government Medians																
Total revenue divided by personal income	0.337	0.335	0.345	0.347	0.346	0.350	0.355	0.361	0.351	0.344	0.359	0.352	0.364	0.354	0.351	0.356
Change 1989–2004																5.5%
Own source revenue divided by personal income	0.244	0.249	0.251	0.244	0.248	0.262	0.276	0.276	0.274	0.261	0.259	0.264	0.270	0.260	0.256	0.260
Change 1989–2004																6.3%

Note: For price of government: Numerator came from U.S. Bureau of Census, The 2010 Statistical Abstract, State and Local Governments—Revenue, by State and State and Local Governments—Expenditures and Debt, by State, 2010, http://www.census.gov/compendia/statab/cats/state_local_govt_finances_employment.html. Denominator came from U.S. Bureau of Economic Analysis, State Personal Income by State, 2009, http://bea.gov/regional/index.htm#state. Statistics Canada, consolidated federal, provincial, territorial, and local government revenue and expenditures, for fiscal year ending March 31, annual.

5. The research on the implicit price of government produced the strongest findings. Rodden's comparison of forty-four countries (2002, 2003) (IMF) and then a smaller panel of twenty-five countries (OECD) found that the magnitude of intergovernmental transfers varied with and predicted larger government size, his measure of the difference between explicit and implicit prices of government, and a condition called fiscal illusion. However, Rodden found that high state-provincial fiscal autonomy related to smaller government size overall, and thus smaller differences between the explicit and implicit price of government, and, it follows, the impact of fiscal illusion.

Both provinces and states fell in the high fiscal autonomy category. If provincial governments' size tops the states', Rodden implies (2002, 2003), intergovernmental transfers must be the most clearly related trend. In the only state research, Marshall's two studies (1989, 1991) and Garand's study (1988) examined the impact intergovernmental revenue had on expenditure per capita and its rate of change. The impact was positive but not statistically significant in Marshall's studies, while positive and statistically persuasive in Garand's study. Garand's study found that the state employee proportion of state population was even more compelling, logically following the intergovernmental grant effect (a higher proportion of grants could lead to higher, relatively permanent government employment). Studies by Dickson and Yu (2000) and Petry and his colleagues (2000) attribute size of government differences across Canadian provinces to intergovernmental transfers. Canadian taxpayer fiscal illusion also may have increased with corporate and other indirect taxation and government borrowing (Dickson and Yu, 2000) or voting power of government employees and the election cycle (Petry et al., 2000).

Boessenkool (2005) recognized the influence of Canadian equalization—intergovernmental transfers—on minimizing economic dislocations when compared to the United States, where equalization programs do not exist. Boessenkool also observed higher, sometimes far higher, tax rates in equalization's receiving provinces than donor provinces. The receiving provinces in Boessenkool's analysis were British Columbia, Saskatchewan, Manitoba, Quebec, New Brunswick, Nova Scotia, Newfoundland and Labrador, and Prince Edward Island. The donor provinces were Alberta and Ontario. (British Columbia has become a donor province since he published his research.) He attributes the difference to the incentive to increase taxes built into equalization formulas.

Called the flypaper effect, this incentive increases the implicit price of government. As a result, the flypaper effect, fiscal illusion theorists say, leads the electorate to see smaller tax prices needed to finance spending programs and to support higher levels of spending than they would if they correctly perceived tax prices and spending. In Canadian provinces, equalization may or may not have a distorting effect on perception, says Coulombe (1999). Equalization, he argues, dampens economic dislocation. Thus, most

Table 8.8 Tax and Spending Responsibility, Canadian and U.S. Governments, 2005

	Canada	United States
Tax Responsibility		
Federal	41.8	57.6
Provincial	45.8	23.4
Local	12.5	19.0
Total	100.0	100.0
Spending Responsibility		
Federal	31.8	51.1
Provincial	47.5	22.0
Local	20.7	26.9
Total	100.0	100.0

Sources: Treff, K., and Perry, D. B., *Finances of the Nation*, Canadian Tax Foundation, Toronto, 2007, p. B:3; U.S. Bureau of Census, The 2010 Statistical Abstract, State and Local Governments—Revenue, by State and State and Local Governments—Expenditures and Debt, by State, 2010, http://www.census.gov/compendia/statab/cats/state_local_govt_finances_employment.html; U.S. Office of Management and Budget, Budget of the U.S., Historical Tables, Table 1.1—Summary of Receipts, Outlays, and Surpluses or Deficits: 2010, 1789–2015.

provinces have higher implicit tax prices with equalization, while states have economic dislocation without equalization. Economic dislocation occurs with economic change; some regions win new and higher-paying jobs, and others lose them. Losing regions face falling incomes and growing unemployment. Government budgets in losing regions must contract with shrinking tax bases. Underinvestment in human and physical capital results; government disinvestment in education and health care as well as infrastructure illustrates this underinvestment in losing regions. Economic change and dislocation often encourage migration from losing to winning regions. Thus, there is higher interstate mobility in the United States than Canada.

The causal chain needs elaboration. Equalization dampens economic change and perhaps relates to mobility. However, equalization may make yardstick competition less possible. Taxpayers may have less information, and vote-seeking politicians may focus strategically to concentrate benefits and make taxes paid less visible to taxpayers. On the other hand, equalization can work as intended to improve information voters have. Equalization can work "to ensure that provincial governments have sufficient revenue to provide reasonably comparable levels of public services at reasonably comparable levels of taxation" (Canadian Constitution of 1982). Voters can more easily compare otherwise heterogeneous jurisdictions as a result. Equalization may also have benefit in creating incentives to increase tax rates where they are too low or in minimizing the impact of living and working in a resource-poor region, reducing the risks in choosing where to live.

The implicit price of government research points toward two sources of tax revolts. First, in the states, economic change and dislocation encourage immobile firms and households to support antitax movements. Second, with equalization, economic change dampens dislocation and discourages immobile firms and households to seek tax price changes through limitation efforts in receiving provinces. In Alberta, Ontario, and now British Columbia, Canada's equalization program donor provinces, firms and households face economic change as in the United States. Most probably feel the pinch of high tax burdens relative to their winning the economic change and dislocation battle. In the equalization donor provinces, Alberta, Ontario, and now British Columbia, we find a laboratory in which we can observe political reactions to economic dislocation in the form of fiscal regime change, citizen initiated or not, as in the states. These reactions combined with the willingness of voters and taxpayers to participate and even protest, plus the openness of leaders to participation and performance management, help predict the route fiscal regime change takes, through conventional or unconventional processes. This discussion of findings explores the participation and performance management dimensions next.

6. In the comparison of provinces and states to reveal the effects of citizen participation on the probability of a tax revolt, sparse evidence exists. Based on the evidence on leader willingness to allow or encourage citizen participation, the comparison shows that provinces are more likely to facilitate citizen participation than states.

Evidence of leader willingness to facilitate citizen participation comes through inferences gained from budget transparency and budget consultation surveys in both Canada and the United States. A web survey of province websites for public consultation updates the information from Ryan-Lloyd, Schofield, and Fershau (2005). See Table 8.9.

All provinces and the federal government have public hearings of one sort or another, except for Alberta. Alberta and British Columbia depend solely on web-based and household surveys. With the same exceptions, all provinces and the federal government allow, perhaps solicit, written submissions. Since online or web-based surveys are characterized as web pages allowing anyone interested to submit answers to both forced-choice, modified forced-choice, and open-ended questions, there is no effort to randomly sample the

Table 8.9 Canadian Prebudget Public Consultations, 2004–2005, Provincial and Federal

Jurisdiction	Parliamentary Committee	Government Organization	Public Hearings/ Community Round Tables	Site Visits	Written Submissions	Online Surveys	Household Surveys
British Columbia	Select Standing Committee on Finance and Government Services		X	X	X	X	
British Columbia		Finance Ministry				X	X
Alberta		Finance Ministry				X	X
Manitoba		Finance Department	X		X	X	
Ontario	Select Standing Committee on Finance and Economic Affairs		X		X		
Ontario		Finance Ministry	X		X	X	
Quebec		Finance Ministry	X		X		
Nova Scotia		Finance Department	X		X		
New Brunswick		Finance Department	X		X	X	
Prince Edward Island		Provincial Treasury	X		X		
Newfoundland and Labrador		Finance Department	X		X		
House of Commons	Standing Committee on Finance		X		X		

Source: Adapted from Ryan-Lloyd, K., Schofield, J., and Fershau, J., *Canadian Parliamentary Review*, 28(3), 44, 2005.

population. Thus, much of the leader willingness in this instance might be called passive—willingness to accept information from anyone interested—but not systematic or active in seeking it. Only British Columbia adds site visits and household surveys; Alberta uses household surveys. Both appear to take an active position in seeking information, to have more leader willingness to allow participation.

Participation evidence on states comes from Forsberg's state budgetary transparency research (2004). She summarizes the data, saying, six states "have no provisions for public input; the rest allow public input at various times, often at the discretion of budget committee chairs." The states therefore have a far less systematic approach than the provinces. In states, legislative leaders have significant discretion to allow public input. State decision makers are more passive in encouraging participation than provinces. States invest particular leaders with significant power to favor some participants over others or to allow participation at all. State budget leaders, Forsberg argues, are more likely to act either capriciously or opportunistically in soliciting participation, both characteristics suggesting high partisanship. Leader willingness to allow citizen participation, on this evidence from states alone, suggests a strategic and narrow definition of citizen participation.

The remainder of the state budget transparency data reveals state budget procedures as cumbersome, complex, and opaque. In fact, consider the frequency of the simplest budget process: an annual budget, accountable executive responsible for the revenue forecast, a single appropriation bill drafted by the executive, a simple majority required for passage of the budget in the legislature, and considerable executive veto power. These characteristics define an executive budget, the focus of continual reform among states since the late 1800s and thought by many to be the essence of "good government." Only four states have even partial transparency, if the executive budget serves as a guide: California, Georgia, New Jersey, and West Virginia. Leader willingness to facilitate citizen participation by the budget transparency standard appears weak in the states.

On the bottom-up question of whether citizens are willing to participate, more evidence exists. The voting evidence favors citizen willingness in the provinces. See Table 8.10.

The minimal differences on World Values Surveys do not permit any conclusive answer; however, a close reading of the trends found in the surveys (shown in Table 8.11) reveals that Canadians have becomes less enamored with protest and people in the United States more. The divergence in "protest potential" deserves more scrutiny.

Perhaps differences come from political culture. A complex answer to the citizen participation puzzle comes in part from comparative studies of deference to authority (Lipset, 1990; Nevitte, 1996). Deference to authority has a unique place in the exit-voice-loyalty triangle (Hirschman, 1970). Where

Table 8.10 Election Turnout, Canada by Province and United States by State, 1997–2006, Median and Average Percentage

	1997	2000	2003[a]	2004	2006
Provinces					
Median	65.6	62.6	68.0	61.2	63.9
Average	66.2	63.0	65.5	60.6	64.7
States[b]					
Median				63.6	43.0
Average				62.5	43.0

Sources: Federal: Elections Canada, http://www.elections.ca/scripts/OVR2006/25/ data_donnees/table_tableau04.csv (accessed August 18, 2007); Provincial: Blake, D., in *Provinces*, ed. Christopher Dunn, 2nd ed., Broadview Press, Peterborough, ON, 2006, p. 138; U.S. Election Project, http://elections. gmu.edu/voter_turnout.htm.

[a] Provincial elections were held in 2003 except for Alberta (2004) and British Columbia (2005); all other columns are federal election turnout percentages. Percentages are assumed to be based on voting-eligible population.
[b] State elections were held along with federal congressional elections in both years, with 2004 also being a presidential election year. The voting-eligible population, used in this table, is the population that is eligible to vote. Counted among the voting-age population are persons who are ineligible to vote, such as noncitizens, felons (depending on state law), and mentally incapacitated persons. Not counted are persons in the military or civilians living overseas.

exit suggests emigration, deference could mean hesitating to protest or use voice; in this case, deference corresponds to loyalty. However, deference could suggest unwillingness to pursue unorthodox methods of voicing support for fiscal policy change propositions. This research assumes that higher deference in Canada would suggest lower Canadian tolerance for revolt.

Based on his analysis, Lipset concludes that Canadians are far more deferential to authority than people in the states. He describes the difference in counterfactual terms: What if the states had not gained independence from Great Britian and what if British North America continued? He observes (1990, p. 227) that the polity

would now be more leftist than the revolution's children, more statist, much more social democratic, more disposed to perceive equality in redistributionist rather than meritocratic terms. It would operate under a parliamentary system, more conducive to third parties. It would be less individualistic and more deferential to authority.

Table 8.11   Hierarchy of Political Action Anchored with Voting

	Political Action	*Percent Taking the Political Action*					
		Canada 1982	*Canada 1990*	*Canada 2000*	*United States 1982*	*United States 1990*	*United States 1999*
Least intense	Voting—consensus estimates of election statistics[a]	~58%			~49%		
	↓						
	Signing a petition[b]	62.2	76.8	73.3	63.4	71.7	81.1
	Joining in boycotts[b]	15.0	22.3	20.5	15.8	19.0	25.7
	Attending unlawful demonstrations[b]	13.5	20.8	19.5	12.7	15.5	21.4
	Joining unofficial strikes[b]	4.7	7.0	7.0	3.2	4.8	6.0
Most intense	Occupying buildings[b]	2.5	3	3.1	1.5	1.5	4.1

Sources: Adapted from Nevitte, N., *The Decline of Deference*, Broadview Press, Toronto, 1996, p. 78; Dalton, R. J., *Citizen Politics in Western Democracies*, Chatham House, Chatham, NJ, 1988, p. 65.

[a] Differences exist across states and provinces and among federal, presidential, provincial, and by- and off-year elections. Consensus estimates follow from adjustments to turnout counts to the percentage of those old enough to vote rather than those either eligible to vote or registered to vote. Source: Elections Canada, http://www.elections.ca/content.asp?section=pas&document=turnout&lang=e&textonly=false; Martinez, U.S. Election Project (Dr. Michael P. McDonald), 2000, http://elections.gmu.edu/voter_turnout.htm.

[b] The World Values Survey asks: "I'm going to read out some different forms of political action that people can take, and I'd like you to tell me, for each one, whether you have actually done any of these things, whether you might do it or would never, under any circumstances, do it." The political actions included all above in the table except for voting.

The Lipset quote suggests propositions to test with the data from the World Values Surveys (WVS) of Canadian and U.S. samples in 1982, 1990, and 1999–2000. In Table 8.12, Lipset's findings appear alongside the last round of the WVS in Canada and the United States.

Table 8.12 Deference to Authority Indicators in the Canada–U.S. Political Culture World Values Survey Differences following Seymour M. Lipset[a]

	Lipset Dimension and World Values Survey Question (years question asked)	Probable Lipset Answer	Agreement with Lipset Answer (in last year the question appeared)		Multiyear Question—Convergence or Divergence Trend	Country Agreeing More with Lipset
			Canada %	U.S. %		
1	**More leftist**					
	Place views on left-right political scale—percentage leftist? (1982, 1990, 2000)	Left	21.1	17.7	Divergence	Canada
2	**More statist**					
	Favor government over private ownership of business (1990, 2000)	Government	20.4	17.4	Convergence	Canada
	Confident in the government (2000)	Yes	42.3	37.8		Canada
3	**View equality in redistributionist not meritocratic terms**					
	Incomes should be made more equal (1990, 2000)	More equal	33.1	29.8	Convergence	Canada
	Is country run for all the people rather than a few big interests looking out for themselves? (2000)	All	48.0	36.7		Canada
4	**Parliamentary government**					
	Confident in Parliament or Congress (1982, 1990, 2000)	Yes	41.1	38.1	Divergence	Canada
5	**More conducive to third parties**					
	Not confident in [existing[b]] political parties (2000)	Not	76.9	77.4		United States[c]

6	**Less individualistic**					
	Does healthy economy require more individual freedom? (1990)	No	36.6	34.7		Canada
	Individuals should take more responsibility for themselves than government (1990, 2000)	No	38.2	30.6	Convergence	Canada
7	**More deferential to authority**					
	Need strong unchecked political leadership (2000)	Yes	23.2	29.5		United States
	Defer to experts outside government (2000)	No	55.8	56.1		United States
	Defer to experts inside government—confidence in civil service (1982, 1990, 2000)	Yes	50.1	54.9	Convergence	United States
	Confident in people in national office (2000)	Yes	65.3	67.1		United States
	Government should be made much more open to the public (1990)	No	3.0	7.1		United States
	Not at all interested in politics (1982, 1990, 2000))	Not at all	22.0	11.1	Divergence	Canada
	Democratic system fairly bad or very bad for governance (2000)	Bad	11.6	10.9		Canada

Sources: Lipset, S. M., *Continental Divide*, Routledge, New York, 1990; European Values Study Group and World Values Survey Association, European and World Values Surveys Four-Wave Integrated Data File, 1981–2004, v.20060423, 2006, 2010.

[a] Based on his analysis, Lipset (1990) concludes that Canadians are far more deferential to authority than people in the states. He describes the difference in the counterfactual—what if the states had not gained independence from Great Britain and what if British North America continued? He observes (1990, p. 227) that the polity "would now be more (1) leftist than the revolution's children, (2) more statist, much more social democratic, (3) more disposed to perceive equality in redistributionist rather than meritocratic terms. It would operate under a (4) parliamentary system, (5) more conducive to third parties. It would be (6) less individualistic and (7) more deferential to authority."

[b] Interpreted here to mean confident that existing political parties are necessary and sufficient to good government. "Not confi-dent" suggests conducive to third parties.

The propositions hold that Canadian respondents in the WVS were

1. More to the left on politics
2. More statist
3. Viewing equality in redistributionist not meritocratic terms
4. Confident of parliament (or the legislature)
5. More conducive to third political parties
6. Less individualistic
7. More deferential to authority

On no dimension are the Canadian-U.S. differences large. On five dimensions of the deference question, however, the table shows that U.S. respondents agree more with Lipset's definitions of deference to authority than Canadian respondents.

Therefore, Lipset's answer to the counterfactual may describe the relative differences between Canadian and U.S. institutions, leaders, and people in the late 1990s. His phrases "more deferential to authority" and "less generally inhibitive of the power of government" suggest that citizen participation is not a good predictor of tax revolts.

The citizen participation aspect of the performance management approach to predicting tax revolts has many signals. The participation research reveals that Canadians participate more, get more encouragement to participate from leaders, have less protest potential, and perhaps resist joining tax revolts as a result. The participation data in states provide a weak but positive inference for tax revolts—low voting in regular elections, an increasing appetite for protest, leader capriciousness or opportunism in soliciting participation, and weak budget transparency.

7. The findings on ex ante vs. ex post fiscal controls are weakest. Both provinces and states have reported performance management-for-results efforts (sometimes called effectiveness and productivity data). The British Columbia, Alberta, Ontario, Quebec, and Nova Scotia efforts are the strongest among provinces, as Table 8.13 shows. The five provinces link planning with budget decision making in a variety of ways.

Table 8.14 reveals the depth and breadth of the purposes and audiences for this performance information. The survey and table do not indicate what impact this information may have had on decision making.

Despite interest—forty-seven out of fifty states report performance management and budget efforts based on statutes and executive orders (Melkers and Willoughby, 1998)—states' undertakings equal if not exceed provincial efforts. Burns and Lee's analysis (shown in Table 8.15) reveals the impact analysts have had with effectiveness or productivity data.

However, no evidence exists to link the ex post fiscal controls in the states with efforts to neutralize TEL support. Rather, the performance data could have an indirect impact in opening government operations to public view by

Table 8.13 Survey Responses on Business Plan–Budget Linkages, Canadian Provinces, 2000

Survey question: Are ministry/departmental business plans linked to or integrated with your jurisdiction's budgeting process?

	BC	AB	ON	QB	NS
If yes, what system or method?	Budget instructions require ministries to provide Treasury Board with performance measures and targets that are tied to ministry goals/ major business areas.	Business planning and budgeting are simultaneously developed, reviewed, and approved. The government's estimates, the government's business plan, and individual business plans are all tabled in the legislature at the same time.	The business planning process requires ministries to align future activities and expenditures with core business objectives. performance measures for each core business reported as part of business planning.	Budget documents identify expenditures according to the activities required to fulfill the business plan.	Business plans outline goals/ priorities as well as the resource requirements by program area. Each program is reviewed and approved by Cabinet subcommittees.
Being developed	SK, MB				
No	MB, NB, PEI				

Source: Office of the Provincial Auditor, Province of Manitoba, 2000.

Table 8.14   Survey Responses on Use of Performance Information, Canadian Provinces, 2000

Survey question: To what extent is information on performance used?					
How Used	*Not Used*	*Somewhat Used*	*Mostly Used*	*Always Used*	*Don't Know*
In decision making by ministries/ departments in relation to:					
1. Reallocation of resources		BC, AB, ON, NS,		PEI	NB
2. Policy development		BC, AB, ON	NS	PEI	NB
3. Program design/ redesign		BC, AB, ON	NS	PEI	NB
In decision making by Cabinet	NS	AB, ON, NB	PEI		BC
In decision making by Ministers of Treasury Board	NS	BC, AB, ON, NB	PEI		
In seeking feedback from elected representatives other than the Government in office	AB, ON, NS, PEI	BC			NB
In seeking feedback from citizens	NS	BC (some ministries), AB			ON, NB, PEI
In decision making by clients	ON, NS				BC, AB, NB, PEI

Source: Office of the Provincial Auditor, Province of Manitoba, 2000.

showing efficient operations and what results they have achieved. Whether efficiency and results convince anyone to stop drives to create government fiscal limitations will become apparent over time.

Discussion and Interpretation of the Results

This research project's findings help explain the absence of Canadian tax revolts in four ways. First, closer scrutiny of tax revolts—tax and expenditure limitation efforts—in the United States paints a different picture than popular opinion would

Table 8.15 Use of Program Analysis in Decision Making, States, 1970–2000

Type of Use	Percentage Use						
	1970	1975	1980	1985	1990	1995	2000
Executive Budget Decisions Based on Effectiveness Analysis							
Substantial degree	15	20	11	21	26	18	31
Some degree	23	59	70	64	64	53	50
Total	38	79	81	85	90	72	81
Executive Budget Decisions Based on Productivity Analysis							
Substantial degree	19	27	21	29	45	30	41
Some degree	32	54	64	67	55	54	44
Total	51	81	85	96	100	84	85
Legislative Decisions Based on Effectiveness Analysis							
Substantial degree	25	20	12	12	9	11	16
Some degree	19	48	66	73	74	72	63
Total	44	68	78	85	83	83	79
Legislative Decisions Based on Productivity Analysis							
Substantial degree	19	20	10	15	13	10	16
Some degree	25	32	56	76	81	69	66
Total	44	52	66	91	94	79	82

Source: Adapted from Burns, R. C., and Lee, R. D., *Public Budgeting & Finance*, 24(3), 11, 2004.

provide. Few were citizen initiatives, although more became institutionalized through referenda. The definition of tax revolts as grassroots efforts describes the aims of limitations supporters rather than the supporters themselves. In efforts limiting the scope of the property tax—the focus of most state limitations—a generally local tax or a tax used to support local expenditures for primary and secondary education, "grassroots" corresponds more to "local" than "citizen initiated." Only two limitations deal fundamentally with state fiscal policy regime change. State tax revolt data can help understand provincial antitax efforts only as state revolts are anti-property tax efforts aimed at local government tax prices, provoked by poor state legislator responsiveness in subsidizing local education systems, and initiated by legislators rather than citizen petition, strangely enough.

Second, Canada's equalization program and its federal-to-province transfers subsidize provincial efforts to confront economic dislocation. Like states, provinces have high fiscal autonomy. Unlike states, provinces have federal transfers that help neutralize the impact of economic dislocation on state support for human capital investment, especially education provided by local governments as in the United States.

Third, the citizen participation aspect of the performance management approach to predicting tax revolts has many signals. The participation research reveals that Canadians participate more, get more encouragement to participate from leaders, have less protest potential, and perhaps resist joining tax revolts as a result. The participation data in states provide a weak but positive inference for tax revolts—low voting in regular elections, an increasing appetite for protest, leader capriciousness or opportunism in soliciting participation, and weak budget transparency.

Finally, provincial efforts to incorporate program and agency performance information in budget decisions and in reports to voters and taxpayers exceed similar efforts in the states. However, neither provinces nor states have aimed ex post fiscal controls toward a goal such as balancing latent, salient opinion about taxes with performance information that produces evidence of value received for taxes paid.

Equalization, citizen participation, and performance management evidence suggests that leaders in the provinces have more means and have made greater effort to deal with the government budget impacts of economic change and dislocation. Many questions remain.

Postscript

Beyond the performance budgeting and fiscal policy approach to tax revolts, a number of other hypotheses appeared to explain the Canadian and U.S. differences in approach to fiscal regime change.

1. Do citizens have much to do with state tax revolts in the United States? Are business interest groups more likely to lead the antitax, tax, and expenditure limitation movements in states?

   Only five citizen initiatives created tax and expenditure limitations of the thirty-one states and thirty-six state limitations from 1978 to 2006. Citizens approved seventeen limitations via referendum, whether begun by citizen initiative or state legislative action. Citizen activity in legislative activity certainly existed in all limitation efforts, especially the limitation efforts that dealt with property tax limitations. However, Daniel Smith's research on antitax measures on statewide ballots in 1996 "questions the wisdom that they were populist undertakings. [Almost all] received the bulk of their financial support from a few wealthy individuals, vested economic interests, [and] out-of-state national nonprofits.... [The] organizations backing the 1996 initiatives were for the most part not grassroots operations" (2004, p. 100). More research on the pivotal support of antitax measures by groups other than what would be defined as citizens groups in the United States and the structure of support for antitax measures in Canada could question the popular belief that antitax efforts grew as popular, citizen-based revolts.

2. Is a tax revolt another form of social movement similar to the environmental and women's rights movements? How does social movement research account for the occurrence of tax revolts in the states and not in provinces?

   While social movements supporting environmental sustainability and women's rights may bear some resemblance to antitax efforts in the United States, Daniel Smith (2004) argues antitax efforts are not social movements. The later limitation efforts in the United States support that claim. However, Graetz and Shapiro (2005) argue that the U.S. federal tax reductions are the fruit of a national movement. State limitation efforts and the federal tax reduction movement may overlap in narratives, exploit similar political opportunity structures, or interlock members and leaders. The movement issue as a research question deserves further scrutiny, especially in the Canada-U.S. comparative perspective.

3. Are tax revolts a product of evolving public opinion spurred by leaders to a right turn politically, a turn well-advanced in the United States but only beginning perhaps in Canada?

   A political right turn in Canada that proceeds in the same direction and to the same degree as the turn in the United States is a phenomenon almost every Canadian political observer has tried to characterize. Some base their views on the shift the right in Canada has made from a position as Red Tories, as Horowitz (1966) developed the term. While the Red Tory idea applies primarily to Ottawa, Jean Crete (2007) has done preliminary research on a province-by-province comparison of parties on a left-right dimension. Crete casts doubt on a Canadian provincial version of the right turn idea. Most of these questions could bottom on political culture in which case research using Douglas and Wildavsky's grid/group measures of culture (1983) applied to fiscal policy questions with random samples in each province and a comparison group of states makes sense.

4. With conditions in Alberta and Ontario so similar to tax revolt predictor conditions in particular states, why are Albertans and Ontarians different? Are Albertans more like taxpayers in Colorado, a tax revolt state, or Texas, a no-revolt state with large resource revenues? Are Ontarians more like citizens in Michigan, a tax revolt state, or New York, a state without a tax revolt? Beyond specific provinces, what does an analysis of matched states provide? Does matching states with provinces, following Boychuk and Vannijnatten's effort to chart cross-border policy convergence, make analytical sense?

   The Boychuk and Vannijnatten effort (2004) might reveal the conditions that exist in Alberta and Ontario—equalization donor provinces left to fend for themselves as economic change occurs. The conditions in Alberta and

Ontario—political culture, business, and wealth-based interest group structure, parliamentary responsiveness to particular interests via political parties, and voter interest in protest—should get incorporated into later stages of this research program. Research using matching groups of provinces and states makes sense.

5. Is health care expenditure the source for differences in state and province tax burdens? Does health care provide a sense of value gained for taxes paid among Canadian taxpayers? Do differences in sentiment about health care service delivery explain the differences in antitax sentiment between states and provinces?

   Public opinion latency and saliency toward health care spending and tax prices might reveal value received for taxes paid in Canada and the opposite in the United States. However, the risks of bias in a survey interview or written questionnaire are quite high. Such research requires a health care service delivery specialist and a public opinion measurement specialist.

6. Finally, is a parliamentary system more responsive than a separation of powers system, especially on fiscal regime change?

   A conversation with federal manager Brian Marson (2007), who was also comptroller in British Columbia in the 1980s and former president of the Institute of Public Administration of Canada, revealed his view: "In our system gridlock doesn't force the [tax] issue onto the taxpayers like it does in the U.S. Here, the executive (which generally also has a majority in parliament/legislature) has the clear accountability to resolve chronic deficits." Many researchers, especially those in comparative politics, make similar observations. This question requires analysis of divided state governments and the strength of so-called veto players. However, U.S. public finance observers have noticed state antitax movements often reacted to state-local fiscal imbalances matched by state legislative unwillingness to respond. Musgrave argued this point in 1979 (p. 698), just after California's Proposition 13 became law. If circumstantial evidence suggests that government structure contributes to state tax and expenditure limitation efforts, what other evidence could researchers find?

References

Adams, Brian E. (2007). *Citizen Lobbyists*. Philadelphia: Temple University Press.

Alm, James, and Mark Skidmore. (1999). Why do tax and expenditure limitations pass in state elections? *Public Finance Review* 27(5):481–510.

Bachrach, Peter, and Morton S. Baratz. (1962). Two faces of power. *American Political Science Review* 56(4):947–952.

Bachrach, Peter, and Morton S. Baratz. (1975). Power and its two faces revisited. *American Political Science Review* 69(3):900–904.

Bergman, Brian. (2004). Ralph Klein. *Maclean's*, February 16, www.thecanadianencyclopedia.com (accessed July 9, 2007).

Berkman, M. G. (1993). *The State Roots of National Politics*. Pittsburgh, PA: University of Pittsburgh Press.

Berry, F. S., and W. D. Berry. (1992). Tax innovation in the states. *American Journal of Political Science* 36(3):715–742.

Blake, Donald E. (2006). Electoral democracy in the provinces and territories. In *Provinces*, ed. Christopher Dunn, 115–144. 2nd ed. Peterborough, ON: Broadview Press.

Boessenkool, Kenneth J. (2005). Letter to Renee St.-Jacques, Expert Panel on the Equalization and Territorial Formula Financing. May 26.

Boothe, Paul, and Reid Bradford. (2001). *Deficit Reduction in the Far West: The Great Experiment*. Edmonton: University of Alberta Press.

Boychuk, Gerard W., and Deborah L. Vannijnatten. (2004). Economic integration and cross-border policy convergence. *Horizons* 7(1):55–60.

Buchanan, James M. (1977). Why does government grow? In *Budgets and Bureaucrats: The Sources of Government Growth*, ed. Thomas E. Borcherding, 3–18. Raleigh, NC: Duke University Press.

Buchanan, James M. (1979). The potential for taxpayer revolt in American democracy. *Social Science Quarterly* 59 (4): 691–696.

Burns, Robert C., and Robert D. Lee. (2004). The ups and downs of state budget process reform. *Public Budgeting & Finance* 24(3):1–19.

Canadian Taxpayers Federation v. Sorbara. (2004). Court File 04-CV-269781 CM1. Toronto: Ontario Superior Court of Justice.

Citizens Budget Commission New York. (2000). *An Affordable Debt Policy for New York State and New York City*. October 18. http://www.cbcny.org/debt1018.pdf (accessed July 31, 2007).

Clemens, Jason, Todd Fox, Amela Karabegovic, Sylvia LeRoy, and Niels Veldhuis. (2003). *Tax and Expenditure Limitations*. Vancouver, CA: The Fraser Institute.

Coase, R. H. (1937). The nature of the firm. *Economica* New Series, 4 (16): 386–405.

Conlon, T. J., D. R. Beam, and M. T. Wrightson. (1995). Policy models and political change. In *The New Politics of Public Policy*, ed. M. K. Landy and M. Levin, 121–141. Baltimore: Johns Hopkins University Press.

Coulombe, Serge. (1999). *Economic growth and provincial disparity*. Ottawa: Renouf Publishing.

Crete, Jean. (2007). Y-a-t-il un lien entre le discourse due gouvernement du Quebec et son activite legislative? Colloque annuel de la Societe quebecoise de science politique, Universite Laval Quebec. May 24.

Cutler, D. M., D. W. Elmendorf, and R. Zeckhauser. (1999). Restraining the leviathan: Property tax limitation in Massachusetts. *Journal of Public Economics* 71(3):313–334.

Dalton, Russell J. (1988). *Citizen Politics in Western Democracies*. Chatham, NJ: Chatham House.

Dickson, Vaughan, and Weiqiu Yu. (2000). Revenue structures, the perceived price of government output, and public expenditures. *Public Finance Review* 28(1):48–65.

Douglas, Mary, and Aaron Wildavsky. (1983). *Risk and Culture*. Berkeley: University of California Press.

Downs, Anthony. (1959–1960). Why the government budget is too small in a democracy. *World Politics* 12:541–563.

European Values Study Group and World Values Survey Association. (2010). European and World Values Surveys four-wave integrated data file, 1981–2004, v.20060423, 2006. Surveys designed and executed by the European Values Study Group and World Values Survey Association. File producers: ASEP/JDS, Madrid, Spain, and Tilburg University, Tilburg, The Netherlands. File distributors: ASEP/JDS and GESIS, Cologne, Germany.

Forsberg, Mary E. (2004). *Let the Sunshine in.* Trenton: New Jersey Policy Perspective. http://www.njpp.org/rpt_transparent.html (accessed August 14, 2007).

Garand, James C. (1988). Explaining government growth in the states. *American Political Science Review* 82 (3), 837–849.

Graetz, Michael J., and Ian Shapiro. (2005). *Death by a Thousand Cuts.* Princeton, NJ: Princeton University Press.

Hill, Edward, Matthew Sattler, Jacob Duritsky, Kevin O'Brien, and Claudette Robey. (2006). *A Review of Tax Expenditure Limitations and Their Impact on State and Local Government in Ohio.* Cleveland, OH: Center for Public Management, Levin College of Urban Affairs, Cleveland State University.

Hirschman, Albert O. (1970). *Exit, Voice and Loyalty.* Cambridge, MA: Harvard University Press.

Horowitz, G. (1966). Conservatism, liberalism and socialism in Canada. *Canadian Journal of Political Science* 32(2):143–171.

Levy, F. (1979). On understanding Proposition 13. *Public Interest* 56:66–89.

Lindblom, C. E. (1959). The science of "muddling through." *Public Administration Review* 19(1):79–88.

Lipset, Seymour Martin. (1990). *Continental Divide.* New York: Routledge.

Lo, Clarence Y. H. (1990). *Small Property versus Big Government: Social Origins of the Property Tax Revolt, Expanded and Updated Edition.* Berkeley: University of California Press. http://ark.cdlib.org/ark:/13030/ft196nb00f/ (accessed July 31, 2007).

Lowery, David, and Lee Sigelman. (1981). Understanding the tax revolt. *American Political Science Review* 75(4):963–974.

MacKinnon, Janice. (2003). *Minding the Public Purse: The Fiscal Crisis, Political Trade-Offs, and Canada's Future.* Montreal: McGill-Queen's University Press.

Mallory, J. R. (1976). *Social Credit and the Federal Power in Canada.* Toronto: University of Toronto Press.

Marshall, Louise. (1989). Fiscal illusion in public finance. Ph.D. Dissertation, University of Maryland.

Marshall, Louise. (1991). New evidence on fiscal illusion. American *Economic Review* 81(5), 1336–1344.

Marson, Brian. (2007). Personal conversation.

Melkers, Julia, and Katherine Willoughby. (1998). The state of the states: Performance-based budgeting requirements in 47 out of 50. *Public Administration Review* 58(1):66–73.

Meltsner, Arnold. (1971). *The Politics of City Revenue.* Berkeley: University of California Press.

Mikesell, John L. (1978). Government decisions in budgeting and taxing. *Public Administration Review* 38(6):511–513.

Miller, Gerald J., W. Bartley Hildreth, and Jack Rabin. (2001). *Performance-Based Budgeting.* Boulder, CO: Westview.

Miller, Gerald J., Weiwei Lin, and Hua Xu. (2006). What can the 'price of government' predict? *State Tax Notes*, January 9, pp. 37–49.

Mullins, D. R. (2003). Popular processes and the transformation of state and local government finance. In *State and Local Finance under Pressure*, ed. D. L. Sjoquist, 95–162. Northampton, MA: Elgar.

Mullins, D. R., and B. A. Wallin. (2004). Tax and expenditure limitations. *Public Budgeting & Finance* 24(4):2–15.

Musgrave, Richard A. (1979). The tax revolt. *Social Science Quarterly* 59(4):697–703.

National Conference of State Legislatures. (2005). State tax and expenditure limits—2005. www.ncsl.org/programs/fiscal/tels2005.htm (accessed September 23, 2005).

National Conference of State Legislatures. (2006). Tax and expenditure limits: The latest. February. www.ncsl.org/programs/fiscal/tels2006.htm (accessed July 18, 2007).

National Election Studies (U.S.). (1998). *American National Election Studies, 1948–1997*. Ann Arbor, MI: Interuniversity Consortium for Political and Social Research.

Nevitte, Neil. (1996). *The Decline of Deference*. Toronto: Broadview Press.

OECD (Organization for Economic Cooperation and Development). (1999). Taxing powers of state and local government. OECD Tax Policy Studies 01. Paris: OECD Publishing.

Office of the Provincial Auditor, Province of Manitoba. (2000). Inter-jurisdictional comparison on trends and leading practices in business planning and performance measurement. Winnipeg: Office of the Provincial Auditor. http://www.oag.mb.ca/reports/STUDYTRANDLPR_DEC00.pdf (accessed August 16, 2007).

Osborne, David E., and Peter Hutchinson. (2004). *The Price of Government*. New York: Basic Books.

Petry, Francois, Louis Imbeau, Jean Crete, and Michel Clavet. (2000). Explaining the evolution of government size in the Canadian provinces. *Public Finance Review* 28(1):26–47.

Phillips, Kevin. (1990). *The Politics of Rich and Poor*. New York: Random House.

Pressman, Jeffrey L., and Aaron Wildavsky (1973). *Implementation: How Great Expectations in Washington are Dashed in Oakland; or, Why It's Amazing that Federal Programs Work at All, This Being a Saga of the Economic Development Administration as Told by Two Sympathetic Observers Who Seek to Build Morals on a Foundation of Ruined Hopes*. Berkeley: University of California Press.

Rodden, Jonathan. (2002). The dilemma of fiscal federalism: Grants and fiscal performance around the world. *American Journal of Political Science* 46(3):670–687.

Rodden, Jonathan. (2003). Reviving leviathan: Fiscal federalism and the growth of government. *International Organization* 57(4):695–729.

Rodden, Jonathan. (2004). Comparative federalism and decentralization. *Comparative Politics* 37(4):481–500.

Ryan-Lloyd, Kate, Josie Schofield, and Jonathan Fershau. (2005). Pre-budget consultations in British Columbia. *Canadian Parliamentary Review* 28(3):43–48.

Sigelman, Lee, David Lowery, and Roland Smith. (1983). The tax revolt: A comparative state analysis. *Western Political Quarterly* 36(1):30–51.

Smith, Dan. (2007). Personal conversation.

Smith, Daniel A. (2004). Peeling away the populist rhetoric. *Public Budgeting & Finance* 24(4):88–110.

Temple, J. A. (1996). Community composition and voter support for tax limitations: Evidence from home-rule elections. *Southern Economic Journal* 62(4):1002–1016.

Teske, P., M. Schneider, M. Mintrom, and S. Best. (1993). Establishing the micro foundations of a macro theory. *American Political Science Review* 87(3):702–713.

Thompson, F., and L. R. Jones. (1986). Controllership in the public sector. *Journal of Policy Analysis and Management* 5(3):547–571.

Treff, Karin, and David B. Perry. (2007). *Finances of the Nation*. Toronto: Canadian Tax Foundation.

U.S. Bureau of Economic Analysis. (2009). Gross domestic product by state. http://bea.gov/regional/index.htm#gsp.

U.S. Census Bureau. (2010). *The 2010 Statistical Abstract*. Washington, DC: Superintendent of Documents. http://www.census.gov/compendia/statab/cats/elections.html.

Wildavsky, A. (1961). The political implications of budgetary reform. *Public Administration Review* 21(1):183–190.

Witte, J. F. (1985). *The Politics and Development of the Federal Income Tax*. Madison: University of Wisconsin Press.

Chapter 9

Debt Management Networks

Gerald J. Miller and Jonathan B. Justice

Why study municipal debt financing and especially the bond sale? The role played by the network of institutions involved in lending funds to localities has important ramifications for the governance of cities and for their accountability, efficiency, and effectiveness. The politics and administration of municipal debt financing have enough visibility and significance that observers of these financings feel justified in pointing out possible abuses. Besides corruption associated with political campaign contributions by investment banks, a deep exploitation argument often emerges. Basic to this chapter's analysis is the observation that exploitation can go either way. Credit market experts can exploit government finance officials' lack of knowledge about financing. Government finance officials can also exploit the banking syndicates' ability to finance almost anything—as long as there is a revenue stream to pay back the bonds—whether for the good of the politician's reelection, the good of a particular group or groups of deserving local interests, or the well-being of the city or state as a whole. This chapter's purpose is to examine the way municipal bond financings work through an understanding of the relationships of the credit market and government participants and to shed light on the exploitation argument.

If financial managers themselves were the sole arbiters of technique in borrowing money from the credit markets, we would expect them to construct strategies that follow an economizing logic based on their reported values. However, attributing the choice of strategy only to the finance officials in the organization borrowing the money oversimplifies the process of financing. Debt issuers formulate and pursue financing strategies with others on a team brought together to sell bonds.

255

Different team members typically have their own goals and interpretations of the political and market environments in which the bonds are to be sold. Those diverse goals and constructions of reality all contribute in some measure to the judgments and choices that define borrowing strategies. Accordingly, understanding how debt issuance strategies are formulated requires focusing on the team involved in the sale, not just the issuer. Particularly important are the routes interpretations take in influencing decisions.

Consider Sbragia's (1983) position. She observed that important links exist between the investment community, the professional finance community, and local policy making. These links suggest much greater interdependence and much less governmental initiative than would otherwise be the case considering the literature on municipal government decision making. If we are to understand policy making, Sbragia argued, much more must be known about these links and their effects on decision-making processes and outcomes.

Research by Pagano (1982) and Pagano and Moore (1985) supports a line of reasoning that holds that public investment decisions have important effects on the economic decisions of private firms. Some firms are relatively direct influences and beneficiaries: underwriters in syndicates of bond buyers as well as the firms whose costs will fall and markets improve as a result of the public investment projects financed by a bond issue. Where these decisions, all essentially economic development ones, do encourage private investment, considerable economic and political development may take place, in turn greatly changing the conditions and expectations of governance.

This chapter outlines an approach for understanding how debt strategies, with their demonstrated implications for governance outcomes, are formulated. The conceptual framework has two broad elements: the need for financial managers to construct knowledge of—to interpret—the realities of political and market environments that are always uncertain and frequently ambiguous, and an interorganizational network model that behaves as a political economy. Financial managers interpret reality with the assistance of teams of advisors and underwriters drawn from networks of debt specialists, and these interpretations guide their judgments about the appropriateness of alternative strategies. Under some conditions, the team members' stability or experience with each other becomes a major factor in the network's success. That experience, in turn, depends on the various bargains struck within the network. These bargains, in turn, reflect the larger pattern of interaction among network members and the outside world.

This framework provides an alternative view to the economizing logic, and in a larger sense, an alternative to rational decision making, and suggests that a bond deal can be more a bargain struck among peer organizations than an application of principal-agent relations and strict means-ends rationality on the issuer's part.

The chapter also includes three empirical applications for this understanding of the decision-making process. First, we show how the framework illuminates prior research on the implications of negotiated vs. competitive sales of debt to underwriters. Second, a simulation using goal-oriented teams of graduate students confirms the framework's utility for understanding the implications for team performance of team stability and other characteristics. Finally, we use the framework to understand how financial managers in the New York Metropolitan Transportation Authority (MTA) and other members of their debt network interpreted a highly ambiguous environment in order to devise a strategy for refinancing $13 billion of outstanding bonds.

We begin by describing the bond issuance process and players, the kinds of decisions that have to be made by issuers with the advice and cooperation of the other players, and the interpretive demands of the process. Next we summarize prior research concerning the choice between competitive and negotiated sales of municipal bonds. Then we lay out the elements of the conceptual framework related to understanding the political economy of debt networks and the role of team composition and stability in shaping decisions. This is followed by reports of the simulation test and the MTA case study, and some concluding remarks.

The Bond Sale Process and Participants

The process of issuing debt requires issuers to make strategic choices in the face of information poverty and the uncertainty associated with the complexity of current economic circumstances, as well as the inherent inability to know the future with certainty. Such situations are somewhat like the cobweb economists use to explain market instability and sellers' imperfect knowledge (Heilbroner and Thurow, 1984, pp. 126–127). That is, markets in constant flux never provide enough certainty—information that lends itself to a patterned image—to compensate for a decision maker's lack of insight. The decision maker constantly decides matters either in terms of the reality of the past, often compounding past error, or through deference to those more likely to be privy to the secrets or nuances of a complex process or system.

Debt decisions are further complicated by the principal-agent issues arising from the competing interests of cost-minimizing issuers and the profit-seeking market participants on their issuance teams. Issuers devising financing strategies must also in some instances cope with normative ambiguity, such as conflicts between the professional norm of cost minimization and political and economic pressures to defer costs to future taxpayers and ratepayers.

Process

There are four steps in the debt issuance process. First, initiation of a sale rests on the choice of the market. Which investors will/should buy the securities? Tax laws, the economic cycle, and the habitual purchasing practices of individuals and institutions combine in various ways. They create choices based on the probability that legislators, interest rates, and consumers will behave in reasonably predictable ways.

The second step in the process involves structuring a debt issue to confront two problems: the predilections of the market chosen and the capacity of the issuer. The market choices put a premium on accuracy, but the ability of the issuer to manage the debt provided in the structure sets limits.

The structure directly connects the market with disclosure of the issue and the issuer, the third step. What facts will be disclosed, and more importantly, what interpretation will be presented for these facts, in the major document for disclosing information, the official statement (OS), and the presentations to ratings agencies?

The final step is the sale, at which time all parties decide the price of the issue. The sale confirms the assumptions made by the team about the structure of the issue and the level of demand for the quantity provided. In viewing the sale another way, it becomes a confirming piece of information about where the sale fell on the cobweb. If the guess about supply and demand resulted in a spiral inward, we can say the team "learned."

Players

Now consider the team involved in the sale of municipal securities. A fairly large group of experts may become involved in either of two types of sale: guaranteed debt and nonguaranteed debt. Guaranteed debt is backed by the full taxing power of a governmental unit, although nominally debt service comes from general, unrestricted revenues. Nonguaranteed debt is usually based on the repayment capacity of a revenue stream, such as water and sewer fee revenue.

Guaranteed debt sales have become ever more tightly regulated by state constitutions and legal codes. As a result, these securities have become homogeneous, commodity-like instruments, requiring little distinction among advisors in their structuring. Differences depend on the creditworthiness of their issuers, as interpreted by rating agencies, and the point in the business cycle at which they are sold.

Interpretations

A nonguaranteed debt sale has become the place where advisors may actually use their creative talents. Because revenue streams may lack history or a basis for forecasting, "the market" must rely on an advisor to depict their earning capacity. Legal interpretations may also be required. Moreover, the market itself has to be analyzed to determine likely purchasers of the securities both initially and in the secondary market. Three basic groups of advisors form the team in a nonguaranteed debt sale: those who interpret the market for the issuer, those who interpret the law for the underwriter/investor, and those who interpret the issuer for the underwriter/investor.

The financial advisor usually leads the effort to interpret the market for the issuer. The financial advisor determines how broad a market can be attracted to a sale or what part of a market is needed for a negotiated private placement. The determination of the market leads directly to the structuring of the security, influencing fundamentally its various features (see Hildreth, 1986; Moak, 1982; Lamb and Rappaport, 1980). In a competitive bond sale, the financial advisor assists the issuer in designing the debt issue structure, preparing documents to disclose information to credit ratings agencies and underwriters who will compete to buy the bonds and the investors underwriters will resell the bonds to, and planning and conducting the actual sale. The underwriter—the initial buyer of the securities from the issuer for resale to investors—in a negotiated bond sale may advise an issuer on the financing, taking over the financial advisor role on the team and changing that role from a formal, legal one to an informal one. By Municipal Securities Rulemaking Board regulation at least, an underwriter may not serve formally as both financial advisor and underwriter.

Bond counsel leads the effort to interpret the structure of the security in terms of applicable law. Many regard bond counsel as the representative of investors, assuring them that the issuer will not default on an obligation by pleading technical defects in the procedures used to authorize or issue the bonds. Yet, Petersen observes (1988, p. 4) that "additional roles of bond counsel in preparing transactions for market and [for] disclosure are extensive, flexible, and subjects of professional debate." The bond counsel may be assisted by counsel for an underwriter in a negotiated sale as well as counsel for any other party, including the issuer, if the structure's complexity demands it.

Finally, the auditor or accounting specialist (CPA) interprets the issuer's financial status, in terms of the structure of the security, for the investor. For example, the CPA interprets the issuer's financial status, as depicted through financial reports. If the revenue stream underlying the security must be forecast, the CPA may also verify the assumptions and calculations made to confirm the stream's contribution to the issuer's ability to repay principal and interest. Assisting or collaborating with the CPA, a consulting engineer, management specialist, or other expert may join in the interpretation of the issuer's financial status or the project being financed.

Disclosure

The three separate areas of interpretation are disclosed primarily through the production of a document, the official statement (OS). The OS is both official—the issuer's authorization of all interpretations made on its behalf by the team members—and a "direct exposition of information concerning the offering" (Petersen, 1988, p. 5).

The ultimate arbiters of the meanings ascribed to the offering, the issuer, and the market, however, remain the rating agencies. By considering the security's structure, the legal interpretation affixed to it, and the financial status of the issuer—as well as relevant economic and managerial information—the agencies determine, essentially, the likelihood that the issuer will repay principal and interest as scheduled.

In summary, the structure of the security and the disclosure of it and the legal status and repayment capacity of the issuer present the market with essential data regarding risk and reward. With these data, theoretically, the market for municipal securities may achieve efficiency by allocating scarce capital among competing uses, assigning appropriate prices (interest payments to the issuer and bond prices and yields to the investor) to structures at particular levels of repayment capacity.

Events and Existing Knowledge of Debt Management Networks

This outline of activity involved in bond sales has deliberately highlighted the range of discretion involved in an issuer's attempt to participate in an efficient market. Such discretion must exist to take account of the vast uncertainty with which an issuer must contend; the bond sale team must guess. The type of team that must surround an issuer, it appears, is the key to surmounting the vast uncertainty that often confounds a sale, and we rely on theory to guide in determining essential factors in comprising the team.

As debt management's importance and complexity have increased, governments' dependence on debt intermediaries such as financial advisors, underwriters (in both their underwriting and informal advisory capacities), and others has grown. Dependent public managers, who nominally head debt management networks in issuing and selling debt to investors, question decisions intermediaries make reluctantly. Consider how these issues arise in the research on method of sale strategies.

The Pennsylvania Negotiated Bond Deal Controversy

Looming debt management problems became apparent in a study of Pennsylvania local government's unique bond sales practices (Forbes and Peterson, 1979). Today, Pennsylvania law directly and indirectly gives preference to negotiated general obligation municipal bond sales to underwriters rather than competitively bid sales. Forbes and Peterson tried to determine whether most governments paid excessive interest costs for the money they borrowed.

Following methods common at the time, the Forbes and Peterson work showed that such might be the case. They found local government's bond net interest cost (NIC) rates were somewhat higher—by 26 basis points or 0.29%—than those paid in other states in the region. However, they also found that (p. 24) "GO negotiated issues in Pennsylvania sell at NICs that are 25 basis points higher than competitively sold GO bonds in Pennsylvania in the same size range."

Their analysis of underwriter spreads—compensation in the bond issue for work done by bankers to sell the securities to investors—revealed larger amounts than was common among New York local governments. Variation in state-specific laws, policies, and procedures suggests little statistical effect on interest costs or underwriter spreads.

Later research modified somewhat the bold assertion of this research. Bland (1985) succeeded in showing that Forbes and Peterson overstated their case, as his research suggested that experience may well inform the negotiation governments pursue with underwriters. In some cases, experience leads to substantial interest costs savings when compared to that paid by less experienced negotiating governments. The differences in costs associated with experience hold up against costs for competitively bid bond sales by local governments in New Jersey and Ohio as well.

Specifically, Bland's analysis suggests that as a negotiated sale issuer's experience increases, interest rates decline. That is, "when all other determinants of NIC are held constant, a negotiating issuer with the experience of four previous sales will obtain an interest rate that is 24 basis points lower than an issuer with no previous experience in the past decade" (p. 236). The difference holds up when experienced negotiators are compared to competitively bid issues. Issuers with experience negotiating sales have interest costs statistically comparable to competitive sale issues getting high demand. Bland infers that, with some market experience, the management team of an issuer is capable of matching wits with the representatives of the underwriting syndicate and is able to negotiate an interest rate comparable to that which could be obtained if the issue were to receive seven or more competitive bids.

Finally, Bland found that negotiating issuers with no experience incur much the same interest costs as do those issues that receive three or fewer bids. Penalties, in other words, accrue to inexperience in making a market for a debt issue—making the issue attractive to a larger number of bidders—as well as to inexperience in dealing with one underwriter through negotiation.

Competing studies have suggested either advantageous or disadvantageous use of negotiated sales. Fruits and his colleagues (2008, p. 16) found "that there is no general advantage of competitive over negotiated issuance processes" in a study of all U.S. municipal new issues over 15½ years after 1990. Robbins and Simonsen (2008, p. 1) found that "persistent use of the same underwriter for negotiated sales is significant determinant of higher interest costs for issuers" among Missouri bond issuers during a one-year period in 2004–2005.

In sum, the Pennsylvania controversy suggests that permanent networks within the municipal bond market for guaranteed debt create excessive interest costs, when compared to competitively bid issues. However, when handling debt issues that are sold less as commodities and more as craftwork, such as nonguaranteed and off-budget enterprise debt, teams relying on negotiated issues seem to learn as time passes, decreasing costs.

This apparent conflict appears rather starkly if a little too simply at this point. The Pennsylvania case involves use of stable routines and stable sets of advisors. Teams come from organizations that work together—form networks—over a large number of bond sales or financial problems to solve. A team and network's relative permanence proves useful, issuers say, for their ability to learn from the past or for their special access to information. However, others argue that relatively permanent teams and networks become insular, self-serving sources of advice for governments. Is the problem this simple?

The Management Literature

The evidence from the literature, especially that on interorganizational networks, suggests conflicting tendencies toward insularity on the one hand or learning on the other. By a network, we mean the "totality of all the units connected by a certain relationship" (Jay, 1964, p. 138; Aldrich, 1979; Tichy, Tushman, and Fombrun, 1979). A network is constructed by discovering all the ties that bind a given population of organizations (Aldrich and Whetten, 1981). Stability evolves through the work of linking-pin organizations that have extensive and overlapping ties to different parts of a network. The links may be thought of as, functionally, communications channels between organizations, resource conduits among network members, and even models to be imitated by other organizations in the population. Thus, an accounting firm might channel information about a reporting standard from rating agencies to bond issuers; the firm might direct clients to financial advisors the firm's members respect as a result of previous bond sales; or the firm itself, through one or more of its many services, might provide many services for the municipal finance office.

All organizations within a network are linked directly or indirectly, and stability depends on the durability of these links. Aldrich and Whetten (1981, p. 391) hypothesize:

> The ultimate predictor of network stability is the probability of a link failing, given that another has failed. This, in turn, is a function of the probability of any one link failing and two network characteristics: the duplication of linkages and the multiplicity of linkages between any two organizations.

The stability of a network implies both the permanence of its membership and the redundancy of its members' ties with others inside and outside that network.

Such redundancy hypotheses find confirmation in the literature on public management. Landau (1969) argued that redundancy tends to ensure performance. Golembiewski (1964) has argued that duplication works, in symbiotic interrelationships, to prevent the exercise of vetoes by powerful subunits.

The Behavioral Literature

The small group literature provides further evidence with which we might generalize to debt management networks. Compensating qualities can substitute for the lack of cohesion in financing teams, a problem some point to as compounding and others as remedying the insularity that grows as the same members continually work with each other (Shaw and Shaw, 1967; Sukurai, 1975; Murnighan and Conlon, 1991).

One of these compensating qualities is heterogeneity. Hoffman (1966) has shown that group members with heterogeneous backgrounds tend to work together more effectively, up to a point, due to the greater diversity of information they bring. Since group membership permanence tends to lead to a homogenizing of views (Sherif, 1935; Festinger, 1950), diversity might counter that tendency.

Diversity may lead to turnover, however. Trow (1960) suggests that turnover leads to a short-run decline in performance as the group undergoes reorganization.

A second quality compensating for either too much or too little cohesion in financing teams is equality of status or, even more likely, settled status. Research shows that groups are more productive when members can avoid status struggle, either because positions of members (who's the leader?) are relatively stable or because the method of cost sharing or surplus sharing is settled (Moulin, 1988).

Finally, the major result of stability is a greater willingness to take risks and greater adaptability. Richly joined networks provide for greater opportunity for trial and error and for the spread of innovation (Aldrich, 1979, p. 282; Terreberry, 1968).

The Knowledge from Actual Practice

Assume a simple situation, a small municipal financing network consisting of a financial advisor, an accounting firm, and a law firm (Miller, 1991; Lemov, 1990). The three are richly joined in the following ways:

- The law firm acts as corporation counsel to the other two organizations.
- The accounting firm audits the transactions of the other two organizations; moreover, auditors have been recruited and have joined the financial advising firm from time to time as principals.
- The three organizations are active in the new-issue market for municipal securities with all other possible participants, and they serve together on a team for a bond sale for an issuer.

An issuer becomes the beneficiary of knowledge about changes made by Congress in tax laws relating to municipal debt, about specific needs for information by rating agencies, and new debt structures that may be designed to appeal to specific segments of the market. The richly joined network ultimately results in the issuer's ability to adjust to complex and changing environments.

Now consider a more complex example. Assume that among a population of law firms that act as bond counsel, the firms tend, as a matter of principle, to differ in their approach to interpreting the law as it regards various creative capital financing structures, with some firms being indulgent, and others strict. Assume, furthermore, that in a population of accounting firms asked to forecast the revenue stream that would generate principal and interest payments for various creative capital financing structures, some firms would tend to be liberal, and others tight. Finally, assume that among a population of financial advisors, the same sort of variation would exist among opinions about the applicability and marketability of debt structures.

Random selection of a combination of these firms by an issuer—through competitive bidding, for example—would yield a team advising the issuer to take a particular course of action, one in which the knowledge each advisor had, as well as the expectation each had of the other's interpretation and its effect on the market for the issue, would play a part. The result would produce a bargain in which a security configured in a unique way was rated and sold.

Now assume a second random selection of firms by an issuer and a second sale. What knowledge does the second team have about the configuration of the first security? What keeps the second team from relying on an incorrect interpretation of what the first team did? What keeps the second sale from "missing the market"?

Consider what factors might encourage learning. We would expect that the number of links among members of the team leads to stability, and stability, in turn, leads either to insularity or to learning and adaptation. An expectations approach helps to understand richly linked organizations in the bond team context. That is, each member of the bond team must be guided in his or her assigned task by expectations of the behavior of others. The financial advisor cannot select a market unless the advisor can expect to have counsel's positive legal interpretation of the structure that would most logically follow the selection of that market. Likewise, the advisor cannot select a market without the expectation that the CPA will interpret the various issuer capacities in such a way as to support the structure the market suggests. No decision made by any member of the team, in the end, can be made in a vacuum, without the knowledge of what the other members are likely to do. Otherwise, the decisions made by the members form an endless iteration—a loop—in which market choice forces structure but is confounded by disclosure leading to a new market and a new structure and interpretations wedded to the previous structure, confounding this new market and structure.

One solution to the problem of expectations is to live with the short-term chaos that lies in individuals getting organized, as the small group literature suggests. Another solution might exist in a richly linked network of organizations. Rich links lead to knowledge of likely behavior under varying circumstances. Assumptions at extremely general levels are shared or at least made widely known through large numbers of activities in which the linked organizations jointly participate. Rich links also provide multiple avenues for testing expectations under widely varying conditions. For example, legal interpretations a bond counsel is likely to submit may be expected based on the legal interpretations the bond counsel has traditionally issued in the capacity of the corporate counsel, as the earlier illustration depicted.

If rich links lead to shared expectations of behavior, these links contribute either to insularity or to learning. Consider the argument for specific types of teams in municipal finance. The negotiated rather than the competitive sale invites the sort of stability and exploitation of existing rich links among potential members of a team. Negotiated sales require the issuer to choose precisely those members who have apparently learned the market as well as each other in terms of the market. A negotiated sale provides an opportunity to choose the market (especially when the sale is privately placed), opening the way or creating the need for innovation (craft work rather than routine technology) in the type of issue structure chosen. The negotiated sale also provides incredible overlap and duplication in the work involved.

Such rich links and the opportunities provided by the negotiated sale invite learning. Stigler (1961) indicated that buyers and sellers accumulate information from their experience in the marketplace, which allows them to obtain more favorable conditions in each successive transaction. More specifically, Bland (1985) found that issuers using multiple, negotiated sales received more favorable terms through each successive sale up to a certain point. He concluded (p. 236): "Local governments with previous bond market experience are capable of assembling a management team that can negotiate an interest rate comparable to what the most sought after competitive issues obtain."

Rich Links and Relative Wealth

Within networks, status, especially that created by wealth, makes possible economies of influence. We would expect that wealth differences encourage or preclude influence, as the case may be. Wealth creates advantage, and lack of wealth results in dependence on sources of information. Such a dependency would reduce creativity, making links among network members and the larger environment poorer rather than richer.

Rich Links and Incentives

Dreams of changing one's status, as well as the appearance of opportunity, create an incentive system that serves to encourage creativity. The poor seek opportunities that help their unique positions, making their information or their energy to gain information valuable to the network. The rich take advantage of opportunities to increase wealth even if it advantages everyone in the network. But, they foresee developing opportunities. They influence the image of events, and they co-opt important skills, broadening their own view and encouraging status changes.

A Recap

A network's stability or instability interacts with the wealth and number of links among its members and the incentives offered by the network to its members. The literature conflicts. One direction the literature takes suggests that the greater the stability, the greater the opportunities for learning, and the greater the amount of learning, the greater the chance for innovation and adaptation. From the literature that takes another direction, we infer that the greater the stability, the more likely network members try to impose their view of the world; this view may or may not be tenable, making risk greater and error more likely.

If an efficient market is one that allocates scarce capital among competing uses, and assigns appropriate prices (interest payments to the issuer and bond prices and yields to the investor) to structures at particular levels of repayment capacity, under what conditions does network stability or instability lead to market efficiency? The answer lies in the test of a network stability model against a network instability model.

Simulating Stable and Unstable Teams

Does stability among bond sale team members, or the market as a whole, have any bearing on minimizing costs or maximizing value? What effect does wealth and the incentive to increase that wealth have on these factors? We explore stability and wealth in an experiment involving relatively knowledgeable and ambitious research subjects. There are three basic propositions in this research:

> Proposition 1: The more stable the group, the faster the learning. That is, the more often individuals work together, the sooner they derive a common view of events, as well as mechanisms for processing and acting on novel events. The common view enables them to see the patterned uncertainties on which they may act profitably.
>
> Proposition 2: The greater the initial equality of resources among members of the group, the greater the learning. That is, the fewer the differences of resource-based status among members, the sooner these differences are settled, the sooner the group is organized, and the sooner the group can process and act on information, to the common benefit of the group's members.
>
> Proposition 3: The greater the willingness of the group to match individual contributions with individual rewards (to provide payoffs proportional to contributions), the greater the learning. Matching risk with reward provides incentives to learn, that is, to get organized to process information.

The simulation stressed the differences in performance associated with stable vs. unstable teams, different levels of wealth, and different methods of compensation. The experiment also simulated competition to achieve a single goal facing uncertainty.

We simulated the stable-unstable team idea with a game. Our research design aimed at isolating the factors gathered from the literature that coexisted with learning in the face of randomness. Basically, we employed a repeated measures research design. The task required subjects to participate in a competitive task ostensibly related to the stability of budgets and the prediction of revenue changes over time that would give them budget surpluses or create deficits.

Subjects undertook the competitive multistep task on teams and received a reward if successful. Some subjects joined teams permanently through the series of steps. Other subjects moved from one team to another each step in the series. Subjects did not know ahead of time the exact amount of the prize for winning each step's competition. They were told the mean and range of the entire set of prizes and that the entire set resembled a normal distribution. Some groups had more resources—were richer—to begin with than others, and some members in some groups had more resources than the others in their group. Groups could distribute the rewards they won in any way they chose, and some rewarded risk taking while others preserved equality.

The research confirmed that stable groups breed insularity and not learning. The more unstable the membership of a group, the faster the learning about taking advantage of mean, range, and the normal distribution of prizes. Unstable teams began by winning less than stable teams, but the winnings in stable groups did not increase over time, while those in unstable groups did.

To measure the impact differing levels of wealth among participants and groups may have had on learning, we removed those groups with unequal wealth from the stable side; there were no such initial allocations among unstable groups. The unstable groups again outperformed the stable groups, although the performance difference was not statistically significant.

Finally, we removed reward structures that did not motivate risk taking. Again, unstable groups outperformed the stable ones.

The small groups here, and their results, give some insight into the mechanics of stable and unstable teams. Unstable teams learn faster how to achieve a single goal in an uncertain problem-solving situation than do stable groups. Why? Consider four groups of explanations.

From the management literature, we read that stronger links among network members led to stability, a trait that might yield learning and adaptability. The inference from this research project suggests otherwise, in fact, the opposite. Very little learning occurred in stable groups we observed. The generalization that network members feather their own nests when there is little uncertainty might hold; it finds confirmation in many cases, such as those described at the front of this piece.

From the behavioral literature, we read that diversity leads to instability, a short-run performance decline and yet long-term effectiveness. We found confirmation for this idea in this research. The generalization, especially to the Pennsylvania local government case, is that competitively bidded sales (and advice) might be just as effective as negotiated sales in all but the most uncertain situations.

From the literature on practice, we surmised that richly joined network members (stable teams) may find it easier than less richly joined members to form an image of an uncertain situation. The question was left open as to whether the image was tenable. The real question, however, may be whether stable teams can change their quickly formed image rapidly if it proves wrong. The evidence from this research suggests otherwise. In fact, unstable teams may well adapt more quickly. The gravity of adaptability is clear in the cobweb illustrated earlier; adaptability prevents an exploding cobweb, a situation in which the reality of the past is the only reality, compounding error.

From debt issuance experience, we read that mutually predictable expectations among team members reduces negotiation effort in understanding social reality. Our research suggests that this may be the case, as evident in the lower initial errors made by stable teams. However, the lower error rates existed only in the short term, as error rates of unstable teams quickly rivaled and then surpassed those of stable teams. We generalize that the diversity inherent in an unstable team may contribute to the useful devil's advocacy that mutually predictable expectations lack.

Finally, the role played by the initial wealth of group members and the group's incentive system became only marginally clearer. Because our findings did not achieve statistical significance, careful generalization is essential. We conclude that rewards and incentives play a role. Rewards may decrease dependence and advantage while increasing the potential for learning. Incentives that are proportionate to risk do seem to encourage learning. Further research will shed light on the interaction among these variables.

In summary, what disciplining strategy does this research suggest for the competitive vs. negotiated bond sale team controversy? Our research sides with competition among members in a debt management network. Competitive bidding over a series of bond sales yields the possibility of an unstable bond sale team. Since unstable teams sense the risks and opportunities in uncertain situations in our simulation, we would expect competitive bidding to change team composition and to relax the lowest common denominator goal of debt management networks, so that the issuer's lowest interest cost goal predominated. Clearly, that seems the case for the vast majority of state and local government bond sales.

Debt Networks and Normative Ambiguity in Practice

Most orthodox government budgeting and finance theories portray principals as fully and completely knowledgeable about ends and means. Principals (bond issuers) employ agents (underwriters, financial advisors, bond counsel) as instruments of implementation. In behavioral or transactional theories there are often information asymmetries between principals and agents, making the relationship a problem of bounded rationality, calculated risk taking, opportunism, and rent seeking. In circumstances where environmental uncertainty (such as about markets for bonds) is compounded by normative ambiguity (such as about relative priorities of major projects or goals, or how to apportion projects' costs across multiple constituencies or multiple generations), debt financing teams and the larger debt networks from which they are drawn can come to seem more like negotiations among equals than hierarchical principal-agent relationships.

We investigated a recent effort by the New York Metropolitan Transportation Authority (MTA)—the nation's largest mass transit service as well as the operator of many bridges and tunnels in the New York Metropitan area—to refinance its debt (Miller and Justice, 2011). The essence of the $13 billion restructuring was to consolidate previous debt issues under a simplified set of bond covenants and lengthen the debt repayment period in order to lower the annual cost of debt service. Stretching out the principal repayment for the MTA's existing debt did appear to comply with conventions calling for matching the period of debt repayment to assets' useful life, but not with injunctions to minimize total costs of debt service. Both as initially formulated in 1999 and as eventually implemented in 2002, this refinancing proposal carried a negative net present value, and so was not one that would be employed if cost minimization were the primary consideration.

Beyond this technical consideration, the proposal drew attention for the role of the investment bank Bear Stearns in developing and promoting the refinancing plan. Bear, a long-standing member of the MTA's debt network, acted first as an informal advisor to the MTA, and later as one of the principal underwriters of the multiple bond issues that implemented the refinancing. The fullest contemporaneous general interest newspaper account of the proposal described it as "a striking example of the way in which Wall Street can shape public policy to its own benefit" (Pérez-Peña and Kennedy, 2000).

At the same time, however, it was evident both at the time and in retrospect that the MTA's financial managers had few other options for raising the funds required to finance the MTA's desired capital spending plans. The MTA was at the time engaged in a massive effort to remediate the consequences of significant deferred maintenance through a series of five-year capital improvement plans. As the agency assembled a strategy for financing its $17.5 billion 2000–2004 capital program, it became clear that federal, state, and city financial assistance would cover a significantly smaller share of this plan than previous five-year plans. At the same time, the MTA's ability to finance capital spending through current resources or to service additional debt was constrained by political and market realities that militated both against toll and fare increases and against generating additional tax revenues. The restructuring was designed to make possible $2 billion in additional debt financing with no increase in annual debt service expenditures, albeit at the cost of significant increases in total interest payments for the existing debt.

Although there has not been a great deal of detailed information available, and MTA officials and their advisers were cautious in their public remarks, there seems to be little doubt that the restructuring plan was conceived and detailed by Bear Stearns. There is no doubt at all that on April 16, 2000, the proposed financing plan was presented for approval to state officials in Albany on the MTA's behalf by Robert Foran of Bear Stearns, acting apparently in an informal advisory capacity but evidently with a very large investment of time and effort. As an informal advisor, the firm would not be precluded from bidding on or negotiating for a large and profitable role in the underwriting of the proposed $12 billion of bond issuance, as it would have been if acting in a formal capacity as financial advisor to the MTA. At roughly 0.6% of issue amount, underwriting fees for the restructuring issues were expected to total as much as $100 million if the deal were executed.

So who was the principal and who the agent? Were the bankers helping themselves or the MTA? Interpretations varied widely. "'It makes me nervous that a private firm has structured a multibillion-dollar deal that will impact on the future of the transit system for three decades, that they thought it up, pitched it, did all this work to flesh it out, lobbied the State Legislature directly, and they're the ones who stand to make tens of millions of dollars off of it,' said Gene Russianoff, staff attorney at the Straphangers Campaign and an ardent critic of the plan. 'They have an inherent conflict of interest'" (Pérez-Peña and Kennedy, 2000, p. B6). Alternatively, other informed observers suggested, this kind of informal advising is in fact a useful way for public agencies to get the benefit of free technical advice from financial experts who are otherwise very expensive.

Bear Stearns was on at least a few occasions prior to this refinancing involved in advising and then doing business with bond-issuing authorities in New York. In 1997, the firm resigned a formal financial advisory role in order to bid on the underwriting for the Long Island Power Authority's acquisition of Long Island Lighting Company (LILCO) assets. Bear Stearns ended up as lead underwriter for that deal, which at $7 billion was the largest municipal issue up to that time (Pérez-Peña and Kennedy, 2000). In 1998, the firm advised the MTA on the creation of a "swaption" structure that enabled the MTA to take advantage of a low-interest-rate environment for outstanding debt that was not yet callable and had already been subject to the one advance refunding permitted by federal law. In return, Bear Stearns was permitted to match the winning bidder and purchase half of the available options when it came in second in a competitive bid process (Kruger, 1998; Sherman, 1998).

Robert Foran in particular had gained the trust of the MTA through a long-standing working relationship, according to at least one well-informed source. Our source argued, in keeping with the debt networks hypothesis, that long-term client-intermediary relationships and institutional knowledge are important in the small world of municipal finance. The MTA, like other issuers, continually gets "free" advice from financial firms in its debt network; the only unusual aspect of this particular proposal was the way in which the pitch was made, which may simply have reflected a desire to have the explanation of the plan given by the party with the most expertise and knowledge of the details of the proposal. As in any case where relationships involve personal trust, reciprocity, and mutual expectations of goal fulfillment, this case may not lend itself to easy analysis within the framework of conventional principal-agent models of public finance.

The irony of this situation, of course, is that the independent public authority device in general, and the financial maneuverings of the MTA in financing its capital program in particular, appear primarily to represent efforts to satisfy the ambiguous demands of voters and ratepayers. Through the fare box and through their elected representatives (and the appointments made by those representatives), citizens demanded that the MTA invest enough to remedy past underinvestment and forestall a future infrastructure crisis. However, they also demanded that the MTA do so without increasing its fares or tax revenues. These demands for a free lunch may effectively have led the agency to become more accountable to the financial markets than to the constituencies more widely recognized as legitimately commanding the fealty of public organizations in a democracy.

After significant political maneuvering, the MTA secured the required approval from the state's Capital Program Review Board in 2001 and executed the restructuring in 2002. The restructuring involved issuing $13.5 billion of refunding bonds in a total of eighteen issues over the course of the year. The restructuring made possible $3 billion in additional, new money borrowing—more than originally anticipated, due to favorable changes in relevant laws and interest rates. It also incurred $4.3 billion in additional debt service obligations over time, however, with a negative net present value of $57 million according to the MTA's 2002 financial report. Bear Stearns participated as manager or comanager in underwriting four of the refunding issues, amounting to $4.25 billion—about 31% of the total refunding issuance. More recently, the fare increase took place anyway (Metropolitan Transportation Authority, 2003a, 2003b), and in 2010 the MTA announced significant service reductions in response to fiscal strain created in part by the significant fixed costs associated with its outstanding debt.

Orthodox observers suggested little controversy in what the leaders of the MTA did. It was said that a good idea is a good idea wherever it comes from, and that MTA's approach constituted "the best way to get free use of this very high-priced talent" (Pérez-Peña and Kennedy, 2000, p. B6). However, the initial reaction from the press, mass transit user groups, and fiscal watchdog organizations was strongly unfavorable. Critics of the restructuring plan objected both to the restructuring's long-term financial implications and to the appearance that the MTA adopted a self-serving proposal from an interested private party without conducting an open and competitive search for solutions.

Finding ambiguity in the ends and means of debt management, financial decision makers interpreted the problems in a rational way. In debt management, they interpreted the situation as one in which a debt restructuring that lengthened the repayment period for existing debt was the best way to raise funds, even at the cost of violating the usual preference of issuers to minimize costs.

As financial decision makers, MTA officials deferred to outside experts, although these outside experts stood to gain by the advice, in restructuring debt to produce funds to finance the capital program. The confluence of their capital program's pressing needs for capital funds, the apparent denial of both financial assistance and fiscal reality by state and local governments and elected officials, and the demands by customers and taxpayers for an impossible free lunch created a circumstance in which uncertainty about markets for debt became only one of a number of problems to solve. The restructuring solution offered by their friends in the bond business enabled the MTA to redefine the problem as a solvable technical one—how to execute the restructuring—rather than an intolerably ambiguous one of how to reconcile the inherently irreconcilable political and economic demands they face.

The finance officials communicated the interpretation in novel ways. In the debt restructuring case, the myth of the ever-wise market prevailed. Where could expertise—wisdom—in financing come from most assuredly but from the financiers themselves, who were willing to put their money at risk to underwrite a public improvement? In a subordinate sense, the choice to borrow, rather than increase costs for transit riders and taxpayers in the short term, was a relatively easy one to make; borrowing would slow the rate of change in the burden transit riders bore, all transit riders would bear the burden of the improvements over the improvements' useful life, and general taxpayers would not bear any new burden at all. In fact, this interpretation was subsequently adopted by the editorial page of the *New York Daily News*, which had initially been among the plan's harshest critics. Only the fiscal watchdogs failed in the event to approve.

Finally, the enforcement of the interpretations relied on methods that countered a textbook view of policy tools and their application. The MTA managers implemented the capital investment financing plan through a debt restructuring, lengthening the repayment period for existing debt and producing no net present value savings. The debt restructuring appears to violate the optimizing assumption that is typically supposed to motivate such debt management plans. On the other hand, the restructuring may have placed the burden of paying for improvements fairly by limiting the burden largely to transit users and spreading the burden over all users through time.

The model of interpretation has meaning as a description of the process that can occur among finance officials. The case study approach suggests that the model has validity. The lingering questions revolve around its counterintuitive implications. That is, can we infer from these findings that finance officials routinely disregard the economizing logic that many expect to govern their decisions? The implications, we argue, do not suggest the primacy of any simple logic, but a complex perception finance officials have for the context in which they decide courses of action.

Consider first the implicit test for theory with which we began. What practical guide for management lies at the heart of this public profession? Is there a rational actor at the heart of the practice of public financial management, this most business-like of fields in public administration? What norms guide this rational actor? From the findings about practice, we can conclude that many rationalities exist. In the situations we examined, a rational actor exists, an actor who optimizes expected utility in the many senses of utility one could generalize from these findings. However, in the orthodox sense of a rational actor and a principal in principal-agent relationships, we found the financial manager behaving quite differently.

References

Aldrich, Howard E. (1979). *Organizations and Environments.* Englewood Cliffs, NJ: Prentice-Hall.

Aldrich, Howard E., and David A. Whetten. (1981). Organization-sets, action-sets, and networks: Making the most of simplicity. In *Handbook of Organizational Design*, ed. Paul C. Nystrom and William H. Starbuck, 385–408. Vol. 1. New York: Oxford University Press.

Bland, Robert L. (1985). The interest cost savings from experience in the municipal bond market. *Public Administration Review* 45:233–237.

Festinger, Leon. (1950). Informal social communication. *Psychological Review 57*: 271–292.

Forbes, Ronald W., and John E. Petersen. (1979). *Local Government General Obligation Bond Sales in Pennsylvania: The Cost Implications of Negotiation vs Competitive Bidding.* Washington, DC: Government Finance Research Center, Municipal Finance Officers Association.

Fruits, Eric, James Booth, Randall Pozdena, and Richard Smith. (2008). A comprehensive evaluation of the comparative cost of negotiated and competitive methods of municipal bond issuance. *Municipal Finance Journal* 28(4):15–41.

Golembiewski, Robert T. (1964). Accountancy as a function of organization theory. *The Accounting Review* 39:333–341.

Heilbroner, Robert L., and Lester C. Thurow. (1984). *Understanding Microeconomics.* 6th ed. Englewood Cliffs, NJ: Prentice-Hall.

Hildreth, W. Bartley. (1986). Strategies of municipal debt issuers. Paper presented at the National Conference of the American Society for Public Administration, Anaheim, CA.

Hoffman, Richard L. (1966). Group problem solving. In *Advances in Experimental Social Psychology*, ed. Leonard Berkowitz, 99–132. Vol. 2. New York: Academic Press.

Jay, Edward J. (1964). The concepts of 'field' and 'network' in anthropological research. *Man* 64:137–139.

Kruger, D. (1998). Salomon is big winner of MTA swaption. *The Bond Buyer*, August 13, p. 32.

Lamb, Robert, and Stephen P. Rappaport. (1980). *Municipal Bonds: The Comprehensive Review of Tax-Exempt Securities and Public Finance.* New York: McGraw-Hill.

Landau, Martin. (1969). Redundancy, rationality, and the problem of duplication and overlap. *Public Administration Review* 29:346–358.

Lemov, Penelope. (1990). For municipal bonds, it's not a plain vanilla world anymore. *Governing*, June, pp. 52–58.

Metropolitan Transportation Authority. (2003a). 2002 annual report. Retrieved November 4, 2005, from http://mta.nyc.ny.us/mta/investor/pdf/2002annualreport_complete.pdf.

Metropolitan Transportation Authority. (2003b). 2003 progress report to investors. Retrieved November 5, 2005, from http://mta.nyc.ny.us/mta/investor/pdf/investor_report_03.pdf.

Miller, Gerald J. (1991). *Government Financial Management Theory.* New York: Dekker.

Miller, Gerald J., and Jonathan B. Justice (2011). Debt Management Networks and the Proverbs of Financial Management: Principles and Interests in the New York Metropolitan Transportation Authority Debt Restructuring. *Municipal Finance Journal 31*(4): 19–40.

Moak, L. L. (1982). *Municipal Bonds: Planning, Sale and Administration.* Chicago: Government Finance Officers Association.

Moulin, Hervé. (1988). *Axioms of Cooperative Decision Making.* Cambridge: Cambridge University Press.

Murnighan, J. Keith, and Donald E. Conlon. (1991). The dynamics of intense work groups: A study of British string quartets. *Administrative Science Quarterly* 36:165–186.

Pagano, Michael A. (1982). The urban public sector as lagging or leading sector in economic development. *Urban Interest* 4:131–140.

Pagano, Michael A., and Richard J. T. Moore. (1985). *Cities and Fiscal Choices: A New Model of Urban Public Investment.* Durham, NC: Duke University Press.

Pérez-Peña, R., and Kennedy, R. (2000). Private promoter for transit debt. *The New York Times,* May 1, pp. A1, B6.

Petersen, John E. (1988). *Information Flows in the Municipal Securities Market: A Preliminary Analysis.* Washington, DC: Government Finance Research Center, Government Finance Officers Association.

Robbins, Mark, and Bill Simonsen. (2008). Persistent underwriter use and the cost of borrowing. *Municipal Finance Journal* 28(4):1–13.

Sbragia, A. M. (1983). Politics, local government, and the municipal bond market. In A. M. Sbragia (Ed.), The municipal money chase: The politics of local government finance (pp. 67–111). Boulder, CO: Westview Press.

Shaw, Marvin E., and L. M. Shaw. (1962). Some effects of sociometric grouping upon learning in a second grade classroom. *Journal of Social Psychology* 57:453–458.

Sherman, L. (1998). N.Y. MTA board to consider entering into the world of swaptions to save on debt. *The Bond Buyer,* June 29, p. 38.

Stigler, George J. (1961). The economics of information. *Journal of Political Economy,* July/ August, 706–738.

Sukurai, Melvin M. (1975). Small group cohesiveness and detrimental conformity. *Sociometry* 38:234–242.

Terreberry, Shirley. (1968). The evolution of organization environments. *Administrative Science Quarterly* 12:590–613.

Tichy, Noel M., Michael L. Tushman, and Charles Fombrun. (1979). Social network analysis for organizations. *Academy of Management Review* 4:507–519.

Trow, Donald B. (1960). Membership succession and team performance. *Human Relations* 13:259–269.

Chapter 10

Auctioning Off the Farm with Tax Incentives for Economic Development[1]

Donijo Robbins and Gerald J. Miller

Traditionally, state and local policy makers offered tax abatements, tax reductions, and other fiscal incentive packages to attract business firms as a way to reverse general economic decline or to redevelop specific, poor, blighted areas. The incentives responded to demand from firms recruited by policy makers. Finance officials designed and constructed the incentives and applied an agency logic in deciding what to do. This chapter explores the agency logic in an intensely pro-business context. The research presented here looks unfavorably on the products and results of finance officials as agents.

Over the past twenty or so years, the redevelopment focus prompting the use of incentives has yielded to efforts to gain strategic economic advantage. Offers of tax and nontax incentives to businesses have escalated. Interlocality competition has grown more intense. Leaders in states and localities often must respond when private firms auction off themselves by topping the incentive packages offered by their rivals. The competition has created an "arms race."

Estimates of the results of the race have produced more debate than agreement. Some argue that the government that outbids another and "wins" the industry will, in the long run, concede more in public funds than the industry will be worth, producing a net loss. Others argue, however, that a net payoff is possible. The literature can be summarized as "you win some, you lose some." High risks and inconclusive research lead us to ask why public officials rely on incentives as an attraction and a retention tool. Winning may have more than one meaning; therefore public officials hesitate to rely on economic analysis alone.

The purpose of this chapter is to investigate empirically the motives and investment patterns of public officials involved in bidding wars. We experiment using a simulated auction with varying conditions and incentives. Our aim is to determine whether governments are able to produce net financial gains from their competitive bidding for business firms. This approach tracks the auction process over time, determining the overall return.

We review the macro-level and micro-level goals of economic development first in this chapter. Next, we introduce the experiment and describe how it worked. The data and findings follow. Finally, we discuss the findings in terms of the macro- and micro-level economic development goals policy makers pursue.

Macro-Level Goals of Incentives

Theory underlying the macro model of government and economic development yields much of the knowledge that exists about public decision makers' behavior. The theory predicts that decision makers will use public financial incentives to encourage private economic development and stimulate growth (Blakely and Bradshaw, 2002; Brace, 1993; Keynes, 1936; Polanyi, 1957; Peterson, 1981; Mollenkopf, 1983; Eisinger, 1988). Attracting new industry brings additional jobs. Basic economic theory suggests an increase in the demand for labor yields higher wages, and higher wages translate into higher demand for goods and services. Business profits increase potentially.

Some research confirms theory. Localities rely on incentives to decrease unemployment, attract new capital investment, and build a larger tax base (Blakely, 1989; Burnier, 1992; Trogen, 1999). Leaders respond with incentives because of economic need, growth expectations, institutional agreements (Clingermayer and Feiock, 1990), or the motivation to improve the locality's competitive economic position (Feiock, 1999). Cities offering incentives grow their economies faster and are simply better off than those that do not (Clarke and Gaile, 1992). Bartik (1991) finds evidence that incentives have some effect on the location of businesses and industries.

In addition, studies assert that incentives show a return. The returns appear when the investment occurs in developing markets and areas exploiting new technologies (Eisinger, 1988) or where the private sector is most competitive (Rosentraub and Przybylski, 1996). Feiock (1999) suggests that offering incentives during economic hardship produces efficient outcomes. Others propose that economic development policies correlate positively with state per capita income growth (Trogen, 1999) and overall investment gains (Kebede and Ngandu, 1999), although little is done for employment (Feiock, 1991). Still others have found benefits when they compared growth in winning jurisdictions with growth in the competing but losing jurisdictions (Greenstone and Moretti, 2003).

Others argue the opposite. These bidding wars have little, if any, effect on industry attraction, they say. David Stockman, former director of the U.S. Office of Management and Budget (OMB), contends that larger national and worldwide economic and demographic forces neutralize the incentives offered by local governments (Greider, 1981). Public efforts are not only irrelevant but wasted (Peters and Fisher, 2004). Bluestone, Harrison, and Baker (1981) suggest that over time, the costs associated with incentives are never recovered; taxpayers lose.

The limited utility view has support. Incentives act only as "swing factors" or "tie breakers" in final location decisions (Watson, 1995) and work only to encourage the retention and expansion of existing local businesses (Kale, 1984). However, some believe that incentives have little effect at all on the location of businesses and industries (Bluestone, Harrison, and Baker, 1981; Wassmer, 1990, as cited in Anderson and Wassmer, 2000; Watson, 1995).

The difficulties associated with the empirical research lie in measuring, determining, and forecasting the locality's net gain in exchanging public dollars for private investment. If traditionally incentives were intended for poverty-stricken areas, then the belief that these incentives improve the economic position of these areas seems plausible. Once the traditional objective of incentives changes, and all governments become involved in the "arms race," efforts made to improve economic position, particularly in poorer areas, deserve analysis.

Micro-Level Goals of Incentives

Macroeconomics analyzes multiple markets and how each reacts to changes in the others. Microeconomic models provide a different analysis; the models look at the individual decision, whether the individual is a corporate board member or executive, an executive or administrator in government, or even an elected official. Since research from the macro view of economic development incentives has produced mixed findings, micro-level research may provide insights that shed light on what weight to give what macro-level findings.

A basic microeconomic principle holds that competitive businesses operate where marginal cost equals marginal revenue. The same applies to localities. The marginal cost of providing public services—including both direct services and subsidies—should equal the tax revenue generated from the new, expanded, or just retained business (Black and Hoyt, 1989). The government should not offer tax incentives when the marginal cost exceeds the marginal benefit. On the other hand, if the marginal cost of public services is less than the tax revenue generated by new or expanded business firms, or less than the net potential lost revenue when a business moves elsewhere, tax incentives are feasible, but only up to a point where marginal cost equals marginal revenue.

The difficulty lies in measuring these costs and benefits. Data files often do not exist in localities. In fact, concession of public dollars may often depend on rival estimates provided by businesses requesting tax concessions.

Public finance and microeconomics explain market structure. Normative public finance assumes an optimal social welfare decision reached by a rational, optimizing public official. Neither sheds light on the motivation of public officials when they do not have perfect information. Neither suggests why public officials support and offer tax incentives when there is no clear evidence that incentives help, and with them officials succeed.

The views held by economists about the behavior of a rational actor also provide no clear direction. Heilbroner (1988, p. 14) points out the "considerable history of controversy into [a] proper definition" of both economics and the rational actor. He outlines both broad and narrow definitions. He acknowledges that some believe economics to be the prescription of optimal decision making, a broad definition. Economic decisions work where the rational actor has limited courses of action available, well-defined and clearly apparent cost and benefit estimates attached to the alternative courses of action, substantial control over the choice made, experience in similar or analogous choice situations, and well-defined goals connected with alternative courses of action in such a simple way that the actor "can understand the effects of what they do on the outcomes" (Taylor, 1996, pp. 225–226).

Heilbroner sides with a narrower definition of economics and the rational actor. As he sees it (1988, p. 14), "economics … is the process by which society marshals and coordinates the activities required for its provisioning." Considerations of the short term, he says, outweigh the long term, and these limited decisions concern consumption and replenishment of worn-out capital (1988, p. 15). A rational actor may separate the economy from the society in terms of the substance—manufacturing, retailing, farming—as well as the technique for coordinating the substantive parts—coordination through markets and price systems. Heilbroner argues that the economic and rational actor approaches to problems can work—can succeed in provisioning society adequately—only when they follow efficiency and equity norms. The rational actor therefore works to provision society in the short term efficiently and equitably.

Public choice ideas and research also lead to predictions about the behavior of public officials. They side with the broader view of rational action. According to Buchanan (1972, p. 17), "The actors who behave 'economically' choose 'more rather than less,' with more and less being measured in units of goods that are independently identified and defined." Therefore, public choice theory may lead to identification and definition of several goods, of which the actor may choose to acquire (or recruit) more rather than less.

Debate centers on whether public officials are rational actors when they decide what to do to compete for business firms. Although some research suggests tax abatements and other incentives are ineffective, it is possible that public officials lack knowledge. They are not aware of others' experiences (Wolman, 1988; Mollenkopf, 1983) or they distrust them (Wolman, 1988; Burnier, 1992). Ohio policy makers say they distrust the research because it does not apply to the real world, where "practical experience tells them that incentives are important because firms routinely request them as a condition for location and expansion" (Burnier, 1992, p. 22). Immediate benefits and remote costs, or spending to stem losses, may suggest ignorance, but may suggest rational ignorance as well (Downs, 1960; Stigler, 1961). The information sources differ, and all may have biases toward particular interests. Only some sources may come from those who share the interest the public official serves first (Noto, 1991, p. 254).

The "real world" and important practical experience may amount to "rent seeking." Coffman argues (1993, p. 595) that rent seeking arises when "government sets an annual [tax] abatement budget," making abatements a scarce resource for which business firms compete. The more discretion the public official has, and the less the official seems bound by hard data suggesting optimal courses of action toward social welfare increases, the greater the incentive for business firms to lobby the official. The rent-seeking official may gain personally, but he or she produces an additional loss of social welfare above the costs of administration and compliance and the excess economic costs of suboptimal public policy (Musgrave and Musgrave, 1989, pp. 277–296; Harberger, 1974, p. 35; Tullock, 1967).

The politics rather than the economics of development incentives may dominate decision making. The community can be a political leader's first concern, and losing a major industry carries a large risk. Noto (1991, p. 252) points out that a major employer moving out forces losses in "citizens' major source of labor income and [is] compounded by the decline in value of a major asset, their houses." At the survival level, political action makes sense, but action at another, social level makes even more. A community, defined as a network of continuing social ties, may allow noneconomic norms of reciprocity and fairness to develop, and Taylor (1996, p. 232) observes that "interactions in [these] networks … are uncoercive, trusting, respectful, … relatively egalitarian [and] contribute to cooperation." A leader, even in good times, might parry threats to the existence of Taylor's community with subsidies to the business firm that contributes to the community's preservation and improvement.

In truly dire straits, the community may benefit by offering a firm a subsidy to bid for time. Noto (1991) identifies this use of incentives with hospice care. The rational leader uses incentives to ease the pain of a community's slow death.

Finally, the politics of incentives confronts the leader directly and professionally with the consequences of error (Noto, 1991, p. 254). If the leader does not provide the incentive, and the firm either moves away or turns down the offer to relocate, the leader faces opposition at a disadvantage; defeat looms large. If the leader grants the concession, the leader also faces opposition and possible defeat for promoting waste, fraud, and abuse. The refusal to grant the concession may hold the greater immediate risk of loss for the leader (Noto, 1991, p. 254; Wolkoff, 1983).

Symbolism, not economics, may motivate public officials to offer incentives to business and industry (Wolkoff, 1992; Kenyon, 1997). Capital is mobile; business firms can pack up and move to a more efficient location. Wolman and Spitzley (1996) argue that private industries are holding communities hostage. Public officials, and more particularly elected public officials, may have to pursue specific actions in order to maintain jobs. "Local officials may be reluctant to pass up the opportunity to attract or retain a high-profile business, finding the political liability resulting from a lost opportunity more damaging than the cost of 'paying too much' to persuade a firm to locate in their jurisdiction" (Kenyon, 1997, p. 21). Political pressure forces locality officials to offer the incentives.

Dependence on incentives is sometimes a result of "monkey see, monkey do," a copycat form of behavior, one rapidly moving from opportunism to necessity. If one government does it, other governments follow (Saiz, 2001), resulting in price wars, or in the case of the public sector, bidding wars (Wolman, 1988). Municipalities offer public dollars in exchange for business to stay alive, to compete with other localities (Bowman, 1988; Burnier, 1992; Clarke and Gaile, 1992; Feiock, 1999), or to defend themselves against regional competition (Grady, 1987).

Governments also use incentives as signals (Wolman, 1988). Incentives demonstrate that the localities are pro-business. That is, important constituencies believe a political leader has to stimulate economic growth and that leaders have the critical levers to pull businesses to the community. If the leader cannot or will not signal growth, he or she can be replaced by a willing member of the growth constituency (Molotch, 1976). Leaders must establish a "record of tangible accomplishments" to prove that the signals bring results (Burnier, 1992, p. 22). The award of incentives followed by the announcement of a new business entering a community, or a business staying, acts as the record the leader needs. The award is a mechanism that shows voters that their government is doing something, actively, even aggressively, to retain and attract industry (Rubin, 1988).

Economic development theory points out a number of instances where a locality's leaders may behave "economically" in choosing or producing "more rather than less" of "independently identified and defined" goods. Not only is the behavior rational in a welfare-enhancing way some of the time (Wolkoff, 1992), but behavior can also be rational in a strategic sense much of the time (Anderson and Wassmer, 1995, p. 742). In social senses, behavior, including manipulating symbols and communicating signals, allows the leader to cope with ambiguous phenomena where consensus does not exist for either ends or means (Feldman and March, 1981; Thompson and Tuden, 1959; Thompson, 1967).

The Research Problem

Practical experience, symbolism, mimicking, and signaling, all with foundations in politics, seem to be guiding the micro-level decision-making process surrounding public involvement in economic development. All of these possible micro foundations help predict what leads officials to make the subsidy decisions they make. The most powerful predictor can lead to a useful criterion by which to judge the results of macro-level economic development incentive studies. In this research, we ask what micro-level goals are more important than traditional welfare economic principles underlying efficient business practices. Politics and economic analyses often compete in the incentive awarding game as the localities themselves compete.

The competition among localities resembles an auction in which localities bid against each other for business (Anderson and Wassmer, 2000; Black and Hoyt, 1989; Siegel, 1997). Business firms have information about short-term and perhaps long-term economic prospects. Government leaders may have difficulty in gaining similar knowledge. Knowledge asymmetry underlies the bidding. However, government leaders may frame the competition as one over economic welfare improvements directly and solely, or they may define success in other ways, particularly the preservation of the sense of community. If differences exist among localities about the definition of success in the auction, the auction may correspond to the sale of a private good, one whose value is subject to different interpretations based on taste, such as a painting. On the other hand, the auction may involve localities that differ only in the knowledge they have of the value of a common good, one whose value may be defined under conditions of uncertainty and probability, such as mineral rights. Localities may behave in aggressive or risk-averse ways in bidding. Yet, multiple governments offer incentives for acquiring or retaining a business firm. The business firm takes the offer that will maximize revenue. Auction forms have distinguishing features, and these characteristics may relate to the surprising behavior found in locality competition for economic development. The locality competition and its resemblance to an auction make the auction an assumption for investigation. We can assume the auction and explore the definitions of winning, characterizing economic development as either a private or common good. We can control certain rival explanations for behavior. In the end, we can relax the auction assumption to explore other forms of interaction among governments and businesses. Auction theory and experimental research therefore can be useful tools to answer the questions about the attribution of rational actor behavior to all the parties in economic development.

Auctions

The politics and economics of economic development incentives may become clearer if the frame of reference changes to decision making in a competitive game with little agreement about the definition of success. Understanding what economic development leaders and specialists actually wish to accomplish in pursuing a competitive strategy over time has importance. Examining the structure and process of the competitive game itself may provide insight. That understanding and insight may provide a firmer micro-level view of economic development subsidy decisions than a social welfare improvement approach (Anderson and Wassmer, 1995, p. 742).

The micro-level view must account for what appears to be one of the most embarrassing decisions most public officials could make, mixing unwillingness, inability, and disadvantage. Being unwilling to gain information, some argue, policy makers "invest blindly, not knowing which economic development policies achieve" what return (Trogen, 1999, p. 256). Others say that these same policy makers do not have the ability "to accurately forecast structural changes in the economy" (Wolkoff, 1990, p. 335). Disadvantage lies in the information asymmetry between a business firm and a locality, and that vulnerability may have fundamental effects on locality leaders' decisions (Wolkoff, 1992). Although the literature supports the idea that it is difficult to predict the return on investment, many government decision makers still get involved in what are economic development wars without all the arms or weapons necessary to win.

Regardless of the rationale, government leaders participate in competitions where the highest bidder wins or acquires an economic asset, the business firm and the social and economic activity that will result over time. These competitions do resemble auctions. An examination of auction dynamics and outcomes can help one understand the dynamics and outcomes of economic development competition.

Milgrom and Weber analyze the competitive bidding process using a first-price auction where the bids are sealed and "the highest bid claims the object and pays the amount he has bid" (1982, p. 1090). Others have examined the same or similar decision processes and have arrived at similar conclusions (Capen, Clapp, and Campbell, 1971, as cited in Thaler, 1988; Wilson, 1977; Bazerman and Samuelson, 1983; Harrison and March, 1984; Cox and Isaac, 1984; Kagel and Levin, 1986; McAfee and McMillan, 1987; Lind and Plott, 1991). Analyzing the auction process for mineral rights on a piece of land, Milgrom and Weber (1982, pp. 1093–1094) argue:

> The value of the rights depends on the unknown amount of recoverable ore, its quality, its ease of recovery, and the prices that will prevail for the processed mineral. The values of these mineral rights to the various bidders can be regarded as equal but bidders may have differing estimates of the common value. Consequently, even if all bidders make unbiased estimates, the winner will find that he has overestimated (on average) the value of rights he has won at auction.

Truly, intent to act in a rational way does not guarantee a rational outcome in mineral rights auctions. As with many auctions, average bids will fall below the value of the object of the auction, the second highest bid will be the closest to the actual value of the object, and the winning bid will exceed the value of the object.

How could a rational actor profit, knowing what mineral rights auction experience teaches? Thaler (1988, p. 200) explains what may be a fairly obvious anomaly: "If you react by optimally reducing your bids, then you will avoid paying too much for [mineral rights] leases, but you will also win very few auctions. In fact, you may decide not to bid at all … [in which case] … you [must] want to switch businesses." The auction phenomenon seems to have every attribute of a rational decision pursued by rational actors. Yet, the auction ends in a less than optimal outcome.

This phenomenon is known as the winner's curse. Although Milgrom and Weber's research uses the private sector, the process of the standard sealed-bid auction, in which the auctioneer/seller sells the goods for a price equal to that offered by the highest bidder, applies to the bidding wars experienced by the public sector. That is, the locality—city, county, state government decision maker—that concedes the greatest amount of tax revenue wins or gains the industry seeking the subsidy.

Anecdotal evidence gives flavor to the winner's curse phenomenon. For example, United Airlines considered Kentucky and Indiana as potential locations for a maintenance facility. Both states decided to bid for the industry by offering subsidies and incentives; both states were competing against each other. The competition ended when Kentucky conceded to Indiana. Kentucky argued that it could no longer compete. Indiana ultimately conceded $341 million in cash, land, and tax abatements (Watson, 1995).

In exchange for $125 million, Toyota moved to Kentucky in 1988. In 1976, Pennsylvania invested $75 million in Volkswagen. Louisville, Kentucky, went head-to-head with Kansas City, Missouri, in 1987 battling for the Presbyterian Church (USA). Louisville yielded over $6 million and a warehouse to the church (Black and Hoyt, 1989). DiamondStar, a joint venture of Chrysler and Mitsubishi, was offered $296 million in tax breaks and $10 million in land from the state of Illinois.

In 1993, Alabama provided $253 million in incentives and tax breaks to attract a $300 million Daimler-Mercedes (now Daimler AG or DAG) sport utility vehicle assembly plant investment (Gardner, Montjoy, and Watson, 2001). Brown, Hudspeth, and Stone (2000, p. 5) estimated the actual incentive package to range from $253 million to $500 million based on many state and local tax and spending promises. Seven years later, Alabama invested $158 million for a $400 million, 1,500-employee Honda plant. In that same year, Alabama approved an additional $119 million improvement package in exchange for an additional 2,000-employee, $600 million expansion for DAG (Anonymous, 1999b; Starner, 2001). One year later, Alabama offered a $118 million incentive package to convince Hyundai to build a $1 billion, 2,000-employee automobile assembly plant in Montgomery (Cason, Hendrick, and Dugan, 2002).

Analyzing these examples and others like them using a competitive bidding approach would shed new light on investment patterns and motives of economic development. To shed light, a simulation we designed applies competitive bidding theory to public economic development investment. The experiment's purpose is to involve those directly and indirectly affected by public sector concessions—professionals who are graduate students in both public budgeting and public financial management courses—in an auction to simulate reality. Once pitted against one another, the experiment participants can help reveal and explain what motivates government leaders to invest as they do.

Research Questions

The explanations for government leader decisions in economic development competition follow at least ten loosely related lines of thought. We list them below as rival explanations:

1. Net gain of marginal benefits (Black and Hoyt, 1989; Rubin, 1988; Feiock, 1999)
2. Ignorance (Wolman, 1988; Mollenkopf, 1983; Burnier, 1992; Downs, 1960; Noto, 1991)
3. Rent seeking (Coffman, 1993)
4. Taste for community (Noto, 1991; Taylor, 1996)
5. Control of political error (Noto, 1991; Wolkoff, 1983)
6. Symbolism (Wolkoff, 1992, Kenyon, 1997)
7. Mimicry (Wolman, 1988, Saiz, 2001)
8. Signals (Wolman, 1988; Molotch, 1976)
9. Fiscal illusion through a leader's "record of tangible accomplishments" (Burnier, 1992) or priority of short-term net benefits over long-term net benefits (Baum, 1987)
10. Deliberate redistribution of tax burdens from capital to labor (Baum, 1987)

The need to control for some explanations while investigating others calls for lab experimentation. The auction assumption also lends itself to experimentation. While experiments can limit the generalization of findings, the trade-off among control, cost, time, and generalizability favors them. We will explain more about this trade-off in the discussion section that follows the findings of this research below.

The Experiment

We chose a laboratory experiment research method because it provides high value in determining the most convincing of the ten explanations for leader behavior. The experiment's purpose was to apply public competitive bidding theory to economic development efforts. The application took place through a game played numerous times over more than a decade, a series of simulated first-price, sealed-bid auctions. Table 10.1 provides many of the features of the experiment, the variations of the basic game played, and the number of auctions in each game.

The extended game was an in-class exercise. Players were graduate students in courses on public budgeting, public financial management, or courses surveying both subjects. The graduate students attended eastern and midwestern U.S. universities. The students were grouped to form city decision-making teams and, in one case (game 13), to form teams for both businesses and cities. The city teams

Table 10.1 Means (Standard Deviations) for Each Group and Respective Round Payoffs, Winning Bids, and Net Payoffs, First Variation, Auction Experiment

	Number of Rounds of Competition	Number of Localities	Definition of Winning	Average Round Payoff	Average Winning Bid	Average Net Return
Game 1	12	6	Not defined	4.67 (1.39)	4.43 (0.50)	0.98 (2.19)
Game 2	10	8	Not defined	4.20 (1.21)	5.86 (1.90)	0.10 (3.89)
Game 3	20	10	Not defined	4.10 (1.23)	5.16 (0.47)	-0.29 (1.84)
Game 4	12	7	Not defined	4.71 (2.43)	5.56 (1.52)	-0.850 (1.45)
Game 5	20	6	Not defined	4.40 (1.43)	5.48 (0.26)	-1.08 (1.43)
Game 6	20	4	Not defined	4.40 (1.43)	5.69 (0.52)	-0.73 (2.48)
Game 7	20	3	Not defined	5.00 (1.17)	5.01 (0.90)	-0.01 (1.25)
Game 8	20	4	Not defined	4.45 (1.50)	4.05 (0.46)	0.40 (1.53)
Game 9	20	5	Not defined	4.50 (1.50)	5.200 (0.64)	-0.70 (1.55)
Game 10	20	5	Not defined	4.30 (1.53)	5.58 (0.55)	-0.16 (2.99)
Game 11	20	5	Not defined	4.50 (1.36)	5.05 (0.50)	-0.30 (1.80)
Game 12	16	4	Not defined	4.59 (1.27)	4.81 (0.63)	-0.22 (1.02)
Game 13a, 2d Variation, Auction	3	3	Win most industry	See Table 10.4		
Game 13b, 3d Variation, Auction	3	3	Win most money	See Table 10.5		

competed with each other in bidding for a business as well as the long-term economic gains or losses the business represented over time (the payoff).

The bids and payoffs represented millions of dollars. Objects (stones or chips) given the participants represented the assets with which each locality began a game and payoffs each winning bidder received in each round of each game. In many of the games, for example, the objects were polished stones, each representing some several hundred thousand dollars. The objects symbolized the scarcity of resources. However, if a group became bankrupt, the administrator of the game took the role of a bank and a willing lender, provided more sources for bidding, and continued the experiment. The bank lending occurred only once in 13 games of 210 auctions. No interest was charged the borrower, and the borrower repaid the loan before reporting the net result of the game.

Participants competed as willing, accountable members of a group. Written instructions told participants to act as if they were officials representing the locality. The officials were to decide as a group the amount to bid. The individual participants contributed in some manner to each of their locality's bids, and each person took responsibility for his or her total gains or losses as well as joint responsibility for the group outcome. Thus, each locality made one bid in each auction with twelve to twenty auctions making up one game. Membership in the groups varied over the games from one to five participants.

The game did not differentiate between retention of existing and attraction of new industry because we assumed that either task would uncover the strategies and behaviors we wanted to observe. We based our assumption on actual, metropolitan area competitions, competitions in which an industry located in a central city might call an auction and force the central city to bid for retention while a peripheral city bids to attract that industry (Anderson and Wassmer, 2000).

The simulation directors structured the game. They determined the amount each individual received, assigned each individual to a group, and by that set the total amount of assets the group held at the start of the game. The group assets represented the budget allocated for economic development, players were told, and the means by which competitors could bid in dollars and declare their estimates of the value of the incentive packages the locality must offer to recruit business firms. Overall locality wealth was heterogeneous; some groups were poor, some wealthy, and others were arranged between the extremes.

The payoffs, the dollar amount simulated to represent the economic return for winning the industry, differed round by round through the thirteen games. Because we wanted to simulate incomplete knowledge of future economic trends, we gave each group no more than general information about the precise value of any payoff. Instead, they were told the range of possibilities and that these possibilities were scheduled to appear in random order. The randomness represented the business cycle distribution of growth and decline among businesses and industries that expand in a cyclical and countercyclical way. With the distribution of the payoffs between the lowest and highest amounts, but not the schedule of their appearance, we attempted to mimic a normal distribution. The normal distribution of payoffs can be thought to include few large payoffs, each representing a trophy company such as a Mercedes-Benz or a Saturn assembly plant. There are only a few in the game, just as there are a few in actual locality competition. Most of the companies considered for incentive packages are small and do not employ as many people as Mercedes-Benz or Saturn.

Each locality (the members of each competing group) discussed an investment strategy in light of available assets. Then, each person in the group stated the amount he or she was willing to risk (invest) via a bid, and each member of the group had to contribute something in each round. The localities (groups of competitors) were not allowed to talk with each other; there were no partnerships, alliances, or other forms of collusion. Each locality submitted a handwritten, sealed bid to the simulation director who acted as the auctioneer. Once all bids were received, the auctioneer awarded the payoff to the locality making the highest bid. The winning bid represented the incentive package chosen by the business being recruited, and the payoff signified the long-term economic or social welfare improvement the winning bid gained.

The winning locality could experience one of three outcomes. Each outcome depended on the difference between the payoff and the bid: a net gain, a net loss, or zero/breakeven. If the winning (highest) bid were $4 million, the bid meant that particular city was willing to concede (or invest) $4 million of assets for a particular payoff they knew would range between $2 million and $7 million. If the payoff was $7 million, the city realized a net gain of $3 million ($7 million − $4 million). If the payoff was $2 million, the city experienced a net loss of $2 million ($2 million − $4 million). With a payoff equal to $4 million, the city broke even on its investment. Although the payoff scheme differed, the highest-bidding city won the industry.

The bidding was repeated for a number of rounds or auctions in each of the thirteen games. The multiple rounds represented cities in continued competition over different industries. The thirteen games differed in length. One game had ten rounds or auctions, two games had twelve auctions, one had sixteen, and nine had twenty. The number of rounds or auctions in the game differed for theoretical and administrative reasons. That is, learning may take place in longer games in contrast to shorter ones due to group development and experience (Shaw and Shaw, 1962; Sakurai, 1975; Murnighan and Conlon, 1991). Evidence of a group's remaining with a losing cause may appear (Mullainathan and Thaler, 2000; Roese and Olson, 1995; Staw, 1976; Staw and Ross, 1978). However, student fatigue may result in little more than perfunctory participation.

At the end of the game, each group calculated its assets, the number of industries gained or auctions won, and its overall, final position. Again, each locality could break even, have a net gain, or a net loss. Moreover, each locality could have gained many, some, or no industries. For example, if a city started the game with $15 million of assets and at the end of the game had $17 million, this particular city had a net gain of $2 million. However, the cities that broke even could differ by the number of industries they had won in the auctions.

This game represented an economic model and therefore represented both a simple and a simplistic one. The game and model controlled certain factors. There were no third-party negotiations, for example, and no private-public or public-public cooperatives. The business firm role did not come into play except through the payoff structure, since the auctioneer worked as the collector of bids and played the neutral role of announcer of bids and payoffs. Further, we assumed that tax concessions are immediate but understand that sometimes, and perhaps oftentimes, tax abatements and other concessions are paid out over a number of years. Finally, the role of conventional politics was not measured, in that no elections were held during the games, and no one could be fired from his or her position.

For this research, we varied the simulation in three ways. The task given groups of students/cities in the first variation was to win; however, there was no clear definition of winning. Sometimes players may have defined winning as attracting the most industry. At other times, competitors may have interpreted winning as having the most money at the end of the game. By leaving the definition of winning open for interpretation, we could determine different strategies for the different perceptions of what to maximize—industry or money.

According to Milgrom and Weber (1982), some localities will win auctions but fall victim to the winner's curse by overestimating the potential investment return of a business. To determine if this theory applied to the public sector, the second variation of the game changed the definition of winning the game to be more explicit—to win the most industries.

The third variation instructed localities that the winner of the simulation was the locality winning the most money in payoffs. We expected the results from the second and third variations to differ significantly—localities would be risk takers with their investments if their mission were to attract the most businesses.

Through the lab work, we asked what micro-level goals were more important to government leaders when they conceded public funds for economic development. Using different variations of the game allowed us to ask, analyze, and eliminate some of the rival explanations.

We reiterate the rival explanations for government leader behavior, listing below what explanations we ignored through controls and the explanations that became our primary focus.

Those ignored through controls:

3. Rent seeking (Coffman, 1993)
4. Taste for community (Noto, 1991; Taylor, 1996)
5. Control of political error (Noto, 1991; Wolkoff, 1983)
6. Symbolism (Wolkoff, 1992, Kenyon, 1997)
8. Signals (Wolman, 1988; Molotch, 1976)

9. Fiscal illusion through a leader's "record of tangible accomplishments" (Burnier, 1992) or priority of short-term net benefits over long-term net benefits (Baum, 1987)
10. Deliberate redistribution of tax burdens from capital to labor (Baum, 1987)

Those focal explanations:

1. Net gain of marginal benefits (Black and Hoyt, 1989; Rubin, 1988; Feiock, 1999)
2. Ignorance (Wolman, 1988; Mollenkopf, 1983; Burnier, 1992; Downs, 1960; Noto, 1991)
7. Mimicry (Wolman, 1988)

The focal explanations concentrated primarily on the rational actor as decision maker. We expected that the localities in the experiment would have net gains in benefits at the end, and we could suggest by that result that they behaved as rational actors. If the net gains did not materialize, the subsidy auction behavior must be justified in a way other than rational actor behavior. The first alternative explanation lies in the auction and the idea of the winner's curse. If we found no net gains, we could argue that the bid winners overestimated the value of the payoff. If the auction is the scapegoat, we can explain the finding as ignorance because the first-price, sealed-bid auction has no provision for learning within each round or auction. Information asymmetry favors the seller or the business firm in the game. The question of private or common goods sold remains unresolved because there is no way to learn whether competitors base their bids on a value dimension they have in common; there is no way to find whether the bidders think they can win by maximizing dollars or the number of firms. The bidders are more likely than not to be aggressive than risk-neutral or risk-averse. If the bid winner who overestimates the value of the payoff differs from round to round and game to game, we can explain the finding as mimicry as well.

Data and Findings

For this research, we present the findings of three major variations in the competitive bidding simulation. The first variation gave poor and rich cities the task of competing for a single firm over several periods. The second variation gave equally well-off cities the task of competing for a number of firms (three cities competed for a single firm, then two firms, and finally three firms) with the object of the competition the effort to win the most firms. In the third variation, we asked the three localities to compete against each other for one firm, then two firms, and finally three firms with the object of the competition the effort to win the most money in payoffs because of winning firms. Each variation and its results are discussed in turn.

First Variation: Over Successive Competitions for One Firm, Winning Not Defined

In the first variation, twelve games were played where one game had ten competitive rounds, two had twelve, one had sixteen, and the remaining eight had twenty. For no other reason than simplicity, throughout the remainder of this chapter, we refer to the groups of students for each game as localities, and to the individual games as competitions. Each of the twelve competitions had a different number of competing localities—the smallest had three and the largest had ten (see Table 10.1). Four of these twelve competitions had localities starting with equal amounts of assets, while the other eight had varying assets. That is, we established starting positions that represented various economic positions: poor, middle, and wealthy localities. Those localities with starting asset amounts between $6.5 million and $10 million are labeled poor; those with assets between $10.5 million and $17.5 million are labeled middle income; and assets between $18 million and $27 million represent upper-income communities. Seventeen (25.4%) of the sixteen localities are labeled poor; thirty-two (47.8%) are middle-income localities; and eighteen (26.9%) are wealthy communities.

Table 10.1 presents the average payoff, average bid, and average net return for each group. Of the twelve games, three (25%) have an overall average net payoff and the other nine (75%) have an average net loss ranging from $0.01 million (game 7) to $1.08 million (game 5).

Next, individual localities were analyzed. We found that of the sixty-seven localities (groups of students), forty-one (61.2%) experienced a net loss, sixteen (23.9%) realized a positive return, and ten (14.9%) broke even. Table 10.2 presents the average starting amount, average bid, average ending amount of assets, average number and percent of rounds won, total investment, and cost per industry grouped by investment return–net loss, net gain, or no change.

An analysis of variance (ANOVA) was used to determine difference among the three investment returns for the variables start amount, bid, and end amount. The analysis revealed that there was no significant difference among the investment returns for the variable start amount. The ANOVA revealed a significant difference of means between net gain and net loss for both the bid and end amount variables. That is, there was a significant difference between the average bids for those communities realizing a net gain and those losing money, a difference of $0.67 million ($F = 12.722$, p-value = 0.000). Those localities experiencing a net loss had an average bid of $4.24 million, whereas those realizing a net gain bid $3.58 million. This significant difference of $0.67 million created a greater difference between the end amounts and the net return, a difference of $7.30 million ($F = 14.38$, p-value = 0.000). Localities with a net gain ended the game with $16.98 million, compared to $9.68 million for localities with a negative return.

A difference of means test revealed that there was no significant difference between payoff and rounds (or industry) won, payoff and percent of rounds won, payoff and total investment, and payoff and cost per industry. Although the bid for a particular

Table 10.2 Averages (Standard Deviations) Grouped by Overall Net Payoff, 12 Games, First Variation, Auction Experiment

	Net Gain	*Net Loss*	*Break Even*	*F or t*[a] *(p-value)*
Start amount	15.563 (4.546)	13.274 (4.378)	13.250 (4.392)	1.639 (0.202)
Bid	3.575 (0.407)	4.242 (0.487)	3.972 (0.341)	12.722 (0.000)*
End amount	16.984 (4.991)	9.683 (4.642)	13.250 (4.392)	14.377 (0.000)*
Rounds (industry) won	3.625 (2.729)	3.366 (2.447)	0	0.348 (0.365)
Percent rounds (industry) won	0.208 (0.136)	0.190 (0.125)	0	0.472 (0.319)
Total investment	16.766 (12.525)	17.043 (13.633)	0	−0.071 (0.944)
Cost per industry	4.690 (1.047)	5.149 (0.859)	0	−0.9934 (0.325)
n	16	41	10	

Note: * denotes significance at an alpha level of 0.05.

[a] An analysis of variance (ANOVA) test was conducted on start amount, bid, and end amount. A difference of means *t*-test was conducted on rounds won, percent rounds won, total investment, and cost per industry. The ANOVA revealed a significant difference between net gain and net loss for the variables bid and end amount. No other differences are significant.

industry was significantly different from the payoff, the total investment (the average total amount invested by each locality) and cost per industry (total investment divided by number of industries won) were not significantly different from the payoff variable.

Furthermore, there was no significant association between the variables start amount and bid ($r = 0.199$, *p*-value = 0.107). In other words, different starting, or income, levels were not associated with the amount a locality is willing to concede.

When income is added to the equation, we found that of the forty-one communities with a negative return on their investment, twenty-two were middle income, eleven were lower income, and eight represented upper income. In addition, half of those with a net gain were wealthy localities and half of those breaking even were middle-income communities. Table 10.3 presents these findings. Overall, we found that investment return and income levels were independent (Chi-square = 5.806,

Table 10.3   Number and Percentage of the Different Income Levels, Grouped By Net Gain, Net Loss, or Break Even; 12 Games, First Variation, Auction Experiment[a]

	Net Gain	Break Even	Net Loss	Total
Poor	3	3	11	17
% of Net Gain	18.75%	30.00%	26.83%	
% of Poor	17.65%	17.65%	64.71%	
% of All	4.48%	4.48%	16.42%	
Middle	5	5	22	32
% of Net Gain	31.25%	50.00%	53.66%	
% of Middle Income	15.63%	15.63%	68.75%	
% of All	7.46%	7.46%	32.84%	
Wealthy	8	2	8	18
% of Net Gain	50.00%	20.00%	19.51%	
% of Wealthy	44.44%	11.11%	44.44%	
% of All	11.94%	2.99%	11.94%	
Total	16	10	41	67

[a] Chi-square is 5.806 with an associated p-value = 0.214 and $df = 4$.

p-value = 0.214); there was no relationship between the amount of money invested and income levels.

Correlation was used to determine if there was a relationship between the winning bid and the next round's bid (next bid = f(winning bid)), as well as a relationship between the immediate return on an investment and the next round's bid (next bid = f(return)). The winning bid and next bid were significantly correlated ($r = 0.336$, p-value = 0.000), suggesting that the subsequent bid would be higher. In addition, the next bid was significantly correlated with the return on investment ($r = -0.265$; p-value = 0.000). This indicates that if the winning bid yielded a positive return, the next bid would be something less than the previous bid. On the other hand, if there was a negative return, a net loss, the next bid would be higher. If there was a net return or payoff of $1, the subsequent bid would decrease by roughly $230,000. If a loss of $1 occured, we would expect the next bid to increase by approximately $230,000.

Overall, there were 210 total competitions played. Analyzing the winning bids from each competition, 115 (54.8%) of the competitions resulted in a net loss, 78 (37.1%) gained, and the remaining 17 (8.1%) broke even. The total payoff for all 210 competitions equaled $941 million, and all of the bids summed up to almost $1 billion ($999.25 million). After 210 competitive rounds of bidding for industry, $58.25 million was lost on all investments.

Second Variation: In One Competition, Win the Most Firms

To vary the competition to test for the symbolic or signaling purpose for which localities use incentives, we asked participants to enter a sealed-bid competition for one firm. We instructed the participants that the winner of the simulation was the locality that won the most firms.

First, three competing localities submitted sealed bids, knowing the range of possible payoffs, to win a single firm. The firm receiving the bids chose the best two of the three bids (the firm did not have to choose the most valuable bids). The two localities surviving this competition bid again, not knowing what the competitor bid the first time. The firm receiving this second set of bids then chose what the firm considered the best bid.

The competition then entered a second phase, where the three localities competed for two firms in the same two-step bidding process. Finally, the competition entered a third phase where the three localities competed for three firms in the same two-step bidding process. The second and third phases attempted to test the idea that firms also compete to win localities as localities compete to win firms.

In all of these bidding rounds, the competitors or the firms did not know the payoffs. In fact, the payoffs were generated from a random number distribution and varied between $5 million and $11 million. As we stated before, the random distribution simulated the inability to forecast precise firm contributions to the local economies where they are located and particularly the precise firm contributions to the local government treasury.

The findings from the second variation are found in Table 10.4. Testing for the implication of bidding for the number of new firms, rather than the amount the firms could add to the local treasury or economy, we found that generally the more firms won, the more money lost. The first winner gained four firms and lost $12 million. The second winner gained two firms and lost $5 million.

Third Variation: In One Competition, Win the Most Money

In a third variation, three localities competed, as in the second variation, for a single firm, then two firms, and then three firms. We instructed the localities that the winner of the simulation was the locality that won the most money represented by payoffs.

By implication, the firms competed among themselves for localities as well. In the directions for the simulation, we instructed firms that not winning a bid competition would result in a 25% loss of assets. By this instruction, we simulated the idea that the innovation or expansion represented by the relocation or retention competitions was essential.

The findings from the second and third variations are found in Table 10.5. In the competition for dollars rather than the number firms, the total won exceeds the total lost, clear winners exist, and three distinct strategies emerge. First, the total

Table 10.4 Variation 2, Auction Experiment: Win the Most Business Firms, Comparison of What Was Won

| | | B1 | | B2 | | | B3 | | | Government Bidding Results | | | | | |
| | | | | | | | | | | Number of Businesses | | | Millions of Dollars | | |
	Bid 1	Bid 2	Payoff	Bid 1	Bid 2	Payoff	Bid 1	Bid 2	Payoff	G1	G2	G3	G1	G2	G3
1st year G1	9														
G2	10	6													
G3	8	10.5	10									1			-0.5
2nd year G1	10	10		10											
G2	10	12	9	10	10						1			-3	
G3	8			8	10	11						1			1
3rd year G1	11	10		11	9		11	11							
G2	10			10	10	8	10				1			-2	
G3	10	12	5	10			10	12	7			2			-12
Total payoff										0	2	4	0	-5	-11.5

Note: In the second year in the bidding for the second business firm (B2), the rules of the simulation permitted the business firm to choose any two bids. The firm chose a bid that was below that of another (notice the choice of the G3 bidder at $8 million). The business firm explained that the choice of the G3 bidder enabled a larger second bid, he thought, which would have been the case had the business firm chosen the two $10 million bids.

Table 10.5 Variation 3, Auction Experiment: Win the Most Money, Comparison of What Was Won

		B1			B2			B3			Businesses Won			$ Millions Won		
		Bid 1	Bid 2	Payoff	Bid 1	Bid 2	Payoff	Bid 1	Bid 2	Payoff	G1	G2	G3	G1	G2	G3
4th year	G1	12	5													
	G2	10	8	10								1			2	
	G3	6														
5th year	G1	12	5		12	9	7				1			-2		
	G2	10	7	8	9	8						1			1	
	G3	0			0											
6th year	G1	7	6		7	6		7	6							
	G2	10	7	11	8	7	8	8	7	6		3			4	
	G3	0			0			0								
Number of businesses											1	5	0			
Millions of dollars														-2	7	0

bid minus the total payoffs was $5 million. Overall, the three cities gained. Second, government 2 (G2) won $7 million. Third, G2 won by, they said, calculating the mean probable payoff of payoffs ranging from $5 million to $11 million, assuming a normal distribution. Government 3 avoided losses by simply standing pat on the assets with which they started the simulation, echoing the common risk-averse strategy that suggests that "nothing ventured, nothing lost." In all three years in the third variation, the first bid in the two-step bidding competition always exceeded the second bid. Bids fell as bidding continued. In contrast, when bidding to win more businesses than money, in the second variation of the game, the second bid in the two-step process usually exceeded the first bid. Bids increased.

In summary, we present the findings in the context of the rival explanations with which we began. We found the auction variation with the most open definition of winning, the first, led to a net loss for the winner about 55% of the time. The number of rounds where the winner had a net gain was just greater than one-third of the time. The second variation's "win the most industries" goal led to consistent losses by winners. The third variation's "win the most money" goal led to consistent gains by winners. Therefore, left to their own goal setting, localities will not have net gains in benefits at the competition's end and cannot be rational actors in the narrow sense that Heilbroner uses (1988).

Since the gains did not materialize, the subsidy grants might be viewed as a function of the winner's curse identified with first-price, sealed-bid auctions. However, when we varied the game to another form, in variations 2 and 3, we found net losses continuing in the second variation but net gains in the third variation. Therefore, the auction technique might matter. Ignorance is an explanation of the localities' bid decisions. However, the open definition associated with the first-price, sealed-bid (first) variation and the "win the most industries" goal definition associated with the second variation combine in a potent way with the auction technique to create the winner's curse. Ignorance is not the only explanation for net losses. Mimicry is also a partial explanation, since we found that the winner who overestimated the value of the payoff differed from round to round over the first twelve games and the first three rounds of the thirteenth. The second three rounds of the thirteenth game revealed a winning strategy, establishing the equally potent combination of a "win the most money" goal definition and an auction form that facilitates goal maximization. The findings suggest that goal definition and auction form interact. The goal definition in the first variation covering twelve games could have been any one of the six goals ignored through the controls used in the experiment.

Discussion

By applying competitive bidding theory to public economic development investment using a simulation game, we find that, on average, localities involved in first-price, sealed-bid, competitive bidding for industry fall victim to the winner's curse—overestimating the payoff from the new industry and conceding too much. In fact, the evidence for the first variation of the game suggests that losses occurred in 55% of the competitions, by 61% of the localities, and in 75% of the games. Overall, it was a negative-sum game where $58.25 million was lost. The second variation yields similar findings. A positive return was realized only when the definition of winning the game changed from most firms to most money.

From the first variation, we find that there is no difference between income levels and what a locality bids; poor and wealthy communities are equally competitive. This differs, somewhat, from Rubin and Rubin (1987). They believe that poor cities—those with poor citizens and high rates of unemployment—are the ones investing more money in expensive economic development incentives. Perhaps as a percentage of total wealth this is true, but our research suggests that there is no difference among varying income levels and the amounts of tax and nontax incentives they are willing to concede.

Anderson and Wassmer's findings offer something similar. They suggest that "when communities are left to their own devices, local economic development incentives are increasingly offered by places that do not fit the 'high unemployment and fiscally blighted' characterization" (2000, p. 174). In other words, there should be a difference between income levels and incentives offered; poorer communities should be investing more since they fit the criteria. Our data suggest otherwise. The original focus on poor areas no longer holds true.

When localities overestimated the payoff and witnessed a negative return on their investment, the subsequent bid was higher because of this loss. The not so rational, additive justification—to make up for a loss, more money must be spent the next time around—becomes acceptable (Staw, 1976; Staw and Ross, 1978). Governments are like gambling addicts, gambling more money in order to make up for the losses faster. Victimized by the winner's curse, localities become more willing to risk their assets. This is apparent in the first two variations of the game.

Possibly, localities believe that they must win industry from other localities. It is not hard to see that economic development incentives get awarded when an election is near, especially when the actual dollar wins and losses will not become known until much later, if ever. The comparison may always be drawn with other communities as well. If those communities are doing well with economic development, the focal community must follow the same strategy. If other communities are doing well even without economic development initiatives, the community's public officials may think they have no choice but to resort to incentives for survival purposes.

Trying to survive, a community might begin the bidding process with a bid that is higher than necessary in order to obtain that one industry. This behavior could, conceivably, be a result of winning a "trophy"; even if the long-run payoff is a net loss, it is viewed as a win. If a city can attract a major industry, then more industry will follow. Perhaps this is why some governments are risk takers, conceding more the next time might make up for past losses.

For example, in 1993, Alabama conceded $253 million to attract one industry, the state's trophy Mercedes-Benz (now Daimler AG). Alabama public officials believed the presence of this one industry would attract additional industry, including steel companies, additional automobile manufacturers, and suppliers, among others. Two related outcomes developed. First, this incentive plan backfired on the governor. Alabama failed to deliver $43 million on time to Mercedes-Benz because state school officials refused to allow the diversion of corporate taxes, earmarked normally for education but promised through negotiations as a subsidy, to the firm to cover construction costs. Government officials turned to the state's pension fund to cover the incentive payout. This maneuver cost Governor Jim Folsom his job (Gardner, Montjoy, and Watson, 2001).

Second, the hope of attracting additional automobile assembly and related industries to Alabama came to fruition almost ten years later in the period from 2000 to 2003. The state offered $158 million in exchange for a 1,500-employee, $440 million Honda auto production facility. Another $119 million was committed to Daimler AG for its 2,000-employee, $600 million Mercedes-Benz expansion, and incentives helped attract three smaller automotive-related firms between 2001 and 2003 (Starner, 2001). Finally, state officials negotiated a $118 million incentive package with Hyundai for a $1 billion automobile assembly plant with 2,000 jobs. Alabama conceded almost three-quarters of a billion dollars for just over 9,000 jobs. One analysis portrayed the Alabama effort as less concentrated on short-term economic and fiscal gains and more on long-term gains and a "positive social and economic image," less the "red-headed stepchild" and more a "world-class" economic star among states (Brown, Hudspeth, and Odom, 2000, p. 160)

According to the local paper in east-central Alabama, *The Daily Home*, Alabama is "telling the rest of the world we're open for business in the automobile industry" (Anonymous, 1999a). However, Samuel Addy, the interim director of the Center for Business and Economic Research at the University of Alabama, believes that *if* additional Honda suppliers locate to the region, *then* Alabama might break even in twenty years (Anonymous, 1999a). This is an if-then statement where politics, not economic analysis, influenced the outcome.

Once a trend is established and copycat behavior ensues, localities may find it difficult to reduce the amount of the initial bid for a firm to a value that will ultimately yield a positive return. Anderson and Wassmer (2000) suggest that this copycat behavior (the use of similar incentives) dilutes the marginal influence of the incentives over time. Such behavior suggests why only sixteen of the sixty-seven localities in the first variation of the experiment experienced a net gain. Milgrom (1989, p. 6) echoes the consequences of less than thoughtful decision making. He argues:

> The most important lessons to be learned from both theory and experiments are that the returns in bidding come from cost and information advantages, that naive bidding strategies can squander these advantages; and that bidders without some advantages have little hope of

earning much profit, but could, with a little bit of carelessness, suffer large losses.

Inexperienced economic development risk takers beware!

The economic development competition is a high-risk one. The experiment revealed how some strategies might lower the risk somewhat. These strategies appear when locality decision makers choose to analyze carefully the agreements they enter with incentives (Hofer, 1994; Blakely and Bradshaw, 2002, pp. 103–153, 281–340). These strategies accord with those followed in high-profile pension investment portfolios (Coronado, Engen, and Knight, 2003; Peterson, 2004). In particular, leaders have methods at their disposal for analyzing exit, voice, and loyalty, that is, in understanding and managing the risks when leaders confront the mobility of businesses, the relatively weaker mobility of voters in a locality, and the desire most voters have for a stable community (Noto, 1991, pp. 253–254; Hirschman, 1970, pp. 120–126; Schneider, Teske, and Mintrom, 1995; Schneider, 1989; Bingham and Mier, 1997; Baum, 1987; Wolkoff, 1983). Leaders also have the means to recapture concessions if firms do not comply with agreements. Finally, leaders have the ability to change the corporate-centered approach they use. They can acknowledge globalization influences, but also the significant power of government intervention has when targeted, clear, and accountable (Robinson, 1989).

The understanding that this research attempts to widen may also encompass the auction-like nature of bidding for business. Seldom must interjurisdictional competition be a first-price, sealed-bid situation. Variations 2 and 3 of the experiment structured competition in two stages rather than one, revealing that bidders might actually offer less in the second stage than the first, lowering risks. Other competitive situations might emerge if the auction literature were considered. For businesses, Milgrom and Weber (1982) have shown that the auction used in the first twelve variations of the experiment, the first-price, sealed-bid method that we believe typifies bidding for business, actually is one of the methods least likely to maximize revenue (Chari and Weber, 1996, p. 829). The one most likely to maximize revenue is an ascending-price, open-outcry or English auction (Milgrom and Weber, 1982, p. 1095). In the government sphere, the simplicity of the open outcry, along with is its accountability potential, has advantages. Most important of the advantages, the information the open-outcry method reveals about single- or multiple-value estimates other competitors have as well as the strategies they pursue reduces the chance of the winner's curse.

This research has yielded insights that many may not find generalizable because of the experimental design. Efficiency in the lab, some say, works against the generalizability of findings (Bozeman and Scott, 1992, pp. 305–306). The research done in field studies has the same problem, however, and almost any study creates doubt about generalizability, as the classic arguments in favor of experimentation contend (Berkowitz and Donnerstein, 1982, pp. 247–249; Cook and Campbell,

1979, pp. 70–73; Kruglandski, 1975, pp. 104–105; Campbell and Stanley, 1963). As Campbell and Stanley state (1963, p. 17):

> Hume's truism [must recognize] … that … generalization is never fully justified logically. Whereas the problems of internal validity are solvable within the limits of the logic of probability statistics, the problems of external validity are not logically solvable in any neat, conclusive way.

The only hope of those pursuing any study is an increase in the understanding of causality, and causality—or internal validity—is the strongest argument for experimental research (Anderson, Lindsay, and Bushman, 1999, pp. 3–5; Bozeman and Scott, 1992, p. 306; Smith, 1989, p. 154). Moreover, the central findings at macro levels of economic development do not ring true to decision makers (Noto, 1991). To anyone else, the sparse, direct, empirical findings conflict. The present micro-level research findings have validity problems, and the Detroit metropolitan area studies by Anderson and Wassmer reveal some of these difficulties, necessary tests, precautions, and concerns (2000, pp. 9–13, 124–128). The micro-level research we have done in labs reveals the individual dynamics that lead to a specific and contrasting set of macro-level outcomes. Above all, we argue that the bidder behavior in experiments revealed the conditions creating a winner's curse. In contrast to Black and Hoyt (1989), our experiments allowed for more realistic assumptions about bidders. The outcomes under these conditions and assumptions amounted to suboptimal economic development. Therefore, we argue that wherever they exist, factors promoting the winner's curse lead to public policy decisions with predictable but unintended economic consequences.

Our research reveals that governments are willing to concede public dollars for an unknown private investment return in order to gain something besides economic welfare improvements. Milgrom's recommendation (1989, 2004) to avoid the winner's curse leads directly to Wolkoff's recommendation that leaders "systematically examine award sensitivity and community benefit flows" to be able to make better decisions "about when, and how much, [incentive] should be awarded" (Wolkoff, 1985, p. 306). Methods of systematic examination have existed for some time (Willis, 1985; Blair and Kumar, 1997; Persky, Felsenstein, and Wiewel, 1997).

Regardless of what the literature suggests—that incentives are negligibly effective—public officials can let their localities fall victim to business firms' optimizing strategies. Perhaps the symbolism and signals surrounding incentives, as well as mimicry, followed by escalating commitment, often explain the decisions made by public officials. One student summed up the game, and perhaps the real world of economic development, with the statement "You have to spend money to make money." The student's view gets support in the news. When officials in South Carolina outbid others in Georgia for Michelin, Stephen Loftin, vice president of governmental affairs for Georgia Chamber of Commerce, said that state legislators' top priority should be strengthening state incentives, arguing, "We don't have to give away the farm, but we do have to do something to compete" (Anonymous, 1999b). In the end, "do something" politics may yield a rationalization of decisions that defies economic analysis.

The research, especially experimental research, agenda has important features. First, the rent-seeking behavior of public officials and the "do something" politics lends itself to lab work. The self-serving politics of economic development suggests variations on the auction method that can reveal important dynamics. Second, the variations among types of auctions representing different competitive positions among localities can lead to sharper and more realistic advice for decision makers and a taxonomy of conditions that predict macro-level outcomes. Third, the experiment run with students, although mid-career professional students, might give way to one with economic development officials. As the parallel in Barber's (1966) experiment with budget officials suggests, face validity for experimental findings should increase.

Summary

Local public officials rely on tax and nontax incentive packages to lever economic development. This reliance is necessary, it is believed, to accomplish macro- and micro-level goals. The research reported here investigates the micro-level or individual goals of economic development officials in using financial incentive packages. We investigated the reasons public officials might have for using tax incentives by giving a group of subjects in a laboratory a certain amount of money representing their total wealth. Here, we used an experiment to analyze the motives and investment patterns of different governments—defined as groups of public administration students as they reacted to an auction of businesses willing to locate in their jurisdictions.

Under a generally unfocused incentive condition, ambiguity, we found that the majority of experimental subjects (who represented governments) fell victim to the winner's curse—overestimating the potential payoff and bidding too much, hence realizing a net loss. We surmise that the object of winning, constructed through the interaction of bidders, was not a quantitatively calculated amount of wealth or jobs but the number of business firms. The bidders sought trophies, and the larger the number, the greater the success. Those in economic development, we found through our review of the reactions of experimental subject winners, portray their efforts as the number of businesses or industries gained, especially highlighting those won in careful and high-stakes competition with rivals. In a sense, winning provides a true sense of development.

We varied the conditions of the simulation. In one variation, we structured the incentive system so that the distribution of money resembled a normal distribution, that the distribution resembled the business cycle, and that the wealth after the simulation dictated the winner. In that variation, we found a calculation strategy among subjects. The calculation strategy involved the recording of the amount and frequency of payoffs from auctions. Those subjects who kept records usually ended as the wealthiest subjects.

The construction of a win-at-any-cost strategy has interest in its contrast with other strategies. This strategy is a nontraditional but rational strategy, nevertheless. Consider the well-known strategies we found that had some success. First, there were signaling strategies. The simulation participant opens with a high bid and in subsequent rounds bids lower, constructing a least-cost or efficiency-dominated strategy. This strategy is a traditionally rational one of gaming the system. Second, there were calculation strategies. The bidders modeled the economic cycle, predicting the distribution of benefits over an economic cycle, and bidding appropriately. This strategy is a rational strategy that seems to lead to the most consistent winners. Finally, symbolic strategies appeared. The bidders desire to win the most business firms irrespective of the business paybacks. This strategy is a go-for-broke/go-broke strategy, the most common winners in the narrow sense of winning the largest number of firms, but it was the most widespread source of losses in paybacks. The symbolic strategies may be a rational strategy defined by a situation in which the payback will be hard to compute, when symbolic action may be necessary.

All of the strategies used in the experiment had some reason for being, according to the participants. Why were there multiple realities? Perhaps to these participants, state and local economic development may be a problem that many different strategies can solve. In the auction literature, as well, Lind and Plott (1991, p. 344) comment: "The difficulty with further study stems from the lack of theory about the behavior of common-value auctions with risk aversion…. Solutions which permit researchers to estimate models of 'subrational' behavior have not been worked out."

A different problem exists in local public policy, decision making, and economic development. So little is known in the context of so many intensely held but differing beliefs that officials may find considerable leeway. "Do something!" may have more resonance than "Don't do it that way!" In a different way of looking at state and local economic development, our participants may have perceived no scarcity of incentives—whether these incentives may have been tax abatements, grants, or spending on behalf of a firm. There may have been no perception of a need to force a go/no-go trade-off in firm acquisition deals or a trade-off among means and firms.

The rational actor problem in economic development business recruitment has room for interpretation. The problem may rest more on what definition of rational action one chooses rather than the phenomena we observed in the experiment. If the Heilbroner (1988) and Taylor (1996) definitions suffice, our experiment shows no overwhelming amount of rational action. When the goal definition of winning is open, the actors define winning as "well-defined choices about provisioning in the short term" only one-third of the time. Buchanan's definition (1972) of economic behavior fits our experimental subjects far more closely. Our game participants, acting rationally, chose more rather than less consistently, and the more or less, we infer, was measured in units they independently identified and defined (Buchanan, 1972, p. 17). The choice of definitions, barring fiscal illusion and the transfer of the locality tax burden to labor from capital (Baum, 1987), is not the locality leader's to make alone. Unless elected to govern as a far-sighted, wise, expert, and judicious leader using his or her own judgment, the elected decision maker acts as the voters expect and delegate. The finance official even further down the agency chain observes these expectations too. The case-by-case analysis required by an expectancy theory of economic development may resist generalization in all but philosophical terms, and this case analysis may be the proper direction research should take.

Endnote

1. Parts of this chapter were published in the *Journal of Public Budgeting, Accounting and Financial Management* (18(3), 307–350, 2006). We thank the editors for permission to use this material. We also thank three anonymous reviewers who asked educated questions and gave acute suggestions, the 175 enthusiastic public administration professionals who took roles in the experiments, and the editors of the journal symposium who knew how to help organize and motivate authors. This paper resulted from presentations at the Association for Budgeting and Financial Management meeting in Kansas City in October 2000 and the Midwest Political Science Association meeting in May 2003.

References

Anderson, C. A., Lindsay, J. J., and Bushman, B. J. (1999). Research in the psychological laboratory: Truth or triviality? *Current Directions in Psychological Science* 8(1):3–9.

Anderson J. E., and Wassmer, R. W. (1995). The decision to 'bid for business': Municipal behavior in granting property tax abatements. *Regional Science and Urban Economics* 25(6):739–757.

Anderson, J. E., and Wassmer, R. W. (2000). *Bidding for Business: The Efficacy of Local Economic Development Incentives in a Metropolitan Area*. Kalamazoo, MI: W.E. Upjohn Institute for Employment Research.

Anonymous. (1999a). Alabama's $158 million for Honda: Initial embrace marks dramatic shift from 1993's Mercedes tiff. The Site Selection Online Insider. www.conway.com/ ssinsider/incentive/ti9906.htm (accessed January 8, 2002).

Anonymous. (1999b). Incentive package makes the difference in Michelin's pick of South Carolina over Georgia. The Site Selection Online Insider. http://www.conway.com/ ssinsider/incentive/ti9910.htm (accessed August 1, 2004).

Barber, J. D. (1966). *Power in Committees: An Experiment in the Governmental Process*. Chicago: Rand McNally.

Bartik, T. J. (1991). *Who Benefits from State and Local Economic Development Policies?* Kalamazoo, MI: W.E. Upjohn Institute for Employment Research.

Baum, D. N. (1987). The economic effects of state and local business incentives. *Land Economics* 63(4):348–360.

Bazerman, M. H., and Samuelson, W. F. (1983). I won the auction but don't want the prize. *Journal of Conflict Resolution* 27(4):618–634.

Berkowitz, L., and Donnerstein, E. (1982). External validity is more than skin deep: Some answers to criticisms of laboratory experiments. *American Psychologist* 37(3):245–257.

Bingham, R. D., and Mier, R. (1997). *Dilemmas of Urban Economic Development.* Thousand Oaks, CA: Sage.

Black, D. A., and Hoyt, W. H. (1989). Bidding for firms. *American Economic Review* 79(5):1249–1256.

Blair, J. P., and Kumar, R. (1997). Is economic development a zero-sum game? In *Dilemmas of Urban Economic Development,* ed. R. D. Bingham and R. Mier, 1–20. Thousand Oaks, CA: Sage.

Blakely, E. J. (1989). *Planning Local Economic Development: Theory and Practice.* Newbury, CA: Sage.

Blakely, E. J., and Bradshaw, T. K. (2002). *Planning Local Economic Development.* 3rd ed. Thousand Oaks, CA: Sage.

Bluestone, B., Harrison, B., and Baker, L. (1981). *Corporate Flight: The Causes and Consequences of Economic Dislocation.* Washington, DC: Progressive Alliance Books.

Bowman, A. O'M. (1988). Competition for economic development among southeastern cities. *Urban Affairs Quarterly* 23:511–527.

Bozeman, B., and Scott, P. (1992). Laboratory experiments in public policy and management. *Journal of Public Administration Research and Theory* 2(3):293–313.

Brace, P. (1993). *State Government and Economic Performance.* Baltimore: Johns Hopkins University Press.

Brown, R. B., Hudspeth, C. D., and Odom, J. S. (2000). Economic development agendas and the rhetoric of local community action: Locating Mercedes Benz in Vance, Alabama. In *Small Town and Rural Economic Development,* ed. P. V. Schaeffer and S. Loveridge, 155–161. Westport, CT: Praeger.

Brown, R. B., Hudspeth, C. D. and Stone, K. L. (2000). *Social Impacts of Large Scale Economic Development Projects in the Rural South: A Longitudinal Re-Study of Vance, Alabama and the Impacts of Mercedes Benz.* Contractor Paper 00-09. htttp://www.rural.org/publications/reports.html (accessed March 2, 2003).

Buchanan, J. M. (1972). Towards analysis of closed behavioral systems. In *Theory of Public Choice,* ed. J. M. Buchanan and R. D. Tollison, 11–23. Ann Arbor: University of Michigan Press.

Burnier, D. (1992). Becoming competitive: How policymakers view incentive-based development policy. *Economic Development Quarterly* 6(1):14–24.

Campbell, D. T., and Stanley, J. C. (1963). *Experimental and Quasi-Experimental Designs for Research.* Chicago: Rand-McNally.

Capen, E. C., Clapp, R. V., and Campbell, W. M. (1971). Competitive bidding in high-risk situations. *Journal of Petroleum Technology* 23:641–653.

Cason, M., Hendrick, D., and Dugan K. (2002). City gets $1B plant. *Montgomery Advertiser,* April 2. www.montgomeryadvertiser.com/1news/business/040202_plant.html (accessed April 2, 2002).

Chari, V. V., and Weber, R. J. (1996). How the U. S. Treasury should auction its debt. In *Handbook of Debt Management,* ed. G. J. Miller, 825–834. New York: Dekker.

Clarke, S. E., and Gaile, G. L. (1992). The next wave: Postfederal local economic development strategies. *Economic Development Quarterly* 6(2):187–198.

Clingermayer, J. C., and Feiock, R. C. (1990). The adoption of economic development policies by large cities: A test of economic, interest group, and institutional explanations. *Policy Studies Journal* 18(4):539–552.

Coffman, R. B. (1993). Tax abatements and rent-seeking. *Urban Studies* 30(3):593–598.

Cook, T. D., and Campbell, D. T. (1979). *Quasi-Experimentation.* Chicago: Rand-McNally.

Coronado, J., Engen, E., and Knight, B. (2003). Public pension funds and private capital markets: The investment practices and performance of state and local pension funds. *National Tax Journal* 56(3):579–594.

Cox, J. C. and Isaac, R. M. (1984). In search of the winner's curse. *Economic Inquiry* 22:579–592.

Downs, A. (1960). Why the government budget is too small in a democracy. *World Politics* 12(4):541–563.

Eisinger, P. K. (1988). *The Rise of the Entrepreneurial State.* Madison: University of Wisconsin Press.

Feiock, R. C. (1991). The effects of economic development policy on local economic growth. *American Journal of Political Science* 35(3):643–655.

Feiock, R. C. (1999). Development policy competition and positive sum growth: Incentive competition and its alternatives. *International Journal of Economic Development* 1(3):238–255.

Feldman, M. S., and March, J. G. (1981). Information in organizations as signal and symbol. *Administrative Science Quarterly* 26(2):171–186.

Gardner, Jr., E. I., Montjoy, R. S., and Watson, D. J. (2001). Moving into global competition: A case study of Alabama's recruitment of Mercedes-Benz. *Policy Studies Review* 18(1):80–93.

Grady, D. O. (1987). State economic development incentives: Why do states compete? *State and Local Government Review* 19(2):86–94.

Greenstone, M., and Moretti, E. (2003). *Bidding for Industrial Plants: Does Winning a 'Million Dollar Plant' Increase Welfare?* Working Paper 9844. Cambridge, MA: National Bureau of Economic Research.

Greider, W. (1981). *The Education of David Stockman and Other Americans.* New York: Dutton Publishers.

Harberger, A. (1974). *Taxation and Welfare.* Boston: Little Brown.

Harrison, J. R., and March, J. G. (1984). Decision making and postdecision surprises. *Administrative Science Quarterly* 29(1):26–42.

Heilbroner, R. L. (1988). *Behind the Veil of Economics: Essays in the Worldly Philosophy.* New York: W.W. Norton.

Hirschman, A. O. (1970). *Exit, Voice and Loyalty.* Cambridge, MA: Harvard University Press.

Hofer, K. (1994). Property tax abatement. In *Case Studies in Public Budgeting and Financial Management*, ed. A. Kahn and W. B. Hildreth, 541–558. Dubuque, IA: Kendall/Hunt.

Kagel, J. H., and Levin, D. (1986). The winner's curse and public information in common value auctions. *American Economic Review* 76(5):894–920.

Kale, S. R. (1984). US industrial development incentives and manufacturing growth during the 1970s. *Growth and Change* 15(1):26–34.

Kebede, E., and Ngandu, M. S. (1999). The economic impact of the Mercedes Benz investment on the state of Alabama. *Journal of Agricultural and Applied Economics* 31(2):371–382.

Kenyon, D. A. (1997). Theories of interjurisdictional competition. *New England Economic Review*, March/April, pp. 13–28.

Keynes, J. M. (1936). *The General Theory of Employment, Interest and Money.* London: Macmillan.

Kruglandski, A. (1975). The human subject in the psychology experiment. In *Advances in Experimental Social Psychology*, ed. L. Berkowitz, 101–147. Vol. 8. New York: Academic Press.

Lind, B., and Plott, C. R. (1991). The winner's curse: Experiments with buyers and with sellers. *American Economic Review* 81(1):335–346.

McAfee, R. P., and McMillan, J. (1987). Auctions and bidding. *Journal of Economic Literature* 25(2):699–738.

Milgrom, P. R. (1989). Auctions and bidding: A primer. *Journal of Economic Perspectives* 3(3):3–22.

Milgrom, P. (2004). *Putting Auction Theory to Work.* Cambridge: Cambridge University Press.

Milgrom, P. R., and Weber, R. J. (1982). A theory of auctions and competitive bidding. *Econometrica* 50(5):1089–1122.

Mollenkopf, J. H. (1983). *The Contested City.* Princeton, NJ: Princeton University Press.

Molotch, H. (1976). The city as growth machine: Toward a political economy of place. *American Journal of Sociology* 82(2):309–332.

Mullainathan, S., and Thaler, R. H. (2000). *Behavioral Economics.* Working Paper 7948. Cambridge, MA: National Bureau of Economic Research.

Murnighan, J. K., and Conlon, D. E. (1991). The dynamics of intense work groups. *Administrative Science Quarterly* 36(2):165–186.

Musgrave, R. A., and Musgrave, P. B. (1989). *Public Finance in Theory and Practice.* 5th ed. New York: McGraw-Hill.

Noto, N. A. (1991). Trying to understand the economic development official's dilemma. In *Competition among States and Local Governments*, ed. D. A. Kenyon and J. Kincaid, 251–258. Washington, DC: Urban Institute Press.

Persky, J., Felsenstein, D., and Wiewel, W. (1997). How do we know that 'but for the incentives' the development would not have occurred? In *Dilemmas of Urban Economic Development*, ed. R. D. Bingham and R. Mier, 28–45. Thousand Oaks, CA: Sage.

Peters, A., and Fisher, P. (2004). Commentary: The failures of economic development incentives. *Journal of the American Planning Association* 70(1):27–37.

Peterson, J. E. (2004). Public employee pension funds. In *Management Policies in Local Government Finance*, ed. J. R. Aronson and E. Schwartz, 501–532. Washington, DC: International City/County Management Association.

Peterson, P. (1981). *City Limits.* Chicago: University of Chicago Press.

Polanyi, K. (1957). *The Great Transformation.* Boston: Beacon.

Robinson, C. J. (1989). Municipal approaches to economic development. *Journal of the American Planning Association* 55(3):283–295.

Roese, N. J., and Olson, J. M. (1995). *What Might Have Been: The Social Psychology of Counterfactual Thinking.* Mahwah, NJ: Erlbaum.

Rosentraub, M. S., and Przybylski, M. (1996). Competitive advantage, economic development, and the effective use of local public dollars. *Economic Development Quarterly* 10(4):315–330.

Rubin, H. J. (1988). Shoot anything that flies; claim anything that falls; conversations with economic development practitioners. *Economic Development Quarterly* 2(3):236–251.

Rubin, I. S., and Rubin, H. J. (1987). Economic development incentives: The poor (cities) pay more. *Urban Affairs Quarterly* 23(1):37–62.

Saiz, M. (2001). Politics and economic development. *Policy Studies Journal* 29(2):203–214.

Schneider, M. (1989). *The Competitive City.* Pittsburgh, PA: University of Pittsburgh Press.

Schneider, M., and Teske, P., with Mintrom, M. (1995). *Public Entrepreneurs.* Princeton, NJ: Princeton University Press.

Shaw, M. E., and Shaw, L. M. (1962). Some effects of sociometric grouping upon learning in a second grade classroom. *Journal of Social Psychology* 57:453–458.

Siegel, B. (1997). Fiscal incentives and the economic development game. *LBJ Journal of Public Affairs.* http://uts.cc.utexas.edu/~journal/1997/siegel.html (accessed May 19, 2001).

Smith, V. L. (1989). Theory, experiment and economics. *Journal of Economic Perspectives* 3(1):151–169.

Starner, R. (2001). Test track: Automobile expansions affirm Alabama's economic development strategy. Site Selection. www.siteselection.com/features/2001/may/al/ (accessed September 4, 2004).

Staw, B. M. (1976). Knee-deep in the big muddy: A study of escalating commitment to a chosen course of action. *Organizational Behavior and Human Performance* 16(1):27–44.

Staw, B. M., and Ross, J. (1978). Commitment to a policy decision. *Administrative Science Quarterly* 23(1):40–64.

Stigler, G. J. (1961). The economics of information. *Journal of Political Economy* 69(3):213–225.

Sakurai, M. M. (1975). Small group cohesiveness and detrimental conformity. *Sociometry* 38(3):340–357.

Taylor, M. (1996). When rationality fails. In *The Rational Choice Controversy*, ed. J. Friedman, 223–234. New Haven, CT: Yale University Press.

Thaler, R. H. (1988). Anomalies: The winner's curse. *Journal of Economic Perspectives* 2(1):191–202.

Thompson, J. D. (1967). *Organizations in Action.* New York: McGraw-Hill.

Thompson, J. D., and Tuden, A. (1959). Strategies, structures and processes of organizational decision. In *Comparative Studies in Administration*, ed. J. D. Thompson, P. B. Hammond, R. W. Hawkes, B. H. Junker, and A. Tuden, 195–216. Pittsburgh, PA: University of Pittsburgh Press.

Trogen, P. (1999). Which economic development policies work: Determinants of state per capita income. *International Journal of Economic Development* 1(3):256–279.

Tullock, G. (1967). The welfare costs of tariffs, monopolies and theft. *Western Economic Journal* 5(3):224–232.

Wassmer, R. W. (1990). Local fiscal variables and intra-metropolitan firm location: Regression evidence from the United States and research suggestions. *Environment and Planning C: Government and Policy* 8:283–296.

Watson, D. J. (1995). *The New Civil War: Government Competition for Economic Development.* Westport, CT: Praeger Publishers.

Willis, K. G. (1985). Estimating the benefits of job creation from local investment subsidies. *Urban Studies* 22(2):163–177.

Wilson, R. (1977). A bidding model of perfect competition. *Review of Economic Studies* 44(3):511–518.

Wolkoff, M. J. (1983). The nature of property tax abatement awards. *Journal of the American Planning Association* 49(1):77–84.

Wolkoff, M. J. (1985). Chasing a dream: The use of tax abatements to spur urban economic development. *Urban Studies* 22(4):305–315.

Wolkoff, M. J. (1990). New directions in the analysis of economic development policy. *Economic Development Quarterly* 4(4):334–344.

Wolkoff, M. J. (1992). Is economic development decision making rational? *Urban Affairs Quarterly* 27(3):340–355.

Wolman, H. (1988). Local economic development policy: What explains the divergence between policy analysis and political behavior. *Journal of Urban Affairs* 10:153.

Wolman, H., and Spitzley, D. (1996). The politics of local economic development. *Economic Development Quarterly* 10(2):115–150.

Chapter 11

Summary

Government budgeting, finance, and financial management practitioners have two important status qualities. They have considerable sway over organizational decision making regardless of subject because they know what resources the organization has available. They also have legitimacy due to expertise; some also have statutory power to decide certain issues. The way they define their practice has particular importance for researchers trying to understand how the government finance world works. In this final chapter, we summarize and discuss the research done to explore finance officials' views on practice in the book.

According to the state and local chief finance officers in our focus-group work, financial management serves three purposes. These include

1. Economic efficiency and financial control
2. Loyalty to the elected governing boards and elected or appointed mayors and chief executives
3. Greater democracy and participation

Economic efficiency and financial control relate back to the reform era alliance's business members, whose arguments were based on "parsimony" or limitation of taxes business firms paid governments. To achieve efficiency and control, CFOs agreed that they must act instrumentally most of the time to achieve consensus priorities, "doing everything possible, with as little help from the taxpayer as necessary, to give citizens what they want."

CFOs supported the loyalty purpose the most often. They argued that finance officers should serve and support purposes established by those they answered to, people we referred to as CFOs' "political masters." CFOs pointed out that their job was to give advice, to produce options for them—to give them what they need to get what they want. We called the loyalty purpose "responsiveness."

Finally, despite strong supporting arguments in public administration, CFOs had significant misgivings about citizen participation, or, what we labeled as "democratization." The public administration line of reasoning defined "citizen" too narrowly, according to CFOs. They argued that participation should involve the important stakeholders in the organization, whether the stakeholder is a taxpayer, an employee receiving a paycheck, the various parties in the debt market, or a vendor in the purchasing system.

The three purposes of financial management practice, we argued, lead to a set of views practitioners have about how the world does work (realism) and could work (pragmatism). Their views of the world, we further argued, lead them to connect problems they faced to a set of logics that they used to solve them. The mechanism for connecting problems and logics is what we call *interpretation*. For example, a CFO could recognize consensus about the definition of a problem implied in the agreement about the need to increase organization performance. The economic efficiency and financial control purpose they serve leads CFOs to search for an optimal solution—they economize—within the boundaries they face, perhaps by investigating the impact on performance more proficient staff and technology upgrades would have. If disagreement about ends or means exists, the CFOs' interpretation leads them to defer to their political masters and stakeholders, the former responsiveness and the latter expert stakeholder participation.

The application chapters in the book illustrated a significant reliance on responsiveness by financial managers. Responsiveness explained much of conventional budgeting, budgeting for nonconventional expenditure, and tax incentive auctioning for business firms.

In contrast, we found stakeholder participation in debt management when credit market experts participated. When so, participation led to the development of debt networks. The debt networks allowed credit market experts to displace political masters and become the group to which financial managers responded.

We also found that deference to political masters, their inaction, and little reliance on citizen participation may shape the conditions for tax and expenditure limitation initiatives and referenda. The Canadian provincial research partly confirmed these well-springs of tax revolt.

The Larger Argument

This book claimed that practice is interpretation of ambiguous government budgeting, finance, and financial management issues. We explained how interpretation works through the series of logics that practitioners say they use.

The simple interpretive process we proposed attributes credibility and legitimacy to finance officials. The ambiguous events that occur lead to a cycle of interpretation—making sense of the events—for the organization. Brute facts and institutional facts help, but considerable ambiguity, in which there is no agreement about ends or means, remains.

Ambiguity enables financial managers to interpret through their own frames of reference—realism, as they defined it. The finance official employs a set of logics to filter ambiguous phenomena. These logics are economizing, responding to the elected elite, or democratizing issues voluntarily or involuntarily, by bringing the appropriate stakeholders into the decision-making process. Using a particular logic, the finance official can interpret ambiguous phenomena in such a way that they can be handled by computation, bargaining, or learning.

How Practical People Do Reality

Realism customarily refers to consensus about the validity and reliability of truth claims, the evidence to support them, and the warrants for both. How do practical people "do" reality? According to March (1994), and later Mouck (2004), they define part of their institutional reality. The rest is defined for them in the rules and expectations for the institution, in what is appropriate for financial managers to do in what situation. Within this reality they define, or these *bounds* as Simon (1947) would word it, financial managers follow appropriate methods—logics—to solve problems. Both methods and problems are dictated by the context finance officials recognize. Finance officials should be called pragmatic problem solvers when they follow these methods.

The research here investigated how practitioners defined and chose an appropriate logic, in other words, how they were pragmatic. For the economizing, responding, and democratizing logics, Thompson and Tuden's work (1959) helps make sense of the dynamics. When consensus exists about both ends and means, practitioners follow an economizing logic. Agreement on means but disagreement on ends tells practitioners to defer—respond—to their political masters who can use compromise. In a third case, there is agreement about ends, but uncertainty about causes and effects and consequently disagreement about means to achieve these ends. Practice calls for investigation for which practical people use experts, experience, their powers of observation, and common sense; they respond to the sources that provoke learning and provide judgment.

Ambiguity is the name given to uncertainty about objectives and about cause and effect, in some if not all cases, disagreement about both ends and means. Practitioners use a responding logic in deferring to their political masters' efforts to interpret and redefine either or both the ends and means to gain compromise or consensus. In conjunction with a responding logic or instead of it when political dithering takes place, practitioners, we argue, must follow a democratizing logic.

Discourse, Logics, and Political Reality

Most public financial managers arguably think of their work as improving government efficiency. When asked, efficiency for what (Waldo, 1948, 201–203), pragmatic public managers say problem-solving. Given a problem to solve, practitioners see themselves as looking for the efficient solution. To practitioners, political masters define problems, and politics is a matter of reconciling different definitions of them.

For example, economic growth with fair distribution of its costs and benefits has dominated political discourse in U. S. government budgeting and financial management since the Articles of Confederation. Derivatives of the problem have included interstate commerce, government promotion of business, slavery to some degree, the regulation of markets, price stability, full employment, and optimal taxation and reform. The essential argument is that a rising tide lifts all boats. Waldo might ask economic growth for what, but, more often than not, fairly distributed economic growth has become an end in itself.

If this consensus exists about ends or the ultimate problem in government budgeting and financial management, economic efficiency—economizing—would be the dominant logic that practical public financial managers use. If a disagreement about which derivative is the subordinate end, e.g., tax reform, practical financial managers would defer, be responsive to what their political masters decided. If political masters dither, citizen participation or other forms of direct democracy, including initiative and referendum, emerge and inspire the definition of ends and means.

The right turn in U. S. politics has produced conflict over both ends and means and created the condition we call ambiguity in government budgeting, finance, and financial management. Consensus does not exist over ends and means. No agreement exists about the meaning of liberty and freedom, much less the appropriate subordinate objectives that follow from the will to achieve fairly distributed economic growth. No agreement exists about whether fair distribution is part of any objective. Conflict has grown over whether government has a role in choosing or providing the means to achieve any objective. Understandably, no applications in this book illustrate practitioner efforts to follow an economizing logic. The applications instead demonstrate efforts to respond to political masters or market expert–dominated networks. The chapter on budgeting for nonconventional spending gave a glimpse at the result. Governments' fiscal control of the governed has increased with the right turn, and governments' fiscal self-control has diminished.

Applications That Illustrate Practice and Logics

The book represented the three logics in chapters on decision making for fiscal policy, budgets for conventional and nonconventional expenditure, citizen participation and revolt, debt management and the auction of tax incentives.

Finance officials as experts rely on a considerable body of information produced by political economists. True to their calling, finance officials express concern for the impact fiscal policies have on target populations. The chapter on fiscal policy impacts argued that there is no consensus about both ends and means in general, political, or government budgeting and financial management discourse. The disagreement centers on perceptions of government action as, metaphorically, Progress or Leviathan. The chapter also catalogued what the expert finance practitioner, acting as an economizer knows and might advise political masters to use when there is agreement about ends but not means.

The tax incentive auction chapter reported a number of ways experiment subjects dealt with ambiguity related to competition to recruit business firms without any certainty about what the return on investment of tax and other economic development incentives might be. There were multiple realities. To these participants, state and local economic development was a problem with many definitions that many different strategies could solve. In a different way of looking at state and local economic development, we sensed in the feedback our participants provided the view that there was no scarcity of business recruitment incentives—whether these incentives may have been tax abatements, grants, or government spending on behalf of a firm. We sensed no perception of a need to examine tradeoffs in firm acquisition deals or a tradeoff among means and firms. There was no perception that a firm was not worth the incentives necessary to win the auction for it.

Our experiment showed multiple rational actions. When the goal definition of winning is open, our game participants, acting rationally, chose more rather than less consistently, and the more or less, we infer, was measured in units they identified and defined themselves.

A different problem exists in local public policy, decision making, and economic development. So little is known in the context of so many intensely held but differing beliefs about what will entice a business firm to relocate that finance officials may find considerable leeway to construct their own reality. "Do something!" may resonate more than "Don't do it this way!"

The choice of definitions, barring fiscal illusion and the transfer of the locality tax burden to labor from capital, is not the finance official's decision to make alone. Unless appointed to office as a far-sighted, wise, expert, and judicious leader using his or her own judgment, the finance official responds to elected decision makers. Elected decision makers act as the voters expect and delegate. If the expectations voters present conflict, leaving "Do something!" the only recognizable common denominator the voters order, finance officials respond to elected officials' construction of reality and act rationally within the limits that reality allows, providing a chance of following an economizing logic.

The conventional budgeting research involved seasoned financial managers in cities in the vanguard of innovative management practices. The research question asked whether they preferred a certification- target–incentive system in whole or in part to traditional budget systems. Our findings reveal that only parts of the C-T-I system have appeared. In this small sample pilot study, five cities used targets with no sub-general fund level carryover of funds from one fiscal year to the next permitted. Two cities had targets with carryovers. One city used carryovers with benchmarked performance measures. One city used performance measures and carryovers, but no targets. One city centered all effort on performance measurement, employed no targets, and allowed no carryovers.

In no case, however, did we find a system we expected. That system would link targets, limiting total spending, to performance measurement, for indications of progress toward getting results, to carryovers, to provide incentives and even breathing room to achieve higher performance. Instead we found a major divide in classifying budget systems. On one side we found those aimed toward savings in different ways. On the other side of the divide, we found performance management systems configured in various ways relative to budgeting systems.

A substantial part of the sample used savings-oriented budget systems, suggesting the pro-business train of thought that has long influenced government budget and finance norms. However, performance management systems benefit from a long tradition of pro-positive government normative thought. We found savings as forced savings programs through line-itemized budget targets. In contrast, we found savings programs that employed targets and funds budgeted in lump sum. Savings, then, had two meanings: essentially high and low responsiveness of both program and financial managers to political leaders.

In the narrower sense of savings as a protection of the tax rate, we found wide use of top-down expense targets. In no case did we find top-down targets used in conjunction with certification of performance. We wondered why because targets unconnected to measurable efforts have little use in managing performance. The most common meaning of budget targets, in fact, refers to contracts for performance in which some effort is made to develop a cost for a preferred level of goods and services agencies will provide, resembling health care cost accounting or "output-purchase budgeting" (Serritzlew, 2006). The budget becomes a contract, and both budgeting and management include considerable effort to monitor performance and apply progressive pressure toward reaching targets (Scheps, 2000).

Besides insights on savings in budgets, the chapter on conventional budgeting among the innovation vanguard reveals the opinions public managers have about integrating budgeting with management. First, a responding logic, what we called a board-of-directors model, may allow a stronger role for budgets. This model invests ultimate accountability in the governing board. The board has a strong incentive to control budgets and management through resource control – the tax rate – approximating target base budgeting: establishing ceilings, restricting within-fiscal year transfers without board approval, and creating board institutions for monitoring and auditing costs. A variation on the board-of-directors model is the adoption of market-type or business-like mechanisms: strategic planning, transaction cost analysis that compares public and private service delivery, asset sales, and government downsizing. In our small pilot group sample, we found no evidence of this radical, market-type model's adoption.

Second, a checks and balances system may allow budget decisions to check and balance management decisions. Top managers and political leaders allow the two systems to exist side by side. The best example is one in which program managers and financial managers have competing interests and incentives. The traditional hierarchical organization strengthens that competition. Centralized organization forces a comprehensive integration at the top manager level at the end rather than the beginning of budget formulation. Financial managers face the competitive context in which, on the one hand, top managers and governing board members agree on ends. On the other hand, with no agreement about ends and means, all may resolve ambiguity in some other way.

Third, a management system may integrate budgeting with other resource systems such as personnel and technology in employing and allocating resources. This decentralized, responsibility center model of performance budgeting requires a strong commitment to decentralized management. The organization's leaders prefer to yield authority to staff expertise in the unit having the responsibility for producing some output. Each responsibility center manager has control over the resources and expertise necessary to produce the output demanded. In this case, the financial manager follows a responding logic, acting as an agent of the responsibility center managers.

Choosing among nonconventional spending tools such as direct spending, tax expenditures, loans, credit guarantees, insurance, mandates, and regulation, finance officials require a criterion, and the nonconventional budgeting chapter explored various alternatives and explained one instance when officials chose one tool over another. In these tradeoffs, the criterion would have much similarity with the logics finance officials use.

The social construction of the target population as deserving or undeserving will influence the choice of the fundamental criterion in any tradeoff. It characterizes the reality constructed around the responsive finance official.

Political leaders are expected to represent constituents' beliefs, preferences, and biases. Sometimes leaders reflect social constructions that are firm. The social construction indicates what tool to use and provides an argument for the suitability of the tool to the context. These leaders however may also reflect views that are not firm, in which case an objective criterion, stipulated by scientific observers knowledgeable in the particular field or professionals in budget control, leads to the choice of the policy tool.

The chapter on nonconventional expenditure budgeting narrated a tradeoff between direct expenditures and tax expenditures that energized partisans and divided the country as change in social welfare policy toward the poor took place in the early 1990s. The criterion for the tradeoff between transfer payments and refundable tax credits was based on the social construction of the poor in the U.S. The choice that resulted, the refundable tax credit, favored poor working parents. Refundable tax credits exist only for those who work, while transfer payments went to anyone defined by law as poor. Shortly after the change in social welfare policy became law, the budget for refundable tax credits almost equaled previous direct spending on transfer payments to the poor.

The research presented in the citizen participation in budgeting chapter revealed the complexity found in efforts to widen involvement. On budgeting being closed to outsiders, we found reasons why officials resist all but extraordinary and isolated instances of true involvement. Conversations with finance officials suggest that most believe in the value of building a community and a sense of belongingness to that community. They believe that education will help citizens have an impact when they participate. However, most officials believe that the republican ideal should guide practice. Community-wide decisions are entrusted to representatives that citizens elect.

Moreover, most officials see participation as a road to increased conflict. Budget participation raises expectations for accomplishments, some of which are beyond reach. Participation, per se, often stands as a repudiation of officials' management skills and policy decisions and creates a defensiveness that almost never wanes.

The budget's accessibility relates to the way the budget frames issues, too often only as inputs—salaries, supplies, and utilities—and seldom as goals to accomplish. Budgets often deliberately hide goals rather than display them in such a way that citizens can subject them to analysis. However, when budgets frame questions in terms of performance, officials' attitudes frequently center on the imperative to seek the best performance for the same tax rate, year in, year out. By revealing that goal, officials invite citizens to define better performance and to guide its measurement.

Financial managers also need answers to questions about what is important enough to perform well. Since performance is a fairly vague concept, citizens help by participating, and incentives are there for officials to share the risk of these decisions with the citizens who do participate.

Finally, accessibility hinges on beliefs officials hold about equity issues and issues about the "interest of the whole community." Related to these issues is the question of who has the right to decide them: representatives who picture themselves as acting in the common interest and against particular interests *or* the particular interests, which participate in the guise of citizens and compete with one another?

Paralleling efforts to widen participation in budgeting, tax revolts force finance officials to respond to changing policies required by a referendum. Tax revolts are direct democracy's "ballot box budgeting." The many tax revolts in the U. S. contrast with the very few, if any, in Canadian provinces, despite their higher provincial tax levels.

The tax revolt chapter's findings help explain the absence of Canadian tax revolts—and the presence of those in the U.S.—in four ways. First, a closer look at tax and expenditure limitation efforts—revolts in the U. S. painted a different picture than popular opinion would provide. Fewer were citizen initiatives than one would expect (Smith, 2004). In efforts limiting the scope of the property tax, the focus of most state limitations, "grassroots" corresponded more to "local" than "citizen initiated."

Second, Canada's fiscal equalization program and its federal-to-province transfers subsidize provincial efforts to confront economic dislocation. Like states, provinces have high fiscal autonomy. Unlike states, provinces have federal transfers that help neutralize the impact economic dislocation has on province financed services.

Third, greater citizen participation may have a neutralizing effect on revolt. Canadians participate more, get more encouragement to participate from leaders, have less "protest potential," and perhaps resist joining tax revolts as a result. The participation data in states provide a weak but positive inference for tax revolts—low voting in regular elections, an increasing appetite for protest, leader capriciousness or opportunism in soliciting participation, and weak budget transparency.

Finally, communicating to taxpayers the value of services they receive could stem revolt. Provincial officials' efforts to incorporate program and agency performance information in budget decisions and in reports to voters and taxpayers exceed similar efforts in the states. However, neither provinces nor states have used results-oriented fiscal controls to balance latent, salient opinion about taxes with evidence of value received for taxes paid.

Equalization, citizen participation, and performance management evidence suggests that leaders in the provinces have more means and have made greater effort to deal with the government budget impacts of economic change and dislocation, causing or stemming from tax revolts.

In the chapter on debt management networks, New York Metropolitan Transportation Authority finance decision makers deferred to outside experts rather than their political masters. These outside experts stood to gain by the advice in restructuring debt to produce funds to finance the MTA's capital program.

The findings indicate that participation can develop into responsiveness. MTA finance officials formed relationships with nominal agents, investment bankers, attorneys, and various others, to borrow money in the credit markets. These relationships changed during the search for a way to finance the MTA's capital plan. What appeared at first to be an effort to widen participation became a reversal of the principal-agent relationship between the MTA officials and investment bankers. As this happened, the MTA responded to the definition of ends held by their nominal agents.

From the findings about practice, we concluded that many rationalities exist. Each of the members of the debt network has a reality within which its people may act rationally. Together, ambiguity forces team members to construct a reality together, one we found in the MTA case to be quite different than the MTA officials' institutional reality.

What Logic Gets Used When?

The cases we chose demonstrated few uses of the economizing logic—the logic of consequence, according to March (194, 2–3). Likewise, finance officials seldom democratize an issue by inviting citizen participation of even the broader stakeholder group type. The most important logic was responsiveness. The character of responsiveness lies in the CFOs' statement that they give their political masters "what they need to get what they want." In cases where no consensus exists about either ends or means or both, finance officials respond by deferring decisions to elected and appointed officials to whom finance officials answer as well as to debt networks, whose members find a consensus together.

Another issue in responsiveness is the question of basic values that work along-side logics to help build interpretations within a constructed reality. These values came up in the context of discussion about superbudgets, nonconventional budget control, and allocation criteria. The criteria used when responding to an elected elite may accord with criteria preferred by the public they represent but may also lead to policies that have extremely damaging impacts on the populations that policies target. What would finance officials do? In the focus groups, finance officers brought up an idea akin to stewardship. They said their ultimate purpose lay in "doing everything possible, with as little help from the taxpayer as necessary, to give citizens what they want." "Which citizens?" is an important question to ask financial managers.

Dithering by an elected elite, or the unwillingness or inability to decide ends or means or both, came up in the tax revolt chapter and especially in the case of California's legislature dithering in the face of the Proposition 13 referendum on June 6, 1978. Dithering creates a vacuum that may lead to voter revolt that, in turn, creates greater ambiguity.

The Place for This Research among Researchers

Studying interpretation is a controversial research methodology. The interpretive approach is one of two competing research traditions or a synthesis of the two. Thompson (2008) tells us there are researchers who follow a technocratic route and others who are constructivists. Some technocrats look for patterns among phenomena that they assume will ultimately form a single pattern. Others test whether, by deduction from first principles, phenomena form a single pattern supposed by the first principles. Both technocratic approaches assume a closed system of thought—a single pattern of relationships among phenomena—from which social scientists can reason rational behavior. While implicit in all research by technocrats, the closed system is most commonly associated with the way mathematicians, some economists, politically ideological movement members, and religious fundamentalists view problems.

Constructivists recognize many logics, multiple rationalities. None of these is anything but an "instrumental rationality" (Thompson, 2008, p. 6). What's more, constructivists view the development of a logic as a matter of social consensus building. For example, some see the system of competitive relationships—zero-sumness, conflict, even intolerance—as the one that should and therefore does exist in Western democratic and capitalist societies. Others see a system of cooperative relationships, of nonzero-sumness, as fundamental to the development of society in the West. In this book, we presented studies about why the multiple rationalities collide and with what result for government budgeting, finance, and financial management.

This book, in following a constructivist path that included technocratic observation techniques, explored a new route through financial management thinking. The new route centers on ambiguity as a motivator for accepting the existence of multiple rationalities, all of which people in organizations socially construct.

Ambiguity and social construction question the assumption about organization consensus held by more orthodox stories of the way the world of government budgeting, finance and financial management works. Consensus becomes an object of research—when and why, so and not—rather than the assumption. Rational action—matching ends and means—becomes a focus of investigation. Research, so far, has led to the argument that managers or anyone else may never know what was intended until they act (Weick, 1980, 19). Looking back, one can force order on the thought process—rationalize acts and decisions—but foresight is a scarce resource.

A lesson comes with shifting the emphasis from conventional and bounded rationality to the supposition that there are multiple rationalities. Research questions in government budgeting, finance and financial management ask what happens in ambiguous circumstances. Ambiguity is the result of disagreement about goals and either disagreement or uncertainty about the means to achieve goals. Studying life under these conditions tends to introduce, rather than ignore, multiple preferences or values in public financial management theory and practice rather than a single one.

Ambiguity leads to an alternative way of thinking about financial management. In this way, anyone can describe public financial decision making without the premise of conscious, far sighted, intended action and without the presumption of the "best interest" of an individual or collection of individuals. Rather, a decision made by an individual, in ordinary circumstances, is relatively random and unpredictable. What gives an otherwise random, unpredictable decision any meaning is either post hoc rationalization, the preemption of an individual's premises through institutional reality, or the logics that practitioners employ in decision making.

Context mattered in this book. Evidence mattered here just as it would to the technocratically inclined researcher. What is unique in this book is the use of constructivist ideas less for argument than for purposes that parallel those used by technocrats. Constructivism can help practitioners find the logic that makes sense of ambiguity and uncertainty, ends and means. In each chapter of the book, we asked whether the problem submitted to an economics or a politics logic in the economizing and agency logics practitioners identified, or should the ends and means be chosen by a bigger, more broadly representative group of people.

The History of Reform and the Political Right Turn

The study of government budgeting, finance and financial management can also develop a sense of realism and escape its reliance on single rationality idealism with more attention to unique contexts and less to deduction from first principles. One of these contexts is the right turn in the U.S. politics.

On the question of whether the right turn has changed social constructions and how that has affected finance officials, we found responsiveness won out. With the right turn, finance officials might respond more to political masters in a small-government-managed-by-the-market enterprise.

Whether the struggle will move in the direction of activist or positive government again is a matter of research. The right turn has not changed the size of government, according to perceptive observers. However, during the turn to the right, the government's reach has expanded gradually with nonconventional spending. Government control of government through budgets has lagged the expansion. The expansion of governments' reach appears superficially to be activist, pro-positive government. Yet, the question of control makes it just as likely that pro-business interests have exploited government. Whether the reform era coalition still exists is an open question. The question of what member of the original reform-era coalition now dominates has saliency. Whether the right turn has led to government managed by the market has become a fair question for debate.

References

March, James G. (1994). *A Primer on Decision Making*. New York: Free Press.

Mouck, Tom. (2004). Institutional reality, financial reporting and the rules of the game. *Accounting, Organizations, and Society,* 29, 5-6, 525–541.

Scheps, P.B. (2000). Linking performance measures to resource allocation. *Government Finance Review,* 16(3), 11–15.

Serritzlew, Soren. (2006). Linking budgets to activity: A test of the effect of output-purchase budgeting. *Public Budgeting and Finance,* 26 (2), 101–120.

Simon, Herbert A. (1947). *Administrative Behavior*. New York: Free Press.

Smith, Daniel A. (2004). Peeling away the Populist rhetoric. *Public Budgeting & Finance,* 24(4), 88–110.

Thompson, Fred. (2008). The three faces of public management. *International Public Management Review,* 9(1), 1–16.

Thompson, James D. and Arthur Tuden. (1959). Strategies, structures, and processes of organizational decision. In *Comparative Studies in Administration*, eds. James D. Thompson, Peter B. Hammond, Robert W. Hawkes, Buford H. Junker, and Arthur Tuden, 195–216. Pittsburg, P.A.: University of Pittsburgh Press.

Waldo, Dwight. (1948). *The Administrative State*. New York: Ronald Press.

Weick, Karl. (1980). The management of eloquence. *Executive,* 6(3), 18–21.

Index